The Status of Religion and the Public Benefit in Charity Law

The Status of Religion and the Public Benefit in Charity Law

edited by

Barry W. Bussey

Anthem Press
An imprint of Wimbledon Publishing Company
www.anthempress.com

This edition first published in UK and USA 2020
by ANTHEM PRESS
75–76 Blackfriars Road, London SE1 8HA, UK
or PO Box 9779, London SW19 7ZG, UK
and
244 Madison Ave #116, New York, NY 10016, USA

© 2020 Barry W. Bussey editorial matter and selection;
individual chapters © individual contributors

The moral right of the author has been asserted.

All rights reserved. Without limiting the rights under copyright reserved above,
no part of this publication may be reproduced, stored or introduced into
a retrieval system, or transmitted, in any form or by any means
(electronic, mechanical, photocopying, recording or otherwise),
without the prior written permission of both the copyright
owner and the above publisher of this book.

British Library Cataloguing-in-Publication Data
A catalogue record for this book is available from the British Library.

ISBN-13: 978-1-78527-266-0 (Hbk)
ISBN-10: 1-78527-266-7 (Hbk)
ISBN-13: 978-1-78527-362-9 (Pbk)
ISBN-10: 1-78527-362-0 (Pbk)

This title is also available as an e-book.

To all religious organisations and charities, and their staff, volunteers and donors, who are on the front line for the public good.

CONTENTS

Acknowledgements   ix

Preface   xi

Table of Cases   xxvii

Part I   Concept and Practice of Public Benefit

Chapter One	Have a Little Faith: The Advancement of Religion and Public Benefit *Juliet Chevalier-Watts*	3
Chapter Two	Religion and Public Benefit: Social Scientific Perspectives and Critiques *Raymond B. Chiu*	21
Chapter Three	The Public Benefit of 'Advancing Religion' as a Charitable Purpose: A Canadian Perspective *John Pellowe*	41

Part II   Advancement of Religion in the United Kingdom

Chapter Four	Religion and Public Benefit in United Kingdom Charity Law *Frank Cranmer*	81
Chapter Five	Back at the Bar: Charity Law, Public Benefit, and a Case of Legal *déjà vu* for the Exclusive Brethren *Bernard Doherty*	101

Part III   Public Benefit and the Advancement of Religion in Canada

Chapter Six	Advancing Religion in a 'Neutral' State: Understanding Religion as a Constitutional Good *Derek B.M. Ross and Ian N. Sinke*	129
Chapter Seven	Making Registered Charitable Status of Religious Organizations Subject to '*Charter* Values' *Barry W. Bussey*	159

Chapter Eight	Just Check the Box: Why Religious Institutions Still Make Canada a Better Place to Live and Flourish *Janet Epp Buckingham*	205

Part IV   Conclusion

Chapter Nine	The Goal of Excluding Religion from the Idea of Public Benefit: Some Aspects of Neo-Secularist Strategies *Iain T. Benson*	225

Contributors	241
Index	245

ACKNOWLEDGEMENTS

I want to acknowledge the exciting opportunity I have in working for an organization (the Canadian Council of Christian Charities) that understands the importance of religious charities in serving and enhancing the greater good. It is my privilege to be engaged in the public debate over the role of law and religion in contemporary society.

To each of the contributors in this volume, thank you for your willingness to participate with such conviction, expertise and eloquence in a lively discussion on a matter that is only going to be more pertinent as time goes on. A special thanks to Amy Ross for her copyediting of the manuscript. Amy is a tremendous asset who is adept at finding the right word or phrase for the appropriate place.

Anthem Press has been a joy to work with. Megan Greiving was instrumental in reaching out to me after my initial enquiry and followed up promptly with helpful replies. Also, Kyra Droog did excellent work in shepherding the peer review process. To the anonymous reviewers, your comments and suggestions were greatly appreciated as we incorporated them into the manuscript.

PREFACE

This book is an apologetic for maintaining the presumption of public benefit for the charitable category 'advancement of religion' in democratic countries within the English common law tradition. The argument consists of three broad fronts. First, there is the quantitative approach that considers practical public benefits, such as church-run soup kitchens or summer camps. Second, there is the qualitative approach that considers the positive effects of religion – both tangible and intangible – in the lives of individuals. Third, there is the political approach that appeals to the notion of pluralism in a free and democratic society, where individuals are free to establish religious communities that engage in the public square. To varying degrees, all of these approaches are canvassed in this book.

To set the stage, it is important to consider the motivation or context for commencing this project. The immediate impetus came from growing academic and political pressure to reform or modernize charity law in Canada – including recurring calls to remove tax exemptions granted to religious charities. This book serves, therefore, as an extended rebuttal to critics of the advancement of religion as a charitable purpose. At the same time, any argument about the merits or deficiencies of advancing religion must necessarily engage with deeper, more fundamental issues. On a philosophical level, then, this book is concerned with the place of religion – and religious institutions – in contemporary society. Hence, this volume has relevance beyond the specific legislative or legal cases analysed in Canada, the United Kingdom or Australia, as it grapples with broader questions related to secularism, civic engagement and liberal democratic freedoms.

Advancing Religion as a Charitable Head

In terms of the political and legal debate surrounding the advancement of religion, charity law in Canada remains dependent on a list of charitable purposes articulated by the British House of Lords more than a century ago.[1] However, as noted above, critics have raised questions regarding the continued inclusion of religion as a charitable 'head' or category. Given the increasing secularization of society, are past presumptions still applicable or, indeed, acceptable? After all, as researcher Don McRae argues, 'the core of the Canadian definition of charity [...] was created in Victorian England and was a product of [...] [a] homogenous, white male-dominated society'.[2] Both Frank Cranmer and Bernard Doherty note in their chapters concerning the United Kingdom that the Charity Commission, under new legislation that abolished the presumption of public benefit,[3] now requires religious charities to provide 'an identifiable, positive, beneficial moral or ethical framework that is promoted by religion which demonstrates that the religion is capable of impacting on society in a beneficial way'.[4] But, as Raymond Chui and Rev. Dr John Pellowe ponder, is it possible for courts or policymakers to recognize and assess spiritual benefits? What, ask Derek Ross and Ian Sinke, might be the constitutional ramifications of retaining or removing the charitable status of religious entities?

Several authors in this volume deal extensively with the *Pemsel* decision; I point in particular to Juliet Chevalier-Watts's article. Although the 1891 *Pemsel* decision, and the 1601 Act[5] of the English Tudor Parliament on which *Pemsel* relied, have come to define charity law, Professor Donovan Waters points out that the idea of Christian 'charity' long predated the 1601 legislation. Indeed, 'the Christian ethical or moral code was concerned [...] with service to the community'.[6] For millennia, Christian organizations have spearheaded good works in numerous fields including education, health and nutrition, elder care, physical welfare and international development.[7] Yet, despite recognizing this lengthy and well-established history, Professor Waters is of the view that the concept of religion being a charitable head has lost its importance in our pluralistic and secular society. He asserts that religion is a matter of belief, not action, and any activities prompted by faith may be more appropriately recognized as charitable in their own right. 'Charity and spirituality', says Waters, 'each *per se*, are as alike as chalk and cheese'.[8] He suggests that it is time to consider them as separate, and religion *qua* religion no longer needs to be considered *a priori* charitable. Instead, we ought to 'rethink the policies that were once enough'.[9]

Though Waters would prefer to take 'religion out of the scope of charity', he concedes that another way to recognize the uniqueness of religion would be to retain the third head as a charitable purpose but abolish the default presumption of public benefit.[10] It is my position that Waters is seeking a solution to a non-existent problem. There are very good reasons why we need the third head of charity – reasons which are outlined in the subsequent chapters. Not least of these is the recognition that, contrary to Water's argument that spirituality can be divorced from action, religious faith and good works are so intricately intertwined in the theology, practice and lives of Christian communities that recognizing religion as charitable speaks to the reality of religion's positive influence in society.

The Role of Religion in Secular Society

However, that is not how many in society see religion. To understand and address the root of their objections is to move beyond charity law into a deeper discussion on the very nature and role of religion. Indeed, there can be little doubt that religion and religious institutions are increasingly challenged by a secular[11] ideology that would deny any place for religious communities outside of their houses of worship. Thus, scholars like Professor Richard Rorty envision an unabashedly 'secularist utopia' in which '[r]eligion will [...] be pruned back to the parish level'.[12]

As a result of this kind of pressure, 'from the point of view of religiously devout people whose consciences and visions of reality are influenced by faith, the public square can indeed seem a cold, suspicious, and hostile place'.[13] So much so, Professor Stephen

L. Carter argues, that 'the modern attitude toward religion in the public square would have crippled the civil rights movement'[14] – an observation that Juliet Chevalier-Watts echoes in the context of charity law in her chapter in this volume.

While 'secular' has long denoted non-sectarian or temporal concerns, as opposed to ecclesiastical beliefs or behaviours, 'secularism' carries more stridently anti-religious overtones. The concept has been around at least since the late nineteenth century when George Jacob Holyoake coined the word 'secularism' in an attempt to untie the moral teachings of the Bible from their spiritual moorings – to rid the public square of religion by converting 'churches and chapels into temples of instruction for the people [...] to solicit priests to be teachers of useful knowledge'.[15] Paul Carus, in the preface to Holyoake's *English Secularism*, described Holyoake's 'secularism' this way:

> Secularism espouses the cause of the world *versus* theology; of the secular and temporal *versus* the sacred and ecclesiastical. Secularism claims that religion ought never to be anything but a private affair; it denies the right of any kind of church to be associated with the public life of a nation, and proposes to supersede the official influence which religious institutions still exercise in both hemispheres.[16]

Secularists hoped that liberal democratic societies would move on from religious superstition and parochial religious rivalries that, in their view, stunted development. In short, and at the risk of oversimplification, the 'secularism thesis' argued that the more educated the populace became, the less religion and its institutions would be needed. For religionists, the idea that religion's societal influence would diminish over time was a cause for concern at the end of the nineteenth century. Carus queried, 'What will become of religion in the future? Will the future of mankind be irreligious [...] or will religion regain its former importance and become again the leading power in life, dominating both public and private affairs?'[17]

The secularism thesis has, for the most part, failed.[18] Yet in key areas of societal influence – notably law, media and academia[19] – religion has been increasingly marginalized, and there remains a preoccupation with the hope that religion will fade away altogether.

Although the sustained pressure of a secularist environment has not eliminated religion, it has meant that religious charities are now obliged to prove their worthiness to maintain special tax-exempt status for their properties or operations and to continue providing government tax incentives to their donors.

Which brings us to the central question to be answered in this book: why should religious charities continue to receive tax exemptions and other incentives such as charitable status?

The answer, in a nutshell, is because we need *all* communities involved in the public good to be treated equally by the state, religious and non-religious working together to build a solid, stable, democratic society that respects pluralism and the rule of law. This is what creates an atmosphere of civil trust necessary to carry on the democratic project of maximizing individual freedom while maintaining civil peace.

While religion has been much maligned by the media and certain professions, it is worth noting religion's enduring influence, despite growing secularization in society. Even though the number of Canadians identifying as Christian has declined over the last four decades, some 67 per cent of Canadians still claim affiliation with either Catholicism or Protestantism.[20] Meanwhile, the Pew Forum Foundation found that the 'other religion' category rose from 4 per cent in 1971 to 11 per cent in 2011, meaning Canadians are becoming more religiously diverse. Likewise, religious charities also retain a strong presence. According to Canada Revenue Agency's (CRA) figures for March 2018, out of 86,234 registered charities across the country, some 33,020 are religious.[21] At the same time, the percentage of those citizens who identify as 'religiously unaffiliated' has risen dramatically to 24 per cent;[22] this group is also known as the 'nones'.[23]

The 'nones' are increasing – but the religious world remains. Professors Michael Barnett and Janice Gross Stein observe that even in the secular West there are 'signs of a religious revival'[24] in the humanitarian field. Barnett and Stein also recognize the prominent role religious organizations had in establishing international aid societies in the nineteenth century, going so far as to say, 'it is only a slight exaggeration to say "no religion, no humanitarianism." '[25] They maintain that while the Christian religion passed the torch to secularism, it did not exit the stage but remained front and centre, and now there is a religious resurgence in the field.[26] Religion continues to play a public role by means of humanitarian involvement, despite the chorus of opposition.

If one steps back – as does Dr John Pellowe in his chapter – to consider the grand mosaic of religious communities engaged in charitable work of many different kinds, it should engender some appreciation for the scope and depth of religious involvement in the common good, from humanitarian work to civic engagement.[27]

Professors Brian Clarke and Stuart Macdonald raise concerns about the impact of declining Canadian church membership on the latter. They point out that it is within the churches that citizens 'become civically engaged. It was there that they would learn how to speak in public, run meetings, engage those with differing viewpoints, and understand the needs of their local community'.[28] With fewer people attending church, there are fewer people being trained in civic engagement. Given that '[c]hurch members tend to join organizations more than those who don't belong to a church',[29] there are fewer individuals to take up the challenge to lead in the religious charitable sector. But, even more, those who are involved with their local churches are also involved 'in a whole host of other organizations'.[30] So, the loss of religiosity is a loss to the greater community.[31] While one could expect the charitable sector to continue operating even without a religious contribution, it would undoubtedly struggle to operate as effectively 'without the depth and intensity of volunteering that has sustained it until now'.[32]

Clarke and Macdonald do not call for a religious revival (in any event 'such a mass change in sentiment is not very likely'[33]); nor do they call for a 're-Christianization of Canadian society', but they argue that 'we as a society need to recognize that the decline in religious affiliation will see involvement in our country's civic life diminish'.[34]

As we recognize both the decline of religiosity and the immense contribution that religious communities and their charities make in Western society, we must take seriously the challenges made by secularists against government tax exemptions and donor tax incentives given to religious communities.

In 2010, Professor Jeffrey Stout was prescient in observing that the secularist insistence on removing religious communities from the public square was bound to have unintended consequences.[35] He pointed out that the desire of 'democratic secularists' to remove religion and its followers from the public square was not going to happen by reasoned argument but by undemocratic means. In other words, coercion. Coercion, in turn, would lead to isolating religious individuals and marginalizing religious communities in order to reduce or eliminate their ability to influence political and social decision making. As Stout elaborates, this marginalization may have the unintended effect of bolstering the divisiveness that secularists fear. Polarization is not what we want – but it is the result of extreme positions. Stout's point is that '[s]ecularist resentment fuels [...] anxiety rather than raising it to self-consciousness. It presents the hateful preacher with a fattened scapegoat, primed for rhetorical sacrifice'.[36] In other words, it contributes to increasing polarization and antagonism, as Stout illustrates in a provocative thought experiment. He calls on readers to suppose they are a preacher in a moderate, Republican-leaning county on a Sunday morning:

> You were raised to love your neighbor, but not to tolerate attacks on faith and virtue. What are you going to make of the claim that atheists make better citizens than theists,[37] or the fantasy of strangling the last king with the entrails of the last priest,[38] or the notion that believers are essentially irrational and intolerant, or the idea that the purpose of a liberal education is to produce as many democratic secularists as possible, or the dream of a day when faith has passed from the face of the earth, or the advice that you should, in all fairness, keep your religious convictions behind the church door while secularists pursue their long-term objectives?[39]

Stout then points out that these well-known secularist statements will be viewed by the preacher as evidence that secularists are enemies, that they plot the eradication of a religious way of life and, ultimately, that they are not committed to democratic ideals or to the American Bill of Rights. The conclusions of the preacher and the congregation are: 'secularists cannot be trusted to hold political office, to educate the children of believers, or to give citizens the news'.[40] The net effect, says Stout, is that secularist resentment 'pushes religious moderates into the arms of their extremist brethren. It further polarizes a political community in which polarization is a primary impediment to democratic action on behalf of the poor and the oppressed'.[41]

In short, the irony of secularist rhetoric against religion is that it creates the very thing that is deemed so distasteful – religious activism in the public square.

But here is the point: the more secularists push against religion's rightful role in the public square, the more such aggression will be resisted. An inevitable pushback from the religious community will become a reality. At that point, as Stout observes, even more extremist religious views become plausible; he goes so far as to suggest it makes 'theocracy more attractive to religious moderates'.[42]

Professor Carter also concurs that dismissing the beliefs of religious citizens 'as racism, sexism, or homophobia does nothing to quiet them. Such insults will simply send those who express the fears rushing into the waiting arms of the next demagogue'.[43] 'What is needed', Carter continues, 'especially from [secular] liberals who pride themselves on a politics of inclusion, is a dialogue that takes the fears seriously, a dialogue that teaches but also tries to learn'.[44]

This plea for respectful dialogue has had success in convincing some secularists to tone down their anti-religious rhetoric, as was evidenced by the *mea culpa* of Professor Richard Rorty,[45] who originally chastised Carter's work. He later conceded:

> instead of saying that religion was a conversation-stopper, I should have simply said that citizens of a democracy should try to put off invoking conversation-stoppers as long as possible. We should do our best to keep the conversation going without citing unarguable first principles, either philosophical or religious. If we are sometimes driven to such citation, we should see ourselves as having failed, not as having triumphed.[46]

Part of keeping 'the conversation going', in my view, is allowing religious charities to continue their important roles in furthering the public good and promoting civic engagement. Though there will remain differences of opinion between power elites and religious charities on many 'culture war' issues such as marriage, gender and the unborn, the reality remains that society needs a plurality of voices and institutions engaged in making society a better place. We do not want, as Professor William Galston observes, 'civic totalism' where the state is plenipotentiary, leaving civil society 'as a political construction possessing only those liberties that the polity chooses to grant and modify or revoke at will'.[47]

The Canada Summer Jobs debate – canvassed in the chapters by Janet Epp-Buckingham and Barry W. Bussey – is a case in point. It involved a federal government programme that gave funding to charities and small businesses to hire students in the summer. For the 2018 season, the government required applicants to attest that they agreed with government ideology on abortion and '*Charter* values'. *Charter* values, as discussed by Bussey and Iain T. Benson in this book, are not constitutionally enumerated rights but are the 'idiosyncrasies of the judicial mind'. Yet government demanded compliance with its worldview in order for the religious charity to receive government funding. The government's support for diversity only extended to those who shared the government's vision. Not surprisingly, this breach of freedom was met with considerable backlash from the religious community.

As an alternative to these kinds of divisive demands for conformity with the views of those in power, Galston suggests we adopt a political pluralism that understands:

> human life as consisting in a multiplicity of spheres, some overlapping, with distinct natures and/or inner norms. Each sphere enjoys a limited but real autonomy. It rejects any account of political community that creates a unidimensional hierarchical ordering among these spheres of life; rather, different forms of association and activity are complexly interrelated. There may be local or partial hierarchies among subsets of spheres in specific context, but there are no comprehensive lexical orderings among categories of human life.[48]

Galston warns that liberal democracies built on political pluralism 'should make us very cautious about expanding the scope of state power in ways that mandate uniformity'.[49]

If only more would heed the calls of Stout, Galston and Carter to respect religion in the public square. But, alas, radical secularists would have religion removed from the public square altogether. Consider Harvard law professor Mark Tushnet's 6 May 2016 blog post, 'Abandoning Defensive Crouch Liberal Constitutionalism'.[50] Tushnet's message is that secular liberals have won the culture wars and no longer need to accommodate conservative religions. Hence, he advocates an aggressive stance not only to challenge legal decisions secularists disagree with, but to take a hard-line approach (i.e. 'you lost, live with it') towards the 'losers' of the culture wars. He does not end there:

> I should note that LGBT activists in particular seem to have settled on the hard-line approach, while some liberal academics defend more accommodating approaches. When specific battles in the culture wars were being fought, it might have made sense to try to be accommodating after a local victory, because other related fights were going on, and a hard line might have stiffened the opposition in those fights. But the war's over, and we won.[51]

Law professor Paul Horwitz rightly challenged Tushnet's 'advocacy of an aggressive, uncompromising consolidation and advance' on 'culture war' issues.[52] Horwitz describes the 2016 US presidential election swing to the right as a vote against the 'idea of having centralized establishment elites entrenching their own power and using it by hook or crook to push their victories into new territories on new positions and take a "hard line" against those "losers"'.[53] In many respects, this is a fulfilment of Professor Stout's and Carter's warning of the unintended consequences of an aggressive secularist rhetoric.

Though there are unique characteristics to American politics that do not always translate into the Canadian landscape, or to other English common law countries, an increasingly polemicized culture is found in these nations. And it is within this polarized culture – left versus right, liberal/progressive versus conservative, secular versus religious – that religious communities are now facing a challenge to their registered charitable status.[54] Therefore, a book that takes seriously the secularist challenges to religious charities maintaining their registered charitable status is long overdue.

Book Summary

The initial chapters provide the theoretical underpinning as to the nature of religion and the benefits of religion to society. The following chapters delve into more concrete examples that illustrate how or why the advancement of religion ought to remain a charitable head and how or why the presumption of public benefit is appropriate, effective and constitutionally sound. They also consider the implications of ignoring or discarding the doctrine of public benefit of the advancement of religion.

Professor Juliet Chevalier-Watts argues that 'charity law is the perfect instrument to enable the most fitting utilization of religion' for society. Law and religion, she points out, are inextricably linked in Western law. Her deep analysis of legal history reveals that all four heads of charity – relief of poverty, advancement of education, advancement of religion and other trusts beneficial to the community – have the common theme of public benefit that justifies the legal and fiscal concessions granted to charities. Religious charities serve functions for the public benefit that governments are unable to provide, and the public benefit doctrine is an effective means of ensuring that charitable religious bodies properly carry out their services.

Raymond Chiu asserts that a narrow understanding of religion results in arbitrary or adverse decisions for religious charities. He argues that policies regarding religion and benefit have been arrived at 'piecemeal, with tacit assumptions' instead of a coherent, social scientific perspective, which the chapter aims to provide. The law needs to understand that religion is a 'phenomenon that centres on the deepest human need for meaning, significance and connectedness'. Chiu distinguishes between spiritual and religious, noting that religiousness is multidimensional, multilevel and multivalent, and that both religion and benefit operate on three levels – societal, organizational and individual. The current legal treatment of religious concepts and levels fails to appreciate the distinct contributions of each layer or the integration between them, instead drawing artificial boundaries or confounding expected effects. For example, organizations may vary in the degree of religious content offered in para-church activities and may 'on the surface appear similar to secular alternatives', but they are still informed by deep religious beliefs and communal bonds. Further, to frame benefits on an individual level puts religious organizations at a disadvantage because they are more holistic.

Rev. Dr John Pellowe's piece in this collection presents a compelling picture of religious engagement and its implications for the betterment of society at large. He argues that religious commitment results in better personal outcomes because it leads practitioners to make more responsible choices. Religion develops and activates prosocial attitudes and behaviours such as empathy, social responsibility and generosity. There are demonstrable community benefits such as social capital and infrastructure. Religion also creates tangible and intangible benefits for the public at large through other-centredness and civic engagement that is foundational for liberal democracy. Pellowe's argument is that given the measurable benefits of religion, it therefore makes sense for government to continue granting charitable status to religious organizations on the presumption that advancement of religion is beneficial. The removal of religious communities from registered charitable status, Pellowe maintains, would have a dramatic and negative impact on our collective good.

Dr Frank Cranmer helpfully contributes the UK experience of moving from the traditional position of advancement of religion as charitable, to the *Charities Act* 2011 which eliminated the presumption of public benefit for that head. In its place is a mandatory statutory public benefit requirement. Dr Cranmer's analysis of the *Hodkin* decision reveals how such a framework functions now in practice. The case involved the Church of Scientology, which was considered a religion, but was denied charitable status because its activities were deemed insufficient to be considered a public benefit. The reader may well see Cranmer's chapter as a cautionary tale of what a regime without the traditional approach to advancement of religion looks like.

Professor Bernard Doherty presents a detailed account of the English Preston Down Trust (PDT) case involving the Exclusive Brethren religious group. In 2006, the PDT was denied charitable status because the Brethren advocate the doctrine of 'separation from evil'. Therefore, their engagement with non-Brethren and the wider public is limited.

The group entered into negotiations with the UK Charity Commission, and in 2014, the Commission announced it would register the PDT on the basis that the group agreed to vary its practices (especially those involving internal discipline of members). Doherty observes that UK charity law has become 'a site of legal contestation and questions of legitimacy for minority religious groups in common law jurisdictions'. One could expect, as Doherty notes, accusations of historic abuse by former members to now be addressed in this context – that is, impacting questions about charitable status. And it may, in turn, 'open the field for all manner of potentially vexatious and financially ruinous claims directed at organisations on historical grounds'. The PDT case 'requires more careful and nuanced discussion, not least in how legislatures and regulators address the distinct sociological and historical contingencies and challenges posed by controversial minority religious groups like the Brethren'.

Derek Ross and Ian N. Sinke argue in their chapter that Canadian constitutional law is not entirely neutral in relation to 'advancement of religion'. Indeed, the Supremacy of God clause in the *Charter of Rights and Freedoms* suggests a religiously positive pluralism in Canada. This is enhanced by the *Charter*'s protection of religious freedom, association, expression and equality and the obligation in *Charter* adjudication to look through a multicultural lens. Ross's and Sinke's observations remind us that Canadian constitutional law does not have a strict separationist view as in the United States. This is important when we consider how different Canadian political voices use the US context when offering commentary.

In Barry W. Bussey's chapter we are reminded of the Canadian Bar Association counsel's argument before the Supreme Court of Canada (SCC) that the tax exempt status of religious communities must be evaluated through the equality lens. Government must not be seen as endorsing a discriminatory position that violates '*Charter* values' by granting registered charitable status to a charity with discriminatory views. The background for this argument is the Bob Jones University (BJU) case that was decided by the US Supreme Court during the Reagan Era. The US Internal Revenue Service took away the Christian university's charitable status due to BJU's racist policies. That case is now being erroneously applied in Canadian courts to remove 'government benefits' such as state accreditation of a Christian law school.[55] Though the BJU case was not specifically mentioned by the SCC in its 2018 Trinity Western University (TWU) law school decisions, Bussey argues that the SCC's reasoning makes no sense but for the BJU analysis and that such analysis is misapplied to religious communities that follow legally acceptable religious practices on fundamental life issues such as marriage.

Professor Janet Epp Buckingham also addresses the TWU law school case but in the context of Canada's educational history and the beneficial role of religious institutions in Canada. She references Peter MacKinnon's *University Commons Divided* which argues that faith-based universities open to the public must comply with secular social norms. This prevailing but illogical argument was embraced by the SCC in the TWU case and, taken to its logical extreme, suggests that religious charities must comply with secular norms or lose charitable status. This is against the founding spirit of charitable endeavours in Canada. Expecting churches to be confined to their four walls limits religious freedom to the much narrower freedom of worship.

Professor Iain T. Benson wraps up our discussion by addressing the reality that Western culture no longer understands or respects the public place of religion in establishing central moral ideas that are essential to make society work. Lost, too, is the recognition of the importance of religion to individual and communal well-being. We no longer allow for different moral viewpoints on issues such as marriage or abortion but face forced conformity under the language of 'equality' or 'non-discrimination'. This sentiment arises when the state is seen as the author of our freedoms rather than liberty being the base condition of all citizens in an open society that maximizes legal space for disagreements. Instead, we are in a setting where law is overtaken by ideology that disparages conscience. We are in a political freefall and we face a future not unlike the communist era that enforced 'atheist pledges'. Benson reminds us that 'secular' must not be held to mean 'non-religious' but rather as a broader description that allows room for religious and non-religious views. Indeed, 'If "secular" means "the opposite of religious" or "non-religious," and if the public realm is defined in terms of the "secular," then the public sphere has only one kind of believer removed from it – the religious believer'. 'The ultimate irony about the proper relationship between charity and religion', Benson observes:

> is that the only relationship that will last is if one is first charitable to religion in order to benefit from the charitable dimensions of religion. This will require a considerable course-correction from the drift of contemporary culture and its aggressive new approaches to law which show a marked tendency towards the denigration of religious communities and their charities rather than the encouragement of both.

Concluding Remarks

The SCC's fondness for the BJU legal analysis, as noted above, along with our polarized cultural moment, and the utilization of the controversial '*Charter*' values' doctrine, has put the charitable status of religious communities in jeopardy unless they conform to the normative moral commitments of power elites in academia, media and the legal profession. The ideology driving the current elites would have religious charities close their doors if they remain non-compliant. This was evident in the 2018 TWU cases as introduced above and described in detail in the following pages. Indeed, as Professor Carter observed, if the same anti-religious secularist position had been as prominent during the Civil Rights Era as it is now, it would not 'accommodate the openly and unashamedly religious rhetoric' of the Civil Rights movement.[56]

Many within the Canadian religious charitable sector felt some trepidation when the Canadian Senate announced in January 2018 the appointment of a Special Senate Committee on the Charitable Sector.[57] Would it address the culture wars? Would it recommend the removal of charitable status of those religious charities that refused to bend the knee to secularist ideological positions, like TWU?

There was considerable relief when the Committee released its report,[58] and it was revealed that the Committee eschewed the call for the removal of advancement of religion[59] as a category. As noted by the Committee, 'if new categories of charitable purposes were added, or existing ones removed, a "culture war" could disrupt the sector'.[60]

However, the Committee did make some recommendations that are disconcerting for religious charities. For example, it recommended that the annual return charities file with Canada Revenue Agency (CRA) include questions on 'diversity representation based on existing Employment Equity guidelines'.[61] Should this Senate recommendation be accepted and implemented, there are a number of questions that will have to be addressed. For example, would the government impose obligations on a religious charity to hire or appoint board members and/or employees not of that faith community in the name of diversity?

Many in the religious community were not willing to compromise their religious convictions to gain government funding for summer jobs for students through the Canada Summer Jobs programme, as mentioned earlier. As a result of the Canadian federal government's imposition of a 'values' test in pursuit of their policy aims, we got to see first-hand just how overreaching government may become. It may well be that a well-intentioned idea will have unintended consequences, a common theme that runs throughout this volume.

The Senate Report referenced the work of Susan D. Philips that charitable status is 'thought to confer legitimacy on an organization, as registered charities are subject to regulatory oversight by the CRA'.[62] As we have seen in the discussions above and will see in the pages following, this approach is bound to cause ongoing struggle for religious communities that do not comply with elite definitions of morality on fundamental human life issues.

Professor Adam Parachin reminded the Senate Committee that charities are intrinsically different from businesses and argued that their distinctive character should be preserved:

> I think that part of what we're investing in with charities is a culture of giving [...] I think there's something profound in us collectively validating, celebrating and recognizing the choice to share and that choice to share through a donation is itself intrinsically important, independently of the goods and services supplied by charities. I think we should worry about preserving that. Market transactions with charities may fund charitable goods and services, but it's not the same thing as the choice to share. I worry about us crowding that out as a defining feature of the sector.[63]

The choice to share is organic within religious communities. In short, it is who they are.

Historically, we have presumed that religion is beneficial. Any suggestion that would either remove the advancement of religion, or advocate the removal of other benefits granted to religious institutions (such as tax exempt status), is predicated on the contrary assumption that religion provides no benefit, or if it does, it only benefits congregants on a Sunday (or Saturday or Friday) morning. This reveals a deeply flawed notion of religion and the role of religion in society by confining religion to a church building or calendar day; it further suggests that a church building cannot be used for any purpose other than prayer and preaching on the designated holy day.[64] All other activities conducted in the church are deemed non-religious, or commercial, even if any revenue generated is used to offset costs and further the mission of the congregation. This lacks appreciation for not only the communal nature of religion[65] but also the holistic nature of religion. Further, it suggests that religious works can be separated from religious beliefs.[66] To see where these flawed assumptions lead, we need only think of Quebec's recent legislation that implies that believers can take off a religious symbol without damaging or sacrificing their beliefs and, indeed, their essence.

Our cultural moment, with its hypersensitive attention to diversity and equality, appears to be harbouring a level of animosity towards the religious community such that it is willing to entertain the removal of religion's registered charitable status. Where, then, is the equality and diversity protection of religious communities that have consistently taken up charitable causes for the common good?

Notes

1 That is, *Commissioners for Special Purposes of the Income Tax Act v Pemsel*, [1891] AC531 (H.L.). In her chapter in this volume, Juliet Chevalier-Watts provides a helpful and more detailed discussion of the *Pemsel* decision, along with the 1601 *Statute of Elizabeth*. See also Ross and Sinke, and Cranmer, who refer to Lord Macnaghten's pivotal decision in their respective chapters as well.
2 Don McRae, presentation to the Special Senate Committee on the Charitable Sector, Ottawa, Monday, 5 November 2018, online: https://sencanada.ca/en/Content/Sen/Committee/421/CSSB/54369-e. See also the Committee's final report, 'Catalyst for Change: A Roadmap to a Stronger Charitable Sector' (Ottawa, June 2019), online (pdf): <https://sencanada.ca/content/sen/committee/421/CSSB/Reports/CSSB_Report_Final_e.pdf> [hereinafter 'Senate Report'].
3 *Charities Act*, 2006 S. 3(2), online: <https://www.legislation.gov.uk/ukpga/2006/50/contents>.
4 Charity Commission, 'The Advancement of Religion for the Public Benefit', Supplementary Public Benefit Guidance, December 2011, online (pdf): <https://www.gov.uk/government/uploads/system/uploads/attachment_data/file/358531/advancement-of-religion-for-the-public-benefit.pdf.>
5 *Statute of Charitable Uses* 1601 (43 Eliz I c 4).
6 Donovan Waters, QC, 'The advancement of religion in a pluralist society (Part I): Distinguishing religion from giving to "charity"' (August 2011) 17:7 Trusts & Trustees 652–67 at 660.
7 This is not, in any way, to whitewash any culpability of religious charities not fulfilling their ideal purposes throughout their service. However, by and large, it is my position, that more good has been realized than not in their public good works.
8 Waters, *supra* note 6 at 665.
9 *Ibid*, at 667.
10 Donovan Waters, QC, 'The advancement of religion in a pluralist society (Part II): Abolishing the public benefit element' (September 2011) 17:8 Trusts & Trustees 729–38 at 738.
11 See Iain T. Benson's discussion of the history and development of secularism in 'Considering Secularism', in *Recognizing Religion in a Secular Society*, ed. Douglas Farrow (Montreal: McGill-Queen's University Press, 2004), 83–98.
12 Richard Rorty, 'Religion in the Public Square: A Reconsideration' (Spring 2003) 31:1 The Journal of Religious Ethics 141–49 at 142 [hereinafter 'Religion in the Public Square']
13 Stephen L. Carter, *Culture of Disbelief: How American Law and Politics Trivialize Religious Devotion* (New York: Doubleday, 1993), 53.
14 *Ibid*, at 214.
15 George Jacob Holyoake, *English Secularism: A Confession of Belief* (Chicago, IL: Open Court, 1896), 119.
16 Paul Carus, 'Publisher's Preface', in *English Secularism*, v–vi [italics added].
17 *Ibid*, at vii.

18 See Peter L. Berger, *The De-Secularization of the World* (Grand Rapids, MI: Eerdmans, 1999); and Ian Ward, 'Democracy After Secularism', (2010) 19:2 Good Society 30–36.
19 Berger states,

> 'There exists an international subculture composed of people with western-type higher education, especially in the humanity and social sciences that is indeed secularized. This subculture is the principle "carrier" of progressive, enlightened beliefs and values. While its members are relatively thin on the ground, they are very influential, as they control the institutions that provide the "official" definitions of reality, notably the educational system, the media of mass communication and the higher reaches of the legal system'. (*The De-Secularization of the World*, 34)

20 Brian Clarke & Stuart Macdonald, *Leaving Christianity: Changing Allegiances in Canada since 1945* (Montreal: McGill-Queen's University Press, 2017) at 7.
21 Government of Canada, 'Charities Program Facts and Figures' (31 March 2018), online: <https://www.canada.ca/en/revenue-agency/services/charities-giving/charities-media-kit/charities-program-facts-figures.htm>.
22 Pew Forum, 'Canada's Changing Religious Landscape' (27 June 2013), online: *Pew Research Centre: Religion and Public Life*, <http://www.pewforum.org/2013/06/27/canadas-changing-religious-landscape/>.
23 Joel Thiessen, 'The Rise of the "Nones"' (3 December 2014), online: *Joel Thiessen, PhD*, <http://www.joelthiessen.ca/single-post/2014/12/03/The-Rise-of-the-Nones>.
24 Michael Barnett & Janice Gross Stein, *Sacred Aid: Faith and Humanitarianism* (Oxford: Oxford University Press, 2012) at 4.
25 *Ibid*, at 4.
26 *Ibid*, at 5.
27 See 'The Public Benefit of "Advancing Religion" as a Charitable Purpose: A Canadian Perspective' in this volume.
28 Clarke & Macdonald, *supra* note 20 at 240–41.
29 *Ibid*, at 241.
30 *Ibid*, at 242.
31 *Ibid*, at 243: 'In short, Canada's charitable and non-profit organizations rely on "a small group of core supporters," among whom weekly attenders are strongly represented. As the pool of those who are religiously active recedes, so too, one can project, will this group of core supporters'.
32 *Ibid*, at 244.
33 *Ibid*.
34 *Ibid*, at 245.
35 Jeffrey Stout, 'The Folly of Secularism' (2010) 19:2 Good Society 10–15.
36 *Ibid*, at 13.
37 See Richard Rorty, *Philosophy and Social Hope* (New York: Penguin, 1999), 170–71: 'we shall not be able to keep a democratic political community going unless the religious believers remain willing to trade privatization for a guarantee of religious liberty'.
38 Spoken by Denis Diderot's character Antistrophe in his poem, 'Les Éleuthéromanes ou Furieux de la Liberté'. Actual wording is, 'Et ses mains ourdiraient les entrailles du prêtre, Au défaut d'un cordon pour étrangler les rois'. See *Oeuvres Completes de Diderot* (Paris: Garnier Freres, Libraires-editeurs, 1875), 16, online: https://archive.org/details/oeuvrescomplte09dide/page/n7?q=Les+%C3%89LEUTH%C3%89ROMANES++ou++Furieux+de+la+Libert%C3%A9.
39 Stout, *supra* note 35 at 13; citations added.
40 *Ibid*.
41 *Ibid*.
42 *Ibid*.

43 Carter, *supra* note 13 at 264.
44 *Ibid*, at 264–65.
45 Rorty, 'Religion in the Public Square', *supra* note 12 at 141–49.
46 *Ibid*, at 148–49.
47 William Galston, 'Religion and the Limits of Liberal Democracy', in *Recognizing Religion in a Secular Society: Essays in Pluralism, Religion, and Public Policy*, ed. Douglas Farrow (Montreal: McGill-Queen's University Press, 2004), 42–43.
48 *Ibid*, at 46–47. This conceptualization of autonomous spheres brings to mind Abraham Kuyper's formulation of 'sphere sovereignty' in *Our Program: A Christian Political Manifesto*, Abraham Kuyper Collected Works in Public Theology (Lexham Press, Kindle Edition), Kindle Locations 1532–39.
49 *Ibid*, at 49.
50 Mark Tushnet, 'Abandoning Defensive Crouch Liberal Constitutionalism' (6 May 2016), online (blog): *Balkinization*, <https://balkin.blogspot.ca/2016/05/abandoning-defensive-crouch-liberal.html>.
51 *Ibid*.
52 Paul Horwitz, 'Doubling Down AND Walking Back on "Abandoning Defensive Crouch Liberal Constitutionalism"' (21 December 2016), online (blog): *PrawfsBlawg*, <http://prawfsblawg.blogs.com/prawfsblawg/2016/12/doubling-down-and-walking-back-on-abandoning-defensive-crouch-liberal-constitutionalism.html>.
53 *Ibid*.
54 See Ian Bushfield, 'Toward A Modernized Charity Framework For Canada: Submission to Special Senate Committee on the Charitable Sector', B.C. Humanist Association (17 September 2018), online: <https://d3n8a8pro7vhmx.cloudfront.net/bchumanist/pages/2297/attachments/original/1537216366/2018_BCHA_CSSB_Submission.pdf?1537216366>.
55 *Trinity Western University v The Law Society of Upper Canada*, 2016 ONCA 518 (CanLII), online: <http://canlii.ca/t/gs9d5>.
56 Carter, *supra* note 13 at 227.
57 Special Senate Committee on the Charitable Sector, online: https://sencanada.ca/en/committees/cssb/ (Hereinafter, 'Committee'.)
58 'Senate Report', *supra* note 2.
59 The British Columbia Humanist Association submitted that the advancement of religion should be omitted or 'expanded to include (i) a religion that involves belief in more than one god and (ii) a religion that does not involve belief in a god' (CSSB, Brief, 1st Session, 42nd Parliament, 17 September 2018, p. 3, online: https://sencanada.ca/content/sen/committee/421/CSSB/Briefs/CSSB_BCHumanistAssociation_e.pdf).
60 'Senate Report', *supra* note 2 at 74, citing prominent charity lawyer Mark Blumberg.
61 *Ibid*, Recommendation 8, at 38–39.
62 *Ibid*, at 65. Susan D. Philips, 'More than stakeholders: Reforming state-voluntary sector relations' (2001) 35:4 Journal of Canadian Studies 182–202.
63 'Senate Report', *supra* note 2 at 90.
64 This thinking is evident in the decision of Justice Gregory M. Warner in *New Minas Baptist Church v Director of Assessment*, 2017 NSSC 72, at paras 122–26:

> I am not satisfied that every activity carried out by a religious congregation is exclusively for a religious or congregational purpose. If a congregation, based on its evangelical or humanitarian beliefs and a recognition of needs in the community, were to construct and operate a seniors' residence, a retail thrift or discount store, or a bakery, other than for the primary benefit of its own congregation, and in competition with similar non-religious operations, it is not conducted exclusively for religious or congregational purposes. The operation of a public service, based on a congregation's religious values, is not synonymous with operation for religious or congregational purposes only. To say

otherwise would be to say that any activity carried out by a congregation or church that involved the use of real property would be exempt from taxation. The word 'religious' has many dictionary definitions. The relevant meaning depends upon context. A broad meaning could be: 'characterized by adherence to a religion'. Another could be: 'of, concerned with, or appropriate to, or teaching religions'. 'Congregational' means 'of or like a congregation'. A congregation is a group of people who come together for religious worship. In ordinary language, use of a church hall for religious or congregational purposes is a use primarily directed to the members of church community [sic], not a use focused on a service to the public community.

While Warner's decision is focused on municipal taxes and land use, this seems to contradict both a Christian understanding of faith in action and the advancement of religion as a charitable head in the sense that a religious charity must provide a public benefit – as the Preston Down Trust case involving the Plymouth Brethren illustrates.

65 See Barry W. Bussey, 'The Right of Religious Hospitals to Refuse Physician-Assisted Suicide' (2018) 85 Supreme Court Law Review (2d) 1 at 211:

It is important to note the communal aspects of religious freedom [...] The principal reason for this is that the accommodation accorded to persons makes little sense if it is not also accorded to groups. Failing to protect the group not only deprives groups of any recognition when it is clear that their associational dimension is important to society but also robs the person of the collective and associational dimension of the right. With respect to religion, this collective dimension of 'communion' (the root concept within the word 'community') is a core aspect of the religion chosen by the individual. A religious believer without other religious believers and their chosen religious group is like a citizen without a country.

66 'The essence of the concept of freedom of religion', said former Chief Justice Brian Dickson of the SCC, 'is the right to entertain such religious beliefs as a person chooses, the right to declare religious beliefs openly and without fear of hindrance or reprisal, and the right to manifest religious belief by worship and practice or by teaching and dissemination. But the concept means more than that', in *R v Big M Drug Mart Ltd.*, [1985] 1 SCR 295, 1985 CanLII 69 (SCC), para 94, online: <http://canlii.ca/t/1fv2b#par94>.

TABLE OF CASES

Adler v Ontario	143
Alberta v Hutterian Brethren of Wilson Colony	137, 189
Berry v St Marylebone Borough Council	99n54
Bob Jones University v United States	xix–xx, 161–64, 167–72, 174–76, 186, 190
Boucher v the King	200n176
Canada (Human Rights Commission) v Taylor	140
Canada Trust Co. v Ontario Human Rights Commission	212
Canadian Magen David Adom for Israel v Minister of National Revenue	211
Canterbury Development Corporation v Charities Commission	9
Carter v Canada (Attorney General)	147, 240n31
Catholic Care (Diocese of Leeds) v Charity Commission for England and Wales & Anor	97n14
Chamberlain v Surrey School District No. 36	187, 231–34
Christian Education South Africa v Minister of Education	229, 233–34
Christian Medical and Dental Society of Canada v College of Physicians and Surgeons of Ontario	228, 237n2, 240n31
Church of the New Faith v Commissioner of Pay-Roll Tax (Scientology case)	3, 11–13
Cocks v Manners	82, 105
Commissioner of Taxation of the Commonwealth of Australia v Word Investments Limited	3, 13–14
Commissioners for Special Purposes of the Income Tax Act v Pemsel	xii, 6–7, 81–82, 131
Dubois v The Queen	133
Egan v Canada	135
Gaum v Dutch Reformed Church	240n31
George Reynolds v United States	176
Gilmour v Coats	82, 105–6
Gosselin v Quebec	133, 151n46
Green v Connally	164
Green v Kennedy	163
Health Services and Support – Facilities Subsector Bargaining Assn v British Columbia	133, 152n74, 153n85
Holmes v Attorney General	92, 100n94, 101–3, 106–7, 110–14, 117
Independent Schools Council v Charity Commission	88, 107, 114

Keren Kayemeth Le Jisroel Ltd v Inland Revenue Commissioners	85
Lalonde v Ontario (Commission de restructuration des services de santé)	151–52n52
Law Society of British Columbia v Trinity Western University (2018)	22, 135, 148, 159, 161–16, 167–69, 171–72, 174–76, 178, 186, 189–90, 191n11, 198n136, 205, 206, 214, 216, 225, 227–28
Liberty Trust v Charities Commission	3, 8–10, 13
Loyola High School v Quebec (Attorney General)	136–37, 214
McBurney v R	129–30, 149
Minister of Home Affairs and Another v Fourie and Another	239n14
Moscow Branch of the Salvation Army v Russia	153–54n109
Mounted Police Association of Ontario v Canada (Attorney General)	142
Mouvement laïquequébécois v Saguenay (City)	132, 145, 147–48, 151n33
Multani v Commission scolaire Marguerite- Bourgeoys	187
National Anti-Vivisection Society v IRC	111
New Minas Baptist Church v Director of Assessment	xxiv–vn64
O'Sullivan v R	155n144
Obergefell v Hodges	170–71, 186
R (Hodkin) & Anor v Registrar General of Births, Deaths and Marriages (2012)	90–91
R (Hodkin) & Anor v Registrar General of Births, Deaths and Marriages (2013)	xviii, 81, 90–91, 94–95
R v Advance Cutting and Coring Ltd	135
R v Big M Drug Mart Ltd	xxv n66, 59, 134, 135–36, 139–40, 233
R v Butler	190
R v Keegstra	140
R v Mills	151n36
R v NS	142–43
R v Oakes	134, 139, 147, 134
R v Registrar General ex parte Segerdal	90–91
R v S(RD)	142
R v Videoflicks Ltd	188
R v Zundel	139, 153n91
Re Greenpeace of New Zealand Inc	10, 13–15
Re Shaw's Wills Trusts	12
Re South Place Ethical Society	86, 91, 94
Re Watson (deceased); Hobbs v Smith and others	104, 106, 111
Reeve and Barisheff, Re	151n52
Reference re Bill 30, An Act to Amend the Education Act (Ont)	143
Reference Re Public Service Employee Relations Act (Alta)	138–39, 142, 153n85
Reference re Same-Sex Marriage	171–72, 212
Saskatchewan Federation of Labour v Saskatchewan	153n85
Saumur v City of Quebec	143

Shergill & Ors v Khaira & Ors	98n32
SL v Commission scolaire des Chênes	132
Syndicat Northcrest v Amselem	133, 135–36
Thornton v Howe	104, 106, 111
Trinity Western University v British Columbia College of Teachers	133, 162, 167, 171, 182, 190, 213, 217, 235
Trinity Western University v Nova Scotia Barristers' Society (2015)	176
Trinity Western University v The Law Society of British Columbia (2016 BCCA)	168, 172–73, 183, 227–28
Trinity Western University v The Law Society of Upper Canada (2016 ONCA)	181, 183
Trinity Western University v The Law Society of Upper Canada (2018 SCC)	161–62, 167–69, 171–72, 174–76, 178, 186, 189–90, 205, 206, 214, 216, 225, 227–28
Vancouver Society of Immigrant and Visible Minority Women v MNR	7, 97n17, 149nn 2, 13

Part I

CONCEPT AND PRACTICE OF PUBLIC BENEFIT

Chapter One

HAVE A LITTLE FAITH: THE ADVANCEMENT OF RELIGION AND PUBLIC BENEFIT

Juliet Chevalier-Watts*

Abstract

The concept of charity is an ancient one, underpinning many aspects of societies. Indeed, charities assist states by alleviating many welfare encumbrances that otherwise would have to be conducted by government agencies. However, there are growing public concerns around granting charitable privileges to organizations whose charitable endeavours are underpinned by intangible belief systems and whose moralistic stance may be contrary to the social policies of the day. This chapter argues that, despite attacks in the media, religion is still as relevant in contemporary society as it was in the past. Religion contributed to the development of Western law and continues to positively influence society in many areas including health benefits and economic gains.

This chapter reviews the legal history of the advancement of religion as a public benefit. The public benefit doctrine, and its presumption, are an effective method of ensuring that charitable religious bodies function legally and benefit their communities. Three cases from New Zealand and Australia are analyzed to support the argument: *Liberty Trust v Charities Commission*, *Church of the New Faith v Commissioner of Pay-Roll Tax* and *Commissioner of Taxation of the Commonwealth of Australia v Word Investments Limited*.

While modern society places challenges at the feet of charity law, these cases illustrate that charity law is equally at home in the new millennium as it was in the seventeenth century. The presumption of public benefit legitimizes the advancement of religion and ensures that a religion's charitable resources are distributed appropriately to its beneficiaries. Charity law, through public benefit, enables religious charities to operate for the public good.

---

* *PhD Candidate; LLM (Distinction); PGCLT; LLB (Hons); BA (Hons) Associate Dean Research, Senior Lecturer in Law Te Piringa – Faculty of Law, University of Waikato; Juliet.chevalier-watts@waikato.ac.nz. Note: this chapter is based on an early draft of a PhD thesis chapter and further makes reference to earlier published articles written by the author.*

Introduction

Charity has early origins in, and is often seen as sustaining, the healthy functioning of society, filling the welfare openings that have been left exposed either as a result of the government policies of the day or shortfalls in government assistance. Thus, it can be said that charity assists with decreasing many of the welfare encumbrances that might otherwise be placed on states while at the same time performing essential roles within a variety of communities. Charity should, therefore, not be underestimated for its value within society.

As will be outlined, there are a number of legally recognized charitable purposes, and the advancement of religion is one such purpose. However, against the backdrop of societies becoming purportedly less religiously inclined and the seemingly growing religious terrorist threats, the relevance of the advancement of religion within a charity context is being questioned. As a result, pressures grow to address public concerns that revolve around granting charitable privileges to organizations whose charitable endeavours are underpinned by intangible belief systems and, indeed, whose religious moralistic stance may be contrary to the social policies of the day.

This chapter demonstrates that religion is still just as relevant in contemporary society as it was in ancient times and, further, that charity law is the perfect instrument to enable the most fitting utilization of religion, under the embrace of advancement of religion.

In undertaking this analysis, this chapter considers the doctrine of public benefit and its role within charity law to ensure the legitimacy of religious charitable purposes, and specifically considers the approach of the Australasian courts to evaluate critically the issues surrounding public benefit and the advancement of religion.

Prior to considering the jurisprudence of Australia and New Zealand, we will set out, briefly, the importance of religion generally within society, to contextualize its relevance. Then we will outline the law relating to charitable purposes, and public benefit, in order to underpin the discussions that follow.

Religion and Society

Religion is undoubtedly of ancient origins, as evidenced in worldwide cave and escarpment paintings and carvings dating back millennia. The Australian Aboriginal religions are tens of thousands of years old, and it is said that the Vedas, the Hindu religious texts, date back 6,000 years.[1] As the notion of religion developed throughout the world, so the numerous belief systems became associated with ceremonies, rituals, sacred objects and writings, as well as shaping and compelling cultural rules regarding, *inter alia*, clothing, marriage, behaviour, food and diet. Indeed, the influence of religions was so strong that it 'often buttressed or became consolidated with the civil power as with the Pontifex Maximus, the Pharaohs, the Aztecs, and many existing religions'.[2] Its effect is still felt today in relation to civil power. For instance, it was said that there was an evangelical surge that helped put Donald Trump in the White House.[3]

With regard to religion and law, specifically Western law, the two concepts of religion and law are indistinguishably interconnected; indeed, Western law cannot be understood in isolation from its religious influences. Every aspect of social and political life was pervaded by religion. With the revival of Roman law in the eleventh and twelfth centuries, the method of studying Roman law texts was the same as scholasticism, which was derived from Greek dialectical reasoning.[4] This reasoning was utilized to 'explain, harmonise, and reconcile the Scriptures'.[5] In addition, the Christian theology of revelation was conjoined with Roman and Greek notions of natural law, and these underpinned the Medieval legal system, as well as various religious notions influencing the content of European civil law, and the common law, in particular through canon law.[6]

It is likely unarguable that religion and law are closely connected, certainly in relation to Western society, but religion within society goes deeper than that. It is asserted that it is religion that underpins that which it means to be human. This is because from early civilizations, humans have sought answers to the meaning and purpose of life, and religion provides some of those answers.[7] Indeed, religion has not only provided answers to the existence and place of humans within the cosmos but is also said to impact beneficially on certain aspects of society, over and above spiritual benefits.

For instance, religion reduces the number of medical terminations, has a lowering effect on divorce rates and assists with judicious payment of debts. There is also further evidence that religiously influenced people are more likely to give to charities and to undertake charity work.[8] Interestingly, religious attendance of once or more a week is also said to have health benefits. A number of studies have revealed that such attendance may increase a person's life span by up to seven years, in addition to boosting a person's immunity, on top of benefits that include decreasing a person's blood pressure, lowering rates of depression and lowering alcohol and narcotic consumption and abuse.[9]

Religious participation also impacts in a positive manner with respect to youth offending and increases the possibility of completing school or college. Such influences often result in improved financial circumstances for society generally, by reducing imprisonment and reintegration expenses. This also then can result in lower unemployment rates, which is likely to reduce state aid to individuals. It is not just the youth who may be advantaged by religious influences. Religiously involved adults are also less likely to be criminally active and, in turn, consequently make fewer demands on state aid and provisions.[10] These many non-spiritual advantages provide numerous benefits as a result of religious observances, not least of which are economic gains for the community. These impacts of religion are said to benefit the American economy to the tune of approximately $2.6 trillion annually; this amounts to about one-sixth of the total economic output.[11]

The economics of charitable giving, and in particular, giving to religious bodies, should therefore not be underestimated, and it is a reflection of the importance of religion in society generally. For instance, in 2016, the total given by Americans to non-secular charitable organizations was $122.9 billion (inflation-adjusted dollars). The next highest amount donated was to education charities, and that amounted to $59.8 billion (inflation-adjusted dollars).[12] In addition, in the United States alone, religion-related businesses and institutions, as well as places of worship, bring in more revenue than Google, Apple and Amazon combined, contributing an impressive $1.2 trillion annually to that nation's GDP. However, this is thought to be a conservative figure; the amount may actually be more than that.[13]

The contribution to society by religion is not just related, however, to identity or economics. Religion has impacted profoundly on 'the contribution of religious organisations, throughout history, to building the constitutional infrastructure [...] of contemporary society',[14] and its impact is said to be beyond estimation.[15] Indeed, many jurisdictions, including New Zealand, Ireland and Canada, are beholden to religious organizations for their role in providing health and educational systems that still exist today.[16] The reality is, therefore, that religious institutions underpin and support national infrastructures, many of which are closely linked to charitable organizations. These include medical institutions and schools and also religious institutes themselves,[17] all of which illustrates the essential role that religion plays within society and through its charitable connections.

What these benefits and relationships suggest, therefore, is that economically and socially, humans would be poorer individually and collectively without the influence of religion throughout society. Indeed, any exclusions of religion within charity law may have adverse consequences for key sections of society, such as hospitals and schools. This would be detrimental not only to the infrastructure of the state generally but also to members of the community who are reliant on such institutions and their support.

This brief foray into the relationship between religion, society and the law has illustrated the fundamental role of religion within society generally. Nonetheless, religion remains the target of consistent and repeated attacks in the media and communities. By way of example, one only has to look to actor and comedian Ricky Gervais, with his millions of followers on Twitter and Facebook, to see the influence of negative press in relation to religion. Mr Gervais is renowned for his criticisms of religion and has observed, in relation to the privileges given to religions granted charitable status, that '[s]ame sex marriage isn't gay privilege, it's equal rights. Privilege would be something like gay people not paying taxes. Like churches don't'.[18] Further, he states that we 'shouldn't even need the word "atheism." If people didn't invent ridiculous imaginary Gods, rational people wouldn't have to deny them'.[19]

Mr Gervais's views are not held in isolation. Famous critics such as Richard Dawkins and Christopher Hitchens[20] are highly vocal in their public criticisms of religion, and brief searches on social media outlets, such as Facebook and Twitter, will reveal equally vociferous and sustained attacks on religion generally.

Against this backdrop, and in conjunction with the apparent darkening cloud forming in relation to religious terrorism facing many communities, it is timely to consider religion's place within society, specifically within the construct of charity law, which this chapter seeks to do.[21] In order to begin this journey, this chapter now sets out, in brief, some of the legal principles associated with charity and religion.

Charitable Purposes and Public Benefit

While much has been written on this matter, it is still important to set out the classifications of charitable purpose, which are rooted in the *Charitable Uses Act* 1601, otherwise known as the *Statute of Elizabeth*.[22] The preamble of this long-repealed[23] Act categorized those purposes that would be legally recognized as charitable, although that list of purposes was said not to be exhaustive.[24] This list of charitable purposes is still recognized in contemporary times. This came about because Lord Macnaghten, in the renowned case of *Income Tax Special Purposes Commissioners v Pemsel*,[25] produced a classification of charitable purposes which found their essence in the aforementioned preamble. Thus, his Lordship confirmed that charity comprises four principle divisions, as follows:[26]

> Trusts for the relief of poverty; trusts for the advancement of education; trusts for the advancement of religion; and trusts for other purposes beneficial to the community, not falling under any of the preceding heads.

Since the recognition of this famous classification, the law of charity has developed, and a number of jurisdictions have added to this list of charitable purposes. For instance, England and Wales now recognizes 13 heads of charity,[27] and Australia has similarly extended its list of recognized charitable purposes.[28] New Zealand, however, retains the original *Pemsel* heads of charity, which are embedded in its Charities Act 2005.[29] New Zealand is not alone in this approach. In the leading Canadian authority of *Vancouver Society of Immigrant and Visible Minority Women v M.N.R.*, the Court observed:[30]

> Canadian courts have consistently applied the *Pemsel* test to determine that question. The *Pemsel* classification is generally understood to refer to the preamble of the *Statute of Elizabeth*, which gave examples of charitable purposes.

What these statutory provisions confirm is a preservation of many of the common law principles.

Of note is that, historically, the common theme that was seen to run through the range of purposes was that they were all of public benefit,[31] even though the *Statute of Elizabeth* does not refer unequivocally to specific public benefit. Nevertheless, the Preamble was seen as recognizing purposes that provided public benefit; thus, 'if there is any thread linking these crude judicial attempts to define charity, it is in the conception of charity as a *public use*'.[32] The effect, therefore, is that for a purpose to obtain charitable status, it must be legally recognized as a charitable purpose, and further, it must be for the public benefit. We turn now to setting out the requirements of public benefit.

In general, those purposes that fall within the first three heads of charity – in other words, those purposes that relieve poverty and advance education and religion – were said to be presumed for the public benefit.[33] For purposes that fall within the fourth *Pemsel* head – that is, purposes that are beneficial to the community – the public benefit is not presumed and must be demonstrated specifically. It should be noted that the United Kingdom has made some considerable legislative modifications to the public benefit doctrine, whereby it is now confirmed that in 'determining whether the public benefit requirement is satisfied in relation to any purpose falling within section 3(1), it is not to be presumed that a purpose of a particular description is for the public benefit'.[34] In other words, the presumption of benefit has been removed for all heads of charity, including the advancement of religion. In New Zealand, and for the most part in Australia, the presumption of public benefit remains.[35]

Thus, public benefit has been infused into charity law by the courts, and the main concern of the courts is to ensure that an entity is not able to 'take advantage of the favoured position of charities in order to carry out what is essentially a private purpose'.[36] In other words, 'it is the element of public benefit that justifies the legal and fiscal concessions granted to charities'.[37] It is generally accepted that there are two components of the public benefit test. This is articulated in the New Zealand High Court case, *Liberty Trust v Charities Commission*:[38]

> It is accepted that in order to have a charitable purpose the entity must be carrying out its purposes for the benefit of the public. This means that the entity must confer a 'benefit' and that it does so in respect of the public or a sufficient section of it.

In other words, the purposes must demonstrate a public benefit, and that benefit should be for the public or a sufficient section of the public.[39] In relation to the advancement of religion, it is 'well settled'[40] that 'a gift for religious purposes is prima facie charitable, the necessary element of public benefit being presumed unless and until the contrary is shown'.[41] Nonetheless, the doctrine of public benefit has been subject to some criticism throughout the years, for instance:[42]

> The concept of public benefit is intangible and nebulous; its effects can only be represented as variable and unpredictable. Imprecision has resulted in illogical and capricious decisions, sometimes impossible to reconcile.

In addition, 'few would regard the [public benefit] and the manner in which it has been applied as wholly coherent and satisfactory'.[43] Such criticisms have done little to assuage the concerns of the public in relation to the continued existence of the advancement of religion as a charitable purpose. However, this chapter asserts that even though this doctrine may be subject to criticism, public benefit provides a legally justifiable and legitimate defence in ensuring that purposes that fall under the advancement of religion will benefit communities, within the confines of the law, through the appropriate allocation of their assets from their charity endeavours. This is so even if cases may be deemed controversial or unpopular in the public view. Therefore, it is argued that the public benefit doctrine, and its presumption, are an effective method of ensuring that charitable religious bodies function as prescribed by law, and as a result, the public will benefit. To illustrate this, we turn firstly to the New Zealand High Court case of *Liberty Trust v Charities Commission*.[44]

Liberty Trust

Liberty Trust was first registered under the *Charities Act* 2005, and its main activity is to provide a mortgage-free lending scheme. This scheme was generally funded by donations, and from that, interest-free loans were made to donors and others. The Charities Commission, as it was at the time,[45] removed the Trust from its charity register, and the Trust subsequently appealed this decision to the High Court.

The Trust seeks:

> to advance the Christian faith by teaching & demonstrating the Bible's financial principles, to assist those in financial difficulty, relieve financial burdens and advance the Kingdom of God. Part of our ministry is lending interest-free to enable New Zealanders to own their own

homes, churches, and ministries without long-term debt, so they can be free to fulfill God's call upon their lives [sic].[46]

The funds are available to all creeds and faiths, with the main message of teaching Biblical financial principles through, among other matters, its loan scheme. Mallon J, in this case, had no concern regarding whether or not the scheme advanced religion;[47] therefore, the issue of interest to this chapter is that of public benefit in relation to whether a mortgage scheme meets the requisite public benefit.

As has been noted, the Trust's purposes include relieving financial burdens, in a hope that Christianity would be advanced as a result of having such burdens alleviated. In other words, recipients of the loans 'can be free to fulfill God's call upon their lives'.[48] This is a commendable approach, although it is not clear how a person should fulfil this requirement. Thus, there may be an argument that the purposes are 'focused too narrowly on its adherents',[49] thereby creating a private benefit, as opposed to a public benefit. Indeed, it might be argued that such a hope is analogous to the circumstances discussed in the New Zealand High Court case of *Canterbury Development Corporation v Charities Commission*. In this case, Ronald Young J stated:[50]

> The applicants' core activities and central focus were to assist and increase the profitability of particular businesses in the hope that there would be an economic lift for the Canterbury region. While the relief of unemployment could be a charitable purpose under the relief of poverty ground, this outcome was too remote from the purposes of the appellants, whose aims were to assist businesses to prosper. The activities were not therefore of public benefit and of direct benefit to a significant part of the public.

In essence, therefore, the purposes need to be more than hopeful, otherwise there would only be an indirect benefit. In relation to the loan scheme, while the aim is to enable 'borrowers to be released from financial burdens and to generously serve and build God's Kingdom',[51] it is not clear precisely how borrowers should serve and build God's kingdom. Therefore, it could be argued that Liberty Trust's loan scheme has a strongly focused private benefit, making the public benefit too remote and making the private benefits perhaps not incidental to the overall public benefit.[52]

However, in answer to this assertion, Mallon J stated that the private benefits reaped from the loan scheme were, in fact, 'seen as part of living as a Christian. An integral part of the scheme is that its benefits are to be shared with others',[53] ensuring that the public benefit element is not rebutted. Indeed, as her Honour asserts:[54]

> These cases are therefore quite different from a private benefit conferred as part and parcel of an activity directed at advancing religion [...] all Christian teaching should be beneficial in the long term for members of the faith so that personal benefit is a necessary element but [...] that is not the end of it.

This suggests, therefore, that the purposes are not 'focused too narrowly on its adherents',[55] although leading a 'Christian life free of the burdens of debt'[56] does suggest that the private benefits are not necessarily incidental. Certainly, this is a grey area because it has been argued that[57]

> there is a line to be drawn between the outworkings of a religious faith that, being ancillary and incidental in nature, can be seen to manifest an organisation's religious beliefs, and those that are disproportionate and unrelated to such an organisation and its beliefs.

There could be grounds for asserting that an interest-free mortgage scheme is not necessarily related to the outworkings of a religious faith. However, Mallon J observed, significantly:[58]

> In terms of the private/public benefits it is difficult to distinguish it from a mass in a Church which is open to the public. A mass in a church may have more ready acceptance as being of a religious nature and for religious purposes than a mortgage scheme that is set up as an example of the Bible's message but that is not the point. On the evidence before me this mortgage scheme is a public example of what is intended to be a Christian approach to money and part of propagating the Christian faith.

Therefore, her Honour's assertions are persuasive as to why a mortgage scheme may demonstrate the requisite public benefit and, importantly, why the public benefit requirement should not be rebutted. Further, just because a purpose may not be readily accepted in the public eye, this does not mean that the public benefit should be rebutted. This point was raised by Elias CJ, for the majority, in the Supreme Court case of *Re Greenpeace of New Zealand Inc*, where her Honour declared that 'unpopularity of causes otherwise charitable should not affect their charitable status',[59] and neither should 'lack of controversy [...] be determinative'.[60]

If popularity, or lack of controversy, were requirements of public benefit, the result would, in effect, exclude 'much promotion of change while favouring charitable status on the basis of majoritarian assessment and the status quo'.[61] Such an approach would, surely, be contrary to the very spirit of charity law, which, in reality, 'should be responsive to the way society works'.[62] If charity fails to respond to the way in which society works, then the law is actually 'likely to hinder the responsiveness of this area of law to the changing circumstances of society'.[63] For example, once upon a time, it would have been inconceivable that purposes such as encouraging the abolition of the slave trade, promoting civil rights or indeed the promotion of environmental protection would be construed as charitable.[64] Nonetheless, charity law has seen fit to find such purposes charitable, even in the face of public criticism. This offers further evidence that charity must evolve to meet the needs of the society of the time, and it is able to do this appropriately through the doctrine of public benefit.

Certainly, it is acknowledged that the *Greenpeace* decision did not refer to the advancement of religion; however, it is submitted that the principles in relation to public benefit are analogous to the assertions in relation to the *Liberty Trust* case. As a result, the latter case demonstrates that public benefit is a useful legal device by which the judiciary may determine the overall benefit to the public, still contained by legal parameters. It represents a rational and practical standpoint which sets public benefit within a contemporary context, whereby financial burdens are of key concern to many in today's society. Reducing such burdens is likely to have benefits overall for society by lessening pressure on individuals and thus mitigating the pressure on society to alleviate those financial worries. As a result, charity law has demonstrated its practical application in a real-world context, underpinned by, and within the confines of, the public benefit doctrine.

Australian jurisprudence echoes New Zealand's pragmatic approach to the utilization of the public benefit doctrine in such a way as to justify the relevance of religion in society but within the confines of charity law. We turn to two cases, both controversial, to assess public benefit and its importance in ensuring that purposes meet stringent charity law requirements while at the same time providing valuable benefit to communities. We begin with *Church of the New Faith v Commissioner of Pay-Roll Tax (Scientology case)*.[65]

The Scientology Case

The question for the High Court of Australia was whether Scientology is a religion. In brief, Scientology was founded by L. Ron Hubbard, and as a self-prescribed religion, it offers 'a precise path leading to a complete and certain understanding of one's true spiritual nature and one's relationship to self, family, groups, Mankind, all life forms, the material universe, the spiritual universe and the Supreme Being'.[66] The High Court, in the *Scientology* case, confirmed the fundamental importance of religion within its legal framework, observing:[67]

> Protection is accorded to preserve the dignity and freedom of each man so that he may adhere to any religion of his choosing or to none. The freedom of religion being equally conferred on all, the variety of religious beliefs which are within the area of legal immunity is not restricted.

I assert that charity law underpins this requirement through the judicious recognition and application of the public benefit doctrine, and as will be addressed, the Court in this case confirmed that public benefit legitimizes Scientology. However, interestingly, the Court makes little explicit reference, if at all, to the doctrine of public benefit. Nonetheless, the doctrine can be implied throughout the judgements so as to validate the legal recognition of Scientology.

It was observed by the Court that the 'law seeks to leave man as free as possible in conscience to respond to the abiding and fundamental problems of human existence'.[68] This suggests that many people struggle with their place in the universe. Some people are able to rationalize their existence through the 'natural order, known or unknowable by use of man's senses and his natural reason',[69] and this provides an adequate answer to the concern of existence. However, not all people find comfort or appeasement in this manner. In those circumstances, 'an adequate solution can be found only in the supernatural order',[70] and this offers a sense of reason for a person's existence in the grand scheme of matters.

Herein lies the implicit recognition of public benefit. The benefit is found in the comfort provided by religion in assisting humans to find their place within their own environment and within the world generally. Such a benefit may not be explicitly measurable, but providing emotional and spiritual succour ensures, among other matters, that humans have sufficient coping mechanisms to deal with life's challenges and are able to function appropriately within society. Charity law already recognizes that finding emotional pleasure in a purpose can be charitable because it satisfies a public benefit.[71] The reason being, as asserted by Vaisey J in *Re Shaw's Wills Trusts*, that promoting and encouraging the arts and graces of life is the 'finest and best part of the human character'.[72] Such a reasoning can be aligned with the benefit, therefore, of religion in promoting spirituality because it can develop, beneficially, a human character.

This reasoning finds support in the *Scientology* case, whereby the Court noted that faith in the supernatural provides a means of rationalizing the sense of inadequacy felt by many humans in relation to their place within mankind generally and also within the universe.[73] Further, religion 'relates a view of the ultimate nature of reality to a set of ideas of how man is well advised, even obligated, to live'.[74] The implication being, therefore, that public benefit may be found in guidance that a religion provides for the beneficial conduct of humans as well as providing a sense of reassurance as to humanity's place in the universe.

Certainly, there may be some scepticism in relation to the emergence of new religions, such as Scientology, when legally recognized religious status confers financial and other advantages. Such a scepticism has been prevalent within Australia since European settlement, not least due to the progress of science. However, religion still retained a foothold within Australia, perhaps in part because of the harsh Australian climate and environment. Religion continued to provide answers and comfort to the settlers in a new and challenging environment, offering relief and guidance. Thus, the public benefit of religion in those circumstances was a pragmatic result of the environment, and religion remains today just as important within Australia as it was to the early European settlers. This, therefore, enables emerging religions to find a place within society, even if there are questions as to the legitimacy of the religion itself.[75]

Indeed, it might be argued that any public benefit in Scientology may be rebutted due to questions raised as to its hoax-like nature or that charlatanism features heavily within its construct. The *Scientology* case explored these issues and provided some perhaps surprising answers to such questions raised.

Murphy J confirmed that the 'truth or falsity of religions is not the business of officials or the courts'.[76] If that were the business of such bodies, then all religions might fail such a test.[77] Instead, religion is seen as giving people 'security and inner strength not to be crushed by the monstrousness of the universe'.[78] Scientology, therefore, sits within the construct of a religion, regardless of whether or not a person may question its truth, because many established religions may also have their truths questioned.

The Court also confirmed that a test of public acceptability in relation to a religion would not, implicitly, be a method of assessing the overall public benefit. This is because nearly all religions begin as a minority interest group, often gathering around the teachings of an inspiring leader. Any subsequent increase in public acceptance is oftentimes gradual and challenging. The Court confirmed that 'a test of public acceptability would create "a danger that a claim's chances of success would be greater the more familiar or salient the claim's connexion with conventional religiosity could be made to appear"'.[79] It could be argued that the proliferation of religions, and religious sects, would therefore create difficulties for 'any test based on public acceptability'.[80] As a result, the public benefit is not to be found in popularity. Rather, it is to be found in the overall benefit it brings to a group that is persuaded of that religion's teachings. This echoes the earlier assertions made in relation to the *Liberty Trust* case, as supported by the findings in the Supreme Court case of *Greenpeace*. Public benefit cannot be assessed on popularity as this may retard the law and cause the charitable sector to suffer overall. The provisions of charity are not always popular, and indeed, oftentimes charity supports those who are sidelined, or who are considered unworthy, by society. That charity provides assistance to such members of society reflects the true nature of charity – non-judgemental and open to all, regardless of perceived worth, which is underpinned by public benefit.

Returning then to the *Scientology* case, it was further argued that Scientology should be denied religious status because it was asserted that it displayed charlatan-type tendencies, or was merely a sham.[81] If this was so, then its public benefit would surely be rebutted. In response, however, the Court observed that 'charlatanism is a necessary price of religious freedom, and if a self-proclaimed teacher persuades others to believe in a religion which he propounds, lack of sincerity or integrity on his part is not incompatible with the religious character'[82] of the religion itself. Indeed, many established religions might fail if faced with such a test.

Therefore, even in the face of stringent criticism and negativity, Scientology found its place within the recognized religions of Australia. While perhaps controversial, it can be argued that the implied public benefit of Scientology ensures that its purposes are constrained within the law, and the law has legitimized its charitable status and will continue to do so. Scientology is, perhaps, a product of contemporary society, and therefore, as considered in the *Liberty Trust* case, this is merely a reflection of the ability of charity law to adapt to new challenges and new requirements, within the constraints of public benefit.

This chapter now considers the second Australian case, *Commissioner of Taxation of the Commonwealth of Australia v Word Investments Limited*.[83]

The Word Case

In this case, Word was established by Wycliffe Bible Translators, Australia, to generate funds for Wycliffe, which is an evangelical body. It spreads the word of God through international missionary work. One of the key questions for the High Court was whether Word could be charitable when it does not engage in charitable activities beyond making profits, which are then directed to charitable institutions that do engage in charitable activities.[84] Such activities suggest that the public benefit may then be rebutted because of the profitability of the organization. In considering this, the Court, *inter alia*, considered a submission by the Commissioner that 'that money subject to charitable trusts is not "applied for charitable purposes" unless actually expended in the field'.[85] In answer to this, and implicit that the public benefit would be met, is that such an approach would be unworkable and, indeed, would be unacceptable. This is because many charities, large and small, operate on the basis of raising money and then choosing other suitable charitable organizations to submit those funds to,[86] thereby ensuring that the public benefit is met.

The High Court asserted that this was likely to be the position in Australia because 'the charitable purpose [...] is often [...] to be found in the natural and probable consequences of the trust rather than its immediate and expressed objects'.[87] The public benefit is therefore implied within the 'natural and probable consequences of the trust', which, in application in the *Word* case, meant that the Court found that it did advance religion.

It might be argued that such implicit recognition of public benefit would extend the doctrine of public benefit beyond its original envisioned connotation. Indeed, this decision has provoked criticism because it has been argued that this decision may be utilized:[88]

> for abusive tax behaviour, as it would seem to open the floodgates for all manner of creative business ventures by religious charities and others, which in future will not need to relate to their charitable purpose.

I would argue, however, that public benefit still has an important role to play in ensuring that charitable purposes are achieved, and if such purposes are not a 'natural and probable consequence' of an entity's activities, then the public benefit will likely be rebutted. Therefore, the doctrine of public benefit may ensure that such 'abusive tax behaviour' does not come to fruition. The *Word* case further reflects the position of charity law within a contemporary society, legitimized by public benefit, whereby the courts now recognize that commercialism is, in reality, a very real part of religions today. Indeed, '[c]ommercialism is so characteristic of organized religion that it is absurd to regard it as disqualifying'.[89] Operating on a commercial basis does not negate public benefit; rather, public benefit can ensure that a religious entity's purposes do benefit the public, notwithstanding its commercial outlook.

Conclusion

I began this chapter by asserting that religion is just as relevant within modern society as it was in ancient times and, in addition, that charity law provides the ideal vehicle to ensure the appropriate function of religion within society, through the doctrine of public benefit. This is because that doctrine legitimizes religion and offers a method of administering a religion so as to satisfy public concerns. The authorities discussed in this chapter demonstrate the relevance of the doctrine in ensuring that, even in the most controversial of circumstances, the charitable sector can benefit generally from a variety of modern purposes.

Ensuring that public benefit is recognized and applied in such a variety of circumstances ensures that charity law remains functional in contemporary society. This assertion finds support in the *Greenpeace* case, wherein Elias CJ noted:[90]

> Just as the law of charities recognised the public benefit of philanthropy in easing the burden on parishes of alleviating poverty, keeping utilities in repair, and educating the poor in

post-Reformation Elizabethan England, the circumstances of the modern outsourced and perhaps contracting state may throw up new need for philanthropy which is properly to be treated as charitable. So, for example, charity has been found in purposes which support the machinery or harmony of civil society[.]

To find otherwise would risk a 'rigidity in an area of law which should be responsive to the way society works. It is likely to hinder the responsiveness of this area of law to the changing circumstances of society'.[91] It is acknowledged that this final point relates specifically to the political purpose doctrine; however, I would assert that such a statement does also relate to the advancement of religion because it has been demonstrated how valuable religions are within society. Thus, to limit their function within charity would be to the disadvantage of society overall.

Indeed, I would argue that religion may be seen as being a part of the 'machinery and harmony of civil society' because of its benefits to society overall, as highlighted earlier in the chapter. Therefore, charity law should continue to acknowledge the advancement of religion, and this can be done effectively through the judicious and efficient utilization of the public benefit doctrine. The doctrine serves as a restraint on purposes that may not meet charitable requirements. Such purposes may include unlawful purposes, or purposes that may be contrary to public policy; thus, the public benefit would be denied and the purpose struck down. Where the public benefit is rebutted, this is likely to be because the subsequent resultant benefits were not established sufficiently.[92]

Therefore, I assert that, overall, the public should feel reassured about the authorities that have been considered in this chapter. This is because 'whilst modern day society places challenges at the feet of charity law […][these] case[s] illustrate […] that the courts recognise that charity law is equally at home in the new millennium as it was in the 1600s'.[93] It could be argued that these decisions actually illustrate the overarching philosophy of charity generally, which is to benefit society overall, even though it might be argued that neither a mortgage scheme nor an unconventional religion nor a commercial entity, could have been anticipated by lawmakers back in the 1600s. Such divisive entities, however, should not automatically be precluded from religious status because, as was evidenced, charitable purposes change as society changes. What a society in the 1600s required was very unlikely to be what a society in 2019 requires. Such contemporary purposes merely reflect charity responding to the changing needs of society, under the effective scrutiny of the public benefit doctrine, which in turn provides legal surety and clarity, which underpins the requirements of the rule of law.[94]

Therefore, the presumption of public benefit legitimizes the advancement of religion and ensures that a religion's charitable resources are distributed appropriately to its beneficiaries. This chapter has demonstrated that charity law, through public benefit, enables religious charities to operate for the public good, as required by law. Therefore, charity law is an appropriate conduit to enable religion to operate for the benefit of society generally, and the doctrine of public benefit enables the charitable resources from religions to be distributed effectively for the public. As a result, the benefits of religion can be realized in multiple communities. Further, the public can be reassured that while religious charities are subject to privileges associated with charitable registration, the public benefit doctrine ensures that the benefits provided by religions to communities are not outweighed by the privileges obtained by being a registered charity.

Notes

1 *Church of the New Faith v Commissioner of Pay-Roll Tax (Scientology case)* [1983] HCA 40, at para 10, *per* Murphy J [hereinafter *Scientology Case*].
2 *Ibid*, at para 11.
3 Brian J. Grim, 'Religion may be bigger business that we thought. Here's why', *World Economic Forum* (5 January 2017), online: <https://www.weforum.org/agenda/2017/01/religion-bigger-business-than-we-thought/> (accessed 8 June 2018).
4 Patrick Parkinson AM, 'Accommodating Religious Beliefs in a Secular Age: the Issue of Conscientious Objection in the Workplace' (2011) 34:1 UNSW Law Journal 281.
5 *Ibid*.
6 *Ibid*.
7 Barry W Bussey 'The Legal Revolution Against the Place of Religion: The Case of Trinity Western University Law School' (2016) 4 BYU Law Review 1136.
8 Niclas Berggren & Christian Bjornskov, 'Is the importance of religion in daily life related to social trust? Cross-country and cross-state comparisons' (2011) 80:3 Journal of Economic Behavior & Organization 461–62, referring to L. R. Iannaccone, 'Introduction to the economics of religion' (1998) 36 Journal of Economic Literature 1465–96; N. Berggren, 'Rhetoric or reality? An economic analysis of the effects of religion in Sweden' (1997) 26 Journal of Socio-Economics 571–96; and R. D. Putnam, *Bowling Alone: The Collapse and Revival of American Community* (New York: Simon & Schuster, 2000).
9 Jeffrey Dorfman, 'Religion Is Good for All of Us, Even Those Who Don't Follow One', *Forbes* (22 December 2013), online: <https://www.forbes.com/sites/jeffreydorfman/2013/12/22/religion-is-good-for-all-of-us-even-those-who-dont-follow-one/#713abffb64d7>, (accessed 8 June 2018).
10 *Ibid*.
11 *Ibid*.
12 Una Osili, 'What influences American giving?' *The Conversation* (25 July 2017), online: <http://theconversation.com/what-influences-american-giving-78800> (accessed 8 June 2018).
13 Kelsey Dallas, 'Economic impact of religion: New report says it's worth more than Google, Apple and Amazon combined', *Deseret News* (14 September 2016), online: <https://www.deseretnews.com/article/865662454/Economic-impact-of-religion-New-report-says-its-worth-more-than-Google-Apple-and-Amazon-combined.html> (accessed 8 June 2018); see also: <http://medfield.wickedlocal.com/news/20160921/economic-impact-of-religion-new-report-says-its-worth-more-than-google-apple-and-amazon-combined> and <https://www.washingtonpost.com/news/acts-of-faith/wp/2016/09/14/study-religion-contributes-more-to-the-u-s-economy-than-facebook-google-and-apple-combined/?noredirect=on&utm_term=.6636b74ca66e>.
14 Kerry O'Halloran, 'Charity and Religion: International charity law reform outcomes and the choices for Australia' (2011) 17:2 Third Sector Review 30.
15 *Ibid*.
16 *Ibid*.
17 E.g. the Catholic Church operates over 10,000 orphanages, 140,000 schools and 5,000 hospitals, as well as 16,000 other health clinics. Caritas, the umbrella organization for Catholic aid agencies, estimated that spending by its associate organizations totalled circa £2–£4 billion; therefore, this is one of the biggest aid agencies globally; see David Paton, 'The world's biggest charity', *Catholic Herald* (16 February 2017), online: <http://www.catholicherald.co.uk/issues/february-17th-2017/a-worldwide-force-for-good/> (accessed 8 June 2018). New Zealand

reportedly has nearly three hundred religious schools throughout the country; see Wikipedia, 'List of Christian Organisations in New Zealand', online: <https://en.wikipedia.org/wiki/List_of_Christian_organisations_in_New_Zealand> (accessed 8 June 2018).
18 Ricky Gervais (5 February 2014 at 19:05), online: *Twitter*, <https://twitter.com/rickygervais/status/431262322300952576?lang=en>.
19 Gervais (3 March 2012 at 05:17), online: *Twitter*, <https://twitter.com/rickygervais/status/175932824518533121?lang=en >.
20 Christopher Hitchens died in 2011, although many of his lectures are still publicly available on YouTube, e.g.: <https://www.youtube.com/watch?reload=9&v=MQox1hQrABQ> (accessed 8 June 2018).
21 While it is not within the remit of this chapter to discuss the issues related to terrorism that have been said to be related to religion, that issue may be a key concern for a number of communities. However, what can be said is that most cases of sectarian violence attributed to religion are, in fact, an oversimplification of complex sociopolitical, geographic, economic and cultural factors; see Elizabeth Shakman Hurd, *Beyond Religious Freedom: The New Global Politics of Religion* (Princeton, NJ: Princeton University Press, 2015) and also William T. Cavanaugh, *The Myth Of Religious Violence Secular Ideology And The Roots Of Modern Conflict* (Oxford: Oxford University Press, 2009).
22 Act (43 Eliz I, c .4) of the English Parliament.
23 Repealed by section 13(1) of the *Mortmain and Charitable Uses Act* 1888 (c. 42). However, as Halsbury's states, that repeal 'expressly preserved the preamble (s. 13(2)). With the repeal of the 1888 Act by the *Charities Act 1960*, the preamble is no longer on the statute book, but the preamble never had any statutory operation, and its final repeal does not affect the authority of the cases decided on it nor the principles on which future cases are to be decided'. See: *Halsbury's Laws of England*, 4th edn, 2001 reissue vol. 5(2): Charities, para 2, fn. 7, p. 8.
24 Hubert Picarda QC, *The Law and Practice Relating to Charities*, 4th edn (Haywards Heath: Bloomsbury Professional, 2010) at 14–16.
25 *Commissioners for Special Purposes of the Income Tax Act v Pemsel* [1891] AC 531.
26 *Ibid*, at 583.
27 *Charities Act 2006*, s. 2(2) and also *Charities Act 2011*, s. 3(1).
28 *Charities Act 2013*, ss 12(1) and 14–17.
29 *Charities Act 2005*, s. 5(1).
30 *Vancouver Society of Immigrant and Visible Minority Women v M.N.R.*, [1999] 1 SCR 10, 1999 CanLII 704 (SCC) at 12, http://canlii.ca/t/1fqmt.
31 Jonathan Garton *Public Benefit in Charity Law* (Oxford: Oxford University Press, 2013) at 1–3.
32 *Ibid*, at 18, citing Gareth Jones, *History of the Law of Charity, 1532–1827* (Cambridge: Cambridge University Press, 1969) at 121.
33 It has been argued that this statement is erroneous. However, it is outside of the scope of this chapter to address that specific point. For further discussions, please see, e.g., Mary Synge, *The 'New' Public Benefit Requirement Making Sense of Charity Law* (Oxford: Hart, 2015); *Independent Schools Council v Charity Commission for England and Wales* [2011] UKUT 421 (TCC); and Juliet Chevalier-Watts, *Charity Law International Perspectives* (Abingdon: Routledge, 2018) at 81 [*Charity Law*].
34 *Charities Act 2011*, s. 4(2).
35 This chapter, therefore, considers the presumption of public benefit because it focuses on Australasian case law.
36 Gino Dal Pont, *Charity Law in Australia and New Zealand* (Melbourne: Oxford University Press, 2000) at 13, citing *Perpetual Trustee Co (Ltd) v Ferguson* (1951) 51 SR (NSW) 256 at 263.
37 *Ibid*.
38 *Liberty Trust v Charities Commission* [2011] 3 NZLR 68 at para 99 [hereinafter *Liberty Trust*], referring to *Re New Zealand Computer Society Inc* HC Wellington CIV-2010-485-924, 28 February 2011 at para 14. This case will be addressed in detail later in the chapter.

39 Debra Morris, 'Charities and the Modern Equality Framework – Heading for Collision?' (2012) 65 Current Legal Problems at 298; see also *Gilmour v Coats* [1949] AC 426 (HL) and *Verge v Somerville* [1924] AC 496 (PC).
40 *Liberty Trust, supra* note 38 at para 99.
41 *Ibid*, referring to Jean Warburton, Debra Morris & N. F. Riddle, *Tudor on Charities*, 9th edn (London: Sweet & Maxwell, 2003), at para 2–048; and included in the footnotes: In the United Kingdom in 2006, legislation was passed requiring charities to be demonstrably for the public benefit (refer to s 3 of the *Charities Act* 2006 (UK), and also see UK Charity Commission, *Analysis of the Law Underpinning the Advancement of Religion for the Public Benefit* (online: <https://assets.publishing.service.gov.uk/government/uploads/system/uploads/attachment_data/file/358534/lawrel1208.pdf>)). It should further be noted that since the decision of the Upper Tribunal Tax and Chancery Chamber in *Independent Schools Council v Charity Commission* [2011] UKUT 421 (TCC), some elements of the Charity Commission for England and Wales Guidance on Public Benefit has been rewritten.
42 Andrew Iwobi, 'Out with the old, in with new: Religion, charitable status and the Charities Act 2006' (2009) 29:4 Legal Studies 630–31, citing G. H. L. Fridman, 'Charities and public benefit' (1953) 31 Canadian Bar Review 539; see also *Gilmour v Coats* [1949] AC 426 (HL) at 443.
43 Iwobi, *supra* note 42 at 630, referring to M. Freeland, 'Charity law and the public/private distinction', in *Foundations of Charity*, ed. C. Mitchell & S. Moody (Oxford: Hart, 2000), 111 and 121.
44 *Liberty Trust, supra* note 38.
45 The Charities Commission was disestablished on 31 May 2012 by the Charities Amendment Act (No 2) 2012. The Commission's core functions were transferred to the Department of Internal Affairs – Charities Services; see Chevalier-Watts, *Charity Law, supra* note 33 at 156.
46 Liberty Trust, 'Questions and Answers', online: <http://www.libertytrust.org.nz/questions> (accessed 25 May 2018).
47 *Liberty Trust, supra* note 38 at paras 91–98.
48 Liberty Trust, 'Questions and Answers', *supra* note 46.
49 *Liberty Trust, supra* note 38 at para 100.
50 *Canterbury Development Corporation v Charities Commission* [2010] 2 NZLR (HC) at para 2.
51 Liberty Trust, 'Principles in Action', online: <http://www.libertytrust.org.nz/principles> (accessed 28 May 2018).
52 Juliet Chevalier-Watts, 'Charitable Trusts and Advancement of Religion: On a Whim and a Prayer?' (September 2012) 43 Victoria University of Wellington Law Review 19–422.
53 *Liberty Trust, supra* note 38 at para 113.
54 *Ibid*, at para 107.
55 *Ibid*, at para 100.
56 *Ibid*, at para 125.
57 Juliet Chevalier-Watts, 'Charity Law, the Advancement of Religion and Public Benefit – Will the United Kingdom Be the Answer to New Zealand's Prayers?' (2016) 47 Victoria University of Wellington Law Review 385–409 at 404, citing Kerry O'Halloran, *Religion, Charity and Human Rights* (Cambridge: Cambridge University Press, 2014), 447.
58 *Liberty Trust, supra* note 38 at para 122.
59 *Re Greenpeace of New Zealand Inc* [2015] 1 NZLR 169 at para 75 [hereinafter *Greenpeace*].
60 *Ibid*.
61 *Ibid*.
62 *Ibid*, at para 70.
63 *Ibid*.
64 *Ibid*, at para 71, referring to, inter alia, *Jackson v Philips* (1867) 96 Mass 539 14 Allen 539 (Mass SC), and Charities Act 2006 (UK), s 2(2)(h).
65 *Scientology Case, supra* note 1.

66 'What is Scientology?' online: *Scientology*, <https://www.scientology.org/what-is-scientology.html?q=> (accessed 7 June 2018).
67 *Scientology Case*, *supra* note 1 at para 8, *per* Mason ACJ and Brennan J.
68 *Ibid*, at para 13.
69 *Ibid*.
70 *Ibid*.
71 *Royal Choral Society v Inland Revenue Commissioners* [1943] 2 All ER 101 and *Re Delius (deceased)* [1957] Ch 299 (Ch).
72 *Re Shaw's Wills Trusts* [1952] Ch 163 (Ch) at 172.
73 *Scientology Case*, *supra* note 1 at para 13.
74 *Ibid*, citing Clifford Geertz, 'An Anthropological Study of Religion', in *International Encyclopedia of the Social Sciences* vol. 13 (New York: Macmillan and Free Press, 1968) at 406.
75 It should be noted that since the arrival of European migrants, and subsequent later migrants to Australia, the dominant religion remains a variety of forms of Christianity. Nonetheless, other religions are prevalent, including the Aboriginal Dreaming, as well as other non-Western centric religions, such as Hinduism, Islam and Buddhism.
76 *Scientology Case*, *supra* note 1 at para 7, *per* Murphy J.
77 *Ibid*.
78 *Ibid* at para 13, citing Carl Jung, *Symbols of Transformation* (London: Routledge, 1956), 231.
79 *Ibid* at para 40, citing *Gillette v United States* [1971] USSC 45 at 457.
80 *Ibid*.
81 *Ibid*, at para 25, per Mason ACJ and Brennan J.
82 *Ibid*, at para 26.
83 *Commissioner of Taxation of the Commonwealth of Australia v Word Investments Limited* [2008] HCA 55.
84 *Ibid*, at para 34.
85 *Ibid*, at para 37.
86 *Ibid*.
87 *Ibid*, at para 38, citing *Baptist Union of Ireland (Northern) Corporation Ltd v Commissioners of Inland Revenue* (1945) 26 TC 335 at 348.
88 Juliet Chevalier-Watts, *Law of Charity* (Wellington: Thomson Reuters, 2014) at 214, citing Kerry O'Halloran, 'Charity and Religion: International Charity Law Reform Outcomes and the Choices for Australia' (2011) 17:2 Third Sector Review 29–44 at 36.
89 *Scientology Case*, *supra* note 1 at para 45, *per* Murphy J.
90 *Greenpeace*, *supra* note 59 at para 70.
91 *Ibid*.
92 *Registration Decision: The Jedi Society Incorporated* (JED494458) 14 September 2015 at paras 45–46.
93 Juliet Chevalier-Watts, 'Charity Law and Religion – A Dinosaur in the Modern World?' (2016) 13 No Foundations: An Interdisciplinary Journal of Law and Justice 124–43 at 135–36.
94 Kathryn Chan, *The Public-Private Nature of Charity Law Divide* (London: Bloomsbury, 2016) at 6.

Chapter Two

RELIGION AND PUBLIC BENEFIT: SOCIAL SCIENTIFIC PERSPECTIVES AND CRITIQUES

Raymond B. Chiu*

Abstract

The legitimacy of public support of religious charitable organizations is tied to a subjective value judgement of the benefit of advancing religion and protecting the religious rights of its members. Despite the variation in treatment across common law jurisdictions, the policy rationale and evaluation method associated with assessing benefit have never been clearly articulated. As a complex aspect of charity law internationally and human rights law in Canada, religion is one of the few heads of charity or enumerated grounds in which privilege or protection is afforded to people on the basis of a pathway of causality from cultural characteristics to effects experienced by individuals, organizations and society at large. In this chapter I explain how the lack of consensus on the question of religion and benefit stems from an insufficient understanding of what the question means. To address this deficiency, I provide social scientific perspectives and critiques in three topical areas: religious concepts and levels, the nature of relationships between levels and the theoretical description of reality. Rather than address the misleading proposition that religion must be instrumentally beneficial, lawmakers should understand that religion is a phenomenon that centres on the deepest human need for meaning, significance and connectedness. In view of the true nature of religion, I conclude that oversimplifying this reality and applying unsuitable tests do a disservice to our shared humanity.

Introduction

The legal discourse is at a crossroads regarding the place of religion within charity and human rights law. Current common law is characterized by an undeveloped policy

---

* Raymond B. Chiu, BASc (University of Toronto), MBA (York University), MTS (Tyndale Seminary, in progress), PhD (DeGroote School of Business, McMaster University), is an assistant professor at the Goodman School of Business, Brock University, where he teaches business ethics. His ongoing research in organizational behaviour and human resource management focuses on religious and spiritual beliefs in the workplace, truth and trust in leadership, the influence of moral beliefs on perception of leaders and ethical objectives in personnel selection.

rationale for maintaining religion as the third head of charity and lack of articulation of the nature of religion and the benefits expected from religious organizations.[1] Interventionalist administrative policies in England and Canada are compelling religious organizations to justify the value of their religious identity and public benefit, without established standards against which such value is to be assessed.

In Canada, interpretations of section 2(a) of the *Canadian Charter of Rights and Freedoms* have led to an emphasis on equal respect and non-discrimination rather than the preservation of religious liberty for groups and individuals.[2] Landmark decisions involving Trinity Western University now place religious organizations on a collision course with administrative bodies who question organizational mandates or policies based on human rights concerns.[3] Judgements of balance, reasonableness and proportionality under the *Charter* will now subject religious organizations to implicit tests of '*Charter* values' – which essentially is another term for perceived benefit and harm – without a full appreciation of the role of religious communities in the maintenance of societal diversity and wellbeing.

Foreshadowing what could happen in other common law jurisdictions (i.e. Canada, Ireland and Australia), England and Wales now have a legal regime in which public benefit must be explicitly demonstrated for any religious organization seeking tax privileges as a registered charity.[4] Regrettably, this change has not appeared to result in better certainty regarding how adjudicators should judge benefit.[5] Some voices suggest that the opposite direction is warranted: that religion should be accepted in a category separate from charity and considered beneficial on its own terms, without having to justify every one of its activities according to utilitarian standards.[6] Although courts in all jurisdictions avoid adjudicating the truth of religious beliefs, implicitly they weigh the value (i.e. benefit or harm) of those claims when they are pressured to allocate scarce tax-related resources or balance human rights interests.

While incremental changes to charity law advance through policymaking and case law, there has been little discussion of the social scientific perspective on religion and its benefits within the legal context. The centuries-old discourse regarding charity revolves around a phenomenon that consists of a relationship between two entities: religion and benefit. Both entities exist on three levels (societal, organizational and individual), meaning a relationship can be inferred from one of the three levels of religion to one of the three levels of benefit. In view of these levels, the legal environment with regard to the third head of charity consists of a conceptualization of religion that has been arrived at piecemeal, with tacit assumptions being made about the relationships between religion and its effects.

Hence, the purpose of this chapter is to critique the legal environment in terms of the ways that religious ideas and connections could be misconstrued or misapplied. I divide my discussion into three subject areas: first, the ideas of concepts and levels; second, the nature of relationships between levels; and third, the theoretical description of reality. Within each subject area, the social scientific perspective is presented with an eye towards its distinctive contributions to our current understanding of religion and benefit. Then, based on the social scientific lens, I embark on critiques of the current legal treatment. To conclude, I outline the overarching implications of the neglect of social scientific realities.

The explanations below are not intended to be a review of case law or the empirical literature. Instead, the focus is on providing a contextual introduction drawn from organizational scholarship and allied fields (social psychology, the psychology of religion, workplace spirituality, etc.). Organizational research (otherwise known as management research, administrative science, etc.) is well suited to the issues identified in this chapter because it is the type of inquiry that takes particular interest in individual and organizational phenomena that are situated in a public (i.e. workplace, marketplace) setting.

Concepts and Levels

Perspective: Religious Concepts and Levels Are Distinct

Religion is a system that encompasses all of life. Psychologists Benjamin Beit-Hallahmi and Michael Argyle remark, 'To most believers religion appears as a total ideology with a sense of the "natural" and the "real," without which it is impossible to conceive the world they inhabit'.[7] Unfortunately, the term *religion* carries considerable negative connotations stemming from a history of having represented institutional dogma rather than a personal experience. Sceptical voices, including the courts, claim that religion involves phenomena without proof. Yet psychologists of religion understand that many aspects of religion are as measurable as any other psychological or sociological phenomenon, particularly its beliefs and practices.[8] Moreover, its doctrines and values are well articulated, and its associated histories and symbols are well documented.

Despite disagreements over the differences between religion and spirituality, scholars have arrived at a consensus in which they recognize a significant overlap between the two. Both are understood to pertain to two elements: the sacred and a search. In the opening of the definitive handbook of the American Psychological Association, Kenneth Pargament and colleagues declare that the term *sacred* is 'used inclusively here to refer not only to concepts of God and higher powers but also to other aspects of life that are perceived to be manifestations of the divine or imbued with divinelike qualities, such as transcendence, immanence, boundlessness, and ultimacy'. Implied in the term *search* is an ongoing journey of discovery and revelation, such that transformations occur in the connection between the individual and the sacred.[9]

Psychologists of religion draw the line between the religious and secular at the point where the religious is indistinguishable from everyday psychological concepts like meaning or hope, or perhaps even a passion for nature or football! Because of the overlap, like other scholars I use *religion* as an umbrella term for the overall phenomenon of both religion and spirituality, and *religiousness* as an attribute of the phenomenon at any level, particularly the individual level (i.e. religiosity). *Spirituality* is a term used to signify a direct personal search for the sacred, whereas religiousness encompasses 'a search for significance in ways related to the sacred'.[10] For example, in an organizational context, mission statements, committee meetings and charitable donations may be considered 'religious' but not necessarily tied to one's individual quest for enlightenment.

Religiousness is considered to be a multidimensional (expressed in diverse ways), multilevel (societal, organizational, individual) and multivalent (positive and negative) concept.[11] At the societal level, religion is understood to originate from culture; there is nothing in religion that can be understood apart from it.[12] A religion is a subculture within the larger culture, or it could even be the dominant driver for a society's culture, and all cultures and organizations are in symbiotic relationship with each other.[13]

At the organizational level, the expression of religion is not a mere carbon copy of the culture-level religion: each type of organization takes on a different function and form. Places of worship focus on maintenance of the religious culture through transmission of doctrine and normative acts of reward and punishment. As for para-church organizations (i.e. relief charities, volunteer associations or faith-based schools), the manifestation of religion is dependent on how the organization approaches integration in the public sphere. Ronald Sider and Heidi Unruh, building on prior work from Stephen Monsma, Thomas Jeavons and others, show that internally there may be explicit religious content incorporated into programming, yet organizations may differ as to the extent to which religious experience among beneficiaries is necessary for the desired external changes in the community.[14] Sider and Unruh's data collection also showed that some organizations with highly religious cultures may not officially communicate their religiousness, whereas other organizations promising spiritual transformation may nonetheless deliver services that on the surface appear similar to secular alternatives.[15]

At the individual level, the conceptualization and measurement of religiousness are highly multifaceted. Because religion is truly a way of life, all aspects of lifelong humanity are reflected in some way through the different methods of assessing religiousness. Peter Hill and Ralph Hood's *Measures of Religiosity* catalogues 126 scales that have been developed up to 1999;[16] for the second edition under compilation, the number of scales being considered is many times the quantity of the first. In the original volume, the categories include religious beliefs, attitudes, orientation, development, commitment, experience and values, as well as measures focused on specific areas such as the afterlife, virtues (e.g. forgiveness) or fundamentalism. The main observation is that there is no one way of measuring a person's religiousness, and the choice of measure implicitly reflects assumptions about what is valued in religion.

Critique: The Concepts and Levels Have Become Confounded

The current legal treatment of religious concepts and levels fails to appreciate the distinct contributions of each layer or the integration between them, instead drawing artificial boundaries or confounding expected effects. This confusion is reflected in the private–public dichotomy that has arisen since the advent of secularism and is also reflected in legal discourse.[17] Social science, however, does not proceed from this starting point, especially when effects (i.e. benefit or harm) are being investigated. The foregoing assumption in social science is that entities at all levels have a potential to affect each other. Individual characteristics, including our personality traits, social values and religious identities, are assumed to have effects at other levels.[18] Contradicting the presumption that religion is a private affair, the Society for Human Resource Management found that nine out of ten workplaces reported some level of religious diversity among their employees, and religious discrimination complaints increased 69 per cent over a 10-year period, a rate faster than claims over race, national origin or sex discrimination.[19] Religious expression is an expected response to the challenges that citizens face in the public sphere, especially in the light of stressful and dehumanizing influences in marketplaces today.[20] Although prayer has been assessed by the courts as mainly private and beyond proof, it is an integral part of religious expression and an important indicator of religious virtue and the benefits that accrue from it.[21]

The multilevel reality of religion is reflected in the discrepancies between the English and Canadian legal approaches to religion. In England, religion is seen as a culture-level phenomenon in which there must be a belief system that is followed by a group of adherents. In Canada, the approach leans towards the individual level. Although in charity law a belief system involving some type of supreme being is typically required, the application of *Charter* rights by the courts have transformed the view of religiousness to a matter of strongly held convictions that may or may not be held by a particular community.[22] Inevitably, trying to apply a particular definition of religion at one level has the unintended consequence of inducing assumptions about the nature of expected benefits. The presumption of benefit focused on the organization or individual level (i.e. the religious charity or individual rights bearer) means that beneficial effects are assumed and evaluated only at a particular level. However, it is not quite clear from the courts which level of outcome is prioritized or how these effects might be different.

When religious rights compete with other priorities (e.g. other parties advocating for tax relief or *Charter* rights), particularly at the individual level, religious organizations are at a disadvantage because religious communities do not usually frame their benefits in such an instrumental way. As I will show in the next section, religion results in a variety of benefits across various levels and types of religiousness. Hence, it is difficult to find the 'pressing and substantial objective' required by the *Charter* to justify discrimination at the individual level without understanding the value of religion as a whole. The study of religion and spirituality from the point of view of sociology, anthropology and theology consistently emphasizes the important role of the collective aspect of religion, whether at the organizational or societal level.[23]

Finally, I must remark that any anticipated application of tests for religiousness or benefit is destined to run up against the complexity identified by Sider and Unruh. They identified 12 different attributes of organizations and their programmes that can vary in terms of religious expression, including lesser-known elements such as board composition, financial sources and physical environment. Commenced in response to US President George W. Bush's 2001 executive order to fund faith-based initiatives, the study was undertaken to address contentions around the legitimacy of state support for religious organizations. The authors' conclusions suggest that one must pay closer attention to the many ways that legitimate organizations can be 'religious' and that operational guidelines, innovative funding mechanisms and private giving at a grass-roots level may be more effective at stewarding funds than a top-down selection of who is worthy of privileged status.[24]

Relationships between Levels

Perspective: Concepts and Levels Are Related in Multiple Ways

Charity law is unique because it extends considerations to certain groups not on the basis of a category (e.g. biological age, company size, etc.) but on an inference regarding the relationship between two subjective entities: an impression of what makes an object truly *religious* and a perception of anticipated *benefit* to the *public*, beyond those individuals who advocate for distinct status. An *inference*, a foundational element of organizational psychology, is a conjecture regarding the manner by which one entity is associated with another.[25] The occurrence of one can be the cause of the other (a *causal* relationship), or the two can occur together without one causing the other (a *correlative* relationship), possibly due to the coincidence of a third or unknown entity.

Religion originates from culture at the *societal* level but is manifest at two additional levels, the *organizational* and the *individual*. Public benefit, which represents effects or outcomes of religious adherence, also exists on three levels. If we apply high-school math to examine the possible permutations, we discover that we are talking about three possible inferences from each of the three levels of religion for a total of nine across all levels. If we were more scientifically rigorous, we could identify more inferences that account for the fact that there are errors or inaccuracies in the way we measure any entity at any level, such as individual religiousness or societal benefit.[26]

The subdivision of the religion–benefit relationship into nine or more inferences may appear excessive. However, social scientific inquiry should proceed with just this type of care to genuinely appreciate religion and its effects, without which its findings become imprecise and meaningless. Within the space available, I touch on research that illustrates each of the nine inferences, but with three caveats. First, many studies show relationships, but it is quite a different matter to conclude proof of cause. Second, my review is by no means comprehensive, yet I do rely on more recent studies and their retrospective reviews. Third, I highlight research that indicates beneficial effects, although researchers are well aware of the negative effects of religion. Most religions do not endorse harm in their core doctrines and scriptures. Hence, the goal of the review is to illustrate the potential of religion to have deeply rooted transformative effects and not to render an unqualified judgement that all religions are always good. For clarity, I label each relationship using the codes R for religiousness, B for benefit and S, O and I for the societal, organizational and individual levels, respectively.[27]

With regard to relationships with *society- or culture-level religion* (RS), the tests involve looking at whether differences in culture across nations or regions predict characteristics of societies, organizations or individuals.[28] In an international investigation of the sociological theses of Max Weber regarding the economic effects of religion (explained more fully later), Rachel McCleary and Robert Barro found that higher belief in hell relative to religious service attendance had significant effects on growth of gross domestic product spanning 1965 to 1995.[29] Looking at provincial-level data from 2001 to 2011, Qunyong Wang and Xinyu Lin added to the mixed evidence of the relationship between religion and growth with the finding that Christianity in particular has significant positive effects on economic growth in China[30] (RS-BS). With regard to relationships with organizations, a study of local audit firms by Thomas Omer and colleagues showed that offices in highly religious US Metropolitan Statistical Areas were more sceptical in their assessments. These firms were more likely to issue audit opinions signalling substantial doubt about their client's ability to continue.[31] Another way of looking at religiousness is to examine religious diversity or pluralism. In prior studies reviewed as well as their own, Navina Lucke and Stefan Eichler affirm the pattern that religious diversity of a developing nation promotes foreign direct investment even while the effect on such investment is the opposite for ethnicity and language[32] (RS-BO). A major study by Michael Bond, Kwok Leung and colleagues revealed relationships between societal and individual characteristics in a cross-cultural survey using one of the few cross-cultural measures focused on worldview beliefs. Conducted across 41 nations, it showed that beliefs grouped by nation can be characterized by two dimensions: dynamic externality, which combines beliefs about the effects of people's efforts with beliefs in a supreme being and the benefit of being religious; and societal cynicism, which involves negative beliefs about human nature and institutions. The dimensions showed high correlations with 70 national and individual indicators, including measures of well-being, job/company/life satisfaction and views on leadership and work. The authors suggested that the negative relationship between dynamic externality and many of the indicators could reflect the human tendency to proactively reach out to external forces when faced with environmental difficulties[33] (RS-BI).

Quantitative research on the external effects of differences between *religious organizations* (RO) is relatively rare, likely because historically the presumption of benefit has been commonplace. There is still considerable sociological and qualitative research on religion, leading sociologist Joshua Yates to conclude that 'a credible body of academic work has profiled the economic impact of religion, the value of religious-inspired social capital, the religious contribution to mutual and humanitarian service, and more'.[34] Initial quantitative studies by two leading figures in the field, Ram Cnaan and Femida Handy, looked at the discrete contributions of churches, with the finding that the social services contributed to the community had an equivalent annual worth per congregation of $145,000 in Ontario and $184,000 in the United States.[35] Later, using conservative valuation methods, Ram Cnaan and Seongho An valued a congregation's contributions to their local urban ecologies at $1.27 M and $2.51 M annually[36] (RO-BS). Religious organizations also affect other organizations, notably commercial firms. In a series of studies in China, Xingquiang Du and colleagues determined that the proximity of a firm to places of worship (e.g. Buddhism monasteries, Taoist temples) predicted benefits in terms of environmental responsibility, philanthropic giving, tunnelling, owner–manager agency costs and earnings management, mirroring the direction of other studies[37] (RO-BO). I will leave to church administrators to review research on the theological, demographic and cultural characteristics that predict effective churches, but it is fair to say that the extent to which people voluntarily attend and support churches is a fairly good indicator that they are satisfied with the benefit they experience. While church attendance is typically an independent variable, Laurence Iannaccone and colleagues observed that churches that emphasize high involvement – frequent attendance and generous giving – also experience the greatest growth in attendance.[38] Attendance, in turn, results in less burden on public resources such as health care, explained in part by the support network that religious communities provide.[39] In a survey of first-generation immigrants across 23 congregations, Jill Sinha and colleagues noted that volunteering within the congregation is positively related to civic engagement, indicating that religious participation also enhances public participation by providing pathways to external opportunities[40] (RO-BI).

Individual-level religiousness (RI) pertains to variations between people on indicators of religiousness. Since the focus of this article is on the public benefit of organizations, this segment will be brief. Looking at the effects of individual observance on Canada's social fabric in 2010, Canada's Survey of Giving, Volunteering and Participating showed that people who attend religious services weekly give substantially more in total to charity and also give more generously to non-religious charities[41] (RI-BS). Individual effect on organizations is a central focus of religion-focused management research. Literature reviews indicate positive and negative effects of religiousness and spirituality related to the enactment of one's religious identity and calling. Much of the negative effects pertain to the challenges of conflicting values and spiritual struggles.[42] With regard to business ethics, Michael O'Fallon and Kenneth Butterfield reported that eight of ten recent studies together show a generally positive relationship between religiousness and ethical decision making[43] (RI-BO). The effect of religion on individuals has been the long-standing focus of research on religiousness. The general message gleaned from reviews is that religion functions primarily through the community to provide a supportive buffer against dysfunctional habits and harmful relationships, thereby transferring an overall benefit to society through the congregation's healthy social capital and capacity for self-care[44] (RI-BI).

Critique: The Complexity of Relationships Is Underappreciated

The examples of research given above are only a slice of a vast literature that has investigated religion over the last century. There are three principles that can be drawn from the explanation provided above. The first is that religion has different effects depending on the relationship in question. Many of these effects are difficult to prove without extensive research, and the plethora of mechanisms that produce them are difficult to discern on the surface, even by the faith communities themselves. Faith communities do not make claims that their religions have beneficial effects resulting from each and every person, measure, circumstance and event, especially when practiced by people who are inevitably needy, fallible and biased. Hence, it befits administrative and judicial bodies to consider whether religious organizations must always demonstrate an obvious benefit.

In reality, religion has a variety of effects across levels, following mechanisms that scholars have for centuries been occupied with trying to explore, theorize and confirm. Some of the most important relationships are not between religion and benefit, but between levels of religion. One could say that the scriptural, historical and liturgical aspect of a religion constitutes the core of its society-level or culture-level existence. The places of worship, religious seminaries and para-church organizations make up the organizational level. Such organizations are formed to simplify the consumption of discrete aspects of this system for the sake of its adherents. Beliefs are drawn from scriptures, interpreted by church-level bodies and enacted by members. Hence, religious beliefs are not simply the idiosyncratic preferences of an individual, as many human beliefs are. They have an important social function, helping organizations define who is accepted into the group and signal what they jointly are required to believe. On the one hand, such doctrines can be considered restrictive and coercive; on the other hand, the fact that most religious organizations make their beliefs open to scrutiny in an open and free society provides a level of transparency, accountability and choice never before contemplated among many secular organizations.

The integrity of the religious system, therefore, depends on all levels of the system. To compromise the integrity of any one level is to do an injustice to the whole system. Not only are there beliefs about individual aspects (life, death, morality) but also beliefs about collective aspects (membership requirements, collective decision making, family well-being, etc.) which are just as important. Yet court and state deliberations that operate at one level run the risk of applying tests that are simply not reflective of what any one religion is about. Legal and political systems are not necessarily equipped to evaluate such complex relationships, and the question remains as to whether the phenomenon of religion is amenable to a legal examination or better left to democratic and marketplace decision-making processes. Although the challenge of understanding religion appears inscrutable, in the subsequent sections I discuss how a more foundational approach can simplify the questions before us.

Theory and Reality

Perspective: Knowledge Comes from Theory Development

At the outset, I introduced the idea that the topic of religion and benefit presents a unique challenge to the legal community. This is the challenge of attempting to make administrative and judicial decisions based on the purported nature of a causal relationship. Considerable attention in social scientific disciplines is paid to ensuring that research methodologies properly handle these types of cause-and-effect questions. My discussion above about concepts, levels and relationships is an example of how scientific methodology pays due attention to making sure that the answer actually addresses the question faithfully.

Religion and benefit are both multifaceted phenomena that are highly susceptible to folk interpretation, meaning that people's subjective and relatively uninformed impressions become the de facto basis for making conclusions about inferences. Each person's perception of religion is shaped by his or her exposure to religious education, spiritual practices and secular influences. By definition, benefit is essentially a moral or ethical concept: it is determined largely by subjective viewpoints of what and who is 'good', which social scientists understand to be driven largely by intuition within a highly influential and self-reinforcing social context.[45] The problem of folk approaches leads us to highlight the nature of scientific theory and a prominent example of it.

Scientific *theory* about religion, like any other phenomenon, is developed with a number of purposes in mind. The first purpose driving theory development is to achieve a basic understanding of the nature of a phenomenon and confirm important relationships associated with it (e.g. what causes and results from religious commitment). Ideally, the concept is measurable and the associated measure (scale, survey, etc.) is reliable and valid, meaning that the measure must be comprehensible, produce consistent readings and correlate with other concepts that are expected to be related. Religious research, which is always a work in progress, gradually builds a body of knowledge that allows the development of a system of scientific laws, for example, that explain how someone's faith at work is related to his or her feelings of purpose and satisfaction. Good theories not only conjecture a relationship but also must explain convincingly the mechanism that activates the relationship. Moreover, good theories addressing causal effects will account for contingencies depending on unique characteristics of the person or the situation.

One important example of religion-related theory was proposed by sociologist Max Weber in his classic work, *The Protestant Ethic and the Spirit of Capitalism*.[46] Weber described how Protestantism in the sixteenth and seventeenth centuries brought a set of unique spiritual and motivational concepts to Western society. It instilled a strong sense of responsibility to pursue work as a spiritual end unto itself – as a calling – and to do this as efficiently as possible. Rather than greed as the motivation, it was driven by a complex set of beliefs that centred on the Calvinist idea of predestination, or the idea that people have already been preselected to salvation by an all-powerful God. This placed the individual in a position of vulnerability in which nothing else could be done except to fashion a particular type of virtuous life as the subjective sign of one's favour before God. The external goal was to work for societal achievements, such as wealth generation, not for personal indulgence but for the enjoyment of meeting the needs of community. Internally, however, the aim was to gain mastery over a life of thrift, restraint, honesty and watchfulness, lifting the devout above the limitations and temptations of the world. Underlying this was a foundation of 1,500 years of moral norms centred on Catholic dominance and Old Testament law, which in themselves were the seed for normative principles that could in the Protestant era be used to motivate the ordering of all of life. Soon this work ethic, Weber lamented, would be entirely secularized as wealth lured people to abandon the religious moorings of their prosperity.[47] I explain next why the basic principles of Weber's theories help us consider the fundamental realities of religiousness.

Critique: The Realities of Religious Effects Are Neglected

By explaining a descriptive view of religion from social science, my hope is to make the case that any decision maker that assesses religious benefit is inevitably faced with the responsibility of adopting a theory that must explain how religions from various cultures in different circumstances have effects in reality. Much like other fields requiring expert evidence, religion is a complex domain that stands out for having attracted significant scholarly attention. Thousands of scholars around the world are engaged in the lifetime study of the psychology, sociology, anthropology, history, literature, theology and cognitive science of religion.

The example of the Protestant Ethic provides a benchmark against which we can examine our paradigmatic assumptions with regard to religion and benefit. Weber's theories are over a century old and have stood the test of time as a starting point for further development of theories adaptable to the power dynamics, experiential processes and cultural divides experienced among the diversity of religious movements today.[48] It does not matter that the theoretical propositions of the Protestant Ethic only apply, albeit imperfectly, to their native historical era, or that they currently are the subject of genuine interest only in non-Western countries such as China.[49] Such theories matter because the transformative potential of such effects – the steady growth in prosperity, order and equality within entire societies – makes the preoccupation of policymaking with discrete problems or day-to-day needs – that is, 'benefits' – seem *vastly inferior* or even scandalous if it transpires without the deep-level beliefs and virtues needed to transform society in the long run. It also does not matter much that such effects do not always occur. It is only crucial that they *could* occur knowing that they are capable of addressing human beliefs and virtues at a level that other social systems cannot.

I end my specific critiques with a prescriptive recommendation, based on the ideas presented above. Due to a neglect of the basic reality of religion along with the theories that support a deeper understanding, I believe that the legal community has basically missed an opportunity for a fuller, more meaningful conversation regarding the nature of the third head of charity. Religion is currently conceptualized as a limited phenomenon defined at the mercy of narrow logic, rather than considering it as a feature that is elemental and essential to our functioning as humans.

In Canada, the courts are now at a point where any vague associations to the supernatural are accepted as if they were religiously inspired.[50] The current definition of religion is equivalent to deeply held convictions that may involve a divine being, although I suggest that the genuine quest to answer ontological questions is a more universal and collective endeavour.[51] This broader scope is reflected in the United Kingdom, where the belief system must be held by a group of adherents, and such a system need only address the place of humanity in the universe, its relationship to the infinite and the requirements for living in conformity. Spirituality does not require a deity but addresses the deep mystery of ultimate questions about existence.[52]

I argue that by its very nature, such endeavours require the act of reaching out to an external source, whether personal or impersonal, along with the engagement of a community of faith, even if the beliefs cannot be objectively assessed for truth. Hence, the community (organization, culture, movement) is integral to the pursuit of any type of religiousness or spirituality, including communities that consider themselves to be spiritual but not religious.[53]

Broader Implications: Does Religion Benefit the Public?

Thus far, I have attempted to interrogate the central challenge to the advancement of religion, 'Does religion benefit the public?' Applying a basic social scientific understanding of the relationship between the various levels of religion and benefit, I have hopefully revealed that the topic presents a complex set of conceptualization problems, causal propositions and theoretical questions that are not easy to solve through intuitive judgement. An inadequate understanding of religion and benefit can lead to a number of unintended consequences and ultimately obscure the reality that religion meets the deep human need for meaning, significance and connectedness that is unachievable by other means. Further to critiques voiced above, I identify three broader consequences that may result from lack of thoughtful engagement into the current realities regarding religion.

Reductionism Oversimplifies Judgement

The social scientific community is in constant struggle with an ideological challenge called reductionism.[54] Reductionism presents three particular problems to the field of psychology that are mirrored in the inadequate treatment of religion by lawmakers. First, reductionism treats the effects of a phenomenon as simply a product of its visible characteristics, when in fact the mechanism is much more complex. Let me use the example of the religious charity where, at the office, people repeat a prayer in the morning, say nice things to each other and think about God occasionally, all in the process of doing their work. An observer finds it difficult to accept that a few token religious distractions have such commendable external benefits, when in reality, the entire system functions on the basis of unseen motivational and social factors that are life-giving and resilient over space and time.

Second, reductionism leads to an extreme form of individualism, an outlook on humanity that sees each person as a fully autonomous and informed author of his or her own fate. The propensity of human rights defenders to juxtapose religious rights against other human rights is an example of this. Yet full self-realization is never apart from the connections that have made our lives what they are now. In most realms of life, human flourishing comes from being bound by culture. Religious freedom is not autonomy, but allegiance, attachment, and affiliation. M. H. Ogilvie adds that the reduction of religion to an interior type of personalized spirituality has the effect of trivializing religion, leading possibly to adverse judicial results.[55]

Finally, and most importantly, reductionism promotes the assumption that elements of religion must have a one-to-one correspondence with their benefits. There is a presumption of mastery over a phenomenon when in fact there is little. When organizational leaders are tempted to provide 'tangible and objective' evidence of benefit based on 'common understanding of enlightened opinion',[56] and can foresee and imagine 'the whole complex of resulting circumstances of whatever kind',[57] the danger of arbitrary decision making arises. More importantly, such a simplified approach results in an instrumentalism that focuses on external indicators of well-being rather than internal social resources cultivated through the free and diverse interaction of healthy human communities.[58] For such reasons, Donovan Waters recommends that religion and charity be separated as distinctly different legal concepts.[59]

Incongruence Confuses Expectation

Incongruence pertains to the misfit between the question and the means used to answer it. One specific manifestation is the mismatch between concepts and levels. As discussed in a previous section, there are numerous relationships that are associated with the influence of religion. By imposing standards based on a limited subset of these relationships, there is the risk of inappropriate expectations about what kinds of religion need to be expressed, what forms of beneficial effect they should have and who the recipients of such benefit should be. The outcome will be judicial tools that are simply out of touch with the nature of religious phenomena and the heavy-handed application of seemingly fair and benign policies.

One example of incongruence is the application of *Charter* rights. Justin Safayeni identified that the balancing of religious freedom with other rights leads to problems reconciling reasonableness and proportionality with minimum impairment.[60] This incongruence puts religion on an unlevel playing field because the prerogatives of religion are spread across the three levels (societal/cultural, organizational and individual), whereas other rights are typically situated at the individual level. Compared at the individual level, religious rights will always lose because the right to abide by a minor ritual or moral rule will always appear less important than rights based on inalienable human characteristics. In reality, the phenomenon of religion crosses levels and only has integrity if there is accordance of belief and behaviour across levels, between the culture of the organization and the participation of its members.

One must not forget that religious organizations are entities that are contingent on the context, regardless of what their core tenets may be. For example, the presence of government-funded services, competition from religious institutions and economies of scale based on population all have effects on the magnitude of the charitable-philanthropic role of a religion. Some minority religious sects or stigmatized types of religious organizations are fighting for financial survival or organizational legitimacy, and hence the reinforcement of their identity may be a higher priority than their external impact. One could argue that the more that an organization's overall viability is in question, the less able they are to display obvious benefit because the urgent concerns of members are impediments to their public participation.

Misconstrual Disrespects Humanity

Since our intuitive theories drive our perceptions and decisions, my examination of theory is a cautionary note about the danger of misconstruing the reality of religion and benefit. The greatest tangible effects of religion do not necessarily accrue from beliefs that directly promote the pursuit of them. Stated another way, it could be *morally hazardous* to encourage organizations to focus solely on the accumulation and disbursement of charitable relief and social services as the means to benefit society. As alluded to in our theory discussion, we know that the development of well-being and prosperity in society is more likely to be complex, value-laden and counterintuitive. As suggested by the Weberian thesis in light of the established models of economic development, human development requires all members to enter a social contract in which they participate in rational collective activity in support of the common good; submit willingly to life-and-death imperatives to curb their hedonic self-interest; allow a long-term perspective to restrain consumption and encourage savings; and become calling-driven, hard-working stewards of their own personal property, all the while upholding the civic institutions and loving relationships that make peaceful joint activity possible.[61] Although religion was a major factor in establishing the worldview beliefs to make these types of outcome possible, Bruno Dyck and David Schroeder remind us that a redemptive moral point of view is required to counter the materialism and individualism brought about by the corrupting influences of progress. Accordingly, we need more than an instrumental policy on charitable donations to make widespread benefit a possibility for the future of society. As I discuss further below, the diversity and freedom to engage in the pursuit of deeper meaning, significance and connectedness are critical to contribute to a prosperous, well-functioning society at a level that is qualitatively and quantitatively different than the resources enabled by tax relief. When judicial or administrative authorities base their decisions on a faulty paradigm, this does an injustice not only to religious communities but also to humanity at large.

As proposed by Sheryl Grana and colleagues, legal decisions have social scientific implications – they influence, and are influenced by, the social context – and as such they should be considered based on an understanding of the current context.[62] Citizens today in common law jurisdictions enjoy a high level of autonomy and religious freedom. Our environment is highly information and technology intensive, facilitating a level of educational enrichment and informed choice never experienced before in history. Members have a multitude of indicators to gauge the effectiveness of an organization, including its impact on personal and family well-being, the quality of internal and external relationships, its standing within a network of religious and secular organizations and so forth. Hence, according to the market perspective of rational choice theory (a basic sociological theory of the advancement of religion), one could surmise that the allocation of funds based on individual choice is the most efficient way of adjudicating public support of various religious groups, especially when people directly experience the workings of such organizations and they primarily receive private funds and not public support. Given that many of our society's laws defer to market-based mechanisms, it behoves the courts to consider why it does not trust these mechanisms in societies that are as free and diverse as Commonwealth nations are. Any discriminatory restrictions based on assessments of benefit could reduce the amount of societal engagement as faith communities entrench and withdraw their contributions, setting in motion a disjointed and unproductive pattern of discourse between religion and the state and increasing the transaction costs between them. It would also signal to other stakeholders locally and globally that the government is taking a risky step with regard to religious freedom. Policy changes could impact non-religious charities, as religious people rationalize where their limited charitable dollars should go. As religious groups become increasingly unable to thrive in the public sphere, they are at risk of becoming more isolated and marginalized.[63]

One option for lawmakers is to improve the information available to the public to make their own judgements of benefit. Efforts from watchdog groups and the accounting profession are already afoot to standardize and improve the type and amount of information available. One of the strengths of the non-profit sector is the professionalization of its core functions, engagement of its membership and the capacity built up over the decades to use various means – social networks, online multimedia, donor travel, etc. – to communicate the nature and extent of its benefits. It would appear that integration of religious schools with access to professional accreditation would be advantageous in this regard, ensuring that people of faith draw from the best in technical knowledge to ensure that their own communities maintain a level of public accountability and credibility.

Returning to the question of theory, I propose that the overall preoccupation with proof is false with respect to legal questions about religion and benefit. In the advancement of education or alleviation of poverty, lawmakers do not go through a process of subjectively judging each and every educational or social programme, deciding perhaps that people do not need to learn fine art or receive grief counselling. To do so would be an affront to the personhood of clients who choose these programmes and the professionals whose job it is to deliver them. Nor do lawmakers conclude that the entire instance of advancing education or alleviating poverty is suddenly void of legitimacy if some people misuse their skills training or social assistance coming from organizations whose basic intent is for the good of humankind.

Religion is a domain of inquiry that taps into sensitive, inclusive and intersubjective ways of looking at life problems. Religion basically addresses *ontological* questions – about who we are, what our purpose is, where life comes from and so on – which ultimately requires that we reach beyond our day-to-day existence to sources of revelation, appreciation and connection outside of ourselves. Kathryn Chan presents a 'wellspring' argument that the strong 'normative universes' of religion are important to motivate the transfer of charitable resources.[64] To that I would add that religiousness does even better – it provides frameworks and tools for addressing key existential dilemmas of human existence. Although it has appeared late on the scene, there is now a growing body of research on religiousness outside purely religious settings, in work, family and public contexts. While religiousness certainly looks different outside the four walls of any place of worship, through normal cognitive processes we automatically access religious ideas that are most useful to us in solving everyday problems. In extensive qualitative research done across a cross-cultural sample, I have found that people draw on religious thoughts to address uncertainties having to do with their self-concept, interpersonal relations, career aspirations or professional practice.[65]

Ultimately, any important life experience must engage with what is real and true, and the religious aspect of life is receptive to such questions. Moreover, since the quest to find such truth is impossible to do alone, by its nature the search for the sacred requires observance in a communal context. Interestingly, it is no surprise that two of the other heads of charity also deal with basic support for human existence: the advancement of education deals with the basic human struggle to gain knowledge – that is, *epistemological* concerns – and the alleviation of poverty pertains to the basic physical needs for well-being – which are *physiological* or *corporeal* concerns. *The advancement of religion is a concept that is more akin to the other heads of charity than many realise.* The role of lawmakers should be to work towards policy that maintains space in society for basic human epistemological, physical/corporeal and ontological strivings or pursuits – the *flourishing of mind, body, and soul* through meaningful protection of the heads of education, alleviation of poverty and the advancement of religion. Without this vision, we run the risk of doing an injustice to the very essence of what it means for humanity to thrive in community.

Conclusion

Elizabeth Mertz, in the opening of her edited volume on *The Role of Social Science in Law*, highlights the precarious place of social science when standing at a distance from a legal profession that, due to its normative and polemical nature, is not designed to engage in nuanced reflection based on theoretical or empirical knowledge. In the judging of issues that have broader social implications, scientific knowledge must be appropriately adapted to the legal issues, used selectively to provide context and carefully structured to act as tools for grasping foreign ideas.[66]

To clarify the contributions of this article, my goal has been neither to provide definitive evidence that religion is beneficial nor to defeat perceived ideological biases that lean toward ruling out religion altogether. Preoccupation with these aims is neither productive nor reasonable. Rather, I hope to provide frameworks and ideas that allow for a disciplined and constructive discourse about what we mean by the words 'religion' and 'benefit'. Additionally, I want to instil a healthy dose of scepticism to slow down the oversimplifying tendencies of lawmakers that seek convenient solutions. Further, I wish to provide a reminder of the underlying importance of such considerations – often unstated in policy guidance or legal decisions – that we are ultimately saying something about what is real and about ourselves as humans whenever we open this topic of discussion.

This chapter is merely a start, as there is great need for a continuation of the discussion, drawing from the extensive literature and also incorporating the abundance of scholarship from major fields (sociology, cross-cultural psychology, the cognitive science of religion, etc.) that have a distinct set of theories and findings that are applicable to religion and spirituality in broader society. Religion is so much more than one can grasp or compartmentalize: it is cultural, supraordinate and extra-worldly, as well as cognitively rich, relationally embedded and normatively potent. Any legal treatment of it inevitably brings the focus back to the central concern of benefit – goodness, worth or value – based on a perception of what religion is as a phenomenon and the potential it has at various levels of human existence.

This chapter is a signal, not just to the legal community but also to all who consider themselves thoughtful, to genuinely wrestle with the nature of religion as we live it. Only then can we be prepared to judge on the behalf of others, in the presence of whatever higher reality is beyond us, what is best for our children, our country and our humanity. Meanwhile, we are wise to tread carefully.

Notes

1 Mark Blumberg, 'CRA's Draft Guidance "Advancement of Religion and Charitable Registration" is Released through ATIP [Access to Information and Privacy]', *Blumbergs* (2017) at 26, online (pdf): <https://www.globalphilanthropy.ca/images/uploads/CRAs_Draft_Guidance_Advancement_of_religion_and_charitable_registration_is_released_through_ATIP.pdf>.

2 Kathryn Chan, 'The Advancement of Religion as a Charitable Purpose in an Age of Religious Neutrality' (2017) 6:1 Oxford Journal of Law and Religion 112–36 at 122.

3 *Law Society of British Columbia v Trinity Western University*, 2018 SCC 32 [2018] 2 S.C.R. 453; *Trinity Western University v Law Society of Upper Canada*, 2018 SCC 33 [2018] 2 S.C.R. 453.
4 Charity Commission, *Public Benefit: Analysis of the Law Relating to Public Benefit: Charity Commission for England and Wales* (2013) at 3, online (pdf): <https://assets.publishing.service.gov.uk/government/uploads/system/uploads/attachment_data/file/587370/Public_benefit_an_overview.pdf>.
5 See Frank Cranmer's assessment of the UK system in this volume: 'Religion and Public Benefit in United Kingdom Charity Law'.
6 Chan, *supra* note 2 at 133; Donovan Waters, 'The Advancement of Religion in a Pluralist Society (Part II): Abolishing the Public Benefit Element' (2011) 17:8 Trusts & Trustees 729–38 at 735 [Part II].
7 Benjamin Beit-Hallahmi & Michael Argyle, *The Psychology of Religious Behaviour, Belief, and Experience* (London: Routledge, 1997) at 97; Peter C. Hill & Ralph W. Hood Jr., eds, *Measures of Religiosity* (Birmingham, AL: Religious Education Press, 1999) at 9.
8 Laurence Binet Brown, *The Psychology of Religious Belief* (London: Academic Press, 1987) at 29.
9 Kenneth I. Pargament et al, 'Envisioning an Integrative Paradigm for the Psychology of Religion and Spirituality', in *APA Handbook of Psychology, Religion, and Spirituality (Vol. 1): Context, Theory, and Research*, ed. K. I. Pargament, J. J. Exline & J. W. Jones (Washington, DC: American Psychological Association, 2013) at 14–15.
10 Brian J. Zinnbauer & Kenneth I. Pargament, 'Religiousness and Spirituality', in *Handbook of the Psychology of Religion and Spirituality*, ed. Raymond F. Paloutzian & Crystal L. Park (New York: Guilford Press, 2005) at 36.
11 Pargament et al, *supra* note 9 at 5–7.
12 This is in particular the viewpoint of the cultural psychology of religion. Jacob A. Belzen, *Towards a Cultural Psychology of Religion: Principles, Approaches, Applications* (Dordrecht, The Netherlands: Springer, 2010) at 17.
13 Dianna L. Stone, Julio C. Canedo, & Shay Tzafrir, 'The Symbiotic Relation between Organizations and Society' (2013) 28:5 Journal of Managerial Psychology 432–51 at 442.
14 Ronald J. Sider & Heidi Rolland Unruh, 'Typology of Religious Characteristics of Social Service and Educational Organizations and Programs' (March 2004) 33:1 Nonprofit and Voluntary Sector Quarterly 109–34 at 112–15. Stephen V. Monsma, *When Sacred and Secular Mix: Religious Nonprofit Organizations and Public Money* (Lanham, MD: Rowman & Littlefield, 2000). Thomas H. Jeavons, 'Identifying Characteristics of 'Religious' Organizations: An Exploratory Proposal', in *Sacred Companies: Organizational Aspects of Religion and Religious Aspects of Organizations*, ed. N. J. Demerath et al (New York, NY: Oxford University Press, 1997), 79–95.
15 Sider & Unruh, *supra* note 14 at 129.
16 Hill & Hood, *supra* note 7 at v–viii.
17 Michael Lounsbury, Nelson Phillips & Paul Tracey, 'Taking Religion Seriously in the Study of Organizations', in *Religion and Organization Theory*, vol. 41 (Emerald Group Publishing Limited, 2014), 3–21 at 6.
18 Deniz S. Ones, Stephan Dilchert, Chockalingam Viswesvaran & Timothy A. Judge, 'In Support of Personality Assessment in Organizational Settings' (2007) 60:4 Personnel Psychology 995–1027 at 1020. Daniel J. Benjamin, James J. Choi & Geoffrey Fisher, 'Religious Identity and Economic Behavior' (2016) 98:4 Review of Economics and Statistics 617–37 at 617.
19 Justina Victor, Evren Esen & Steve Williams, *Religion and Corporate Culture: Accommodating Religious Diversity in the Workplace* (Alexandria, VA: Society for Human Resource Management, 2008).
20 Karen C. Cash & George R. Gray, 'A Framework for Accommodating Religion and Spirituality in the Workplace' (2000) 14:3 Academy of Management Executive 124–33 at 125.
21 Chan, *supra* note 2 at 118 discusses rulings that conclude how private religious rites such as prayer do not satisfy the public benefit test. Bruno Dyck, at 146–48, reviews empirical research on the virtuous effects of religious devotion including prayer, in 'God on Management: The World's

Largest Religions, the "Theological Turn," and Organization and Management Theory and Practice' in *Research in the Sociology of Organizations*, vol. 41 *(Religion and Organization Theory)*, ed. Paul Tracey, Nelson Phillips & Michael Lounsbury (Bingley: Emerald Group, 2014), 23–62.
   See also *Re Hetherington* [1990] Ch 1 (Ch). *Gilmour v Coats* [1949] AC 426 (HL) 446.
22 Blumberg, *supra* note 1 at 7, outlines Canada Revenue Agency's requirements for religion, although M. H. Ogilvie, at 319, notes how Supreme Court of Canada judgements engaging the *Charter* differ from charity law. See Ogilvie, 'The Meaning of Religion and the Role of the Courts in the Adjudication of Religious Matters: An English and Canadian Comparison' (2015) 23:1 Canadian Bar Review 303–26.
23 Consider, e.g., Penny Edgell's review of the latest sociological thinking on religion: 'A Cultural Sociology of Religion: New Directions' (2012) 38 Annual Review of Sociology 247–65 at 250.
24 Sider & Unruh, *supra* note 14 at 131.
25 John F. Binning & Gerald V. Barrett, 'Validity of Personnel Decisions: A Conceptual Analysis of the Inferential and Evidential Bases' (1989) 74:3 *Journal of Applied Psychology* 478–94 at 478.
26 *Ibid*, at 479.
27 The nine relationships are as follows: RS-BS (societal religiousness to societal benefit); RS-BO (societal religion to organizational benefit); RS-BI (societal religion to individual benefit); RO-BS (organizational religiousness to societal benefit); RO-BO (organizational religiousness to organizational benefit); RO-BI (organizational religiousness to individual benefit); RI-BS (individual religiousness to societal benefit); RI-BO (individual religiousness to organizational benefit); and RI-BI (individual religiousness to individual benefit).
28 Strictly speaking, the characteristics of a nation or region do not predict characteristics of each and every organization or individual, only the organizations or individuals as a group within each nation or region, on average.
29 Rachel M. McCleary & Robert J. Barro, 'Religion and Economy' (2006) 20:2 Journal of Economic Perspectives 49–72 at 67.
30 Qunyong Wang & Xinyu Lin, 'Does Religious Beliefs Affect Economic Growth? Evidence from Provincial-Level Panel Data in China' (2014) 31 China Economic Review 277–87 at 277.
31 Thomas C. Omer, Nathan Y. Sharp & Dechun Wang, 'The Impact of Religion on the Going Concern Reporting Decisions of Local Audit Offices' (2018) 149:4 Journal of Business Ethics 811–31 at 811.
32 Navina Lucke & Stefan Eichler, 'Foreign Direct Investment: The Role of Institutional and Cultural Determinants' (2016) 48:11 Applied Economics 935–56 at 938, 951.
33 M. H. Bond et al, 'Culture-Level Dimensions of Social Axioms and their Correlates across 41 Cultures' (2004) 35:5 Journal of Cross-Cultural Psychology 548–70 at 558–561.
34 Milton Friesen, *Religion and the Good of the City: Report 2: The State of Research and Influence* (Hamilton, ON: Cardus Social Cities, 2017), 9.
35 Ram A. Cnaan & Femida Handy, 'Comparing Neighbors: Social Service Provision by Religious Congregations in Ontario and the United States' (2000) 30:4 American Review of Canadian Studies 521–43 at 538–39.
36 Ram A. Cnaan & Seongho An, 'Even Priceless has to have a Number: Congregational Halo Effect' (2018) 15:1 Journal of Management, Spirituality & Religion 64–81 at 64.
37 Xingquiang Du reviews the literature on similar studies of religious influence in Du et al, 'Does Religion Mitigate Earnings Management? Evidence from China' (2015) 131:3 Journal of Business Ethics 699–749 at 699–701.
38 Laurence R. Iannacconte, Daniel v A. Olson, & Rodney Stark, 'Religious Resources and Church Growth' (1995) 74:2 Social Forces 705–32 at 726.
39 Harold G. Koenig & David B. Larson, 'Use of Hospital Services, Religious Attendance, and Religious Affiliation' (1998) 91:10 Southern Medical Journal 925–32 at 931.
40 Jill Witmer Sinha, Itay Greenspan & Femida Handy, 'Volunteering and Civic Participation among Immigrant Members of Ethnic Congregations: Complementary NOT Competitive' (2011) 7:1 Journal of Civil Society 23–40 at 37.

41 Martin Turcotte, 'Charitable Giving by Canadians (Canadian Social Trends)', *Statistics Canada*, 2012, at 30, online (pdf): <https://www150.statcan.gc.ca/n1/en/pub/11-008-x/2012001/article/11637-eng.pdf>.
42 Stephen T. Carroll, 'Addressing Religion and Spirituality in the Workplace', in *APA Handbook of Psychology, Religion, and Spirituality (Vol. 2): An Applied Psychology of Religion and Spirituality*, ed. K. I. Pargament, J. J. Exline & J. W. Jones (Washington, DC: American Psychological Association, 2013), 599–603.
43 Michael J. O'Fallon & Kenneth D. Butterfield, 'A Review of the Empirical Ethical Decision-Making Literature: 1996–2003' (2005) 59:4 Journal of Business Ethics 375–413 at 378–79, 385, 390, 392, 394.
44 Linda M. Chatters, 'Religion and Health: Public Health Research and Practice' (2000) 21 Annual Review of Public Health 335–67 at 342.
45 Raymond B. Chiu & Rick D. Hackett, 'The Assessment of Individual Moral Goodness' (2017) 26:1 Business Ethics: A European Review 31–46 at 33; Jonathan Haidt, 'The Emotional Dog and its Rational Tail: A Social Intuitionist Approach to Moral Judgment' (2001) 108:4 Psychological Review 814–34 at 818.
46 Max Weber, *The Protestant Ethic and the 'Spirit' of Capitalism and Other Writings*, trans. Peter R. Baehr & Gordon C. Wells (New York, NY: Penguin Books, 1905/2002).
47 See also Carroll, *supra* note 42 at 596–97 and Hei C. Kim, 'Relationship of Protestant Ethic Beliefs and Values to Achievement' (1977) 16:3 Journal for the Scientific Study of Religion 255–62 at 256.
48 Edgell, *supra* note 23 at 248.
49 Joy Kooi-Chin Tong, *Overseas Chinese Christian Entrepreneurs in Modern China: A Case Study of the Influence of Christian Ethics on Business Life* (London: Anthem Press, 2012), 2–4.
50 Donovan Waters tracks the history of religion through common law courts to the present day. See Waters, 'The Advancement of Religion in a Pluralist Society (Part I): Distinguishing Religion from Giving to "Charity"' (2011) 17:7 Trusts & Trustees 652–67 [Part I].
51 Ogilvie, *supra* note 22, reviews the Canadian definition of religion by Iacobucci J in *Syndicat Northcrest v Amselem*, 2004 SCC 47, [2004] 2 S.C.R. 551 [*Amselem*].
52 Ogilvie, *supra* note 22, reviews the UK definition of religion by Lord Toulson in *R (Hodkin) v Registrar General*, [2013] UKSC 77, [2014] AC 610 [*Hodkin*].
53 Linda Mercadante finds that the spiritual-but-not-religious hold beliefs about what has authenticity, representativeness and integrity much the same way that people in traditional religions do. See Mercadante, *Belief without Borders: Inside the Minds of the Spiritual but Not Religious* (New York: Oxford University Press, 2014) at 9.
54 H. Putnam, 'Reductionism and the Nature of Psychology' (1973) 2:1 Cognition 131–46 at 131, 140, 142.
55 Ogilvie, *supra* note 22 at 320.
56 This is language from the analysis supporting the Charity Commission's guidance on public benefit, citing *National Anti-Vivisection Society v IRC*, Charity Commission, *supra* note 4 at 10. See also *National Anti-Vivisection Society v IRC* [1948] AC 31 at 49 (Lord Wright) [*Anti-Vivisection Society*].
57 *Anti-Vivisection Society*, *supra* note 56 at 47.
58 Both Chan and Waters provide further discussion regarding the problem of reducing charitable giving to the mere redistribution of material wealth. See Chan, *supra* note 2 at 134. Waters, 'Part I', *supra* note 50 at 666.
59 Waters, 'Part II', *supra* note 6 at 730.
60 Justin Safayeni, 'The Doré Framework: Five Years Later, Four Key Questions (and some Suggested Answers)' (2018) 31:1 Canadian Journal of Administrative Law & Practice 31–51 at 38.
61 Bruno Dyck & David Schroeder discuss the moral virtues necessary to counter the materialism and individualism of conventional management. See 'Management, Theology and Moral Points of View: Towards an Alternative to the Conventional Materialist-Individualist Ideal-Type of Management' (2005) 42:4 Journal of Management Studies 705–35 at 724–25.

62 Sheryl J. Grana, Jane C. Ollenburger & Mark Nicholas, *The Social Context of Law* (Upper Saddle River, NJ: Prentice Hall, 1999) at 3.
63 Chan, *supra* note 2 at 134, identified these types of problems arising from framing public benefit in ways that religious communities do not recognize.
64 Chan, *supra* note 2 at 128.
65 I explain four ways by which religiousness addresses the existential uncertainties in the workplace. See R. B. Chiu, 'Beliefs that Matter: Workplace Religiousness and Spirituality across Cultures' (Doctoral thesis, McMaster University, 2017), 158–62, online: http://hdl.handle.net/11375/22117.
66 Elizabeth Mertz, ed., *The Role of Social Science in Law* (Farnham: Ashgate, 2008), xiv.

Chapter Three

THE PUBLIC BENEFIT OF 'ADVANCING RELIGION' AS A CHARITABLE PURPOSE: A CANADIAN PERSPECTIVE

John Pellowe*

Abstract

Advancing Religion as a charitable purpose provides Canada with public benefits that represent a very high value to all Canadians, whether of faith or not. These benefits can be sorted into four categories.

First, religion results in *better personal outcomes* that reduce demand on the state's resources for the justice system and rehabilitation, social support and health care, due to fewer marital breakdowns, stronger families and social networks, rejection of unlawful behaviour, higher school attendance and graduation, and better mental/physical health and well-being. Religion improves quality of life, increases a sense of personal efficacy and promotes greater contribution by individuals to society.

Second, religion develops and activates *prosocial attitudes and behaviours*, such as empathy, social responsibility, forgiveness, honesty, kindness, friendliness, generosity and concern for others, that improve public civility and result in high levels of generosity and volunteerism that benefit both religious and secular charities and individual Canadians, whether religious or not.

Third, religion has *tangible community benefits* in terms of social capital, infrastructure and neighbourhood viability and a 12-times return on investment related to tax concessions. Places of worship, due to their low overhead and their ability to use volunteers, produce a socio-economic value of about 4.5 times their operating budgets to their local neighbourhoods.

Fourth, religion creates *tangible and intangible benefits for the public at large*. Religion and the freedom of religion form the bedrock of modern liberal democracies. Religious freedom is seen as a prototypical freedom that has led to freedom of assembly, speech and the press. Religion has contributed to the development of public policy and has been linked to greater economic output, improved business ethics, greater environmental responsibility and a reduction in illegal business practices.

This chapter ends with a non-spiritual explanation of how religion is thought to produce such significant results.

* *MBA, DMin, CEO, Canadian Council of Christian Charities.*

Introduction

Religion benefits those who are religious, but a significant body of research shows how religion also benefits those who are not religious. The well-being of every Canadian, whether of faith or not, is significantly enhanced because religion is part of our society. Two literature surveys have already been done citing significant research in the United States.[1] The abundance of research canvassed in this chapter will demonstrate that the same benefits apply to Canada as well.

To prove that religion benefits even the non-religious, I will draw on a substantial body of academically rigorous research, much of it by Canadian organizations and academics, with the rest coming from the United States and, to a lesser degree, Europe and Asia.

A significant portion of the Canadian research was conducted by Statistics Canada. Its surveys are repeated regularly, which allows for confidence both in the consistency of certain results over time and in the trends of other results that are unfolding. For example, its *Giving, Volunteering, and Participating Survey* has been repeated every three years since 1997, and each new set of results has validated the previous results. Other regular surveys of Canadians were conducted between 1975 and the present by various pollsters including Statistics Canada, the World Values Survey, Angus Reid Polling and Canadian sociologist Reginald Bibby. Some additional studies in recent years are not part of a regular series but replicate findings from older studies dating as far back as the early 1950s. In only a few minor instances has more recent research led to questioning or at least nuancing the results of the older research, mostly due to improvements in methodology. However, nothing of significance was found in error.

We can be confident, therefore, that while the religious composition of Canada may be changing, the public benefit of religion remains the same over time. We know the relationships between religion and public benefit reported here are not temporary aberrations, and they are not out of date. They have remained consistent over many decades.

What is changing is the overall impact of religion on society. The declining number of religious Canadians lessens religion's impact because a smaller percentage of the population is transmitting the benefits to the general population. The effects of the decline in religion's impact are already noticeable. The number of donors to charity is declining (dropping by a third between 1990 and 2014);[2] public civility is declining (the polarization of society has resulted in closed minds on all sides of the issues of the day, and the rise in hostility is plainly evident in both the news and social media);[3] and volunteering is declining (between 2004 and 2013, the percentage of Canadians who volunteered declined marginally from 45 per cent to 44 per cent of the population, but the average number of hours volunteered declined 8 per cent from 168 hours to 154 hours).[4]

Given the decline in Canadian religiosity, Canadian sociologist Kurt Bowen gave a prophetic word to Canada in his 2004 book, *Christians in a Secular World: The Canadian Experience*:

> If the expanding body of the Non-Religious is our guide to the future, we may reasonably expect that life satisfaction will decline, concern for others will diminish, marriage will grow

more fragile, family and friendship networks will shrink, volunteering will become less frequent, and we will grow ever less generous in our so very affluent world. In a word, our civility is threatened. If this is the victory that secularism and the Enlightenment have wrought, then we have no cause to celebrate.[5]

Declining religiosity is not only a challenge to the religious but also a challenge to the non-religious who are or will be feeling the negative consequences if the decline is not reversed. This chapter defines the public benefits of advancing religion, but by doing so it also highlights what society risks losing if current downward trends in religiosity continue.

My goal in writing this chapter is to help religious and non-religious Canadians alike fully appreciate the value religion contributes to Canadian society. I also want those working in religious organizations to be inspired by the breadth of the impact they have and to focus on raising up people who take their faith seriously and apply it in every aspect of their lives.

Sociologist Joshua Yates (University of Virginia) notes that the great challenge we face in evaluating the contemporary contributions of religion is that each facet of its contributions is typically assessed in isolation from the others. As a result, he says we 'easily miss a comprehensive picture of religion's possible impact on a community and it may be far greater than we have thought'.[6] While many of the benefits have been evident for years, the enormity of the benefits in their totality has not generally been appreciated. This chapter is my attempt to bring the assessments all together in one place to provide a comprehensive overview of how religion benefits even the most atheistic person in Canada.

It must be noted that, given the historical and demographic significance of Christianity in North American society, the research presented in this chapter primarily relates to the Christian faith. However, research related to other religions has been drawn upon when available. The focus on Christianity should not be problematic since the strongest factor in relation to charitable giving is not *which* religion a person follows but *how* religious a person is. This conclusion was noted by Robert Putnam, professor of public policy at Harvard, and David Campbell, associate professor of political science at the University of Notre Dame.[7] It is also borne out by a number of other papers cited in this chapter.[8]

This chapter does *not* compare religious people to non-religious people. That comparison is misleading as far as determining the benefits of religion because not all people who claim to belong to a religion are statistically similar. Studies that compare the religious to non-religious people, without further distinctions, often find there are no differences between them. An example is a 2008 Barna study.[9] While Barna found little or no difference between 'born again' Christians and the general population in their divorce rates, the methodology was based on reported religious beliefs, not religious practice. The study's methodology notes that religious attendance was explicitly excluded from consideration. The choice to exclude attendance patterns is significant because study after study shows that those who attend a place of worship at least once per week are statistically very different from all others (as will be shown). It is thus very surprising that Barna chose not to consider it. We will see from other research on divorce that their results would have been quite different had they factored in attendance at worship services.

Knowing that not all people who claim to be religious are the same, sociologists use a spectrum to study the effect of different degrees of religiosity on attitudes and behaviour. In his research, Canadian sociologist Kurt Bowen uses the following nomenclature, which I have adopted:

1. Very Committed (people who attend a place of worship *at least* once per week);
2. Less Committed (people who attend a place of worship monthly but less than weekly);
3. Seekers[10] (people who say they are religious but who rarely or never attend religious services); and
4. Non-Religious (people who are not religious and never attend a place of worship).[11]

Comparing these four categories shows the significant positive effect religion has on people who take their faith seriously, as demonstrated by at least weekly attendance at a place of worship. The Very Committed are distinguishable from all other Canadians. They have a very distinctive psychological profile of prosocial values and sense of well-being. The Less Committed and the Seekers have profiles much more in common with the Non-Religious than with the Very Committed.[12]

Better Personal Outcomes

Religion enhances people's personal outcomes with the result that many social costs are minimized and their ability to contribute to society is maximized. A systematic review of nearly eight hundred studies (mostly from recent years) shows conclusively that higher levels of religious involvement and practices are an 'important protective factor that buffers or insulates individuals from deleterious outcomes' and that those same factors are responsible for 'promoting an array of prosocial behaviours and thus enhancing various beneficial outcomes'. The study's authors conclude, 'Researchers are now in a position to cite hundreds of quality studies in peer-reviewed journals that indicate a striking correspondence between religiosity and general health and well being'.[13] Several reasons why this is so are outlined here.

More Responsible Choices

First, religious commitment is linked to more responsible choices among all age groups. When it comes to youth, many studies over the years have found that youth participation in religion correlates with lower rates of juvenile delinquency, better school attendance and increased probability of graduating from high school.[14] As religious socialization rises, so too does educational attainment.[15] Furthermore, delinquency is minimized when both a mother and her child have high religiosity, but when either the mother or the child is very religious and the other is not, the child has a higher rate of delinquency.[16]

Religion affects other choices too. For example, a three-year study of 13,000 high school women found that the 'intensity of the individual's religious commitment (religiosity) can be powerfully influential' in determining who becomes a teenage mother.[17]

Religiosity encourages good behaviour, and religious people who are involved in the life of a youth will model and mentor the social skills and coping mechanisms that help youth avoid or resist the common causes of delinquency. Margaret Vaaler's PhD dissertation found that religion improves relationships between parents and children by bringing them closer together and causing them to communicate more, which creates very supportive relationships between them. Religious family members are more involved with each other.[18] I believe this research suggests that attitudes, behaviours and choices are more likely to be discussed at home, giving youth the benefit of their parents' greater knowledge and wisdom when making their choices.

Religion therefore has a 'protective effect' on religious youth that reduces their likelihood of engaging in destructive behaviour. These factors have positive economic benefits for communities by reducing incarceration and rehabilitation costs, as well as encouraging greater employment and productivity.[19] Religion has also been shown to be more effective than secular treatment programmes in returning addicted youth to normal, productive lives.[20]

In essence, youth who are religious make choices that have long-term positive consequences for their lives. Research from the Harvard T. H. Chan School of Public Health shows that children and youth who attend weekly religious services report greater life satisfaction and positivity in their twenties and are less likely than others to smoke, use drugs or make poor sexual activity choices. And when youth do get sick, the research shows that youth in very religiously committed families have better skills in solving health-related problems than those whose families attend church less often [21]

Religion's positive effects are seen in adult's choices as well. Religiously involved adults are less likely to commit crimes or misuse prescription drugs, and (like religiously active youth) more likely to make wise choices for positive long-term outcomes.[22] Local congregations help adults cope with their adult roles and responsibilities, and provide them with the attitudes and interpersonal skills required for 'optimal functioning with marriage and employment'.[23]

An epidemiologist reports that large, well-designed longitudinal research studies have associated religious service attendance with greater longevity, less depression, less suicide, less smoking, less substance abuse, higher survival rates of cancer and cardiovascular disease, less divorce, greater social support, greater meaning and purpose in life, greater life satisfaction, more charitable giving, more volunteering and greater civic engagement.[24] Other studies add even more to this list. Compared with never attending worship services, attendance at least weekly is associated with more forgiveness and lower probabilities of premature sexual initiation. Weekly attendance is also possibly associated with lower probabilities of post-traumatic stress disorder, prescription drug misuse and sexually transmitted infections (STIs). In comparison, little difference was found between less-than-weekly attendance and never attendance of services, except for the character outcomes. Other studies support these conclusions.[25]

When it comes to reconciliation between marriage partners, religion has the strongest relationship with success, and sharing the *same* religious commitment between partners significantly increases the chances of that success.[26] It has also been found that both men and women who attend religious services regularly are less likely to commit acts of domestic violence than others. Among men, the study found that this protective effect of religion was evident only in those who are committed to the point of attending weekly.[27]

Numerous studies report that religious attendance and/or devotion are positively related to indicators of marital quality and success – including happiness and satisfaction, adjustment and duration[28] – and negatively related to divorce.[29] Studies suggest that religion helps partners cultivate a sense of higher purpose and values centred on loving, caring for and being sensitive to the needs of each other.[30] Religion stimulates spouses to become more open to accommodation and compromise with their partners, thereby improving their conflict resolution skills.[31] These values supplant egocentric attitudes and behaviour.[32]

Places of worship are thought to help cultivate successful marriages in several ways. They limit couples' isolation through their integration into a worshipping community. In such a community, people develop confiding relationships (making it more difficult to hide abuse). Those relationships also provide social support, coping assistance and opportunities for emotional release, potentially buffering the effects of stressors on the risk of violence. The evidence clearly shows that religious attendance is inversely associated with the perpetration of domestic violence, among both men and women.[33]

Greater Opportunity

Beyond more responsible choices, churches further provide people with greater opportunities for participation and self-development they may not otherwise have had in their lives. As religion helps people better understand who they are (for example, they are someone who was lovingly created by God), people who 'occupy low-status and marginal positions in society can be reassured of their own self-worth and inspired to action'.[34] With a healthy self-image and sense of self-efficacy, they learn that they have a place in the world and that they have the ability to contribute to it in positive, meaningful ways.

Churches can create a greater sense of personal potential by providing people with creative roles in the production of events and selection of songs to perform, as well as coaching people to be able to perform those songs. A church environment can give people greater fulfilment and self-esteem as they participate in leadership, governance and volunteer support roles.[35] People who may never have an opportunity to lead elsewhere in their lives can gain valuable experience leading programmes or serving on church boards. One study noted that a good predictor that an inner-city youth will successfully escape the ghetto is their attendance at church (as opposed to just having religious beliefs). The researcher found that attendance positively affects allocation of time, school-going, work activity and the frequency of socially deviant behaviour.[36]

At the Parliament of Religions held in August 2015, Ela Bhatt, Chancellor of Gujarat Vidyapith University, stated that religion can particularly empower women and raise their dignity because they are disproportionately affected by poverty. Religion can unite women and give them the capacity to work together to lift themselves out of poverty. Religion is a shared community that allows women to act as a group in a way that many other organizations cannot. Because the journey to empowerment is closely intertwined with personal development within religions, the inclusion of women in religion is of great importance.[37]

Religion has been linked positively to educational attainment, occupational achievement, work orientation and income.[38] It has been found that as levels of religious socialization rise, there is a corresponding rise in educational achievement.[39] The importance of religion is evident in a study that found that the effect of religious values is consistently more significant than the effect of socio-economic status when predicting both the level of student performance and changes in their grades.[40]

Improved Health

A clear, strong and consistently beneficial link between religion and health (both physical and mental) has been established by research in the health, social and behavioural sciences extending over the past one hundred years. This fact, along with an excellent overview of the literature on this topic, is provided by Linda Chatters in 'Religion and Health: Public Health Research and Practice'.[41] A literature review by Lawrence Gary of Howard University suggests a number of social functions of religion that contribute to the healthy socialization experiences of religious people, which, I believe it is reasonable to conclude, contributes positively to mental health. These functions include psychological affirmation, social support, identity formation, political involvement and creativity. Religion fosters psychological well-being by providing a source of personal comfort and consultation, as well as offering emotional and social support through advice, material aids and services, exchanges of services and other assistance. Social intercourse is enhanced by participation in congregational meals, sports games, sharing, rehearsals, trips and informal gatherings. A sense of identity can be developed as the individual is linked to the past and future, and gains group values, a place in the universe and a sense of recognition or 'somebodiness'. Political agency is enhanced through education and advocacy, while many religious traditions promote creativity through the development of spiritual music, plays and rich and poetic teachings.[42]

The beneficial link between religion and health applies to children as well as adults. Significant longitudinal research following children from 8 to 14 years shows that attending church weekly as a child has long-lasting benefits on mental health and other health issues.[43] This finding is very relevant in Canada today, as 63 per cent of Canadian millennials are reported to be at high risk for mental health issues, the terrible cost of which is seen in the fact that suicide is now the second-leading cause of death among Canadians 15–24 years old, second only to accidental deaths.[44]

Finally, as with other age groups, empirical research suggests religion is associated with better health and well-being in adults.[45] One study showed that diastolic blood pressure for men was almost 5 mmHg lower among the group that had high religious attendance and who rated religion as highly important to themselves when compared to the non-religious group. The authors noted that a reduction of a population's mean blood pressure by as little as 2–4 mmHg could reduce cardiovascular disease by 10 per cent to 20 per cent.[46]

Religion has a positive effect on physical health because religious teachings often include practices related to living a healthy lifestyle and sometimes explicitly consider character or respect for the body as an integral part of the religion's beliefs.[47] Religious *attendance* shows the strongest relationship to good health, and religious *coping* is a prominent predictor for successful recovery and survival in clinically ill populations.[48]

There is a wealth of literature all supporting the positive linkage between religiosity/spirituality and mental health.[49] In fact, 100 studies have demonstrated positive effects of religious involvement on rates of suicide, drug use, alcohol abuse, delinquent behaviour, marital dissatisfaction, psychological distress and depression.[50]

Psychology professors Hill and Pargament note that social scientists have had limited success trying to describe the effect of religion using only psychological and social explanations. The psychology professors suggest that religion may be of an entirely different order than psychosocial factors, and rather than working indirectly through traditional psychosocial factors, religion may have its own direct effect on health. They conclude: 'Already, there is evidence that religion and spirituality are distinctive dimensions that add unique explanatory power to the prediction of physical and mental health'.[51]

Sociologist Joshua Yates offers a possible reason why the social scientists have been unsuccessful in their quest for completely secular explanations. Yates speculates that perhaps one of the most significant contributions that religion makes to our mental well-being is that it helps people grapple with the possibility that tragedy in life is a fundamental, deep and persistent feature of our human experience. He asks: 'How can our governments foster a mysterious sense of our need to appreciate the fabric of our finitude? They can't', he concludes, 'But religion can and does'.[52] It is apparent that religion helps us make sense of our lives, leading to better mental health.

Increased Longevity

As well as improving mental and physical health, religion also increases longevity. A study of 21,000 case files from the US National Health Interview Survey showed that people who never attend religious services exhibited almost twice the risk of death in the study's eight-year follow-up period when compared to the Very Committed. This translates into a seven-year difference in life expectancy at age 20.[53] The relationship between frequent religious service attendance and lower mortality risk is found even in the most rigorous studies.[54]

For instance, a study by Tyler VanderWeele, professor of epidemiology at the Harvard T. H. Chan School of Public Health, using the Nurses' Health Study of 74,534 women from 1992 to 2012, showed that Very Committed women were 30 per cent less likely to die in the 16-year period of his study than non-religious women. The study also showed that Very Committed women were five times less likely to commit suicide. VanderWeele found that religion increases social support, discourages smoking, decreases depression and helps people have a more optimistic or hopeful outlook on life.[55]

Economic Impact of Better Personal Outcomes

Finally, religion has a positive, measurable economic impact. The better choices and greater opportunity brought about by religion have significant benefits for the broader society. Sociologists studying the effect of religion on human behaviour and health have estimated that the American economy benefits by about $2.6 trillion annually – or about one-sixth of its total economic output – due to reduced welfare and social support costs, reduced incarceration and rehabilitation costs, and increased employment and productivity.[56]

Prosocial Attitudes and Behaviours

We are reminded by Canadian researchers who published their findings between 2001 and 2014 that faith-based congregations help people to explore and cultivate deeply held beliefs, to participate in rituals of meaning, to find comfort in their times of deep pain and sorrow, and to foster relationship in community.[57] Beyond these listed benefits of being part of a faith-based congregation, there are many more direct benefits to individuals that help them in turn provide significant benefits to the public.

Good Citizens

The first benefit is the development of good citizens. Throughout history, human societies have depended on prosocial behaviour to ensure their survival. Cultures, therefore, are centred on the practices, norms and institutions that foster prosocial attitudes and actions.[58] All institutions that develop or promote prosocial citizens provide an important public benefit, and places of worship are just such institutions.

The citizens who form Canada's civic core are those prosocial people who are caring, kind, generous, selfless and community-oriented. They are other-centred and have a worldview that stresses responsibility and connectedness. They give, volunteer and pursue goals that benefit local communities and the greater good beyond themselves. Canada's religiously committed adherents share all these traits and form a vital part of Canada's civic core.[59]

It must be acknowledged that religion is not *necessary* to instil prosocial attitudes and behaviours in people. Most non-religious people have prosocial attitudes and behaviours to some degree, and there are some among the non-religious who are more prosocial than certain religious people. However, as will be shown, research on the linkage between religion and prosocial attitudes and behaviours demonstrates that Very Committed religious people, as a group, are markedly more likely to have prosocial attitudes and behaviours than non-religious people, as a group. Canadian sociologist Reginald Bibby has explained the relationship between religion and prosociality this way: 'People who don't believe in God can be good. But people who believe in God are more likely to *value* being good, enhancing the chances that they *will* be good'.[60]

Princeton University sociologist Robert Wuthnow states that compassion, altruism and charity are core tenets of the main world religions,[61] especially those that are of the monotheistic tradition.[62] Wuthnow explains that the Hebrew Scriptures teach that people are created in the image of God and are for this reason deserving of all the caring and kindness that can be given them. The Scriptures also teach that loving others is a duty we owe to God. The Koran teaches that those who give to charity guard themselves from evil. Buddhist thought, particularly in the Mayahana tradition, elevates compassion above all other virtues. And Christianity emphasizes love of neighbour, acts of mercy and charity for the needy.[63]

Remembering that there will always be individuals from both non-religious and religious groups who will be strongly prosocial, Canadian sociologist Kurt Bowen summarizes his research of 20 years of surveys by Statistics Canada and others, saying:

> The Very Committed put a distinctively high value on the importance and quality of their relationships with others. Compared to the Non-Religious, notably more of the Very Committed say they value a sense of belonging (69% vs. 53%), friendliness (80% vs. 63%) and kindness (85% vs. 71%). The Very Committed are even more likely to stress the importance of forgiveness (73% vs. 43%), generosity (71% vs. 42%), and concern for others (80% vs. 58%). Moreover, they are more inclined to disapprove of vengeance, to think we should forgive those who hurt us, and to believe that we ought to put our trust in others, even when we cannot be certain of reciprocation. This impressive, consistent, and cumulative set of differences suggests that the Very Committed are much more likely than other Canadians to be concerned with the welfare of others. Though various secular moralities can and do preach the same virtues, it is the overwhelming Christian ranks of the Very Committed who most frequently and consistently endorse that ethic of forgiveness and concern for others.[64]

Good Behaviour

Secondly, in conjunction with producing good citizens, religion contributes to good behaviour. Kurt Bowen has detected an increased 'gentleness among the Very Committed that sets them apart from other Canadians'.[65] For example, the Very Committed care about justice but are careful to advocate in lawful ways. When it comes to protest, the Very Committed are twice as likely to support a boycott or attend a legal demonstration as the Non-Religious. But as to illegal forms of protest, only 20 per cent of the Very Committed would join an unofficial strike or occupy a building, compared to 50 per cent of the Non-Religious.[66]

The Very Committed are law-abiding people who avoid antisocial behaviour. They are more likely than the Non-Religious to strongly agree that cheating, buying stolen goods, lying and accepting a bribe are never justified. Across six forms of antisocial behaviour that were studied, the Very Committed are the most likely to strongly disapprove of the behaviours while the Non-Religious are the least likely to disapprove of them. Bowen concludes: 'The common thread underlying these findings on both protest and permissiveness is that religiosity is intimately linked to civility'.[67]

The civility of the Very Committed extends to their close relationships. For example, the rate of marital breakdown among the Very Committed is half that of the Non-Religious (14 per cent vs. 33 per cent), and the Very Committed are embedded in a much more stable and extensive network of close relationships than the Non-Religious.[68]

Attendance at worship services has been found to have the greatest impact on marital stability, and when both spouses attend worship services regularly, they have the lowest divorce rate of all.[69] These factors add to social stability and the availability of people who can provide support to those in need, without their having to resort to a social agency.

Canadians value our international reputation for being a nation of caring, kind, generous, selfless and community-oriented people, and this is who the Very Committed religious people are. They contribute significantly to earning that reputation for Canada. As we've noted, they tend to be other-centred, committed to working through family and other relationship problems, and are willing to sacrifice their own preferences for the greater good. The result is a strong, stable social network for families and communities that strengthens Canada's social fabric.

Giving and Volunteering

The third prosocial benefit, which is closely related to good citizenship and good behaviour, is the promotion of giving and volunteering. When it comes to practical altruism, Very Committed religious people have a distinctive commitment to giving and volunteering. Kurt Bowen notes, 'Though we overwhelmingly agree that voluntary and charitable organizations are crucial to our collective well-being, only about a third of us actually volunteer in community organizations. [...] Religiosity is one of the major social forces affecting the volunteering levels of Canadians and it is the most influential factor bar none in determining how much we give to charity'.[70]

The reason the Very Committed are so much more generous than anyone else has very much to do with the religion they follow. Very Committed and Non-Religious givers do not differ in their motivation for giving: both groups embrace altruistic and humanitarian reasons for giving. But underlying the altruism and humanitarian motivations for giving to others is the fact that 74 per cent of the Very Committed say they have a core religious motivation to give. Religious people have a basic orientation to community and concern for the welfare of others. Bowen writes: 'The inescapable conclusion is that religious motivations and high religious commitment have a profound impact on charitable giving'.[71]

Bowen noted that the higher giving by the Very Committed cannot be attributed to any greater privilege than the Non-Religious because their incomes and educational attainments are similar to other Canadians. At every income and educational level, the Very Committed give far more to charity than the Less Committed and the Non-Religious. And in fact, the greatest gap between Very Committed and Non-Religious givers occurs at the lowest income and educational levels. At the lowest levels, the Very Committed give 10 times more than the Non-Religious, and at the highest levels of income and education, they still give five times more. Bowen concludes: 'The central, inescapable conclusion is that religiosity has the largest beta weight (0.336) and hence has the greatest impact on how much we Canadians give to charity'.[72]

After an extensive review of about 550 different studies, sociologist Pamela Wiepking reports that a positive relationship between church membership and/or frequency of church attendance on the one hand and secular and religious philanthropy on the other appears in 'almost any article in which this relationship was studied'.[73] Wiepking then cites 30 studies as examples.

The relationship between religiosity and philanthropy has been observed the world over, including in reports and studies by Giving Australia (2005);[74] Canadians Reed and Selbee (2001),[75] Bowen (1999),[76] and Berger (2006);[77] Bekkers (2003) in the Netherlands;[78] Chang (2006) in Taiwan;[79] and Reitsma, Scheepers and Grotenhuis (2003) in Western Europe.[80] Research on individual religious giving includes studies by Finke, Bahr and Scheitle,[81] Hoge,[82] Donahue,[83] Hoge, Zech, McNamara and Donohue,[84] Wuthnow,[85] Chaves and Miller,[86] and an entire issue of *Review of Religious Research*.[87]

A Taiwanese study found such positive benefits from religion that it recommended increasing the tax breaks for donations to religious organizations to encourage greater participation in religious activities.[88]

The biggest impact on the amount donated to charity as adults was having been active in a religious organization as a youth. Youths who were active in a church gave more than double to charity as adults than did adults who were not active in a religious organization as youths.[89]

A 2018 study by Imagine Canada found that 91 per cent of people who attended a place of worship at least once a week were donors, virtually the same percentage (90 per cent) as those who attended monthly. Where they differed though, was in how much they gave. A 47 per cent of weekly attenders are in the top 25 per cent of all givers in Canada, giving an annual average of $1,284, while only 28 per cent of the monthly attenders were in the top 25 per cent of Canadian donors.[90] There really is something distinctive about weekly attenders.

Turning our attention to the Non-Religious, the effect on philanthropy of having no religion is that all the numbers are markedly lower. Only 76 per cent of the Non-Religious are donors – they give a yearly average of only $313 – and only 12 per cent of them are in the top 25 per cent of Canadian donors.[91] The weekly attenders mentioned previously really are Canada's superstar donors. But their generosity doesn't happen spontaneously.

It turns out that the Very Committed tend to plan their giving in advance as part of their religious responsibility to care for others, often deciding to give a percentage of their income each week.[92] Those who plan their giving as a fixed percentage of their income give an average of 3 per cent more of their income to religious and non-religious charities than those who do not plan their giving in advance.[93]

In addition, Statistics Canada has shown that as of 2004, the 19 per cent of Canadians who are Very Committed fund 74 per cent of all donations to religious charities and more than 20 per cent of all donations to secular charities.[94] This is true in the United States as well.[95]

Indeed, it is not only religious charities that benefit from the liberality of the Very Committed. Canadian social surveys reveal that the Very Committed give more to secular charities than do the Non-Religious or, indeed, anyone else. Bowen reports that the median donation by the Very Committed to secular charities is almost double that of the Non-Religious. The one-third of Canadians who were religious (the Very Committed *and* the Less Committed) together provided more than 40 per cent of all the funds raised by secular charities, while the 40 per cent of the population who were non-religious gave only 30 per cent of the donations received by secular charities.[96] (Other Canadians fit into the 'seeker' or 'spiritual' part of the religiosity scale.) When a non-religious person receives assistance from a secular charity, they benefit from the gifts of time and money made by religious people who learned to be generous in their places of worship. The fact is, religious Canadians give sacrificially to ensure that secular goals for the common good are achieved.

According to Bowen, if everyone gave like the Very Committed give, the total value (at the time) of all charitable donations would rise from $5 billion to $12 billion. He said, 'Without the Very Committed, all Canadians and our network of charities and non-profit organizations would be much diminished'.[97] Religious ideals inspire generosity that is much greater than it otherwise would be.

As with charitable giving, survey results show that a core group of individuals provide most of the hours volunteered. Roughly 10 per cent of Canadians account for more than 75 per cent of all volunteer hours. The Very Committed give almost double the volunteer hours per year than the hours given by the Non-Religious, and a greater percentage of the Very Committed volunteer for secular organizations than the Non-Religious do (35 per cent to 25 per cent).[98]

As the evidence shows, Advancing Religion leads directly to a strong charitable sector that cares for citizens in need.

Tangible Community Benefits

Not only do religious people contribute to Canadian society as individuals, but most, if not all, religions have a very strong communal aspect. I conclude from the evidence that many benefits accrue to all Canadians because places of worship *create synergy* as individual members live out their faith together and accomplish something much greater together through their places of worship than they could achieve on their own.

A significant body of academic work has profiled the economic impact of religion as a communal phenomenon, the value of social capital generated by the religiously inspired, the religious contribution to mutual and humanitarian service, and more.[99] This section considers the socio-economic benefits of the communities that gather in places of worship.

Places of worship benefit their local communities through four means, each of which will be canvassed in greater detail below:

1. A positive contribution of social capital.
2. A multiplier effect (the 'Halo Effect') that produces benefits far greater than their budgets.
3. An exceptionally high return on society's investment through the tax system.
4. An improvement in the area's Neighbourhood Viability Index.

Positive Social Capital

An Imagine Canada report contains this summary statement about religious organizations and their communities:

> Religious organizations are more likely than other nonprofit and voluntary organizations to have a local community focus. Often at the heart of their communities, religious organizations can act as a point of initial contact for people new to a neighbourhood. Perhaps contrary to expectation, religious organizations tend to serve the public, regardless of faith. Religious organizations are less likely than nonprofit and voluntary organizations in general to have membership restrictions or to serve a specific segment of the population. In fact, more than two-thirds of religious organizations say that both members and non-members benefit from their services.[100]

A study of 46 Ontario churches supports what Imagine Canada reported. The study concluded that non-members were four times more likely to use a church's community programmes than the church members were.[101]

Congregations provide an accessible environment that is rich in opportunities to build bonding social capital (relationships within a group). Drawing on survey work by others, a research team reports that people trust other people in their place of worship more than they trust co-workers, neighbours and people of their own race. Attending or joining a place of worship therefore hastens the formation of trust and bonding social capital.[102] They also found that participating in volunteer activities within a place of worship, whether serving internal needs of the organization or reaching out to and serving the public, builds bridging capital (relationships between groups) with the surrounding community and increases volunteering externally and civic participation.

Many places of worship connect with outside groups and support their programmes, often providing them with use of their building space. Nancy Ammerman, a sociologist at Boston University, studied congregational life in the United States. She writes:

> Everywhere you look among the congregations we interviewed, there are scout troops and nursery schools, senior centers and sports leagues – all existing independently of any single congregation, but often housed and supported by religious groups in cooperation with others in the community. In addition, there are arts organizations that use religious buildings for rehearsals, performances and lessons. Congregations support formal and informal programs of tutoring, after-school care, and literacy classes. They contribute to programs of education and service provision that surround issues as diverse as AIDS, unwanted pregnancies, handicapped persons, adoption, and more. They support and refer parishioners to counseling centers of all sorts. And they cooperate with others in delivering spiritual care to people in hospitals, nursing homes, on college campuses, and even in police and fire departments.[103]

Ammerman observes that 'the largest proportion of congregational energy goes into providing relief for people in need, but nearly as much is directed at the education and self-improvement of others who may be less immediately needy'.[104]

Canadian and American research both show that local churches are truly a blessing to their surrounding communities, not only spiritually but also socially and economically. In *American Grace*, Robert Putnam noted that religious people make good neighbours, commenting: 'Good neighborliness and involvement in religiously based social networks are highly correlated in every survey we have examined, even when we hold constant everything from demographic and ideological factors to general religiosity and general sociability'.[105]

Another contribution congregations make to their neighbourhood's social capital is that they serve as important links in the delivery of the services and activities of other organizations that make their communities a better place in which to live.[106]

The 'Halo Effect'

In addition to social capital, a second tangible community benefit can be found in the 'Halo Effect'. This phenomenon was illustrated by a Canadian research study called The Halo Project, which analysed places of worship in the Greater Toronto Area (GTA) representing different religious traditions. The project was jointly supported by the City of Toronto's Research and Analysis Unit, Toronto Parks and Recreation, and Toronto Water, along with other organizations including the Canadian Council of Christian Charities, the Evangelical Fellowship of Canada and Cardus. The study examined 10 places of worship in the City of Toronto and determined the difference between what a place of worship spends and the higher value that it provides to its local community. The difference is referred to as the Halo Effect. The researchers used the same principles to calculate the benefit provided to the community as are used when analysts calculate the benefits of hosting world events in Canada. The Halo Effect of having a place of worship in a large urban community is almost five times its annual budget.[107]

A follow-up study included 26 congregations in Ontario, British Columbia and Quebec, including four rural or small-town communities. The Halo Effect for this group was less than in the GTA but still three times their annual budgets. When these results are applied to all the religious congregations in Canada, they produce an annual benefit of about $17.5 billion, equivalent to 1.1 per cent of the GDP.[108]

A third study by Michael Daly was done of four churches in Ontario: one small-town church and three rural churches (Parry Sound, Auburn, South Mountain and Southampton). Although they made a lesser economic contribution than the big-city congregations, the small-town/rural churches still made a significant contribution to their communities and, in fact, outperformed the big cities almost 3:1 in the value of the 'social capital and care' they contributed to their communities.[109]

These three studies of the economic impact of local places of worship on their communities round out several other studies in recent years, both in Canada and in the United States, that have reviewed the contributions that faith communities or local religious congregations make to the cultural, spiritual and social lives of their surrounding neighbourhoods, which also found positive results.[110]

So, large and small, urban and rural, local congregations have a significant effect on the quality of life in their communities.

Religion's Return on Investment

Third, religion offers a meaningful return on investment. Advancing Religion as a head of charity provides an outstanding tangible return on investment (ROI) to Canada. Some people feel that public support for religious charities through tax concessions given to places of worship is unfair, as non-religious people are thereby supporting religious charities through the tax system. These objections can be properly assessed by doing a cost/benefit analysis that considers both the cost of the tax concessions and the significant benefits identified by The Halo Project.

A 2017 analysis of 16 congregations calculated an ROI for places of worship. It calculated the total amount of 'lost' taxes in terms of municipal property tax, provincial and federal sales tax, and the provincial and federal personal income tax credit for receipted donations. The amount was then compared to the socio-economic benefit contributed by those congregations, and the result was a return on investment that is 12 times higher than the 'lost' taxes.[111] The fact is, those taxes are not lost but are invested, and Canada's investment in religious charities through the tax system provides an outstanding return on investment to all taxpayers, reducing the burden taxpayers would otherwise have to pay to obtain equivalent benefits for the public.

Neighbourhood Viability Index

Fourth, religion is an important indicator when it comes to neighbourhood viability. When a place of worship closes, the neighbourhood suffers. Two political scientists looked at the effect of a church closing on its surrounding community using a Neighbourhood Viability Index, which measures the neighbourhood's well-being in terms of residential tenure, home ownership, educational attainment and other similar factors. They were concerned that neighbourhoods in major metropolitan areas that experience decline and disinvestment would be adversely affected by the closure of places of worship. They report that places of worship are often regarded as important social actors because they are typically the last community group to leave a neighbourhood.

They found that for each closure of a geographically oriented congregation (e.g. Roman Catholic, Episcopalian, Orthodox Jewish), there is a corresponding decrease in neighbourhood viability over the following decade of 10 per cent for departing Roman Catholic churches and 7.5 per cent for the others. They also found that for each closure of a congregation characterized by bridging capital (i.e. the church is involved in social concerns beyond the congregation and active in its neighbourhood), there is a corresponding decrease in neighbourhood viability over the following decade of 2.5 per cent. The authors conclude that the presence of a place of worship contributes positively to a neighbourhood's viability and that congregational closures often lead to the socio-economic collapse of their neighbourhoods.[112]

A good example is the closure of St Matthias Anglican Parish in Guelph, Ontario. Michael Wood Daly recounts:

> Guelph Planning Department officials as well as some City Councillors have expressed concern about the City's capacity to replace programs and services once offered by the church. Even in the short time the congregation has been closed, the community has gone lacking and the City has been unable to allocate sufficient resources to replace those programs and services that have been lost.[113]

Benefits for the Public At Large

The following benefits accrue to society as a whole as opposed to individuals: other-centredness, civic engagement, early intervention and recovery, improved availability of community services, foundational freedom, pluralism, public discourse, economic growth and support for government policy.

Other-Centredness

The positive impact of religion on the public was observed in the early nineteenth century by Alexis de Tocqueville, who argued that religious values were the impetus that moved people away from self-interest and towards civic engagement.[114] Tocqueville's observation is highly relevant because social scientists are concerned that today's individualism is undermining civic engagement.[115] Religion (especially worship) reminds people that they are not the 'centre of the universe' and that they are responsible for supporting the greater good.[116] It is a powerful corrective to individualism's negative consequences and promotes a kind and caring society by helping people learn how to communicate better and trust one another.[117]

Civic Engagement

There are several definitions of 'civic engagement', but the one that seems most appropriate for this topic refers to a person who is 'working to make a difference in the civic life of our communities [...] promoting the quality of life in a community'.[118] People who have prosocial characteristics are the most likely to engage this way and, as we have seen above and will discuss further below, religion is the most significant mechanism our society has that develops prosocial attitudes and behaviour.

It is no surprise, then, that two Canadian academics who noted a trend in declining civic engagement since 1945 linked that decline to waning church attendance.[119] They report that membership in organizations that serve others (churches, service clubs, Scouts) is down while membership in organizations that serve their own members (sports, arts) is up.

They explain that civic engagement and church attendance are linked because, in addition to instilling prosocial attitudes and behaviours, the local church used to be where people learned to become civically engaged; it was there that they learned to speak in public, run meetings, respectfully engage those with different viewpoints and understand the needs of their local community. A local church equipped people to be change agents in their community. If a nation wants its citizens to be civically engaged, a flourishing religious subculture is an easy way to achieve that goal.

A Social Buffer

Places of worship are 'recognized as therapeutic communities and resources for both the prevention and amelioration of mental and physical health problems'.[120] Religious congregations transfer an overall benefit to society through the congregation's healthy social capital and capacity for self-care as each religious community cares for its own and for those who come to it for assistance. (When personal problems arise, people are more likely to seek assistance from a member of the clergy than from a mental health professional.)[121] In some cases, early intervention and support may prevent problems from worsening and becoming more costly for society, and in other cases congregational support may augment public, social and medical services and speed recovery or resolution, again minimizing the cost to society.

The nature of religion is that it deals with deeply personal issues. There is an expectation of shared intimacy between people that permits them to discuss aspects of their lives they might not be willing to share elsewhere. People can receive advice and encouragement from others that helps them deal with life's issues, perhaps settling things without needing to resort to public support services.

Nancy Ammerman found that as congregational members care for each other 'through thick and thin', they 'pick up much of the first-line social service delivery that might otherwise have to be done by government agencies'.[122]

In this way, places of worship act as a kind of buffer between the state's support services and the public's needs. Whether it be additional support through medical treatments or longer-term health issues, or dealing with dysfunctional relationships, poverty or addictions, religious communities are often part of the solution.

Improved Availability of Community Services

Indeed, the impact of a religious community's support for those in need can be significant. Researchers have documented that not only does religion increase the supply of community services, but it also reduces the demand for them.

As an example, one study of more than 500 admissions to Duke University Medical Center found that patients who attended church weekly or more often were significantly less likely to have been admitted to the hospital in the previous year, more likely to have had fewer hospital admissions overall, and more likely to have spent fewer days in the hospital than those who attended less often (11 days compared to 28 days). These associations retained their significance after controlling for other factors. The study's authors believe that attendance at church worship services results in less burden on public resources, such as health care, in part because of the support network that religious communities provide.[123]

The benefits of religion reduce the demand for government and community services and, therefore, increase the availability of those services for the non-religious public.

Foundational Freedom for Liberal Democracy

Canadian society further benefits from the free practice and expression of religious belief because religion and religious freedom are foundational to the other freedoms that are characteristic of liberal democracies. To curtail religious freedom is to compromise the basic liberty of the nation. As Thomas Farr of the Berkley Center for Religion, Peace & World Affairs asserts:

> Any state that protects religious liberty thereby limits itself. Religious liberty empowers religious actors both to perform services that might otherwise be carried out by the state, and to adhere to an authority beyond the state. For this very reason, authoritarian governments might understandably permit some secular assembly and speech, while banning or restricting religious assembly and speech. Such has been a pattern throughout history – from Stalin, Mao and Hitler, to Mexico's Plutarco Calles and Syria's Bashar Assad.[124]

Derek B. M. Ross, Executive Director of Christian Legal Fellowship, agrees with Farr's point about authoritarian governments. He writes: 'Religion is beneficial to the public because it nurtures independent thought, outside of the machinery of the state'.[125]

Farr reports that sociologists Brian Grim and Roger Finke have shown high statistical correlations between religious liberty and the presence of the other fundamental freedoms that ensure the longevity of democracy, including civil and political liberty, freedom of the press and economic freedom. Grim and Finke also found that religious freedom is highly associated with overall human development and the absence of violent religious extremism.[126]

Former Chief Justice Dickson of the Supreme Court of Canada reflected this same idea when he stated in *R v Big M Drug Mart* that 'an emphasis on individual conscience and individual judgment [...] lies at the heart of our democratic political tradition [...] Religious belief and practice are historically prototypical'.[127] That is to say, religious freedom blazed the trail for many other freedoms including freedom of assembly, freedom of speech and consequently of the press.[128]

It is good for everyone that our society encourages the institutions that bring people of faith together for a public, communal expression of their faith. That they can do this is a demonstration that they live in a free and democratic society. This is why the European Court of Human Rights stressed that the autonomous existence of religious communities is indispensable for pluralism in a democratic society – a position that has been adopted by the Supreme Court of Canada.[129]

Contribution to a Pluralistic Culture

Writing for the World Economic Forum, Brian Grim (President of the Religious Freedom and Business Foundation) and Jo-Ann Lyon (General Superintendent of the Wesleyan

Church) argue that religious freedom allows minority groups, including women, to have a voice in and contribute to society, making it a more pluralistic culture. They report research by the Pew Foundation that found a correlation between higher restrictions on religious freedom and greater gender inequality across countries in all five major continents. Their conclusion is that '[t]o close the gender gap, strengthen economies and empower women, it is imperative that religious freedom become a factor that is taken seriously and acted upon'.[130]

The law has recognized that there is a public benefit even when religious charities are closed to the public. Although most places of worship are open to the public, an English judge ruled that there is public benefit even in a synagogue that is not open to the public because it allows persons to 'mix with their fellow citizens'.[131] The judge recognized that places of worship provide a useful service to the broader community by helping to preserve and advance minority cultures and ethnicities, thus increasing pluralism.

The black church in America is a good example of this type of public benefit. While enforced segregation is deplorable, the development of black churches in the United States gave the black population an institution that preserved their culture and provided a community hub in which black culture could continue to develop. It served as the centre of activism and community organization, and as a voice for the community in the wider society. Dr Peniel Joseph, founding director of the Center for the Study of Race and Democracy, notes that black churches published newspapers; raised money to build schools and colleges; and helped organize libraries, insurance companies, and anti-poverty efforts. Joseph writes that historically, black churches helped sustain black communities against the ravages of Jim Crow, poverty and racial violence that shaped African-American life during a very difficult period in history.[132]

Religion and Women

Special mention should be made of how religion has led to the development and empowerment of people to maximize their human potential. Society benefits when everyone is able to contribute for the good of all from their own experience, education, talents, and other personal attributes. A good example of how religion can empower people and promote pluralism is the promotion of women's rights and opportunities across a variety of religious traditions.

Indeed, in a written statement to the United Nations Fourth World Conference on Women in 1995, the Bahá'í International Community stated that in the treatment of women, '[f]oremost is the principle of the oneness of humankind. It lies at the heart of the exhortation that we should treat others as we ourselves would wish to be treated, an ethical standard upheld in some form by every religion'.[133]

Religious leaders of different faiths are currently making diligent efforts to advance women's rights in Ethiopia.[134] In 2016, religious leaders developed a 13-point call for action to end harmful traditional practices and gender-based violence in Ethiopia, including rejecting violence against women, child marriage and the practice of female genital mutilation (FGM). They are now preaching to prevent such violence in their congregations. UN Women Ethiopia Deputy Representative Funmi Bologun explains:

> Religious leaders are fundamental allies in driving the advancement of women's rights in Ethiopian society. [...] Where patriarchal traditions and cultural practices condone discrimination against women, true interpretation of religion has the power to break the barriers and unlock human potential. Programmes such as this [a UN training initiative involving religious leaders], aiming to build the capacity of religious leaders on women's rights, are critical in order to reduce the social acceptance of violence against women and to change discriminatory attitudes and behaviours.[135]

Similarly, Nicholas Kristof, a columnist for the *New York Times*, describes how religion is improving the lives of women in Africa. Though not unequivocal in his commendation, Kristof praises the positive contributions of 'conservative [churches] led by evangelicals'. He notes that Pentecostal congregations in particular 'encourage women to take leadership roles, and for many women this is the first time they have been trusted with authority and found their opinions respected. In rural Africa, Pentecostal churches are becoming a significant force to emancipate women'.[136]

In 2016, in an event organized by UN Women Myanmar, prominent leaders of four religions (Buddhism, Christianity, Islam and Hinduism) gathered to jointly state that no religion justifies discrimination or violence against women. Al Haj U Aye Lwin, Chief Convener of the Islamic Centre of Myanmar, claimed that it is not religion that teaches discrimination but its (mis)interpretation. According to Hla Tun, Coordinator of Sanatan Dharma Swayamsevak Sangh, the empowerment of women empowers the community as a whole in its social and economic development. Jean D'Cunha, Head of UN Women Myanmar, spoke of the power of faith to effect change and stressed that discrimination and violence against women is not just a women's issue but one that also hurts other members of society and a country's overall development. 'Religious leaders with their strategic reach and influence, together with women and men laity, can draw on the transformative potential of religion to end discrimination and violence against women and girls and foster genuine peace and harmony', she said. 'For religion speaks to the core of our beings, and inspires our meaning systems and relationships, including relationships of gender justice and equality'.[137]

Manini Sheker, a PhD candidate at the University of Sussex, agrees about the transformative power of religion. She says, 'From the mass mobilization of Christian women to end fourteen years of civil war in Liberia to the founding of Islam-inspired grassroots organizations to advance women's empowerment and civic dialogue in Bosnia-Herzegovina, faith-inspired movements are playing a critical role in safeguarding women's rights'.[138]

Contribution to Public Discourse

Legal scholar Kathleen Brady notes that religious groups play a prophetic role and help the broader society when they develop and communicate new ideas that contribute to the common good of the whole society and push the larger community forward.¹³⁹ For example, the now mainstream Canadian values of equality and human dignity were developed from the Christian theology that all humans are created in the image of God.¹⁴⁰ Religion promotes its values of freedom of conscience, justice and mercy for the good of all. Brady reminds us that:

> Religious groups speak to us not only about the divine but also about the social and civic concerns of the larger community, and our collective progress depends upon the range of insights that different traditions provide. [...] Indeed, religious groups do more than speak to us about social and political truth. Religious communities seek to live out their social visions in their internal community life, and it is in this form of witness that the power of new ideas may be most evident. Religious groups not only speak a prophetic word, but they model it in their internal life.¹⁴¹

Erin Wilson, Director of the Centre for Religion, Conflict and the Public Domain at the University of Groningen, recognizes that people who have identified as religious, such as Martin Luther King Jr., have led movements for inclusion. Likewise, religious development organizations such as World Vision International have developed training programmes to promote gender equality and to reduce gender-based violence. They are examples of the good that religion can do for society.¹⁴²

Effects on Business and the Economy

It is also worth noting that the presence of religion in a society constructively impacts business practices and economic growth. Sociologist Joshua Yates reports that 'a credible body of academic work has profiled the economic impact of religion and more'.¹⁴³

Religious freedom is a key ingredient to peace and stability, which is particularly important for business because where stability exists, there are more opportunities to invest and to conduct normal and predictable business operations, especially in emerging and new markets.¹⁴⁴ One study found that the presence of proselytizing Protestant faiths – that is, faiths competing for adherents – was associated with economic development throughout the world.¹⁴⁵ A notable finding of a study of 143 countries is that 'religious freedom—taken as the inverse of religious restrictions and hostilities—is one of only three variables that remains a significant predictor of GDP growth. The study found that religious freedom is correlated with economic global competitiveness.¹⁴⁶

In a series of studies in China, Xingquiang Du and colleagues used a sample of 11,357 observations of business valuations from the Chinese stock market for the period of 2001–2011 and found 'strong and robust' evidence to show that religion is significantly negatively associated with the extent of 'earnings management', suggesting that religion can serve as a set of social norms to mitigate corporate unethical behaviour. The proximity of a business to places of worship (e.g. Buddhist monasteries, Taoist temples) predicted benefits in terms of greater environmental responsibility and philanthropic giving, as well as a reduction of illegal business practices. Their results mirrored the findings of other studies.¹⁴⁷

Other Chinese research looked at provincial data from 2001 to 2011 to study the impact of religion on economic growth. The authors connect religion to the economy through religion's influence on political preference, quality of governance, human capital, education and work ethic. They report that 'among the different religions, Christianity has the most significant effect on economic growth. This conclusion is consistent among different estimators and robust with stability over time'.[148] Here is an indication that at least one religion definitely influences the national economy. The authors don't rule out that other religions may have a similar effect; they just can't make a positive declaration on that matter.

Finally, as a support to the business community and economic success, eight of ten recent studies have found a generally positive relationship between religiousness and ethical decision making,[149] and three studies suggest that organized religion helps to improve government stability by increasing social capital and stimulating economic growth.[150]

Support for Government Policy

Another major benefit to the public at large is that religious support networks augment government programmes, such as receiving refugees. Statistics Canada reported that in 2011 there were 7,400 government-assisted refugees, and in addition, another 5,500 refugees were supported by private groups which, according to Statistics Canada, were mostly Christian churches.[151] In fact, a newspaper reported that churches dominate the roster of 100 organizations pre-approved by the federal government to work with refugees. The article stated that with determined volunteers and a built-in donation base, faith-based organizations are well suited for refugee work.[152]

Faith-based sponsors tend to sponsor marginalized people who might be overlooked by the government's refugee programme. For example, 90 per cent of the Syrian refugees who came to Canada through private sponsorship (mostly by Christian churches and individual Christians) were from vulnerable ethnic and religious minorities, while only 5 per cent of those sponsored by the federal government came from those minorities. One Christian group, Hay Doun of Montreal, alone sponsored 25 per cent of all Syrian refugees arriving since 2013, continuing a service it had already been providing for 10 years as they sponsored both Christians and Muslims alike.[153]

Once refugees arrive in Canada, government studies show that privately sponsored refugees tend to fare better than their government counterparts.[154]

More broadly, a Canadian survey showed that half of new Canadians receive material support, help finding a job and new language instruction from faith-based communities, and more than 60 per cent rely on those same groups to form a community and relational network after they arrive in Canada.[155]

A study of 500 first-generation immigrants to the United States found that they made good use of ethnic religious congregations, quickly building trust with their co-attendees (as reported above, people trust fellow believers at their place of worship more than they do others) and developing social networks in those congregations. The study shows that volunteering within the congregation is significantly related to civic engagement and that participating in volunteer activities, as opposed to simply attending, is associated with volunteering outside the congregation and civic participation. Volunteering within a place of worship helps immigrants not only build bonding capital but also bridging capital and is thus very helpful in integrating new immigrants into their new host community.[156]

Why Religion 'Works'

As sociologist Joshua Yates wrote, we can measure inputs and outputs, as we have done throughout this chapter, but the real question of great interest is the idea of formation and how religious communities shape people so they develop characteristics and practices that yield public benefit. He asks: 'How are these communities forming people into valued neighbours, community leaders, active citizens, and in some cases, tireless advocates? The relationship of all these dynamics has been significantly underexamined'.[157]

Religion is Comprehensive

A starting point to understanding religion's effect on people is its comprehensive nature. Religion is a single system than encompasses all of life. Psychologists have noted: 'To most believers, religion appears as a total ideology with a sense of the "natural" and the "real", without which it is impossible to conceive the world they inhabit'.[158]

Religion Provides Strong Motivation

The secular concept of altruism describes the scenario when a person does something of benefit for someone else without any discernible benefit in return. But it does not explain *why* people do altruistic deeds. Some see altruism as irrational, and some say it doesn't really exist. Even believers in altruism concede that it is comparatively rare. Civil communities can create the mechanisms for altruism and encourage it, but they don't have the ability to teach altruism and create within people an intrinsic norm of altruism.

Religious communities are different; they are communities in which norms are not just taught but also internalized. Religion supplies the *why* for altruistic behaviour.[159] In fact, religion is so powerful because it isn't just about attending a worship service. Ninety-four percent of religiously committed Canadians say they draw their personal identity from their faith and religious belief. Religion is both an identity and a worldview.[160] While most studies use weekly attendance at a worship service as a proxy for religiosity, it appears that the importance of a person's religion to them and the internalization of that religion are the real factors in the difference between the Very Committed and the Non-Religious. High levels of personal devotion are associated with friendlier and more cooperative interactions with others, including higher levels of listening, more control of disappointment and more control of anger.[161]

Religion Shapes Identity

To the extent that individuals are involved in a place of worship or a religious belief system, a socializing influence is exerted upon them.[162] Even singing in the choir has a positive effect on people, as they work together to perfect a song and then, through the song, proclaim a shared religious value or norm.[163] Church-sponsored young adult groups support positive socialization by helping people to develop social skills and to reaffirm their self and group identity.[164] Those who rank religion as a major part of their identity are more likely to use their religion to find meaning in their daily lives[165] and thus are more likely to produce its benefits in the world around them.

The 'secret sauce' of religion is that adherents believe there is a Higher Power, gods or God that is external to themselves. Religious people understand that the world does not revolve around them but that they are part of something bigger than themselves. Their fundamental worldview is that life is lived in community and there are communal responsibilities, to religious and non-religious people alike. That perspective turns the focus of religious people outward and inspires them to find fulfilment in serving others.

Two sociologists from the University of Akron and a professor of medical humanities at Stony Brook University wrote a book called *Habits of the Heart*.[166] Their research found experiencing God's love directly was the only variable that significantly predicted a benevolent person.[167] Within the Very Committed, those who experience divine love most frequently are the most benevolent people of all. They are the most likely to agree that 'all people share an unbreakable bond of humanity'. Only 39 per cent of people who do not feel God's love directly strongly agree with the statement that they should contribute to making the world a better place, while 65 per cent of those who most frequently and directly experience God's love strongly agree with that statement.[168]

Places of Worship Have Self-Reinforcing Social Networks

Regular attendees at worship services enjoy larger in-person social networks and more frequent in-person social contacts than any other persons.[169] Religious groups promote informal exchanges of tangible support and socioemotional support.[170] They also offer pastoral counselling, formal programmes for learning life skills and other practical supports.[171] Regular attendees report receiving more social support than others, on average, and are more likely to perceive their support networks as reliable and satisfying.[172]

Places of Worship Drive Behaviour

The reason religiosity is so crucial is that good intentions, beliefs and attitudes alone are not enough to drive behaviour.[173] Believing it is important to care for others is only weakly correlated with caring behaviour. What matters more are habits and practices accumulated over time and then activated by circumstances that cue caring behaviour. Prosocial behaviours are taught, modelled and practised in a mutually reinforcing community environment located within local places of worship where caring behaviours are observed in others, needs are highlighted, opportunities to act are presented and relational networks reinforce prosocial behaviour. The religious doctrines of responsibility for one's neighbour, of valuing each person as God's creation regardless of social status and of self-sacrifice for the greater good work together with the practices learned by participating in the congregation's religious programmes to drive the prosocial concern for the welfare of others to tangible action. Practising one's religion is the mechanism that converts attitudes and beliefs into habits and regular practices.[174]

A group of researchers from University of Notre Dame's Department of Sociology came up with a helpful metaphor for places of worship when they noted that congregations function as *schools* for learning formative skills and values that are conducive to philanthropic behaviour.[175]

Places of Worship Build Strong Family Bonds

The more religious a couple is, the closer their children feel to them and the more the children describe their homes as happy, warm, accepting and communicative. Family solidarity is positively linked to the frequency of attendance of high school students at religious services.[176]

Religion promotes the idea that positive relationships among family members are desirable. Most religions encourage marriage, procreation and loving relationships within the family; they also provide parent–child interactive activities such as family camps or retreats that facilitate bonding between them and give opportunities to discuss religious teachings and family issues.[177]

Simply put, shared religiosity promotes strong spousal and familial ties and has significant positive effects on the quality of parent–child relationships, including the level of a father's involvement with his children, whether married or divorced, and the father's spending time monitoring his children, praising and hugging them and simply being with them.[178] As previously noted, loving, supportive relationships within a family equip children and youth to make better choices and form better habits, and then to continue them into adulthood.

Places of Worship are Coherent and Cohesive

A place of worship combines in one cohesive environment a coherent package in which all elements work together to achieve their intended result. Sermons are reinforced with opportunities to act on them. Many congregations have a small group programmes in which congregational members meet in groups of about 10 people to build strong relationships between them and give them opportunity to discuss their faith and its application in life. Values are discussed and modelled in community for both children and adults. As noted previously, people who occupy low-status and marginal positions in society are reassured of their self-worth and their intrinsic ability to contribute to the public good.[179]

Religion is Unique in How it Works

Michael McConnell, professor of law at Stanford University, addresses the issue of whether the public benefits of religion are just the sum of individual religious practices (which might be replicated without religion) or are the product of the practices working synergistically together. His description of how the practice of religion works as a single, holistic, comprehensive system is a great explanation of what makes religion so effective at producing prosocial people who do great good for Canadian society:

> Religion bears resemblances to, and has differences from, a wide variety of other human concerns. Religion is a special phenomenon, in part, because it plays such a wide variety of roles in human life: it is an institution, but it is more than that; it is an ideology or worldview, but it is more than that; it is a set of personal loyalties and locus of community, akin to family ties, but it is more than that; it is an aspect of identity, but it is more than that; it provides answers to questions of ultimate reality, and offers a connection to the transcendent; but it is more than that. Religion cannot be reduced to a subset of any larger category. In any particular context, religion may appear to be analogous to some other aspect of human activity – to another institution, worldview, personal loyalty, basis of personal identity, or answer to ultimate and transcendent questions. However, there is no other human phenomenon that combines all of these aspects; if there were such a concept, it would probably be viewed as a religion.[180]

Conclusion

Carl Juneau, with more than 28 years' experience in the regulation of charities through the Canada Revenue Agency's Charities Directorate and the Tax Policy Branch of the federal Department of Finance, wrote about the public benefit of Advancing Religion, stating:

> Beyond faith, [religion] has taught us to respect human life; it has taught us to respect property; it has taught us to respect God's creation; it has taught us to abhor violence; it has taught us to help one another; it has taught us honesty. In essence, what makes religion 'good' from a societal point of view is that it makes us want to become better – it makes people become better members of society.[181]

Juneau's assessment points to a final benefit of Advancing Religion: it makes us want to become better people and it shows us how. In an ideal world, all people of faith would become outstanding paragons of virtue, but in the real world, faith communities do not claim that each and every adherent of their faith will manifest the beneficial effects of their religion, because people are inevitably fallible.[182] Nevertheless, the positive effect over time that religious organizations have on individuals has been proven by impartial academic research and is a tremendous public benefit for Canada.[183]

As law professor Matthew Harding declares, there is 'most clearly an argument for applying a presumption of benefit to religions that have enriched the lives of large numbers of adherents over long periods of time'.[184] Likewise, Canada's federal minister of finance wrote to the Canadian Secular Alliance in 2012 about the presumed benefit of Advancing Religion, arguing that 'providing charitable status for the advancement of religion is based on the presumption that religion provides people with a moral and ethical framework for living and plays an important role in building social cohesion'.[185]

Based on the research reported in this chapter, it is reasonable to conclude that the presumption of benefit is well founded.

The charitable purpose of Advancing Religion benefits the Canadian public, both individuals and communities, and it benefits our nation by increasing civic engagement, economic output and social infrastructure. Advancing Religion does all this by producing citizens who bolster our international reputation for civility, generosity and kindness.

Notes

1 Pat Fagan, '95 Social Science Reasons for Religious Worship and Practice', *MARRI (Marriage and Religion Research Institute)* (2012), online: <http://marri.us/research/research-papers/95-social-science-reasons-for-religious-worship-and-practice/>; 'Why Religion Matters Even More: The Impact of Religious Practice on Social Stability', *The Heritage Foundation* (2006), online <https://www.heritage.org/civil-society/report/why-religion-matters-even-more-the-impact-religious-practice-social-stability>.

2 David Lasby & Cathy Barr, '30 Years of Giving in Canada – The Giving Behaviour of Canadians: Who Gives, How, and Why?' (Ottawa: Rideau Hall Foundation and Imagine Canada, 2018) at 6, online (pdf): <https://www.rhf-frh.ca/wp-content/uploads/2018/04/RHF_30years_Report_eng_FNL.pdf>.

3 For a thoughtful discussion of public civility, see this post by Eric Sigurdson, 'Civility, the Rule of Law, and Lawyers: the 'glue' that binds society against social crisis – is incivility the 'ugly new normal' in government, politics', *Sigurdson Post*, 25 November 2016, online: <http://www.sigurdsonpost.com/2016/11/25/civility-the-rule-of-law-and-lawyers-the-glue-that-binds-society-or-social-crisis-is-incivility-the-ugly-new-normal-in-government-politics-and-the-law/>.

4 Martin Turcotte, 'Volunteering and charitable giving in Canada', *Statistics Canada* (2015) at 4, online (pdf): <https://www150.statcan.gc.ca/n1/en/pub/89-652-x/89-652-x2015001-eng.pdf?st=t8AeXsJT>.

5 Kurt Bowen, *Christians in a Secular World: The Canadian Experience* (Montreal: McGill-Queen's University Press, 2004), 288 [Bowen, *Christians in a Secular World*].

6 Joshua Yates, 'The Social Impact of Religion', in *Religion and the Good of the City: Report 2: The State of Research and Influence* (Hamilton, ON: Cardus Social Cities, 2017) at 11, online: <https://www.cardus.ca/research/social-cities/reports/religion-and-the-good-of-the-city-report-2/>.

7 David E. Campbell & Robert D Putnam, 'Charity's Religious Edge: The most religious Americans actually give more money to secular causes than do secular Americans', *Wall Street Journal Online* (10 December 2010), online: <https://www.wsj.com/articles/SB10001424052748703766704576009361375685394>.

8 Jeffrey Dorfman, 'Religion is good for all of us, even those who don't follow one', *Forbes* (22 December 2013), online: <https://www.forbes.com/sites/jeffreydorfman/2013/12/22/religion-is-good-for-all-of-us-even-those-who-dont-follow-one/#25189cd964d7>; David R. Williams et al, 'Religion and Psychological Distress in a Community Sample' (1991) 31:11 Social Science and Medicine 1257–62.

9 The Barna Group Ltd, 'About the Research', in *New Marriage and Divorce Statistics Released* (31 March 2008), online: *Barna* <https://www.barna.com/research/new-marriage-and-divorce-statistics-released/>.

10 Seekers who never attend a worship service may be called 'Spiritual' in some studies because they are not seeking an organized religious experience.

11 Bowen, *Christians in a Secular World*, *supra* note 5 at 44.

12 *Ibid*, at 99.

13 Byron R. Johnson, Ralph Brett Tompkins & Derek Webb, 'Objective Hope: Assessing the Effectiveness of Faith-Based Organizations: A Review of the Literature', (Baylor University,

2008) at 5, 7, 22, online (pdf): *Baylor Institute for Studies of Religion (ISR Report)*, <https://www.baylor.edu/content/services/document.php/24809.pdf>.

14 See: Dorfman, *supra* note 8; Dorfman based his story on research reported in Christopher Ellison & Robert A. Hummer, eds, *Religion, Families, and Health: Population-Based Research in the United States* (New Brunswick, NJ: Rutgers University Press, 2010).

See also: Todd W. Hall, 'Christian Spirituality and Mental Health: A Relational Spirituality Paradigm for Empirical Research' (2004) 23:1 Journal of Psychology and Christianity 66–81; Diane R. Brown & Lawrence E. Gary, 'Religious Socialization and Educational Attainment Among African Americans: An Empirical Assessment' (1991) 60:3 Journal of Negro Education 414–15; Ying Chen & Tyler J. VanderWeele, 'Associations of Religious Upbringing with Subsequent Health and Well-Being from Adolescence to Young Adulthood: An Outcome-Wide Analysis' (2018) American Journal of Epidemiology, https://doi.org/10.1093/aje/kwy142; Byron R. Johnson, 'A Better Kind of High: Religious Commitment Reduces Drug Use Among Poor Urban Teens' (Baylor University, 2008), online (pdf): *Baylor Institute for Studies of Religion (ISR Research Report)*, <http://www.baylorisr.org/wp-content/uploads/ISR_Better_High.pdf>; David B. Larson & Bryon R. Johnson, 'Religion: The Forgotten Factor in Cutting Youth Crime and Saving At-Risk Urban Youth' (1998), online: *The Manhattan Institute* <https://www.manhattan-institute.org/html/religion-forgotten-factor-cutting-youth-crime-and-saving-risk-urban-youth-5880.html>.

15 Brown & Gary, *supra* note 14 at 421.

16 Lisa D. Pearce & Dana L. Haynie, 'Intergenerational Religious Dynamics and Adolescent Delinquency' (2004) 82:4 Social Forces 1553.

17 Allan F. Abrahamse, Peter A. Morrison & Linda J. Waite, 'Beyond Stereotypes: Who Becomes a Single Teenage Mother?' (1988) The Rand Population Research Center, National Institute of Child Health and Human Development, 7.

18 Margaret Lommen Vaaler, 'Familial Religious Involvement and Children's Mental Health Outcomes' (DPhil Dissertation, University of Texas at Austin, 2008) <http://hdl.handle.net/2152/18357>.

19 See Chapter 1, Juliet Chevalier-Watts, 'Have a Little Faith: The Advancement of Religion and Public Benefit'.

20 Andrew C. Kenney, 'Teen Challenge's Proven Answer to the Drug Problem', summary of Aaron T. Bicknese, 'The Teen Challenge Drug Treatment Program in Comparative Perspective' (PhD Dissertation, Northwestern University, 1999), online (pdf): <http://acadc.org/wp-content/uploads/pdf/NW_study.pdf>.

21 Harvard T. H. Chan School of Public Health, News Release, 'Religious upbringing linked to better health and well-being during early childhood' (2018), online: <https://www.hsph.harvard.edu/news/press-releases/religious-upbringing-adult-health/>; Pearce & Haynie, *supra* note 16; Christian Smith, 'Theorizing Religious Effects among American Adolescents' (2003) 42 Journal for the Scientific Study of Religion; Acheampong Yaw Amoateng & Stephen J. Bahr, 'Religion, Family, and Adolescent Drug Use' (1986) 29:1 Sociological Perspectives; Sharon Scales Rostosky, Mark D. Regnerus & Margaret Laurie Comer Wright, 'Coital Debut: The Role of Religiosity and Sex Attitudes in the Add Health Survey' (2003) 40:4 Journal of Sex Research 358–67.

22 Chevalier-Watts, *supra* note 19.

23 Brown & Gary, *supra* note 14 at 413–14.

24 Tyler J. VanderWeele, 'Physical Activity and Physical and Mental Well-Being in Church Settings' (2017) 107:7 American Journal of Public Health 1023–24; Harold Koenig, Dana King & Verna B. Carson, *Handbook of Religion and Health*, 2nd edn (Oxford: Oxford University Press, 2012); Tyler J. VanderWeele, 'Religion and Health: A Synthesis', in *Spirituality and Religion Within the Culture of Medicine: From Evidence to Practice*, ed. J. R. Peteet & M. L. Balboni (New York: Oxford University Press, 2017), 357–402 [VanderWeele, 'Religion and Health'];

Harold Koenig et al, 'The Relationship Between Religious Activities and Cigarette Smoking in Older Adults' (1998) 53A:6 Journal of Gerontology: Medical Sciences M426–M434.

25 See Chen & VanderWeele, *supra* note 14; Y. J. Wong, L. Rew, & K. D. Slaikeu, 'A systematic review of recent research on adolescent religiosity/spirituality and mental health' (2006) 27:2 Issues in Mental Health Nursing 161–83; A. J. Weaver, K. J. Flannelly, & A. L. Strock, 'A review of research on the effects of religion on adolescent tobacco use published between 1990 and 2003' (2005) 40:160 Adolescence 761–76; J. W. Yeung, Y. C. Chan, & B. L. Lee, 'Youth religiosity and substance use: A meta-analysis from 1995 to 2007' (2009) 105:1 Psychology Reports 255–66; D. E. Davis et al, 'Research on religion/spirituality and forgiveness: A meta-analytic review' (2013) 5:4 Psychology of Religion and Spirituality 233–41; Rostosky, Regnerus, & Wright, *supra* note 21.

26 Howard Wineberg, 'Marital Reconciliation in the United States: Which Couples Are Successful?' (1994) 56:1 Journal of Marriage and Family 80–88.

27 C. G. Ellison, J. P. Bartkowski & K. L. Anderson, 'Are There Religious Variations in Domestic Violence' (1999) 20 Journal of Family Issues, cited in Christopher G. Ellison & Kristin L. Anderson, 'Religious Involvement and Domestic Violence among U.S. Couples' (2001) 40:2 Journal for the Scientific Study of Religion 270.

28 Ellison & Anderson, *supra* note 27; E. E. Filsinger & M. R. Wilson, 'Religiosity, Socioeconomic Rewards, and Family Development: Predictors of Marital Adjustment' (1984) 46 Journal of Marriage and the Family 663–70; G. L. Hansen, 'The Effect of Religiosity on Factors Predicting Marital Adjustment' (1987) 50 Social Psychology Quarterly 264–69; M. G. Dudley and F. A. Kosinski, 'Religiosity and Marital Satisfaction: A Research Note' (1990) 32:1 Review of Religious Research 77–86.

29 Vaughn R. A. Call & Tim B. Heaton, 'Religious Influence on Marital Stability' (1997) 36:3 Journal for the Scientific Study of Religion 382–92; Kristin T. Curtis & Christopher G. Ellison, 'Religious Heterogamy and Marital Conflict: Findings from the National Survey of Families and Households' (2001) 23:4 Journal of Family Issues 551–76; Timothy T. Clydesdale, 'Family Behaviours among Early U.S. Baby Boomers: Exploring the Effects of Religion and Income Change, 1965–1982' (1997) 76:2 Social Forces (University of North Carolina Press) 605 at 611.

30 W. R. Schumm, 'Beyond Relationship Characteristics of Strong Families: Constructing a Model of Family Strengths' (1985) 19 Family Perspective, 3; J. Scanzoni & C. Arnett, 'Enlarging the Understanding of Marital Commitment via Religious Devoutness, Gender Role Preferences, and Locus of Marital Control' (1987) 8 Journal of Family Issues 136–56; D. B. Larson & J. W. Goltz, 'Religious Participation and Marital Commitment' (1989) 30:4 Review of Religious Research 387–400.

31 A. Mahoney, et al, 'Marriage and the Spiritual Realm: The Role of Proximal and Distal Religious Constructs in Marital Functioning' (1999) 13 Journal of Family Psychology 321–38.

32 T. B. Heaton & E. L. Pratt, 'The Effects of Religious Homogamy on Marital Satisfaction and Stability' (1990) 11 Journal of Family Issues 191–207; J. Stacey, *Brave New Families: Stories of Domestic Upheaval in Late Twentieth Century America* (New York: Basic Books, 1990).

33 Christopher G. Ellison & Kristin L. Anderson, 'Religious Involvement and Domestic Violence among U.S. Couples' (2001) 40:2 Journal for the Scientific Study of Religion 269–86.

34 Nancy T. Ammerman, 'Doing Good in American Communities: Congregations and Service Organizations Working Together' (Hartford: Hartford Institute for Religious Research, Hartford Seminary, 2001), 4, online: <http://hirr.hartsem.edu/orw/orw_cong-report.html#religiousscene>; Brown & Gary, *supra* note 14 at 414.

35 *Ibid*, at 412. See also: J. Cone, *For <y People: Black Theology and the Black Church* (Maryknoll, NY: Orbis, 1984); C. E. Lincoln & L. H. Mamiya, *The Black Church in the African American Experience* (Durham, NC: Duke University Press, 1990); M. D. Williams, *Community in a Black Pentecostal Church: An Anthropological Study* (Pittsburgh, PA: University of Pittsburgh Press, 1974).

36 R. B. Freeman, 'Who Escapes? The Relation of Church Going and Other Background Factors to the Socioeconomic Performance of Black Male Youths from Inner-City Tracts', in *The Black Youth Employment Crisis*, ed. R. B. Freeman and H. J. Holzer (Chicago, IL: University of Chicago Press, 1986), 2, 16

37 Ela Bhatt, 'Religion can empower women and raise their dignity' (14 August 2015), online: *The Elders*, <https://theelders.org/news/%E2%80%9Creligion-can-empower-women-and-raise-their-dignity%E2%80%9D>. For more on women and religion, see section 4 of this chapter.

38 J. Coleman, T. Hoffer & S. Kilgore, *High School Achievement: Catholic, Public, and Private Schools Compared* (New York: Basic Books, 1982); Z. S. Blau, *Black Children/White Children: Competence, Socialization, and Social Structure* (New York: The Free Press, 1981); G. Lenski, *The Religious Factor: A Sociological Study of Religion's Impact on Politics, Economics, and Family Life*, revised edn (Garden City, NY: Doubleday, 1963); Mark D. Regnerus, 'Shaping Schooling Success: Religious Socialization and Educational Outcomes in Metropolitan Public Schools' (2000) 39:3 Journal for the Scientific Study of Religion; Regnerus, 'Making the Grade: The Influence of Religion Upon the Academic Performance of Youth in Disadvantaged Communities', (Baylor University, 2001), online (pdf): *Baylor Institute for Studies of Religion (ISR Report)*, <http://www.baylorisr.org/wp-content/uploads/ISR-Making-Grade_071.pdf>.

39 Brown & Gary, *supra* note 14.

40 S. L. Hansen & A. L. Ginsburg, 'Gaining Ground: Values and High School Success' (1988) 25 American Educational Research Journal 18–19, 25, online (pdf): <https://files.eric.ed.gov/fulltext/ED268069.pdf>.

41 L. M. Chatters, 'Religion and Health: Public Health Research and Practice' (2000) 21 Annual Review of Public Health 335.

42 Brown & Gary, *supra* note 14 at 412.

43 Chen & VanderWeele, *supra* note 14.

44 Carmen Chai, 'Why more Canadian millennials than ever are at 'high risk' of mental health issues', Global News (2 May 2017), online: <https://globalnews.ca/news/3417600/why-more-canadian-millennials-than-ever-are-at-high-risk-of-mental-health-issues/>.

45 VanderWeele, 'Religion and Health', *supra* note 24

46 David B. Larson et al, 'The Impact of Religion on Men's Blood Pressure' (1989) 28:4 Journal of Religion and Health.

47 L. K. George, C. G. Ellison & D. B. Larson, 'Explaining the relationships between religious involvement and health' (2002) 13:3 Psychological Inquiry 190–200.

48 M. A. Musick, J. S. House & D. R. Williams, 'Attendance at Religious Services and Mortality in a National Sample' (2004) 45:2 Journal of Health and Social Behaviour 198–213; George, Ellison & Larson, *supra* note 47; T. J. Vanderweele et al, 'Attendance at religious services, prayer, religious coping, and religious/spiritual identity as predictors of all-cause mortality in the Black Women's Health Study' (2017) 185:7 American Journal of Epidemiology 512–22.

49 See Todd W. Hall, 'Christian Spirituality and Mental Health: A Relational Spirituality Paradigm for Empirical Research' (2004) 23:1 Journal of Psychology and Christianity 66–81; Theodore J. Chamberlain & Christopher A. Hall, *Realized Religion: Research on the Relationship Between Health and Religion* (Philadelphia, PA: Templeton Foundation Press, 2000); H. G. Koenig, ed., *Handbook of Religion and Mental Health* (New York: Haworth Pastoral Press, 1998); D. B. Larson, J. P. Swyers, & M. E. McCullough, *Scientific Research on Spirituality and Health: A Report Based on the Scientific Progress in Spirituality Conferences* (Bethesda, MD: National Institute for Healthcare Research, 1998); T. G. Plante & A. C. Sherman, eds, *Faith and Health: Psychological Perspectives* (New York: Guilford Press, 2001); L. M. Chatters, 'Religion and Health: Public Health Research and Practice' (2000) 21 Annual Review of Public Health 335–67 at 339–41; Christopher Ellison et al, 'Religious Involvement, Stress, and Mental Health: Findings from the 1995 Detroit Area Study' (2001) 80:1 Social Forces 215–49. A special section on 'Religion, Spirituality, and Health' was published in the January 2003 edition of *American Psychologist*.

50 John Gartner, Dave B. Larson, & George D. Allen, 'Religious Commitment and Mental Health: A Review of the Empirical Literature' (1991) 19:1 Journal of Psychology and Theology; Chamberlain & Hall, *supra* note 49; see also Peter C. Hill & Kenneth I. Pargament, 'Advances in the Conceptualization and Measurement of Religion and Spirituality: Implications for physical and mental health research' (2003) 58:1 American Psychologist 64–74; William R. Miller & Carl E. Thoresen, 'Spirituality, religion, and health: An emerging research field' (2003) 58:1 American Psychologist 24–35.
51 Hill & Pargament, *supra* note 50 at 71.
52 Yates, *supra* note 6 at 14.
53 Robert A. Hummer et al., 'Religious Involvement and U.S. Adult Mortality' (1999) 36:2 Demography 273–85.
54 Chen & Vanderweele, *supra* note 14 at 2355.
55 Harvard University T. H. Chan School of Public Health, News Release, 'Frequent religious service attendance linked with decreased mortality risk among women,' *Journal of the American Medical Association Internal Medicine* (16 May 2016), online: <https://www.hsph.harvard.edu/news/press-releases/religious-service-attendance-womens-mortality-risk/>.
56 Rodney Stark, *America's Blessings: How Religion Benefits Everyone, Including Atheists* (West Conshohocken, PA: Templeton Press, 2012); Ellison & Hummer, *supra* note 14.
57 Michael Wood Daly, 'Dollars and $ense: Uncovering the Socio-Economic Benefit of Religious Congregations in Canadian Society' (Toronto, ON: Sphaera Research, 2017) at 4 [Daly, 'Dollars and $ense'].
58 Irina Feygina & P. J. Henry, 'Culture and Prosocial Behaviour', in *The Oxford Handbook of Prosocial Behaviour*, ed. David A. Schroeder & William G. Graziano (Online Publication Date: March, 2014), see abstract online: <https://doi.org/10.1093/oxfordhb/9780195399813.013.009>.
59 Ray Pennings & Michael Van Pelt with Stephen Lazarus, 'A Canadian Culture of Generosity: Renewing Canada's Social Architecture by Investing in the Civic Core and the "Third Sector"', Cardus Discussion Paper (2 October 2009) at 12, online: <https://www.cardus.ca/research/social-cities/reports/a-canadian-culture-of-generosity/>.
60 Reginald Bibby, 'Good Without God, But Better With God?' Project Canada, Press Release #10 (8 October 2007), online (pdf): <http://www.reginaldbibby.com/images/PC_10_BETTER_WITH_GOD_OCT0807.pdf> (emphasis added).
61 Robert Wuthnow, *Acts of Compassion: Caring for Ourselves and Helping Others* (Princeton, NJ: Princeton University Press, 1991) [Wuthnow, *Acts of Compassion*].
62 Edward L. Queen, *The Religious Roots of Philanthropy in the West: Judaism, Christianity, and Islam*, Working Paper Series #96-4 (Indianapolis, IN: Indianapolis University Center on Philanthropy, 1996).
63 Wuthnow, *Acts of Compassion*, *supra* note 61 at 122, 139.
64 Bowen, *Christians in a Secular World*, *supra* note 5 at 283.
65 *Ibid*, at 204.
66 *Ibid*, at 203.
67 *Ibid*, at 205.
68 *Ibid*, at 115, 139.
69 Call & Heaton, *supra* note 29 at 390
70 Bowen, *Christians in a Secular World*, *supra* note 5 at 284.
71 *Ibid*, at 179–80.
72 *Ibid*, at 166–72.
73 Pamela Wiepking, 'Who Gives? A Literature Review of Predictors of Charitable Giving' (2010), 5–6, online: *Erasmus University Rotterdam*, <https://www.researchgate.net/publication/228709185_Who_Gives_A_Literature_Review_of_Predictors_of_Charitable_Giving>.
74 Australian Government Department of Family and Consumer Services, *Giving Australia: Research on Philanthropy in Australia* (2005), online (pdf): <https://www.cbd.int/financial/charity/australia-givingreport.pdf>.

75 P. Reed & K. Selbee, *The Religious Factor in Giving and Volunteering* (Ottawa: Statistics Canada Research Report, 2001).
76 Kurt Bowen, 'Religion, Participation, and Charitable Giving: A Report' (Canadian Heritage, Canadian Centre for Philanthropy, and Volunteer Canada, 1999), online (pdf): <http://www.imaginecanada.ca/sites/default/files/www/en/giving/rp_1997_religion_participation_and_charitable_giving_en.pdf>.
77 Ira E. Berger, 'The Influence of Religion on Philanthropy in Canada' (2006) 17:2 Voluntas 115–32.
78 R. Bekkers, 'Trust, Accreditation, and Philanthropy in the Netherlands' (2003) 32 Nonprofit & Voluntary Sector Quarterly 596–615.
79 Wen-Chun Chang, 'Determinants of Religious Giving in an Eastern-Culture Economy: Empirical Evidence from Taiwan' (2006) 47:4 Review of Religious Research, 363–79.
80 J. Reitsma, P. Scheeper & M. Te Grotenhuis, 'Dimensions of Individual Religiosity and Charity: Cross-National Effect Differences in European Countries?' (2006) 47:4 Review of Religious Research 347–62.
81 R. Finke, M. Barr & C.P. Scheitle, 'Toward Explaining Congregational Giving' (2006) 35:3 Social Science Research 620–41.
82 D. Hoge, 'Introduction: The Problem of Understanding Church Giving' (1994) 36:2 Review of Religious Research 101–10.
83 M. J. Donahue, 'Correlates of Religious Giving in Six Protestant Denominations' (1994) 36:2 Review of Religious Research 149–57.
84 D. Hoge et al, *Money Matters: Personal Giving in American Churches* (Louisville, KY: Westminster John Knox Press, 1996).
85 R. Wuthnow, *The Crisis in the Churches: Spiritual Malaise, Fiscal Woe* (New York: Oxford University Press, 1997).
86 M. Chaves & S. L. Miller, eds, *Financing American Religion* (Walnut Creek: Alta Mira Press, 1999).
87 *Review of Religious Research* (1994), 36.
88 Chang, *supra* note 79 at 363.
89 Lasby & Barr, *supra* note 2 at 55, 84.
90 *Ibid*, at 27.
91 *Ibid*.
92 Ryan Lincoln, Christopher A. Morrissey & Peter Mundey, 'Science of Generosity: Religious Giving: A Literature Review' (Department of Sociology, University of Notre Dame, 2008), at 8, online (pdf): <https://generosityresearch.nd.edu/assets/9286/religious_giving.pdf>; Hoge, *supra* note 82 at 101–10.
93 Paul G. Schervish & John J. Havens, 'Social Participation and Charitable Giving: A Multivariate Analysis' (1997) 8:3 Voluntas 235–60.
94 Don Hutchinson & Faye Sonier, 'Advancing Religion as a Charitable Object' (2008), at 5, online (pdf): *Evangelical Fellowship of Canada*, <http://files.efc-canada.net/si/zmisc/AdvancingReligionAsACharitableObjectCanadaRevenue.pdf>, citing 'Caring Canadians, Involved Canadians: Highlights from the 2004 Canada Survey of Giving, Volunteering and Participating – no.71-542-XIE' (2004) at 13, online (pdf): *Statistics Canada*, <https://www150.statcan.gc.ca/n1/en/pub/71-542-x/71-542-x2006001-eng.pdf?st=R_PHjHe6>.
95 Campbell & Putnam, *supra* note 7.
96 Bowen, *Christians in a Secular World*, *supra* note 5 at 174–75.
97 *Ibid*, at 181.
98 *Ibid*, at 180.
99 Yates, *supra* note 6 at 11.
100 Barbara Brownlee et al, 'Understanding the Capacity of Religious Organizations: A synthesis of findings from the National Survey of Nonprofit and Voluntary Organizations and the National Survey of Giving, Volunteering and Participating' (Ottawa: Imagine Canada,

2006), at 53, online (pdf): <http://sectorsource.ca/sites/default/files/resources/files/understanding_capacity_religious_orgs_report.pdf >.

101 Femida Handy & Ram A. Cnaan, 'Religious Non-Profits: Social Service Provision by Congregations in Ontario' in *The Non-Profit Sector in Canada: Roles and Relationships*, ed. K. G. Banting (Montreal: McGill-Queen's University Press, 2000).

102 Saguaro Seminar, 'Social Capital Community Benchmark Survey: Executive Summary' (Cambridge, MA: John F. Kennedy School of Government, Harvard University, 2001), reported in Jill Witmer Sinha, Itay Greenspan & Femida Handy, 'Volunteering and Civic Participation among Immigrant Members of Ethnic Congregations: Complementary NOT Competitive' (2010) 7:1 Journal of Civil Society, online (pdf): <http://www.baruch.cuny.edu/mspia/centers-and-institutes/center-for-nonprofit-strategy-and-management/documents/SinhaGreenspanHandy_VolunteeringandCivicParticipationamongImmigrantMembersofEthnicCongregati.pdf>.

103 Ammerman, *supra* note 34 at 10.

104 *Ibid*, at 12.

105 See Sam Reimer & Michael Wilkinson, *A Culture of Faith: Evangelical Congregations in Canada* (Montreal: McGill-Queen's University Press, 2015), 23, quoting Putnam & Campbell, *American Grace: How Religion Divides and Unites Us* (New York: Simon & Schuster, 2012), 476.

106 Ammerman, *supra* note 34.

107 The full Halo Project report for Toronto can be accessed online: *The Halo Project* <https://www.haloproject.ca/phase-1-toronto>.

108 Daly, 'Dollars and $ense', *supra* note 57 at 3, 19.

109 Michael Wood Daly, 'Regenerating Rural Places of Faith Halo Study' (Toronto, ON: Sphaera Research, 2016). Note that social capital and care includes the value of social programme space, the value of volunteer time and social programme in-kind support.

110 Daly, 'Dollars and $ense', *supra* note 57 at 4.

111 Michael Wood Daly, *Taxing Faith: Halo Impact and the Consequences of Taxing Places of Worship* (2019) [manuscript submitted for publication].

112 Nancy T. Kinney & Todd Bryan Combs, 'Changes in Religious Ecology and Socioeconomic Correlates for Neighborhoods in a Metropolitan Region' (2016) 38:3 Journal of Urban Affairs 409–28, <https://doi.org/10.1111/juaf.12211>.

113 Daly, 'Dollars and $ense', *supra* note 57 at 8.

114 Reimer & Wilkinson, *supra* note 105 at 22.

115 R. N. Bellah et al, *Habits of the Heart: Individualism and Commitment in American Life* (Berkeley: University of California Press, 1996); R. D. Putnam, *Bowling Alone: The Collapse and Revival of American Community* (New York: Simon & Schuster Paperbacks, 2000).

116 Ammerman, *supra* note 34 at 3.

117 Ammerman, *supra* note 34.

118 Thomas Ehrlich, ed., *Civic Responsibility and Higher Education* (Westport, CT: The Oryx Press, 2000), vi, online: <https://archive.nytimes.com/www.nytimes.com/ref/college/collegespecial2/coll_aascu_defi.html>.

119 B. Clarke & S. MacDonald, *Leaving Christianity: Changing Allegiances in Canada since 1945* (Montreal: McGill-Queen's University Press, 2017) at 239–41.

120 L. M. Chatters, 'Religion and Health: Public Health Research and Practice' (2000) 21:335–67 Annual Review of Public Health 343–44, 352.

121 Neal Krause et al, 'Church-Based Social Support and Religious Coping' (2001) 40:4 Journal for the Scientific Study of Religion 639.

122 Ammerman, *supra* note 34 at 4.

123 Harold G. Koenig & David B. Larson, 'Use of Hospital Services, Religious Attendance, and Religious Affiliation' (1998) 91:10 Southern Medical Journal 931, online:

<https://www.researchgate.net/publication/13500645_Use_of_Hospital_Services_Religious_Attendance_and_Religious_Affiliation>.

124 Thomas Farr, 'Is Religious Freedom Necessary for Other Freedoms to Flourish?' (7 August 2012), online: *Berkley Center for Religion, Peace & World Affairs, Georgetown University*, <https://berkleycenter.georgetown.edu/essays/is-religious-freedom-necessary-for-other-freedoms-to-flourish>.

125 See chapter 6, Derek B. M. Ross, 'Advancing Religion in a "Neutral" State: Understanding Religion as a Constitutional Good'.

126 Farr, *supra* note 124.

127 *R v Big M Drug Mart Ltd.*, [1985] 1 SCR 295, para 122–23.

128 See Barry W. Bussey, *The Legal Revolution Against the Accommodation of Religion: The Secular Age v The Sexular Age* (DPhil dissertation, Leiden University, 2019) [publication forthcoming].

129 Ross, 'Advancing Religion in a "Neutral" State', *supra* note 125.

130 Brian Grim & Jo-Ann Lyon, 'Religion holds women back. Or does it?' (17 November 2015), online: *World Economic Forum*, <https://www.weforum.org/agenda/2015/11/religion-holds-women-back-or-does-it/>.

131 Matthew Harding, 'Religion and the Law of Charity: A liberal perspective' (2014) 29:2 Journal of Law and Religion 252, https://doi.org/10.1017/jlr.2014.2.

132 Peniel E. Joseph, 'Why the Black Church Has Always Mattered' (19 June 2015), online: *The Root*, <https://www.theroot.com/why-the-black-church-has-always-mattered-1790860217>.

133 Bahá'í International Community, 'The Role of Religion in Promoting the Advancement of Women' (13 September 1995), online: *Bahai.org*, <https://www.bahai.org/documents/bic/role-religion-promoting-advancement-women>.

134 'Religious leaders at the forefront of ending gender-based violence in Ethiopia' (31 August 2016), online: *UN Women*, <http://www.unwomen.org/en/news/stories/2016/8/religious-leaders-at-the-forefront-of-ending-gender-based-violence-in-ethiopia>.

135 *Ibid*.

136 Nicholas Kristof, 'Religion and Women', *New York Times* (10 January 2010), online: <https://www.nytimes.com/2010/01/10/opinion/10kristof.html>.

137 'Religions uphold the equality and dignity of women, religious leaders say in seminar organized by UN Women Myanmar' (5 March 2016), online: *UN Women*, <http://asiapacific.unwomen.org/en/news-and-events/stories/2016/03/iwd-myanmar>.

138 Manini Sheker, 'Can religion be a positive force for social change?' (5 July 2016), online: *Open Democracy*, <https://www.opendemocracy.net/transformation/manini-sheker/can-religion-be-positive-force-for-social-change>.

139 Kathleen Brady, 'Religious Group Autonomy: Further reflections about what is at stake' (2006) 22:2 Journal of Law and Religion 164.

140 Ross, *supra* note 125.

141 Brady, *supra* note 139 at 167, 169.

142 Erin K. Wilson, 'The "religion or secularism" debate on women's equality obscures the real problem: patriarchy' (2017), online (blog): *London School of Economics and Political Science*, <http://blogs.lse.ac.uk/religionglobalsociety/2017/03/the-religion-or-secularism-debate-on-womens-equality-obscures-the-real-problem-patriarchy/>.

143 Yates, *supra* note 6 at 14.

144 Brian J. Grim, Greg Clark & Robert Edward Snyder, 'Is Religious Freedom Good for Business?: A Conceptual and Empirical Analysis' (2014) 10:4 Interdisciplinary Journal of Research on Religion 4.

145 Robert Woodberry, 'The Missionary Roots of Liberal Democracy' (2012) 106 American Political Science Review 244–74.

146 Grim, Clark & Snyder, *supra* note 144 at 13.

147 Xingqiang Du et al, 'Does Religion Mitigate Earnings Management? Evidence from China' (2014) 131:3 Journal of Business Ethics, also reported in chapter 2, Raymond Chiu, 'Religion and Public Benefit: Social Scientific Perspectives and Critiques'.

148 Qunyong Wang & Xinyu Lin, 'Does Religious Beliefs Affect Economic Growth? Evidence from Provincial-Level Panel Data in China' (2014) 31 China Economic Review 277–87, reported in Chiu, *supra* note 147.

149 Michael J. O'Fallon & Kenneth D. Butterfield, 'A Review of the Empirical Ethical Decision-Making Literature: 1996–2003' (2005) 59:4 Journal of Business Ethics 375–413, reported in Chiu, *supra* note 147.

150 Lori G. Bearman & Solange Lefebvre, eds, *Religion in the Public Sphere: Canadian Case Studies* (Toronto: University of Toronto Press, 2014); Putnam, *Bowling Alone*, *supra* note 115; Francis Fukuyama, 'Culture and Economic Development', in *International Encyclopedia of the Social and Behavioural Sciences*, ed. N. J. Smelser & Paul B. Baltes (Oxford: Pergamon, 2001).

151 Douglas Todd, 'Refugee changes pressure religious groups in Canada', *Vancouver Sun* (23 June 2012), online: <https://vancouversun.com/news/staff-blogs/refugee-changes-pressure-religious-groups-in-canada>.

152 Brent Wittmeier, 'Church groups play vital role in bringing refugees to Canada, bridging cultural gaps', *Edmonton Journal* (9 December 2015), online: <https://edmontonjournal.com/news/politics/church-groups-play-vital-role-in-bringing-refugees-to-canada-bridging-cultural-gaps>.

153 Lee Berthiaume, 'Few ethnic minorities among Syrians sponsored by Canadian government', *Ottawa Citizen* (22 September 2018), online: <https://ottawacitizen.com/news/politics/few-ethnic-minorities-among-syrians-sponsored-by-canadian-government>.

154 Wittmeier, *supra* note 152.

155 'Faith and Immigration: New Canadians rely on religious communities for material, spiritual support' (2018), online (pdf): *Angus Reid Institute* <http://angusreid.org/wp-content/uploads/2018/07/2018.06.22_CardusWave1_2018.pdf>.

156 Sinha, Greespan, & Handy, *supra* note 102 at 37.

157 Yates, *supra* note 6 at 12.

158 Benjamin Belt-Hallalmi & Michael Argyle, *The Psychology of Religious Behaviour, Belief, and Experience* (London, UK: Routledge, 1997), 97, quoted in Chiu, *supra* note 147.

159 Kathryn Chan, 'The Advancement of Religion as a Charitable Purpose in an Age of Religious Neutrality' (2017) 6:1 Oxford Journal of Law and Religion 129, 132.

160 Ray Pennings, 'Faith plays a big role in how Canadians see the world', *National Post* (17 May 2017), online: <https://nationalpost.com/news/religion/canada-is-not-the-secular-society-that-we-thought-it-was>.

161 Philip Morgan, 'A Research Note on Religion and Morality: Are Religious People Nice People?' (1983) 61 Social Forces 683–92.

162 C. G. Ellison & D. A. Gay, 'Region, religious commitment, and life satisfaction among Black Americans' (1990) 31 The Sociological Quarterly; Lincoln & Mamiya, *supra* note 36; E. D. Smith, *Climbing Jacob's Ladder: The Rise of Black Churches in Eastern American Cities* (Washington, DC: Smithsonian Institution, 1988), 1740–877; G. Washington & W. Beasley, 'Black Religion and the Affirmation of Complementary Polarity' (1988) Western Journal of Black Studies 12.

163 Lincoln & Mamiya, *supra* note 35; E. Southern, *The Music of Black Americans: A History*, 2nd edn (New York: W.W. Norton, 1983); W. T. Walker, *Somebody's Calling My Name: Black Sacred Music and Social Change* (Valley Forge, PA: Judson, 1979).

164 N. Boyd-Franklin, *Black Families in Therapy: A Multisystems Approach* (New York: Guilford Press, 1989); D. P. Hopson & D. S. Hopson, *Different and Wonderful: Raising Black Children in a Race-Conscious Society* (New York: Prentice-Hall, 1990); E. P. Wimberly, *Pastoral Care in Black Churches* (Nashville, TN: Abingdon, 1979).

165 Peter L. Berger, *The Sacred Canopy* (Garden City, NY: Doubleday, 1967); Clifford Geertz, 'Religion as a Cultural System', in *The Interpretation of Cultures*, ed. C. Geertz (New York: Basic Books, 1973).

166 Matthew T. Lee, Margaret M. Poloma & Stephen G. Post, *The Heart of Religion: Spiritual Empowerment, Benevolence, and the Experience of God's Love* (Oxford: Oxford University Press, 2013).
167 *Ibid*, at 200.
168 *Ibid*, at 193.
169 C. G. Ellison & L. K. George, 'Religious Involvement, Social Ties, and Social Support in a Southeastern Community' (1994) 33:1 Journal for the Scientific Study of Religion 46–61; D. E. Bradley, 'Religious Involvement and Social Resources: Evidence from the Dataset "Americans' Changing Lives"' (1995) 34 Journal for the Scientific Study of Religion, 259–267.
170 R. J. Taylor & L. M. Chatters, 'Church Members as a Source of Informal Social Support' (1988) 30:2 Review of Religious Research; Ellison & George, *supra* note 169.
171 R. J. Taylor et al, 'Mental Health Services within Faith Communities: The Role of Clergy in Black Churches' (2000) 45 Social Work.
172 Ellison & George, *supra* note 169; Bradley, *supra* note 169.
173 Mark Chaves, 'Rain Dances in the Dry Season: Overcoming the Religious Congruence Fallacy' (2010) 49:1 Journal for the Scientific Study of Religion 1–14; Timothy T. Clydesdale, 'Family Behaviours among Early U.S. Baby Boomers: Exploring the Effects of Religion and Income Change, 1965–1982' (1997) 76:2 Social Forces 605–06, 626.
174 Reimer & Wilkinson, *supra* note 105 at 23.
175 Lincoln, Morrissey, & Mundey, *supra* note 92 at 8.
176 Judson T. Landis, 'Religiousness, Family Relationships, and Family Values in Protestant, Catholic, and Jewish Families' (1960) 22 Marriage and Family Living; Howard M. Bahr & Thomas K. Martin, 'And Thy Neighbor as Thyself: Self-Esteem and Faith in People as Correlates of Religiosity and Family Solidarity among Middletown High School Students' (1983) 22 Journal for the Scientific Study of Religion; Lisa D. Pearce & William G. Axinn, 'The Impact of Family Religious Life on the Quality of Mother-Child Relations' (1998) 63:6 American Sociological Review.
177 William v D'Antonio, 'Family Life, Religion, and Societal Values and Structures', in *Families and Religions: Conflict and Change in Modern Society*, ed W. D'Antonio & J. Aldous (Beverly Hills, CA: Sage, 1983); Arland Thornton, 'Reciprocal Influences of Family and Religion in a Changing World' (1985) 47:2 Journal of Marriage and Family 381–94; Douglas A. Abbott, Margaret Berry & William H. Meredith, 'Religious Belief and Practice: A Potential Asset in Helping Families' (1990) 39 Family Relations; Martin A. Johnson, 'Family Life and Religious Commitment' (1973) 14:3 Review of Religious Research 144–50; W. Bradford Wilcox, 'Religion, Convention, and Paternal Involvement' (2002) 64:3 Journal of Marriage and Family; Pearce & Axinn, *supra* note 176.
178 Pearce & Axinn, *supra* note 176; Valerie King, 'The Influence of Religion on Fathers' Relationships with Their Children' (2003) 65:2 Journal of Marriage and Family; Wilcox, *supra* note 177; J. P. Bartkowski & X. Xu, 'Distant patriarchs or expressive dads? The discourse and practice of fathering in conservative Protestant families' (2000) 41 Sociological Quarterly.
179 Ammerman, *supra* note 34 at 3; M. Johnson, *supra* note 177.
180 Michael W. McConnell, 'The Problem of Singling out Religion' (2000) 50:1 DePaul Law Review 42.
181 Carl Juneau, 'Is Religion Passé as a Charity?' (2002) 17:2 The Philanthropist, online: <https://thephilanthropist.ca/2002/07/is-religion-passe-as-a-charity/>.
182 Chiu, *supra* note 147.
183 *Ibid*.
184 Harding, *supra* note 131 at 253.
185 John Longhurst, 'Church, state, and tax receipts', *Winnipeg Free Press* (6 January 2013), online: <https://www.winnipegfreepress.com/arts-and-life/life/faith/church-state-and-tax-receipts-209772051.html>.

Part II

ADVANCEMENT OF RELIGION IN THE UNITED KINGDOM

Chapter Four

RELIGION AND PUBLIC BENEFIT IN UNITED KINGDOM CHARITY LAW

Frank Cranmer*

Abstract

In the United Kingdom, the advancement of religion had been traditionally regarded as charitable; however, after 2000, legislation in all three jurisdictions removed that presumption. The Charity Commission for England and Wales subsequently consulted on draft supplementary guidance on the advancement of religion and public benefit, and, though the draft was on the whole helpful rather than the reverse, there were several areas in which it was either unclear or capable of improvement. Its deficiencies – and the outcome of the consultation – are examined in some detail. Next is a review of the Commission's more recent decisions on the registration of religious charities before and after the entry into force of the Charities Act 2006, beginning with the decision on the Unification Church. The series is interrupted by a discussion of the Supreme Court's judgement in *R (Hodkin & Ors) v Registrar General of Births, Deaths and Marriages* [2013] UKSC 77, in which the UKSC held that, contrary to an earlier judgement of the Court of Appeal in 1970, Scientology was to be regarded as a religion. There follows a discussion of the two post-*Hodkin* registration cases: the *Preston Down Trust* and *Temple of the Jedi Order*. The survey concludes with a discussion of the possible future of the registration of charities in England and Wales; in particular, the apparent dissonance between the description of religion given by Lord Toulson in *Hodkin* and the Charity Commission's rejection of the claim that Jediism amounted to a religious belief for the purposes of charity law.

Charitable Purposes and Public Benefit

In the United Kingdom, the advancement of religion has traditionally been regarded as charitable. The Preamble to the Statute of Charitable Uses 1601 included 'the repair of Churches' as a charitable purpose[1] and in *Pemsel*,[2] Lord Macnaghten generalised that purpose into 'trusts for the advancement of religion' as the so-called 'third head' of charity.[3] But parallel to its expansion in *Pemsel* had been the requirement that, in order to

---

* B.A., M.A., LL.M., S.Th., Fellow of St Chad's College, University of Durham and Honorary Research Fellow, Centre for Law & Religion, Cardiff University. I should like to thank Professor Russell Sandberg, of Cardiff University's School of Law and Politics, Robert Meakin, a Charity & Social Enterprise partner at Stone King LLP, and the anonymous reviewer for their helpful comments. Any remaining inadequacies are mine.

be charitable, a religious trust had to confer some element of benefit on the public. *Cocks v Manners*[4] – which predates *Pemsel* – and *Gilmour v Coats*[5] determined that a bequest to an enclosed religious order was not for the public benefit and therefore not charitable. In *Cocks*, Sir John Wickens V-C put it like this:

> It is said, in some of the cases, that religious purposes are charitable, but that can only be true as to religious services tending directly or indirectly towards the instruction or edification of the public.[6]

Likewise, said Lord Denning MR:

> The word 'advancement' connotes to my mind the concept of public benefit […] When a man says his prayers in the privacy of his own bedroom, he may truly be concerned with religion but not with 'the advancement of religion'.[7]

Even so, the public benefit test in English and Scots law had always been a fairly minimalist one because of the general presumption that the advancement of religion would be for the public benefit *in the absence of evidence to the contrary in the instant case*. That changed decisively, however, with the enactment of the Charities and Trustee Investment (Scotland) Act 2005 and, for England and Wales, the Charities Act 2006. Both maintained 'the advancement of religion' as a charitable purpose but raised the bar considerably on public benefit.

England and Wales

The current statutory provisions for England and Wales are contained in the Charities Act 2011, which consolidated the earlier legislation, including the 2006 Act. Under it, the position is as follows:

> 4 The public benefit requirement
>
> (1) In this Act 'the public benefit requirement' means the requirement in section 2(1)(b) that a purpose falling within section 3(1) must be for the public benefit if it is to be a charitable purpose.
> (2) In determining whether the public benefit requirement is satisfied in relation to any purpose falling within section 3(1), *it is not to be presumed that a purpose of a particular description is for the public benefit.*
> (3) In this Chapter any reference to the public benefit is a reference to the public benefit as that term is understood for the purposes of the law relating to charities in England and Wales.[8]

The Charity Commission's sectoral *Guidance: The Advancement of Religion for the Public Benefit* – of which more below – interprets this as requiring 'an identifiable, positive, beneficial moral or ethical framework that is promoted by religion which demonstrates that the religion is capable of impacting on society in a beneficial way'.[9] In short, the 2006 and 2011 Acts finally abolished the presumption of public benefit in England and Wales.

Scotland

Until 1990, there had been little statute or case law in Scotland that related specifically to charities. The law of charities had largely been derived from the law of public trusts and, for the purposes of taxation, the English definition of 'charitable' had been imported into Scots law.[10] The Law Reform (Miscellaneous Provisions) (Scotland) Act 1990 introduced limited reform; the more radical reform came with the enactment of the 2005 Act. Its provisions grew out of the recommendations of the Scottish Charity Law Review Commission chaired by Jean McFadden, which was set up by the Scottish Executive[11] in March 2000 to develop proposals on modernising charity law. The Commission's key recommendations were to establish a new regulator for Scottish charities, bringing together all the current functions except for direct tax, and to set out a new inclusive series of principles to define charitable purposes.[12]

Perhaps the most critical difference between the Scots and English statutes is that the s.5 of the 2005 Act introduced a formal 'charity test'.[13] Moreover, s.8 abolished explicitly any prior presumption of public benefit:

(1) No particular purpose is, for the purposes of establishing whether the charity test has been met, to be presumed to be for the public benefit.
(2) In determining whether a body provides or intends to provide public benefit, regard must be had to –
   (a) how any –
      (i) benefit gained or likely to be gained by members of the body or any other persons (other than as members of the public), and
      (ii) disbenefit incurred or likely to be incurred by the public, in consequence of the body exercising its functions compares with the benefit gained or likely to be gained by the public in that consequence, and
   (b) where benefit is, or is likely to be, provided to a section of the public only, whether any condition on obtaining that benefit (including any charge or fee) is unduly restrictive.

So, henceforward, the test was to be this: do the *outputs* of the charity – what it does on the ground – actually benefit the public?[14]

Northern Ireland

The basic legislation for Northern Ireland is the Charities Act (Northern Ireland) 2008 as amended by the Charities Act (Northern Ireland) 2013. Section 3 of the 2008 Act *as originally enacted* stated that, in determining whether the public benefit requirement was satisfied in relation to any charitable purpose, it was not to be presumed that a purpose of a particular description was for the public benefit; and, for the purpose of determining whether or not an institution provided or intended to provide public benefit, it reproduced the text of s.8(2) of the Charities and Trustee Investment (Scotland) Act

2005 quoted above. The obligation to balance the benefit 'gained or likely to be gained by members of the body or any other persons (other than as members of the public)' against the disbenefit 'incurred or likely to be incurred by the public' proved, however, to be unworkable in practice, and the 2013 Act amended the 2008 Act by substituting a new s.3 in the same terms as s.4 of the Charities Act 2011 for England and Wales.[15]

The Influence of the Scottish Act

Perhaps inevitably, given that it was the first new charity statute of the three, the Scottish Act had a degree of influence on the way the law developed in England and Wales and in Northern Ireland. One effect was an attempt by the Charity Commission for England and Wales in the draft general guidance on public benefit to import into English law the Scots law notion of 'disbenefit'. It then disappeared – but seemed to remain in the background of Charity Commission thinking.

Another effect was to import a tendency to confuse *objects* and *outputs*. The traditional position in English charity law had been that, in order to decide whether or not a trust might be registered as a charity, one looked at the objects of the trust. Therefore, when applying the more stringent test of public benefit under the 2006/2011 legislation, one should in principle still look at the objects and ask the question, 'are the objects of the trust charitable and therefore for the public benefit?',[16] but there has been an increasing tendency to think in terms of outputs in England and Wales as well as in Scotland. The two approaches might possibly amount to the much same thing in practice, but they are rather different in terms of methodology.[17] As we shall see, the Preston Down Trust was originally registered as a charity on the basis of its objects, but the Charity Commission withdrew its charitable status on the basis that its outputs in terms of its activities in the community were not, on balance, of sufficient benefit to the public to satisfy the terms of the Charities Act 2011.

The Commission's Recent Decisions on Registration

In the 1980s there was considerable public disquiet about the activities of the Unification Church founded by Sun Myung Moon and commonly known as the 'Moonies'. Two of its organisations – the Holy Spirit Association for the Unification of World Christianity and the Sun Myung Moon Foundation – had been registered in England and Wales as charities for the advancement of religion. At the end of a libel action brought by a member of the Unification Church against the *Daily Mail*,[18] the jury added a rider that the tax exemptions of the Church should be investigated – which, of course, rested on its charitable status. The Attorney General applied to the Charity Commission for the removal of the two charities from the register, but the Commissioners took the view that they could not do so without a decision of the court – and no application to the court appears to have been pursued.[19]

In 1999, in *Church of Scientology*,[20] the Commissioners rejected an application to register the Church as a charity for the advancement of religion. They accepted that 'Scientology claimed to profess belief in a supreme being' and, though the nature of the supreme being was 'not similar to the god of the Judaeo-Christian tradition', that claim was sufficient because it was 'clear that English law does not enquire into the nature, worth or value of religious beliefs, nor concern itself with the truth of the religious beliefs in question'.[21] However, they concluded that Scientology was not a religion *for the purposes of English charity law*[22] and that, even if it were so, public benefit could not be presumed, given the relative newness of Scientology and the public and judicial concern expressed about it. Moreover, its central practices – auditing and training – were of their nature private rather than public; that fact, and the practice of requesting donations in advance of auditing and training sessions, led to the conclusion that any benefit flowing from Scientology as advanced by the Church was of a private rather than a public kind.[23]

In *Sacred Hands*,[24] in which the applicant organisation was a Spiritualist church whose application for registration had previously been rejected in 2001, the Commissioners concluded that the Sacred Hands Spiritual Centre met the criteria of belief in a supreme being, worship of that being, advancement of religion (because it advertised its services and they were open to the public) and public benefit. As to the last of these:

> As the organisation had met the first three criteria, the Commissioners considered that the necessary public benefit would be shown unless there was reason to consider that Spiritualism was not for the public benefit. The Commissioners did not consider that there was any evidence which established that Spiritualism was not for the public benefit.[25]

The Commission's overall conclusion on public benefit was hardly surprising, given that the parent body of Spiritualism, the Spiritualists' National Union, had been registered as a charity in 1971.

In *Good News for Israel*,[26] registration was refused to an applicant company whose objects were the advancement of the Jewish religion and of the public understanding of the Jewish religion, 'particularly but not exclusively, by promoting the awareness of and observance of the doctrine of *Aliyah* (i.e. the return of the Jewish people to the land promised them by God)', the advancement of mutual understanding and good relations between the Christian and Jewish religions and the relief of poverty among orphans, 'particularly those of the Jewish religion'.[27] The Commission concluded that the second and third objects were exclusively charitable; however, *Keren Kayemeth* had established that settling Jewish people in Israel was not a charitable purpose for the advancement of religion because it involved considerations that were not exclusively charitable; therefore, 'the Commission did not accept that the establishment of the State of Israel meant that the settlement of Jewish people in the Holy Land can now be accepted as furthering a religious purpose when previously it could not' and assistance to return could not be considered to be exclusively concerned with the advancement of religion.[28]

The Charity Commission and the Abolition of the Presumption

Once the 2006 Act was in place, the Charity Commission for England and Wales as reconstituted by the Act had to consider from first principles how charities would have to operate under the new legislation. As to the advancement of religion, Kathryn Chan points out that, in order to be recognised as a charity at common law, a religious trust had both to '"advance" religion and advance "religion"',[29] and notes that in *Re South Place Ethical Society* the Chancery Division had held that 'religion required "faith in a god and worship of that god"'.[30] But that requirement was superseded by the clarification in s.2(3)(a)(ii) of the 2006 Act that 'religion' includes 'a religion which does not involve belief in a god' – so the *South Place Ethical Society* definition having been overturned and the presumption of public benefit having been abolished, the Commission had to consider what to put in their place.

In 2008, the Commission consulted on a draft of supplementary *Guidance* on the advancement of religion and public benefit, and though the draft was on the whole helpful rather than the reverse, there were several areas in which it was either unclear or capable of improvement.

The Role of the Regulator

The draft declared at section B5 that the Commission 'is the regulator of charities [...] It is not the regulator of religion itself and cannot make subjective or value judgments as to the truth or worth of religion or religious beliefs'. On the other hand, at section B8 the draft also stated that, in some cases, 'we might ask the trustees to change the way in which they are carrying out their charity's aims in order to meet the public benefit requirement; sometimes, it will be because the trustees are acting in breach of trust'.

That was perfectly acceptable in relation to matters such as accounting and record-keeping. But if a question ever arose as to whether the trustees were acting in accordance with the teachings of the religion in question, matters of doctrine would inevitably start to arise – probably to be determined, ultimately, by the courts. It should be remembered that one of the issues on which the *Free Church Case*[31] had been decided was whether or not the majority of the Church that had agreed to union with the United Presbyterian Church of Scotland still held to the doctrines of the Free Church as founded by Thomas Chalmers and David Welsh at the Disruption in 1843.[32]

The Nature of 'Religion'

According to the draft, in order for a movement to be regarded as a religion, followers or adherents had to believe in something that has the attributes of either a personal creator god or gods, a supreme being or a divine or transcendental being, entity or principle. The accompanying *Analysis of the law underpinning The Advancement of Religion for the Public Benefit* relied heavily on the Commission's decision not to register the Church of Scientology as a charity[33] (of which more below):

> 2.17 Leaving context (including case law) aside, *'religion'* does not today have a plain and unambiguous meaning which is generally accepted. Dictionary definitions of 'religion' often quoted suggest it can mean (i) belief in some superhuman controlling power entitled to obedience, reverence and worship; or it can mean (ii) a system defining a code of living (especially as a means to achieve spiritual or material improvement).

2.18 The Commission's *Scientology* decision effectively concludes that – on the authorities – the first, and not the second, is the meaning it has in English law.

The draft appeared to assume that little or nothing had changed since 1999. No doubt the Commissioners' decision was correct in law at the time; but the view of 'religion' on which it was based appeared to have been overwritten by s.2(3)(a)(ii) of the 2006 Act.[34]

Furthermore, the draft seemed to focus on religion as *belief* and ignore religion as *action*. On page 19, the draft suggested that 'pastoral and missionary work should clearly and explicitly relate to the particular form of religious teaching and practice and be distinguishable from purely secular and/or social work in similar fields' – which ignored the fact that social welfare programmes carried out by organisations such as the Salvation Army were the result of what they regarded as a religious imperative[35] and that, though secular organisations might do very similar and equally valuable work, their motivations were different. In most religions, *faith comes first, action follows*. The Commission, however, did not seem to grasp the idea of pastoral work as an outworking of faith: it appeared to think that pastoral work had to be overtly 'religious' in order to be pastoral.

Finally, the draft said at section C3:

> Advancing religion does not mean advancing a political purpose in the name of religion, nor does it mean advancing a particular viewpoint which is held by a religious person or which perhaps refers to extracts from religious texts which serve to promote that viewpoint.

In principle, trusts established for a political purpose cannot be charitable,[36] and pacifism was cited as a possibly political purpose. The draft concluded that, though a religion might include pacifism as part of its beliefs, an organisation set up solely to promote, for instance, a boycott on paying tax for weapons would not be 'advancing religion'.

No one would have quarrelled with the bar on 'advancing a political purpose in the name of religion'; however, the objection to 'advancing a particular viewpoint which is held by a religious person' was much more problematical. Leaving aside the fact that most Christian denominations regard their primary function as to advance a particular viewpoint held by a religious person named Jesus, Christian Science, for example, is based very specifically on the teachings of Mary Baker Eddy in *Science and Health with a Key to the Scriptures*. So what was the Church of Christ, Scientist, doing if it was not 'advancing a particular viewpoint which is held by a religious person'?

The Outcome of the Consultation

In the event, the *Guidance* that was finally issued[37] took account of many of the criticisms expressed during the consultation.[38] It made it clear that in order to be charitable, though an organisation advancing religion had to demonstrate belief in a supreme being or entity, it did not have to use that terminology in its objects: for Buddhists, for example, 'supreme being or entity' was inappropriate because Buddhism is a 'realised' religion rather than a 'revealed' one. Nor was it obligatory to talk of 'worship' if that expression was inappropriate for the religion in question. The *Guidance* also made it clear that it was not necessary for a faith-community to proselytise in order to 'advance' religion; advancement might include the 'personal and social effects' of religious practice. Crucially for organizsations such as the Salvation Army, the guidance accepted that 'for many, the separation of religious and secular work is not easy, or even possible, as secular and/or social work in these similar fields is in fact an outworking of the religion'.[39] It also stated specifically that Christian Science healing was not 'dangerous or damaging'.[40]

The Aftermath

In October 2011, the Upper Tribunal (Tax and Chancery Chamber) held that the Commission's *General Guidance on Public Benefit*, on *Public Benefit and Fee-Charging* and on *The Advancement of Education for the Public Benefit* were defective as a result of a judgement on fee-charging by independent schools operated by charitable trusts.[41] The result was that the Commission also withdrew its text on fee-charging in *The Advancement of Religion for the Public Benefit* because it included a passage on the 'ability to pay any fees charged' as an element in determining whether or not benefit was 'to the public or a section of the public'.[42] At the time of writing, the text remains on the Commission's website but has still not been revised some eight years on.[43]

The Charity Commission's Registration Decisions after 2006

In *The Gnostic Centre*,[44] the objects of the applicant trust were the following:

> To advance the Gnostic religion for the benefit of the public in accordance with the statement of beliefs/articles of faith as set out in the schedule. Most important in this endeavour will be the celebration of our religious rituals, such as the Gnostic Mass, to which all members of the public will be invited to attend. Also there will be courses seminars, events, workshops and publications involving anybody in the public wishing to improve their inner life and learn about our religion. Our research methods can be scholastic, involving research on source documents and the like, as well as spiritual involving meditation and other spiritual disciplines.[45]

In considering whether The Gnostic Centre was advancing religion for the public benefit, the Commission considered that the characteristics of a religion for the purposes of charity law are:

1. Belief in a god (or gods) or goddess (or goddesses), or supreme being, or divine or transcendental being or entity or spiritual principle, which is the object or focus of the religion (referred to as 'supreme being or entity');
2. A relationship between the believer and the supreme being or entity by showing worship of, reverence for or veneration of the supreme being or entity;
3. A degree of cogency, cohesion, seriousness and importance; and
4. An identifiable positive, beneficial, moral or ethical framework.[46]

The Commission concluded that though Gnosticism as advanced by the Centre satisfied a number of the essential characteristics of a religion for the purposes of charity law, it had not demonstrated that it met all the necessary characteristics of a religion,[47] given that it had not identified a positive, beneficial, moral or ethical framework that was being promoted. Therefore, it had not been demonstrated that The Gnostic Centre was established for the advancement of religion as understood in charity law.

In *The Druid Network*,[48] the objects of the applicant unincorporated association were: 'To provide information on the principles and practice of Druidry for the benefit of all and to inspire and facilitate that practice for those who have committed themselves to this spiritual path'.[49] The Network provided information about Druidry, put interested members of the public into contact with their local groups, advertised public rituals and supported members in providing them, assisted in the establishment and running of new groups, supported the organization of a public ritual at mid-winter and mid-summer at Stonehenge, produced a newsletter, provided a forum on its website and supported environmental projects. The majority of the work was carried out through its website.[50]

The application for registration was accepted. The board members who considered the application accepted that 'the sincerely-held belief of spirit within and arising from nature as an essential and core element of belief within Druidry, as promoted by the Druid Network, represented a divine being or entity or spiritual principle for the purposes of charity law'[51] and concluded that the Network had demonstrated a sufficient belief in a supreme being or entity to constitute a religion for the purposes of charity law, evidence of worship of, reverence for and veneration of the supreme being or entity, a sufficient element of core practices and beliefs to satisfy the tests of cogency, cohesion, seriousness and importance of their religious beliefs, and evidence of an identifiable positive ethical framework that was capable of having a beneficial impact on the community at large.[52]

In *The Way of the Livingness*,[53] the applicant trust had as its objects included advancing The Way of the Livingness as a religion by encouraging and facilitating 'Soul-full religious practice' through living by its principles, providing buildings for religious practice, instruction and contemplation, conducting religious ceremonies, 'raising awareness and understanding of religious soul-full life by the development of the key principles relating to self-love and energetic integrity', education, mediation, harmonious union and study, visiting the sick and dying, working for 'reconciliation, truth telling and harmonious union' and promoting retreats.

The Commission concluded that the trust was not established for exclusively charitable purposes and could not be registered because The Way of the Livingness appeared to be a form of theosophy which the court had decided was not a religion as charity law understood that term.[54] And even if it were not a form of theosophy, the Commission was still not satisfied that it came within the definition of religion in charity law. Moreover, the second object (raising 'awareness and understanding of religious soul-full life') was not charitable.[55] In reaching its conclusion, however, the Commission confirmed that it was 'neither its role nor intention to judge the inherent worth of the Trust for the Way of the Livingness, but only to consider the narrower question of whether it met the test laid down in law for registration as a charity'.

In contrast to the success of the Druids, the Charity Commission rejected the application of *The Pagan Federation*[56] because it was not

> absolutely clear that Paganism in the broadest sense [...] involves belief in a supreme being which is the object or focus of the beliefs [...] where there are some followers whose understanding of the divinity cannot be categorised in the forms identified above and the principles are open to honourable and reasonable interpretation. It suggests that there is some scope for followers to simply view Paganism as a philosophy or way of life.[57]

The Federation stated that Pagans had three principles: love for and kinship with nature, a positive morality and recognition of the Divine in both its female and male aspects. The Commission doubted whether this amounted to a 'religion' or whether it was merely 'a multitude of similar but diverse beliefs and practices encompassing a broad range of traditions focused on celebrating nature'.[58] Although it accepted that the Federation upheld particular values that might be capable of having a positive and beneficial impact on the public, it concluded:

> the extent of the beneficial impact on the public of all of the paths and traditions promoted by the Pagan Federation is open to question. Whilst the Pagan Federation may encourage individuals to uphold particular values and promote individual responsibility and integrity, it appears that individuals are free to develop their own guidelines.[59]

The Federation appealed to the Charity Tribunal in November 2012 but subsequently withdrew its appeal.[60]

Hodkin and the Definition of 'Religion'

Defining, or at least describing, 'religion' in English law then took a further twist when Louisa Hodkin and her fiancé, both Scientologists, wished to marry in a Church of Scientology chapel in central London and decided to contest the refusal of the Registrar General of Births, Deaths and Marriages to register the chapel as a place of worship – and it is that to which we now turn.

In *Hodkin*,[61] the chapel in question was not registered under s.2 of the Places of Worship Registration Act 1855 as a 'place of meeting for religious worship' and was not, therefore, a 'registered building' for the purposes of s.26(1)(a) of the Marriage Act 1949.[62] No application could be made under the 1949 Act for it to be registered merely for the solemnization of marriages; and when the Church of Scientology Religious Education College Inc (the second claimant and owner of the chapel) applied to the Registrar General to register it under the 1855 Act, she refused to do so on the grounds that the chapel was not, in fact, a place for 'religious worship'. She cited in support of her refusal the previous decision of the Court of Appeal in *Segerdal* that had upheld her predecessor's refusal to register another Scientologist chapel as a 'place of meeting for religious worship'.

The claimants argued that the understanding of Scientology as a religion had developed since 1970, that the meaning of a place 'for religious worship' in what was now a more obviously multifaith society had broadened, that the effect of the Human Rights Act 1998 and the Equality Act 2010 meant that the distinction drawn by the Court of Appeal in *Segerdal* between Buddhism and Scientology was no longer tenable and that the Registrar General's practice of registering Buddhist and Jain temples as places of religious worship but not registering Scientology chapels was discriminatory. Ouseley J dismissed the claim, primarily because he regarded himself as bound by *Segerdal*, but suggested that his decision might be properly appealed: 'Forty years on from *Segerdal*, the Court of Appeal may find the route at least to reconsider its decision in *Segerdal* with the fuller material now available'.[63]

The claimants duly appealed and were successful. The definition of 'worship' espoused by the Court of Appeal in *Segerdal* had been 'something which must have some at least of the following characteristics: submission to the object worshipped, veneration of that object, praise, thanksgiving, prayer or intercession',[64] and the Court had suggested in 1970 that 'the governing idea behind the words "place of meeting for religious worship" is that it should be a place for the worship of God'.[65]

The Supreme Court rejected those assumptions.[66] Lord Toulson described 'religion' as:

> a spiritual or non-secular belief system, held by a group of adherents, which claims to explain mankind's place in the universe and relationship with the infinite, and to teach its adherents how they are to live their lives in conformity with the spiritual understanding associated with the belief system. By spiritual or non-secular, I mean a belief system which goes beyond that which can be perceived by the senses or ascertained by the application of science [...] Such a belief system may or may not involve belief in a supreme being, but it does involve a belief that there is more to be understood about mankind's nature and relationship to the universe than can be gained from the senses or from science. I emphasise that this is intended to be a description and not a definitive formula.[67]

On that basis, he concluded that 'the meaning given to worship in *Segerdal* was unduly narrow, but even if it was not unduly narrow in 1970, it is unduly narrow now'.[68]

For the purposes of *charity law*, Lord Toulson's 'description' did not, of course, address the issue of whether or not the activities of a particular religion would be for the public benefit. He noted that, though the definition of religion in the Charities Act 2011 had removed the uncertainty created by Dillon J's judgement in *South Place Ethical Society* about whether religious charitable trusts excluded faiths such as Hinduism and Buddhism, it had no direct application to s.2 of the Places of Worship Registration Act 1855: 'It did, however, widen considerably the scope of what kinds of belief might be held to be "a religion" beyond the Judaeo-Christian assumptions implicit in *Segerdal*'.[69]

The Commission's Decisions on Registration Post-*Hodkin*

Subsequent to the decision in *Hodkin*, the Commission has considered two cases of charitable registration for the advancement of religion.

The Preston Down Trust

The Preston Down Trust operates a group of chapels that belong to the Exclusive Brethren.[70] Traditionally, the Exclusive Brethren associated only with each other: for example, they would not eat or drink with those with whom they did not share 'table fellowship' and their services of Holy Communion were not open to non-members of the denomination. And if they decided that a member had transgressed the rules of the church community, s/he might be 'disfellowshipped' – in which case, the rest of the family could not associate with that person. They had noticeboards outside their Gospel Halls advertising the times of services; but the Charity Commission's understanding was that that represented the limit of their engagement with the general public. In 2012, therefore, the Commission decided that it was unable 'to satisfy ourselves and conclusively determine that Preston Down Trust is established for exclusively charitable purposes for public benefit and suitable for registration as a charity'[71] for the following reasons:

> We are aware that Preston Down Trust provides a meeting hall with a notice board identifying it as a public place of worship with contact details and that is consistent with an agreed protocol with the Valuation office in order to qualify for rate relief. We question whether this is sufficient to demonstrate meaningful access to participate in public worship as opposed to simply providing an opportunity without wider advertising of service times and opening hours. We also have concerns about the lack of public access to participation in one of the key religious services provided by Preston Down Trust, that of Holy Communion.
>
> The beneficial impact of the Preston Down Trust is perhaps more limited than other Christian organisations as the adherents limit their engagement with the wider public, arising as a consequence of the doctrines of their religion. It raises a concern as to whether Preston Down Trust is established primarily for the benefit of its followers or adherents. The extent to which Preston Down Trust encourages followers or adherents to conduct themselves in the wider community to put the values held by the religion into practice in such a way as to lead to the moral or spiritual welfare or improvement of society is uncertain. The evidence is [sic] relation to any beneficial impact on the wider public is perhaps marginal and insufficient to satisfy us as to the benefit to the community.
>
> Like the court we must balance the benefit and disadvantage in all cases where detriment is alleged. We are aware of some public criticism, which we have discussed with the applicants, in connection with (1) the disciplinary practices of shutting up and withdrawal and (2) the effects of the doctrine and practice of separation on family, social and working life. We ought to make it clear that we do not have any evidence before us at this time to demonstrate disadvantage which may serve to negate public benefit.

In doing so, the Commission felt that it was possible to distinguish the *Preston Down* application from the earlier decision in *Holmes*[72] that a trust for the Exclusive Brethren was charitable.

The Brethren appealed that decision to the First-tier Tribunal (Charity). Negotiations then took place between the Commission and the Brethren, and in 2014, in a very lengthy decision, the Commission agreed to register the Trust.[73] It did so on the basis of the Brethren's agreement to a revised statement of their doctrines and practices – in particular, on their interrelation with the wider community – set out in a draft Deed of Variation appended to the Commission's decision. The deed incorporated as part of the trust purposes statements of the Brethren's Core Doctrine and Faith in Practice[74] – the second of which set out a much-modified statement on 'separation':

Within the parameters set out above, the principle of separation permits inter-personal communication and social interaction with non-Brethren (including former Brethren) and service to them – because we seek to do good to all in the world, as opportunities arise. Those in fellowship must ultimately exercise their own judgment in the practice of separation both from those (family, friends, colleagues) they leave when joining the Brethren community, and from those (family, friends, colleagues) who choose to leave the Brethren community. They exercise this judgment based upon their understanding and appreciation of Holy Scripture, the guidance provided in Ministry (now including this statement of doctrinal principle), and the exemplary practice of fellow members of the community.

The Commission was satisfied that if the Trust applied for and was registered on the basis of the amended documentation, the Commission would be able to regulate it;[75] if, however, the trustees did *not* comply with the trusts, the Commission would be able to regulate on the basis of breach of trust and, if the trustees were unable to comply with and carry out the trusts, the Commission might regulate on the basis that a *cy-près* occasion had arisen and would apply the trust property for charitable purposes of a similar nature.[76]

The Temple of the Jedi Order

Most recently, in *Temple of the Jedi Order*,[77] the Order applied to be constituted as a Charitable Incorporated Organisation (CIO) and be entered on the register of charities. The purposes of the proposed CIO were to advance the religion of Jediism for the public benefit worldwide, in accordance with the Jedi Doctrine, and to advance such charitable purposes (according to the law of England and Wales) as the Trustees saw fit from time to time.[78]

The Commission concluded that, having considered the statute law and the cases, Jediism did not meet the characteristics of a religion for the purposes of charity law,[79] since Jediism did not involve belief in a god. Yet the statutory definition of religion included religions which did not involve belief in a god, such as Buddhism and Jainism.[80] The Jedi Doctrine stated that Jedi believed 'In the Force, and in the inherent worth of all life within it'. Its Teachings stated that Jedi 'are in touch with the Force. We are open to spiritual awareness and keep our minds in tune with the beauty of the world' and that 'Jedi believe in eternal life through the Force. We do not become obsessed in mourning those who pass. We may grieve at their passing but we are content, knowing that they will forever be a part of the Force and so always a part of us'.[81] The definition of Jediism also stated that 'The Jedi religion is an inspiration and a way of life for many people throughout the world who take on the mantle of Jedi' and The Order acknowledged that there was 'some scope for followers to simply view Jediism as a philosophy or way of life'.[82]

On that basis, the Commission was not satisfied that the observance of the Force within Jediism was characterised by the belief in one or more gods or spiritual or non-secular principles or things that were necessary in order to constitute a religion in charity law: 'Despite being open to spiritual awareness, there is scope for Jediism and the Jedi Doctrine to be advanced and followed as a secular belief system. Jediism therefore lacks the necessary spiritual or non-secular element'.[83] The Commission also noted that in *Hodkin*, Lord Toulson had excluded secular belief systems from his description of religion.[84]

Nor was the Commission satisfied that Jediism as promoted by the Order demonstrated sufficient coherence and a sufficiently distinct set of beliefs, principles and practices to demonstrate the promotion of ethics or morals that could be shown by evidence to be for the benefit of the public. It was not sufficient to advance spirituality or spiritual beliefs on their own, nor that there was a presumption that individuals would behave in a way that impacted beneficially on society.[85] There was also a lack of clarity as to what beliefs, principles and practices were promoted[86] and insufficient evidence that moral improvement was central to the Order's beliefs and practices – particularly as the Jedi Doctrine could be accepted, rejected and interpreted by individuals as they saw fit.[87] Nor was there sufficient evidence of Jediism directly promoting moral improvement within society generally.[88]

In summary, the Commission concluded that there was insufficient evidence that the purpose of the Order was the promotion of moral or ethical improvement for the benefit of the public.[89] There was insufficient evidence to demonstrate the beneficial effects of the Order,[90] and the Commission was not satisfied that Jediism and the Jedi Doctrine were sufficiently structured so as to have a beneficial impact.[91] In short, it was not satisfied that the public benefit requirement had been met, either for the advancement of religion or for the promotion of moral or ethical improvement.[92]

Conclusion: So Where Next?

Kerry O'Halloran has characterizsed the replacement of the public benefit *presumption* with a mandatory statutory public benefit *requirement* as 'a step change in charity law and a challenge to all other common law jurisdictions',[93] while Kathryn Chan suggests that because the English common law tradition has shied away from articulating the public benefit of religion and has simply assumed that 'it is good for man to have and to practise a religion',[94] the resulting vagueness makes the continued charitable status of religious trusts vulnerable to calls for its abolition.[95] Russell Sandberg goes further, arguing recently that the result of the Charity Commission's refusal to register the Temple of The Jedi Order is that our understanding of the definition of religion for the purposes of charity and registration law is now 'hideously confused'[96] – a criticism that could equally be levelled at its refusal to register the Pagan Federation.

In Sandberg's view, though the influence of *Hodkin* has been significant in relation to the 'faith in a god' test from *Re South Place Ethical Society*, it has seemingly been ignored in relation to the 'worship of a god' test, and, instead, 'a questionable distinction has been made between religion and a lifestyle choice and it has been suggested that the first cannot exist entirely online'. Furthermore, in relation to the requirement of 'cogency, cohesion, seriousness and importance':

> a requirement that a religion needs to be 'distinct' has been added to the ECHR case law and the Commission seems to have been operating from an assumption that religions can be

objectively described, are obligatory upon members and members are uniform in how they manifest their religion.[97]

Not only would I agree with Sandberg about the hideousness of the confusion, I would suggest that part of the problem in the United Kingdom – not just in England and Wales – is that there is no overall working definition of 'religion' that applies universally and consistently for purposes such as charitable status, trusts, tax law and employment rights. So, for example, were the Church of Scientology to reapply to the Charity Commission for registration as a charity, what would be the outcome? We know that Scientology is a 'religion' because that is what the Supreme Court decided in *Hodkin*, but would the Commission accept that its activities provided sufficient public benefit for recognition?[98]

Moreover, because the public benefit test was not applied to charities already in existence when the 2006 Act came into force, glaring inconsistencies persist. To take a very extreme example, The National Fund[99] was set up with an anonymous donation of £500,000 in 1928 with the object of creating a fund that either on its own or combined with others would be sufficient to discharge the National Debt. Pigs might fly, and the result is that The National Fund currently has total assets of some £480m, accrues income at a current annual rate of some £7m, spends roughly £1m on administration *and makes no charitable disbursements whatsoever.*[100] There are understandable technical reasons for that situation, the most blindingly obvious of which is that a mere £480m will never pay off the UK National Debt in a month of Sundays; and the Charity Commission has said the future of the charity is 'of serious concern' and that it is trying to ensure that the charity's assets are put to good use.[101] The point at issue for the present discussion, however, is this: *what conceivable public benefit does the National Fund as presently constituted provide*? The answer, surely, is 'zilch' – but, having been established before 2006, the charity benefits from the presumption of public benefit.

Finally, might it be that, in considering the right to manifest under Article 9 of the European Convention on Human Rights[102] and the domestic consequences – including any possible public benefit from religious belief and practice – that flow from it, rather too much judicial emphasis has been placed on the *forum externum* and rather too little on the *forum internum*? It is perfectly possible, for example, to be an observant Orthodox Jew while rarely going anywhere near a synagogue: by keeping kosher, by observing the commandments and by performing the prescribed prayers. Indeed, for a lone Jew in a very isolated community that may well be the only option, given that a *minyan* of ten adult men is a necessary prerequisite for most kinds of corporate worship.[103] And how does that approach fit with the conclusion of the European Court of Human Rights in *Eweida and Others v United Kingdom*[104] that 'there is no requirement on the applicant to establish that he or she acted in fulfilment of a duty mandated by the religion in question'?[105]

As to the Commission's critique of Jediism that the Doctrine could be accepted, rejected and interpreted by individuals as they saw fit,[106] are other 'established' religions very different? A poll of 1,499 Anglican *clergy* in the United Kingdom conducted by YouGov for Westminster Faith Debates in 2014[107] revealed that only 83 per cent agreed with the statement 'There is a personal God', while three per cent preferred 'There is some sort of spirit or life force' and two per cent were 'not sure "God" is more than a human construct'.[108] Both the latter are perfectly tenable views but not, surely, views that sit very comfortably with regular public recitation of the Nicene Creed. And by the same token, 'though there is scope for Jediism and the Jedi Doctrine to be advanced and followed as a secular belief system',[109] the same could be said of some other religious groups, such as the Quakers[110] and, possibly, the Unitarians. But no one, so far as I am aware, has seriously suggested that the beliefs and practices of the Religious Society of Friends or of the General Assembly of Unitarian and Free Christian Churches do not amount to 'religions' – or that they are not for the public benefit.

Perhaps the House of Commons Public Administration Committee should have the last word:

> 85. Parliament should be under no illusion about the scale of the task it presented to the Charity Commission when it passed the Charities Act 2006, which required the Commission to produce public benefit guidance without specifically defining 'public benefit'. This has had the effect of inviting the Commission to become involved in matters such as the charitable status of independent schools which has long been a matter of party political controversy.
>
> 86. *In our view, it is for Parliament to resolve the issues of the criteria for charitable status and public benefit, not the Charity Commission, which is a branch of the executive. In this respect the Charities Act 2006 has been an administrative and financial disaster for the Charity Commission and for the charities involved, absorbing vast amounts of energy and commitment, as well as money.*[111]

And the Committee's conclusion?

> 93. *We recommend that the removal of the presumption of public benefit in the 2006 Charities Act be repealed, along with the Charity Commission's statutory public benefit objective. This would ensure that no transient Government could introduce what amounts to substantive changes in charity law without Parliament's explicit consent. If the Government wishes there to be new conditions for what constitutes a charity and qualifies for tax relief, it should bring forward legislation, not leave it to the discretion of the Charity Commission and the courts.*[112]

Further comment is superfluous.

Notes

1 The list in the Preamble also includes 'Mariages of poore Maides'.
2 *Commissioners for Special Purposes of Income Tax v Pemsel* [1891] AC 531; 3 TC 53 [hereinafter *Pemsel*].
3 [1891] 3 TC 96. The full list is 'trusts for the relief of poverty; trusts for the advancement of education; trusts for the advancement of religion; and trusts for other purposes beneficial to the community, not falling under any of the preceding heads'. It was the 'fourth head' that included at least a kernel of 'public benefit'.
4 (1871) LR 12 Eq 574 [hereinafter *Cocks*].
5 [1949] AC 426 [hereinafter *Gilmour*].
6 *Cocks, supra* note 4 at 585.
7 *National Deposit Friendly Society Trustees v Skegness UDC* [1958] 2 All ER 601.
8 Emphasis added.

9 *The Advancement of Religion for the Public Benefit* (London: Charity Commission, 2008 as amended 2011) 11 [hereinafter *Guidance: Advancement of Religion*].
10 By *Pemsel*, *supra* note 2, and *Inland Revenue v City of Glasgow Police Athletic Association* [1953] UKHL 1, [1953] AC 380.
11 Now the Scottish Government.
12 Scottish Charity Law Review Commission, *Charity Scotland* (Edinburgh: The Stationery Office, 2001): the summary report is available online (pdf) at <http://www.gov.scot/Resource/Doc/1136/0010186.pdf>. Before the enactment of the 2005 Act, charities in Scotland were, in effect, regulated by what was then the Board of Inland Revenue, now HM Revenue & Customs.
13 '(1) A body meets the charity test if – (a) its purposes consist only of one or more of the charitable purposes, and (b) it provides (or, in the case of an applicant, provides or intends to provide) public benefit in Scotland or elsewhere'.
14 So e.g. in *Catholic Care (Diocese of Leeds) v Charity Commission for England and Wales & Anor* [2010] EWHC 520 (Ch), Briggs J explained, at para 97, 'An organisation which proposes to fulfil a purpose for the public benefit will only qualify as a charity if, taking into account any disbenefit arising from its *modus operandi*, its activities nonetheless yield a net public benefit'.
15 In Ireland, the Charities Act 2009 made provision on very similar lines to those of the 2005 and 2008 Acts in Great Britain; critically for the present discussion, however, s.3(4) makes special provision in relation to religion that 'It shall be presumed, unless the contrary is proved, that a gift for the advancement of religion is of public benefit' and s.3(5) provides that the Charities Regulatory Authority established under the Act 'shall not make a determination that a gift for the advancement of religion is not of public benefit without the consent of the Attorney General'.
16 On which point, see P. Luxton, *Making Law? Parliament v The Charity Commission* (London: Politeia, 2009), in which he argues, at 18, that 'once a purpose has been admitted as charitable it is necessarily a purpose for the public benefit. This applies to all the purposes listed in s.2(2) of the Charities Act 2006, and all the purposes previously held charitable under the fourth head [of charity]. To require an institution whose purposes are charitable (e.g. for the advancement of education) to show that such purposes are for the public benefit is to apply to such institution a test that according to the law it has already passed. It is, to put it bluntly, nonsense'. See online (pdf): <http://www.politeia.co.uk/wp-content/Politeia%20Documents/2009/June%20-%20Making%20Law%3F/'Making%20Law'%20June%202009.pdf>.
17 In Canada, e.g., in *Vancouver Society of Immigrant and Visible Minority Women v MNR* [1999] 1 SCR 10, 1999 CanLII 704 (SCC), the Court was of the view that it was an examination of the *purposes* of the charity – the equivalent of 'objects' in England and Wales – that was the appropriate method of determining charitable status rather than *outputs* – in England and Wales, 'objects'.
18 *Orme v Associated Newspaper Group Ltd* (1981), *The Times*, 4 February.
19 Balcombe AJ [Lord Justice Balcombe], *The Attitude of the Law to Religion in a Secular Society* (Oxford: Oxford Centre for Postgraduate Hebrew Studies, 1989), 15.
20 *Decision of the Charity Commissioners for England & Wales made on 17 November 1999: Application for registration as a charity by the Church of Scientology (England and Wales)* [hereinafter *Church of Scientology*].
21 *Ibid*, at 25.
22 *Ibid*, at 1. In doing so, the Commission relied in particular on *Bowman v Secular Society* [1917] AC 406, *Keren Kayemeth Le Jisroel Ltd v Inland Revenue Commissioners* [1931] 2 KB 465, [1932] UKHL TC_17_27, *United Grand Lodge v Holborn Borough Council* [1957] 1 WLR 1080, *R v Registrar General ex parte Segerdal* [1970] 2 QB 697 [hereinafter *Segerdal*], *Re South Place Ethical Society* [1980] 1 WLR 1565 (Ch) 1571 and *Gilmour*, *supra* note 5.
23 *Church of Scientology*, *supra* note 20 at 48.
24 *Decision of the Charity Commissioners to register Sacred Hands Spiritual Centre as a charity: 5 September 2003*.

25 *Ibid*, 5.1.4.
26 *Application for registration of Good News for Israel: 5 February 2004*.
27 *Ibid*, 3.1.
28 *Ibid*, 6.2.9.
29 K. Chan, 'Advancement of Religion in an Age of Religious Neutrality' (2017) 6:1 Oxford Journal of Law and Religion 116.
30 *Ibid*, at 117.
31 *General Assembly of the Free Church of Scotland v Lord Overtoun: Macalister v Young* [1904] AC 515.
32 See also *Shergill & Ors v Khaira & Ors* [2014] UKSC 33, arising from a dispute in a group of Sikh *gurdwaras* and, in part, about 'the extent to which the court can and should refuse to determine issues of religion or religious belief in legal proceedings', at para 1.
33 *Church of Scientology*, *supra* note 20.
34 '(3) In subsection (2) – (a) in paragraph (c) 'religion' includes – (i) a religion which involves belief in more than one god, and (ii) a religion which does not involve belief in a god'.
35 For example, 'Love your neighbour as yourself' (Lev 19:18; Mt 22:39).
36 *National Anti-Vivisection Society v IRC* [1948] AC 31. See also Charity Commission for England and Wales (2010), *Regulatory Case Report: The Atlantic Bridge Education and Research Scheme, Registered Charity Number 1099513*. The objects of Atlantic Bridge included 'The furtherance of public education on both sides of the Atlantic, in areas of common interest, focusing particularly but not exclusively on free trade, economics, health and science' and 'Research into relations between Europe and North America and their implications for the international community with the aim to raise cultural awareness and improve links'. The Commission concluded that, though Atlantic Bridge was established as a charity with exclusively charitable purposes and was capable of operating for the public benefit, its educational objects had not been advanced by its activities because, inter alia, 'these activities promote a particular point of view which is not uncontroversial, and are consequently not educational' (at para 36) and that its activities 'may lead members of the public to call into question its independence from party politics. The promotion of the Special Relationship is not the purpose of this Charity, nor can it be. The Commission has made clear to the trustees their legal and regulatory responsibilities and that the Charity's current activities must cease immediately' (at para 37).
37 *Guidance: Advancement of Religion*, *supra* note 9, online (pdf): <http://webarchive.nationalarchives.gov.uk/20100321015216/http://www.charitycommission.gov.uk/Library/publicbenefit/pdfs/pbreligiontext.pdf>.
38 For a longer analysis of the changes, see F. Cranmer, 'Religion and Public Benefit' (2009) 11:2 Ecc LJ 203–5.
39 *Guidance: Advancement of Religion*, *supra* note 9 at 24 and 26.
40 *Ibid*, at 28.
41 *Independent Schools Council v The Charity Commission* [2011] UKUT 421 (TCC).
42 *Guidance: Advancement of Religion*, *supra* note 9 at 4.
43 See online (pdf): <https://assets.publishing.service.gov.uk/government/uploads/system/uploads/attachment_data/file/358531/advancement-of-religion-for-the-public-benefit.pdf>. It now begins with the caveat, in bold: '**This guidance is currently under review. It no longer forms part of our public benefit guidance and should now be read together with our set of 3 public benefit guides. It will remain available to read until we publish replacement guidance.**'
44 Charity Commission for England and Wales, *Application for Registration of The Gnostic Centre: 16 December 2009*.
45 *Ibid*, at para 5.
46 *Ibid*, at para 23.
47 Notwithstanding the fact that Irenaeus wrote *Adversus Haereses*, a refutation of the teachings of Gnosticism, in about 180 CE.
48 *Application for registration of The Druid Network: 21 September 2010*.

49 *Ibid*, at 5.
50 *Ibid*, at 7.
51 *Ibid*, at 31.
52 *Ibid*, at 64.
53 Charity Commission for England and Wales, *The Way of the Livingness, The Religion of the Soul Trust: 24 August 2011*.
54 In *Berry v St Marylebone Borough Council* [1958] 1 Ch 406, in which the Theosophical Society sought charitable exemption from local property taxes. On 20 June 2016, the Commission registered the Theosophical Society in England as a charity but, as it explained in its Annual Report for 2016–17, at 8, 'for promoting moral or ethical improvement and the advancement of education for the benefit of the public' – not as a charity for the advancement of religion.
55 On a purely technical point, the Commission also concluded that the dissolution clause in the Trust Deed might allow the Trust's assets to be applied for non-charitable purposes.
56 Charity Commission for England and Wales, *Letter to the Pagan Federation, dated 4th October 2012*.
57 See S. Owen's 'Defining Pagan Religions through Charity Law', paper presented at the American Academy of Religion meeting in Atlanta, Georgia, in the Contemporary Pagan Studies Group and Indigenous Religious Traditions Group, 23 November 2015, at 5.
58 *Ibid*, at 5.
59 *Ibid*, at 4.
60 See *Charity Tribunal Register of Cases: Table*, updated March 2018, online: <https://www.gov.uk/government/publications/charity-appeals-register-of-tribunal-cases/charity-tribunal-register-of-cases>.
61 *R (Hodkin) & Anor v Registrar General of Births, Deaths and Marriages* [2012] EWHC 3635 (Admin) [hereinafter *Hodkin* 2012].
62 In Scotland, where registration is of marriage *celebrants* rather than *buildings*, there had been no such problem: her brother David had earlier been married in a Scientology ceremony in Edinburgh: *R (Hodkin) & Anor v Registrar General of Births, Deaths and Marriages* [2013] UKSC 77 at para 2 [hereinafter *Hodkin* 2013].
63 *Hodkin* 2012, *supra* note 61 at para 102.
64 *Segerdal*, *supra* note 22, *per* Buckley LJ.
65 *Segerdal*, *supra* note 22, *per* Lord Denning MR.
66 *Hodkin* 2013, *supra* note 62.
67 *Ibid*, at para 57.
68 *Ibid*, at para 61.
69 *Ibid*, at paras 54, 55.
70 Now known as the Plymouth Brethren Christian Church. They should not be confused with the much larger group of 'Open' Brethren, of whom perhaps the best-known member in recent years was the New Testament scholar Frederick Fyvie Bruce.
71 *Preston Down Trust – application for registration as a charity*: Letter from the Commission's Chief Legal Adviser and Head of Legal Services to Mr Julian Smith, of Farrer & Co, advisers to the Trust.
72 *Holmes v Attorney General* (1981) *The Times* 12 February [hereinafter *Holmes*].
73 Charity Commission of England & Wales, *Application for Registration of The Preston Down Trust: 3 January 2014* [hereinafter *Preston Down Trust*].
74 *Ibid*, at 96.
75 *Ibid*, at 97.
76 *Ibid*, at 98.
77 Charity Commission for England and Wales, *The Temple of The Jedi Order: Application for Registration: Decision of The Commission 16 December 2016* [hereinafter *Temple of the Jedi Order*].
78 *Ibid*, at 4.
79 *Ibid*, at 14, 15.
80 *Ibid*, at 15.
81 *Ibid*, at 16.

82 *Ibid*, at 17.
83 *Ibid*, at 18.
84 *Ibid*.
85 *Ibid*, at 40, 42.
86 *Ibid*, at 43.
87 *Ibid*, at 44.
88 *Ibid*, at 45.
89 *Ibid*, at 48.
90 *Ibid*, at 54.
91 *Ibid*, at 46.
92 *Ibid*, at 60.
93 K O'Halloran, *Religion, Charity and Human Rights* (Cambridge: Cambridge University Press, 2014), 171.
94 Or as the Court expressed it in *Holmes*, *supra* note 72, 'it is better for man to have a religion – a set of beliefs that take him outside his own petty cares and leads him to think of others – rather than to have no religion at all'.
95 Chan, *supra* note 29 at 119, citing *Gilmour*, *supra* note 5 at 459.
96 R. Sandberg, '*The Farce Awakens*: Why the Charity Commission's decision on Jediism reveals a need to revisit the definition of religion', *Law & Religion UK* (22 December 2016), online: <http://www.lawandreligionuk.com/2016/12/22/the-farce-awakens-why-the-charity-commissions-decision-on-jediism-reveals-a-need-to-revisit-the-definition-of-religion>.
97 *Ibid*.
98 For further analysis of this point, see R. Sandberg, 'Clarifying the Definition of Religion under English Law: The Need for a Universal Definition' (2018) 20:2 *Ecc LJ* 132–57.
99 Registered charity no. 1046814.
100 For the current position see online: <http://beta.charitycommission.gov.uk/charity-details?regid=1046814&subid=0>.
101 David Ainsworth, '£475m Charity Which Spends Nothing on Cause "Trying to Close for Nine Years"' (4 April 2018) *Civil Society*.
102 Freedom of thought, conscience and religion.
103 I am grateful to David Frei, External and Legal Services Director of the United Synagogue, for confirming that point: he added that, historically, there were 'communities' in Eastern Europe where no *minyan* was ever present.
104 [2013] ECHR 37.
105 *Ibid*, at para 82.
106 *Temple of The Jedi Order*, *supra* note 77 at 44.
107 *4th YouGov Survey (of Anglican Clergy) (fieldwork 14 August – 9 September 2014)*, at 23, online (pdf): <http://cdn.yougov.com/cumulus_uploads/document/5f5s31fk47/Results-for-Anglican-Clergy-Survey-08092014.pdf>.
108 My suspicion is that if the question were put to a large sample of Anglican *laypeople*, the proportion of agnostics would be rather higher.
109 *Temple of The Jedi Order*, supra note 77 at 18.
110 See, e.g., David Boulton, ed., *Godless for God's Sake: Nontheism in Contemporary Quakerism* (Dent: Dales Historical Monographs, 2006).
111 House of Commons Public Administration Select Committee, *The role of the Charity Commission and 'Public Benefit': Post-legislative scrutiny of the Charities Act 2006* (Third Report of Session 2013–14 Volume I), 29–30 (emphasis in original).
112 *Ibid*, at 31 (emphasis in original).

Chapter Five

BACK AT THE BAR: CHARITY LAW, PUBLIC BENEFIT, AND A CASE OF LEGAL *DÉJÀ VU* FOR THE EXCLUSIVE BRETHREN

Bernard Doherty*

Abstract

In 2012, the Charity Commission for England and Wales rejected the Preston Down Trust (PDT) application for charitable status because it concluded that doctrines of the Plymouth Brethren Christian Church (PBCC) as practiced by the PDT did not meet the public benefit requirement in charity law. This came as a result of the removal of the presumption of benefit in the Charities Act 2006 (now Charities Act 2011). On January 8, 2014 the Charity Commission reversed its 2012 decision following political controversy and negotiations with the PBCC.

This chapter contextualizes the PDT case within the wider controversies which have surrounded the PBCC over the last half-century, including the 1981 pre-reform case (*Holmes v Attorney General*). It reviews the political fallout of the PDT decision, as well as the PBCC's efforts to better establish its public benefit in the face of possible deregistration, and the ways in which the Charity Commission has sought to ensure that the PDT abides by its stated purposes.

This case study provides a framework for analysis of future cases involving other religious minorities in a similar predicament. The chapter concludes by noting that the question of undesirable state interference needs to be considered, especially when there is public criticism of controversial minority religious groups. The PDT case, whatever its merits or flaws, clearly highlights a series of problem areas in charity law reform in England and Wales and raises a series of issues which other common law jurisdictions would be well advised to consider as they tackle reforms.

Introduction

On 7 June 2012, the Charity Commission for England and Wales rejected an application by the Preston Down Trust (henceforth PDT) for charitable status on the grounds that it was 'not satisfied it was able to determine conclusively that the doctrines and practices of

---

* B.A. (Ancient History, Macquarie University), M.A. (Early Christian and Jewish Studies, Macquarie University), Ph.D. (Macquarie University); Course Director at the School of Theology, Charles Sturt University, Canberra.

the PBCC [Plymouth Brethren Christian Church] as practised by PDT met the public benefit requirement in charity law and, consequently, that PDT was not established for exclusively charitable purposes for the public benefit'.[1] This trust was operated by the Plymouth Brethren Christian Church (PBCC), then better known as the 'Exclusive Brethren', a conservative evangelical Protestant group known for their strict adherence to a doctrine known as 'separation from evil'.[2] The Commission's decision letter established that the chief legal ground on which this decision was reached related to the removal of the presumption of benefit in the Charities Act 2006 (now consolidated in the Charities Act 2011) and the Commission's opinion that the 1981 High Court case involving the Brethren, *Holmes v Attorney General* (1981), could no longer be regarded as a precedent in a post-reform legal context.[3] The letter also noted the Commission's awareness of 'public criticism' of the PBCC and that it must 'balance the benefit and disadvantage in all cases where detriment is alleged', though it qualified this by noting that 'we do not have any evidence before us at this time to demonstrate disadvantage which may serve to negate public benefit'.[4] This became the first post-reform instance of charitable status being refused to an established religious group.[5] The Commission's original decision was reversed on 9 January 2014, following considerably political controversy and confidential negotiations between the PBCC and the Commission. The PDT case, while settled outside of court and not a legal precedent, highlights a series of problem areas in charity law reform as this has occurred in England and Wales and some have seen its resolution as partially, if not entirely, unsatisfactory.

The final PDT decision and how the Commission approached this specific case raises a number of interesting questions regarding the assessment and regulation of religious charities and the public benefit requirement following widespread reforms to charity law in various common law jurisdictions over the past decade and a half. It also highlights some of the differences which have emerged between the models adopted by different common law jurisdictions.[6] Indeed, as was noted when this matter was raised in the House of Commons' Public Administration Select Committee (PASC), both the Office of the Scottish Charity Regulator (OSCR) and Australian Charities and Not-for-profits Commission (ACNC) had registered PBCC trusts with little comment despite the group's sometimes negative public image in both jurisdictions.[7]

In particular, the PDT case demonstrates one approach which charity regulators might adopt to address the historically vexing question of alleged or established 'detriment and harm' as this relates to assessing questions of public benefit, particularly when this relates to charities seeking registration under the traditional head for the advancement of religion. Moreover, from a wider sociological and historical perspective, the PDT case provides an intriguing case study of how charity law has become a site of legal contestation and questions of legitimacy for minority religious groups in common law jurisdictions. It represents the latest episode in a series of controversies involving the Brethren's negotiation of its 'mode of insertion'[8] into society in different common law jurisdictions.[9]

This chapter provides a case study of the PDT decision and has four brief aims. First, it discusses the earlier pre-reform legal case between the Commission and the Brethren (*Holmes v Attorney General*) to establish the *status quo ante* before legislative changes removed the presumption of benefit under the Charities Act 2006.[10] Second, it outlines the progression of the PDT case and the legal questions addressed in the negotiations between the Brethren and the Commission and discusses the case law rationale for the decision on each question. Third, it contextualizes the PDT case against the more recent history of the Brethren and seeks to highlight some of the ways by which this context, in particular the 'public criticism', helped to fuel controversy around this case – including factors which might be relevant when considering other controversial religious groups accused of 'detriment and harm' to either their members or the wider community. Finally, it looks at the aftermath and political fallout from the PDT decision and the ways in which the Commission has sought to ensure that the PDT, and by implication the PBCC, has abided by its stated purposes.

While this case has attracted significant attention from legal commentators, both at the time and since,[11] little has been written with a view to contextualizing the PDT furore against the wider controversies which have surrounded the Brethren over the last half-century and the bearing these may have had on the Commission's decision.[12] Instead, legal scholars, who have generally been critical of both the original decision and the subsequent resolution, have looked at this case through the focused lens of charity law reform. As will be narrated below, for the Brethren and their critics, the PDT case was in many ways a case of legal *déjà vu*, and the kinds of external pressures and legal questions which came to bear on the Commission during the PDT case appear to have been remarkably similar to the *Holmes* case in 1981.

A Case of Legal *Déjà Vu*?

The Brethren's history of dispute with the Charity Commission for England and Wales over their charitable status dates to the early 1970s and a series of court cases relating to the division of property between different Brethren factions following what is probably best described as a schism in the group in 1970.[13] While historians are divided as to the exact facts surrounding this schism, and the Brethren have litigated against some authors who have penned accounts of these events which they deem to be slanderous, in a simplified narrative, the proximate cause was allegations of untoward behaviour by then world leader James Taylor Jr (1899–1970) during a visit to Aberdeen, Scotland, in early 1970.[14]

The seeds of this schism, however, had been sown much earlier in the tightening of group behavioural standards which had begun under earlier leader James Taylor Sr (1870–1953). One well-informed former Brethren historian has described the 'substantial haemorrhaging and public notoriety'[15] of the Brethren from the 1950s through to the 1970s, arguably reaching its apogee with moves by conservative MP Gresham Cooke to seek legislative action against the group through a private member's bill in 1964 (an action rejected by the Wilson government).[16] These events have been treated at length by various authors. What is more important in the present context is that as a direct result of one of these cases, in the words of the Commission's 1974 report, 'evidence arose which raised a doubt as to whether certain of the doctrines and practices of the Exclusive Brethren might not be contrary to public policy'.[17]

Under section 6 of the then-current Charities Act 1960, the Commission instigated a semi-judicial inquiry into the Brethren and appointed H. E. Francis, QC, to gather evidence for whether or not the Brethren's activities were contrary to public policy and, if this was established, to determine 'whether they were so contrary to the public policy as to render the trust non-charitable'.[18] A legal basis for a religious charity's presumption of benefit to be rebutted on public policy grounds had long existed in charity case law following the so-called morality test[19] set out in *Thornton v Howe* and later reiterated in *Re Watson*.[20] This test maintained, in the words of Justice Plowman quoting the earlier case, that:

> Having regard to the fact that the court does not draw a distinction between one religion and another or one sect and another, the only way of disproving a public benefit is to show, in the words of Romilly MR in *Thornton v Howe*, that the doctrines inculcated are—'adverse to the very foundations of all religion, and that they are subversive of all morality'.[21]

No religious group has at that time or since been denied registration on this ground, and courts have proven reluctant to pursue such an inquiry.[22] As such, this inquiry was almost unprecedented.[23] Francis submitted his report in November 1975, and while the report itself was given limited circulation – with the Brethren understandably later seeking to ensure that it was kept confidential[24] – its most damning allegations were publicized in a press release issued by the Commission in May 1976 which singled out Francis's opinion that the Brethren doctrine of 'Separation from Evil' – as implemented during James Taylor Jr's tenure as leader from 1959 to 1970 – was:

> A harsh and harmful doctrine, calculated and in fact operating to disrupt family ties and perfectly normal and proper business, professional and social relationships, and to cause widespread distress and anguish among many deeply religious and decent people.

Francis went on to conclude that the Brethren 'cannot be regarded as charitable, because the advancement of such a religion, far from being beneficial to the community, is inimical to the true interests of the community'.[25] Importantly, much of Francis's evidence – described as a 'large volume of statements and letters received from people all over the country'[26] – came in the form of unsolicited evidence provided by former members of the group who had left or been expelled during Taylor's tenure as leader (estimated by some scholars to have been in the thousands).[27] This situation was to reoccur in the PDT case, though it is unclear whether evidence was solicited or unsolicited by the Commission in this case. It is reasonable to surmise that some of the evidence came from some of the same individuals as in the early case.

In response to Francis's report, the Commission decided that until these concerns were addressed by either the High Court or Parliament they would maintain the *status quo* and neither register new Brethren trusts nor deregister the current trust.[28] Unsurprisingly, on receipt of the report, the Brethren's counsel agreed that the issue should not be one decided by the Commission but rather by the courts or Parliament, and members of the Brethren began privately lobbying parliamentarians on grounds of freedom of religious worship.[29] Moreover, the Brethren's counsel pointed out their opinion that 'the inquiry was unfair in that they had no opportunity to examine, test or counter the evidence submitted to Mr. Francis'.[30] As such, in 1977, several members of the Brethren took out a writ against the Charity Commissioners and Francis challenging both the validity and legality of the inquiry itself and the subsequent decision to freeze further registration of Brethren trusts (*Rule and Others v Charity Commissioners of England and Wales and Another*). Matters of due process were also raised by Scottish MP Malcolm Rifkind in parliament on 1 August 1978, with a motion signed by 320 MPs calling for the 'powers of the Charity Commission' to be 'altered so that the charitable status of religious bodies and churches cannot be removed by the Commission' unless these groups 'have been found to have objects and practices inconsistent with charitable status by a court of law'.[31]

The Brethren members' 1977 legal action was dismissed on 10 December 1979 by Justice Fox on the grounds that the inquiry and the subsequent hiatus in registrations were within the powers granted to the Charity Commissioners and that 'one can now only regard this Report as a document of no real importance at all. It has no legal consequences, *nor in the event did it satisfy the Charity Commissioners as to the validity of its main conclusions*'. Furthermore, Justice Fox pointed out that 'the Brethren have immediately available to them a means of obtaining a full investigation by the Court of the effect of the doctrine of separation from evil and of determining once and for all whether any of their doctrines are of such a nature that they affect charitable status'.[32]

Unsurprisingly, the Brethren appealed this decision, but in the meantime a clerical error within the Commission led to the temporary registration and subsequent cancellation of a new Brethren trust in Feltham. The Brethren subsequently appealed to the High Court seeking a 'declaration that the Commissioners had no jurisdiction to decide that they had made a mistake and to remove the Trust from the register, that the Trust was at the date of that decision a valid charitable trust, and that the Trust was entitled to be registered'.[33] Under the presumption of benefit (approach) then operating regarding religious trusts, this placed the Commission in a difficult legal bind regarding the burden of proof and the likelihood of a successful rebuttal.

Since the clerical error registering the Feltham trust had legally recognized an identical object as for the public benefit, it now fell to the Commission to rebut this – an outcome which would have been unprecedented and, given the Commission's own prior public admission that it was not satisfied with Francis's conclusions – unlikely of success. As Woodfield observed regarding the rebuttal of public benefit with reference to the differences between the two important charity cases of *Gilmour v Coats* and *Cocks v Manners*:[34]

> Where an object has previously been held not to be beneficial to the public, the onus rests on the party seeking charitable status to establish the existence of such a benefit. However, *where the object has previously been recognised as potentially benefiting the public, the onus shifts to the party denying charitable status to rebut the presumption of benefit*.[35]

Under such conditions the Solicitor General chose not to challenge any of the evidence presented by the Brethren and their supporters.[36] In the words of Justice Walton, the 'evidence was all one way'.[37] On 11 February 1981, Justice Walton gave his verdict in the Brethren's favour, examining three issues in his verdict.

First, Justice Walton examined whether the Brethren were an enclosed type of organization of the type excluded under *Gilmour v Coats* – Justice Walton ruled no on the grounds that (on the evidence provided) Brethren meetings other than the Lord's Supper and administrative meetings were open to well-disposed outsiders and that the group engaged in street preaching and thus was not an enclosed organization comparable to the closed religious order dealt with in *Gilmour v Coats*.[38]

Second, the question was raised whether Brethren street preaching of Christian doctrine as espoused by the Brethren might be considered for the public benefit. In assessing this, Justin Walton cited the 'morality test' in *Thornton v Howe* and *Re Watson*, ruling that – despite not examining the extensive written ministry of James Taylor Jr at any length – 'there was not the slightest reason to suppose that there was anything remotely adverse to the very foundations of all religion or subversive to all morality'.[39] This was an unsurprising finding, and a number of legal scholars have noted what Peter Edge has called the 'nebulous'[40] nature of what might constitute 'doctrines adverse to the very foundations of all religion, and […] subversive of all morality'.[41] It is interesting to note, however, that Justice Walton did not examine Taylor's written extensive ministry – whereas John Romilly MR had done this in *Thornton v Howe*, concluding that Joanna Southcott was a 'foolish ignorant woman, of an enthusiastic turn of mind',[42] and Justice Plowman had sought expert opinion in *Re Watson* about the value of Hobbs's writings which were found to have no 'intrinsic worth'.[43]

Third, Justice Walton ruled specifically that the implementation of the doctrine of Separation from Evil – in particular, communal discipline – was not contrary to the public interest (i.e. public policy). Interestingly on this third point, however, Justice Walton only heard evidence from the Brethren themselves describing the nature and purpose of communal discipline and concluded, 'No evidence had been put before him concerning very serious allegations which had been made against the Brethren elsewhere and he was not, therefore, entitled to pay any regard to them judicially'.[44] Like Justice Romilly before him, Justice Walton himself was far from sanguine in expressing his personal opinion of the Brethren, chiding their 'Pharaisaical [sic] position of being blown up with their own pride' and suggesting that the description of their disciplinary practices 'may very well put the matter in a much more favourable light than it wears in reality'.[45]

Unfortunately, Justice Walton's entire judgement in *Holmes* has not been made publicly available, only the brief summary in *The Times* Law Report and quotations in an article by the late sociologist Bryan Wilson and the Commission's annual reports. This whole episode is, of course, quite interesting from a jurisprudence perspective, but what the documentation in the Charity Commissioner's reports only obliquely reveals is the wider social context in which this was taking place and the interests that were at play. Without going into great detail, during this period both the tabloid media and aggrieved former members of the Brethren had drawn public attention to what they considered its unchristian practices.[46]

The Preston Down Trust Decision

In 2009, under the then Charities Act 2006, members of the local Brethren first attempted to register the PDT to operate the meeting hall at Torquay in Devon.[47] After some initial negotiations between the local Brethren and the Charity Commission, on 7 June 2012 the Commission rejected the application on the grounds noted above. In a submission later tendered before PASC in the House of Commons, the Commission elaborated on its rationale, noting:

> Preston Down Trust promotes particular beliefs and practices, in particular the doctrine of separation which is central to their beliefs and way of life and this has the consequence of limiting their engagement with non-Brethren and the wider public. The evidence we were given showed that the doctrine of separation as preached by the Trust requires followers to limit their engagement with the wider public, and there was insufficient evidence of meaningful access to participate in public worship.[48]

The initial issue, then, was, like *Holmes*, related to the question of public benefit as it related to a religious community who, in the phrase of the late sociologist Bryan Wilson, 'have remained within the wider society, withdrawing from it mentally, socially and politically, although still involved in the world's economic activities'.[49] As such, this decision has wider implications for closed religious communities – as was later discovered through a leak of internal Commission documents.[50] Unsurprisingly, the Brethren appealed to the First-tier Tribunal (FTT) on 19 June 2012, with an already registered Brethren charity with identical purposes – the Horsforth Gospel Trust – joining the appeal.

In later documentation, including the official summary of its final 2014 decision, the Commission noted that this case turned on four legal questions of unequal weight:

(1) the purposes of the PDT;
(2) whether these purposes were exclusively charitable;
(3) whether the purposes were for the public benefit and not just for the Brethren community; and
(4) were there elements of detriment, harm, public disadvantage or disbenefit which might outweigh any public benefit.[51]

It is important to note in this last instance that, before the original decision was made, the Commission explicitly noted that it was 'generally aware of allegations with regard to detriment and harm which might militate against public benefit, but had no direct evidence of this and therefore did not take this into account in its 2012 Decision'.[52] From a legal perspective this is unsurprising – the Commission's official guidance then in operation – which was to prove so contentious in a subsequent parliamentary inquiry and had already caused controversy in the 2011 *Independent Schools Council v Charity Commission for England and Wales* Upper Tribunal decision[53] – contained little regarding detriment and harm which could be easily applied to the Brethren (see below). However, this matter of detriment and harm was to loom large in subsequent discussion and debate and has remained, arguably, the most contentious point among critics of the Commission's decision. Before turning to the four points of law considered, it is important to briefly turn to what can be said of the negotiations.

Realizing the significant freedom of worship and financial impacts the PDT decision might have on the entire Brethren community, as had been the case in *Holmes*, the Brethren and other concerned evangelical Christian groups began an extensive public lobbying campaign of local members over the six months between June and December 2012, which one critical Labour MP Paul Flynn later went on to call 'bullying'.[54] Several MPs from the Conservative Party voiced their support for the Brethren in what they saw as an unjust attack on a Christian group and expressed their feelings to the Commission.[55] On 5 February 2013, the Brethren and the Commission agreed, with the consent of the FTT and support of the Attorney General, to a three-month stay in proceedings and began negotiating a way forward – this stay was subsequently extended on a number of occasions. However, the Commission also made clear its preference that the 'matter be dealt with authoritatively and independently in the FTT'[56] perhaps, as Decker and Harding have suggested, in order that the Commission not be seen to be acting contrary to state policy regarding religious difference and diversity.[57] Political expedience and financial costs were clearly contingent factors here, with the June 2013 PASC report noting that the Committee considered the financial burden on both the Commission and the Brethren to have been unjust and politicians on both sides of parliament weighing in on the issues at stake.[58]

Most notable here were the contrasting interventions of conservative MP Peter Bone and conservative peer Baroness Elizabeth Berridge. In a speech given during an otherwise quite positive discussion of religion in the United Kingdom moved by Lord Indarjit Singh in the House of Lords on 22 November 2012, Baroness Berridge, who had family connected with the Brethren, cited unpublished findings by two British academics, one of whom, Jill Mytton, had left the Brethren in the late 1960s, regarding poor mental health outcomes for ex-members.[59] Berridge quoted former Australian Prime Minister Kevin Rudd's comment calling the Brethren a 'cult', and insisted that the Charity Commission hear evidence from ex-members anonymously. In a move never likely to succeed, Berridge also opined that she believed 'there needs to be a church-led inquiry into the Exclusive Brethren; a theological and psychological inquiry chaired by a former Archbishop'. She concluded by acknowledging that the 'religion and public benefit guidance needs to be clarified, but we also need clarity on the outer limits of what is acceptable behaviour for all religious groups'.[60] In a dramatic sitting of Parliament around a month later, the outspoken Member for Wellingborough, Peter Bone, brought a private member's bill before the House of Commons, passionately denouncing the treatment of the Brethren as religious persecution and seeking the reintroduction of the presumption of benefit for religious charities – decrying what he called the 'creeping secularism in society'.[61] While the bill's first reading was initially supported by 166 MPs, it never got a second reading – and has been seen as a political stunt.[62] While certainly dramatic at the time, and attracting some media attention, these parliamentary actions had no long-term effects other than to further politicize the PDT case. In the meantime, legal scholars were beginning to speculate about the legal questions the negotiations might consider.[63]

The confidential negotiations between the Brethren and the Commission have been the subject of some speculation by lawyers, but more so by some former members of the Brethren who questioned aspects of the Commission's January 2014 decision.[64] Writing in an appendix to a fellow ex-member's autobiography in 2015, one concerned former member of the Brethren and retired academic, Dr Ian McKay, wrote, for instance, of Brethren approaches to academics and of payments received – subtly impugning the honesty of some of those who subsequently wrote opinions (though failing to note the rigours imposed on expert testimony).[65] McKay also raised the issue of the Brethren's threatened legal action against Jill Mytton whose preliminary research had been cited by Baroness Berridge and which the Brethren had analysed by other experts who found it methodologically wanting; for the Brethren this was a matter of confronting what they considered very serious and defamatory claims. Writers more sympathetic to the Brethren have noted the equally extensive lobbying campaign which was waged by some former members both online and in person – which saw a number of politicians on both sides of parliament making critical remarks on the case.

Without being privy to all the details, it is notable that expert testimony was sought by both the Commission and the Brethren's counsel as to the nature of the Brethren's beliefs and practices as this related to the legal questions under consideration.[66] Some witnesses were certainly paid, as is usual practice, for their services, others chose not to be and one withdrew from the process over concerns about restricted access to Brethren ministry.[67] Unsolicited evidence, as discussed below, was also received and weighed by the Commission from former members of the Brethren and from members of other branches of the Brethren movement concerned about being tarred with the same brush as the PBCC.[68] Only one of the expert reports prepared (the author is aware of at least three) was directly cited in the Commission's decision, that of the respected sociologist Professor Eileen Barker, who was approached directly by the Commission due to her established expertise. It appears unlikely that expert testimony by academics other than that of Barker, and perhaps that of ecclesiastical law expert Norman Doe,[69] was seriously considered in the proceedings. While some acrimony and speculation has followed in the wake of the PDT decision among those unhappy with the result, the actual negotiation appears to have been undertaken in good faith by both parties. The subsequent report is relatively transparent regarding legal rationale adopted by the Commission, and, rather than indulging in fruitless speculation, it is more worthwhile to address the four legal matters it considered: charitable purpose, public benefit, the extent of public benefit and detriment and harm.

Charitable Purpose

The Commission here was concerned that the Brethren's doctrine of 'progressive revelation'[70] (though the Brethren do not use this term) might mean that the purposes of the trust might be subsequently changed and thus no longer for the public benefit.[71] In essence, this meant that in order for the Commission to reverse its original decision, from this point onwards the Brethren were bound to adhere to the stipulations summarised in Schedule 2 of the Deed of Variation, in particular with regard to their treatment of former members and members under communal discipline.[72] Were the current leader, Bruce David Hales (1950–), or future leaders to institute rules which changed these conditions in 'an irremediable non charitable way',[73] then the trust could be considered in breach and the PDT's assets could be applied *cy-près* to another charity with similar goals. While critics of the decision have questioned the Brethren's willingness to change with reference to often harsh past disciplinary practices,[74] this condition was arguably a powerful legal incentive to comply. Moreover, over one hundred other Brethren trusts with identical purposes have been re-registered since the January 2014 decision;[75] as such, any identified violation of these purposes poses a significant financial risk to the Brethren as a whole – of which the group was, and is, clearly aware.[76]

Public Benefit

After examining further evidence provided by the PDT and others following the initial determination, the Commission found that the PBCC was, according to the purposes set forth by the PDT, on the whole for the public benefit 'through its instruction and edification of the public in a Christian way of life'.[77] The Commission held, following its own (problematic) guidance, that the Brethren had demonstrated its aims in three ways.[78] First, it provided sufficient public access to worship, with the Commission noting that 'the requirement to be a well-disposed person and adhere to their dress code does not prohibit public attendance and is common to some other religions'. Second, the Brethren practice of street preaching was seen as charitable, for it involved the 'distribution of religious publications and the spreading of the word of God' to those outside of the Brethren fold – not directly citing but certainly supporting the earlier finding in *Holmes* that nothing in Brethren teachings failed the 'morality test'. Third, the Commission considered the Brethren's limited but demonstrably evolving involvement with the wider community during periods of disaster relief, by holding 'pie days' at their meeting rooms and fundraising for non-Brethren charities. Two out of three of the reasons provided by the Commission were almost identical to those already established in the *Holmes* case. The third, however, is interesting and has received a sceptical reception by some former members, who, like the Commission itself, have questioned the Brethren's motives.[79] Regardless, since this time the Brethren have increased their degree of engagement with the wider community, in particular through the Rapid Relief Team (RRT) which has become an increasingly visible presence at community events and providing food for emergency services personnel at times of natural and man-made disasters – perhaps most visibly following the Grenfell tower tragedy in 2017.[80]

Extent of Public Benefit

The further question raised was how far the public benefit provided by the PBCC extended – notably, was any benefit accruing from the PDT merely for the Brethren or to 'a sufficient section of the public'?[81] Because of the Brethren's sociologically 'introversionist'[82] nature it was clear to the Commission that it was 'more difficult to demonstrate benefit to the wider community'.[83] To demonstrate how it met this requirement the Brethren provided extensive documentation to show how they lived their lives as contributing members to the local community through disaster relief, assisting the needy, and sizable financial donations to other registered (and non-Brethren) charities. While the Commission still concluded that the Brethren predominantly operate for the benefit of their own members, this minimalist interaction was considered to be not so negligible as to exclude them in light of earlier pre-2006 judicial decisions considered relevant by the

Commission (especially *Neville Estates v Madden* – a case, incidentally, usually cited alongside the Australian case involving the Brethren, *Joyce v Ashfield Municipal Council*, though the latter was notably not cited).[84]

Detriment and Harm

This was arguably the most interesting and controverted of the issues raised in the wake of the initial 2012 PDT decision and remains the point most often discussed by those who disagree with the Commission's decision and who are familiar with the Brethren's history. According to the Commission's original guidance for charities for the advancement of religion, detriment and harm considerations related largely to charities operating internationally (e.g. missionary organizations) whose purposes might be illegal or pose an unacceptable risk to their workers in other jurisdictions; to charities whose activities might be deemed dangerous to either mental or physical health; or to the promotion of violence or hatred towards others.[85] It appears from this guidance, as O'Halloran suggests,[86] that the Commission had in mind here religious groups like the Jehovah's Witnesses or the Christian Scientists who hold specific controversial beliefs about health, though it might also be suggested that the phrase 'a religion can be potentially damaging to a person's mental health, for example because of the techniques that it uses'[87] had other contentious New Religious Movements in mind.

Unlike in *Holmes*, however, the Commission did not base its deliberation about detriment and harm on a 'morality test' or public policy approach derived from *Thornton v Howe* and *Re Watson* but instead opted for the approach in *National Anti-Vivisection Society v IRC*, whereby after 'the whole terms and effects of the particular trust have been considered and if its object involves consequences which, when duly weighed, are found injurious to the community, the trust cannot be charitable'.[88]

As noted above, when the initial decision was made by the Commission in 2012, negative evidence pertaining to the Brethren's practices was not considered – for reasons discussed below. However, following the Commission's refusal to register and the subsequent appeal by the Brethren, evidence had come to light and the Commission decided that this should be considered. Likely due to the manifest problems associated with any 'morality test' approach and the Commission's (arguably premature) dismissal of *Holmes* as a precedent on the grounds that it was decided predominantly on the basis of the now defunct presumption of benefit,[89] the Commission based its decision on the test established in *National Anti-Vivisection Society v IRC*, which assessed whether a charity's 'objects involve consequences which, when duly weighed, are found injurious to the community'.[90] This test, however, has two parts, only one of which was relevant to the earlier June 2012 decision:

> The court, we conclude, has to balance the benefit and disadvantage in all cases where detriment is alleged and is supported by evidence. But great weight is to be given to a purpose which would, ordinarily, be charitable; before the alleged disadvantages can be given much weight, they need to be clearly demonstrated. There is, we think, a considerable burden on those seeking to change the status quo.[91]

Because the initial determination in 2012 did not find there was sufficient public benefit for the PDT to be charitable on other grounds, the Commission apparently did not deem it necessary to move to the second limb of this test and determine any question of disbenefit.[92] The circumstances, however, had changed in the interim period.

The nature of the evidence of alleged detriment and harm produced was listed in s.89 of the Commission's decision and was presented to the Brethren during the negotiations.[93] This included allegations pertaining to the all-encompassing nature of Brethren beliefs, the harsh treatment of members placed under communal discipline, the treatment of former members who left the group and the impact of the group's practices on children – particularly with regard to education.[94] None of these claims were anything new and had been levelled at the Brethren in various contexts over previous decades.[95] In response, the Commission did note:

> In making its representations PDT indicated that some of the allegations must be of an historic nature but did acknowledge past mistakes in relation to its Disciplinary Practices. They further demonstrated a willingness to make amends for these and to do what they could as a Christian organisation to ensure, as far as it was consistent with its religious beliefs, it would act with Christian compassion in the future, particularly in its dealings with disciplines of the Disciplinary Practices and in its relations to former members of the Brethren.[96]

What is most interesting, however, regarding the final conclusions of the Commission is that they did note this finding:

> The Commission considered that there is evidence to support the view that there are elements of detriment and harm which are in real danger of outweighing public benefit, although given as noted above that the evidence was untested by cross examination, it could not come to a concluded view of its extent or whether it indeed outweighed public benefit in the first sense.[97]

As was the case under the earlier decision in *Holmes*, once again the question turned on the nature of evidence. However, while in the early case this had been because the Solicitor General had not challenged the evidence provided by the Brethren, in the PDT case, the question was one of the situation where the Brethren's solicitors could not cross-examine those making claims of detriment and harm against the Brethren. Interestingly, given subsequent criticism of the decision, Baroness Berridge's earlier request that former members be permitted to give their evidence anonymously would likely have done little to address the substantive question of detriment and harm as it would still have prevented the Brethren's legal counsel from testing the validity of claims made.

In response to the summary of allegations put to it and the Commission's request, the Brethren addressed these issues in the Deed of Variation – in particular with reference to a clearer statement of their disciplinary practices and the treatment of ex-members. What was eventually included was a summary of Brethren disciplinary practices which, while criticized historically by some former members, was comparable to those implemented by various mainline denominations.[98] In both instances, the Brethren set out in the Deed of Variation that with reference to Disciplinary Practices these would be 'mitigated by compassion',⁹⁹ and the documents outlined in a clear and binding way (arguably for the first time outside their internal writings – though *Holmes* did discuss these matters¹⁰⁰) the nature and procedure of Brethren Disciplinary Practices. While then, unlike *Holmes*, the evidence examined in the PDT negotiations could certainly not be considered to be 'all one way', in reality the determination on detriment and harm was largely a return to the pre-reform *status quo ante* though with the proviso that Brethren agree to address concerns raised.

The Decision

On 14 January 2014, the Commission announced that 'it agreed that it would register the PDT on the basis of the attached draft Deed of Variation'.¹⁰¹ More importantly, however, the Commission noted that it 'was satisfied that if PDT applied for and was registered on the basis of this amended documentation, the Commission would be able to regulate PDT'.¹⁰² The Commission also noted in its penultimate paragraph the legal consequences which might ensue should the PDT fail to comply.

As is so often the case regarding the Brethren, the decision was met with mixed reactions. A member of the PDT trust, in a rare interview for the camera-shy Brethren, noted the group's relief at the decision and the thoroughness of the Commission's examination. Among some of the more vocal former members who had lobbied politicians and made submissions to the Commission, the response was initially hopeful, though tempered with a degree of scepticism.¹⁰³ Among politicians the result was mixed. Those who had supported the Brethren's campaign – mainly conservatives – were pleased, whilst at least one who had raised concerns about the Brethren, Labour MP Paul Flynn, chastised the Commission for what he called a 'uniform surrender under lobbying done for commercial reasons'.¹⁰⁴ Conservative peer Baroness Berridge commended the Commission on its hard work, though also encouraged former Brethren to report any concerns they had to the Charity Commission. A major online website for ex-members, Wikipeebia.com, has since featured a direct link where visitors can 'Report a Breach' regarding the PDT decision.¹⁰⁵

The Brethren in Conflict

That this case should have attracted so much attention highlights not only the controversial nature of the Brethren but also the way in which the changes first introduced in the Charities Act 2006 and the lack of clarity about questions of public benefit as these related to religion could become a point for political, as well as legal, controversy. As had been the case in other jurisdictions over the last two decades, the PDT case highlights once again how the Brethren's 'mode of insertion'¹⁰⁶ into society has made them a useful group for politicians to utilize in wider cultural debates regarding the status of religion in modern societies. It also raises further questions about whether 'public criticism' should be given serious weight in such legal determinations.

While it is not entirely clear whether the Commission was aware of the extent before it handed down its original decision, Kenneth Dibble's reference to 'public criticism' in his original letter suggests that this may have been one downplayed factor behind the Commission's original decision. As alluded to above, since the 1960s, the Brethren had been involved in a long-running and acrimonious series of disputes with former members. Among other consequences, this has created a significant pool of often aggrieved former members who monitor the activities of the Brethren, some of whom have formed a cohesive international online network centred on a series of websites.[107] This is a point strongly noted in a recent study by Italian lawyer and sociologist Massimo Introvigne, who emphasized the influence of the 'so-called anti-cult movement' in the Charity Commission campaign.[108]

While Introvigne is partially correct in highlighting the organized network of individuals operating against the Brethren, the reasons for their success here, I suggest, were far more political and context-specific than is the case with many other controversies surrounding minority religions to which Introvigne compares the PDT case. As was the case with previous controversies involving this group in Australia and New Zealand, certain often valid concerns held about past Brethren practices by former members were linked to other contingent political factors surrounding the case. Indeed, the PDT case was clearly utilized for ulterior political motives about the wider debates over the role and function of the Charity Commission playing itself out in the post-reform context,[109] particularly in the wake of criticisms of the Upper Tribunal decision in *Independent Schools Council* and later the 'Cup Scandal' exposed by *The Times* in January 2013.[110]

What differentiated the criticisms of the Brethren which emerged during the PDT case from the allegations uncovered by H. E. Francis which led to the *Holmes* case was the scope for criticism and the mobilization strategies open to critics of the group. While in previous years the Brethren had been able to litigate against critical authors and journalists who attacked them, in the PDT case this was no longer a realistic option. Despite some attempts during the context leading up to the PDT case, the Brethren were not able to effectively legally temper criticism from a series of critical websites which have served as a platform for mobilizing criticism against the group from aggrieved former members.[111]

While most legal scholars ignored these websites, the comments on blogs of some legal commentators were utilized as a platform by vocal former Brethren to argue against the PDT's registration.[112] In the wake of the January 2014 decision, these same former Brethren continued to influence the court of public opinion through the repetition of earlier claims made against the Brethren in media reports and online. Unfortunately, subsequent media reports attacking the Commission by suggesting political machinations on the part of the Brethren were less circumspect in acknowledging similar actions on the part of their opponents or recognizing how all parties were socially constructing the PDT case to aid their wider personal or political campaigns. This aspect, however, was clearly apparent to some legal commentators.[113]

In this context, the Brethren found themselves, as had earlier been the case in political controversies in Australia and New Zealand, a group whose strict beliefs and unpopularity, coupled with their visibility in lobbying, made them a useful political tool for conservatives to champion and critics to malign – more so, I suggest, because as a small community well known for not voting in parliamentary elections, they were perceived to be – at least by those unfamiliar with their history – an easy target for political point-scoring. In Britain, this manifested itself most clearly when *The Times* published a series of articles critical of the Brethren in early 2015.

The Aftermath

On 17 March 2015, *The Times* published the first of two lengthy front-page articles based on 'leaked documents' purporting to demonstrate an 'extraordinary lobbying campaign waged by the Brethren to win political support' to overturn the Charity Commission's original decision.[114] Repeating a series of allegations familiar to observers of the Brethren in other jurisdictions, this article included a series of accusations about the group. The inventory of images presented was a classic example of a prefabricated presentation of a socially constructed view of the Brethren as a wealthy, secretive and sinister 'cult' cosying up to conservative politicians: a depiction familiar from early controversies in other common law jurisdictions.[115] What these reports did not mention, however, was that following earlier controversies in Australia and New Zealand, the Brethren had been clearly transparent in their campaign to secure registration for the PDT with members even appearing before the PASC committee.

For the Brethren, the original PDT decision had not been an idle matter but an existential threat to their ability to practice their faith, and the lobbying undertaken by the group was open to anyone who cared to analyse the publicly available parliamentary documents. Internal documents from within the Brethren cited in the article – coupled with the 3,000 letters sent to politicians by members of the group – only serve to highlight just how dire they believed the situation was. Claims that some MPs wrote to Tribunal judge Alison McKenna seeking to influence the decision, while a poor decision on their part, can similarly be viewed as elected representatives representing their constituents. That said, subsequent allegations about campaigning by Brethren members on behalf of conservative MPs[116] do (arguably) raise some questions of *quid pro quo* and how far charities of any stripes should be involved in political campaigns, though it could also be argued that to restrict or exclude individual citizens – purely by virtue of their membership in an unpopular religious group – from exercising rights taken for granted in democratic countries runs counter to their human rights.

Following its purported exposé, *The Times* published a series of letters to the editor where Brethren defended their status and challenged the assertions made about their beliefs. Meanwhile, the besieged chairman of the Charity Commission, William Shawcross, wrote to the paper defending the 'independent and robust' nature of its investigation and highlighting that it was the Commission who had first put on record the 'detriment and harm' caused by the doctrines and practices of the Brethren. Shawcross reiterated that the Commission would 'make public the conclusions of our monitoring of those Brethren halls that we registered as charities. If any member of the public has evidence relating to these charities, we would be glad to receive it'.[117] Shawcross's defence, however, was not well accepted in all quarters, with the chief executive of the industry organization Association of Chief Executives of Voluntary Organisations (ACEVO) Sir Stephen Bubb criticizing the Commission for essentially financing organizations they believed caused detriment and harm and demanding a full explanation of who had been involved in making the decision.[118] In light of media and public scrutiny, the question worth raising is: what did the ongoing monitoring find?

The post-registration monitoring, and freedom of information reports published by the *Third Sector*, suggested that – second only to the Royal Society for the Prevention of Cruelty to Animals (RSPCA) – the PDT had been the subject of the most complaints to the Commission.[119] More clarification, however, established that none of the nine complaints about alleged breaches received actually related to the PDT but to other Brethren Gospel Hall trusts which had been re-registered in the wake of the PDT decision. In February 2016[120] and again in August 2017,[121] the Commission published reports outlining its monitoring – as well as re-registering over one hundred other PBCC Gospel Trusts under identical conditions to the PDT. The first report, published in 2015, found that the Brethren were continuing to engage with the wider community in a variety of ways – though it was recommended that for sizeable grants to other charities (e.g. for the purpose of an air ambulance) the PDT draw up a grant-making policy.

Some complaints about awareness of the Deed of Variation by other gospel trusts were received, but no action was taken by the Commission. However, the Commission did advise that 'the trustees could do more to be open about this very important document'.

The Commission suggested, moreover, that the Deed of Variation be posted on the PBCC's website, noting that 'this might help dispel speculation and suspicion which appears to exist about members and the public being prevented from viewing the document'. One researcher who regularly attended a Brethren meeting in Liverpool between 2015 and 2017 attested to the author that the Deed of Variation was highly visible in the foyer of this meeting room and that he was provided with a copy on his first visit.[122] The group continued their street preaching, providing the Commission with times and locations where this took place. In terms of access to meetings, no evidence was found of members of the public being refused access, though this may be a purely academic point, as the report also noted that 'in practice only one new person had attended a meeting of the charity since it was registered'.[123] The question of signage advertising service times, which had been a matter raised in previous disputes, had been resolved and the Commission verified this through site visits.

With reference to complaints, the 2016 report noted that the Commission had not received any complaints about the PDT. Moreover, it noted that the Commission had been proactive in contacting individuals who had previously raised concerns about the Brethren, noting that 'they had no complaints to raise about PDT',[124] though some complaints were clearly received about other Brethren meeting rooms. However, the substantive issues identified by the Commission were related to various bureaucratic compliance requirements and not related to the controversial topic of detriment and harm. The Commission's first report concluded that it had 'not identified any significant issues relating to the charity's compliance with the DoV and found the trustees were taking steps to ensure it was a well run charity'.[125]

The second report was issued on 29 August 2017. Unlike the earlier 2016 report, which dealt only with the PDT, this second report dealt more widely with PBCC Gospel Hall trusts. Of the over 100 Gospel Hall Trusts re-registered under the same Deed of

Variation, 24 were selected for monitoring, comprising those which the Commission had received complaints about and a selection of others. As with the earlier PDT case, the Commission again sought out and utilized information from former members, media documents and in most cases inspection visits 'to explore issues we had identified during the course of our engagement and to gain additional assurance and verification of information'.[126] Once again some concerns were raised about access to the Deed of Variation, but the Commission noted that they 'found no evidence that any members were prevented from accessing a copy of the DoV, which is also available on the Commission's website'.[127] While a small number of former members continued to raise concerns, upon investigation the Commission found 'that they [the PBCC] had acted in accordance with the requirement for compassion in the DoV in those particular matters'. Regarding the bureaucratic compliance matters raised in the 2016 report, the Commission noted that while it acknowledged the value of the centralised Universal Service Team (UST), this did not remove the responsibility of individual trusts.[128]

This demonstrates a clear awareness by the Brethren that their charitable status cannot be taken for granted, as well as the ways in which they are now seeking to present (and defend) their activities and engage more proactively with the wider public – a situation, interestingly, which has spread to other common law jurisdictions like Australia where the presumption of benefit aspect of charity law for religious groups remains in place.[129] However, what this, and some of the stronger recommendations about the awareness regarding the Deed of Variation, may also indicate is how *ad litteram* the Commission has been in seeking to hold the Brethren to their express purposes – a degree which it could be suggested places a far greater emphasis on compliance and regulation to the detriment of the original purposes of the PDT as a charity established for the advancement of religion. This compliance approach may already be leading to some undesirable consequences – such as potentially encouraging the Brethren to litigate against critical former members campaigning against them.[130]

Conclusions

In reality, the PDT decision of January 2014 was in many aspects a return to the *status quo ante* of *Holmes*, which permitted both the Charity Commission and the Brethren an opportunity to circumvent an expensive and no doubt controversial test case for the already beleaguered Tribunal. However, the Commission's decision is not a legal precedent, and while in some ways binding, were the Commission to claim that any PBCC Gospel Hall Trusts were in breach, this would likely result in further expensive litigation. As such, the legal issues addressed by the Commission, while interesting, do not permit the Brethren to return to pre-PDT *status quo*. Thus, it is worth reviewing, by way of conclusion, how the decision has been received by some legal scholars and suggesting some of the pros and cons of the Commission's approach.

How the Commission's decision has been viewed by scholars has been mixed. Some scholars, notably Matthew Harding, in his advocacy for an autonomy-based liberal approach to charity, considered that the PDT decision had 'something to commend it' by the fact that it took an evidential approach that seemed to weigh the potential harm against potential benefit and found the latter to outweigh the former.[131] In particular, the decision clearly considered concerns raised by former Brethren about detriment and harm and sought through negotiation to find a workable solution which took these matters into account in a way which recognized religious diversity without providing groups like the Brethren *carte blanche* under the guise of charitable status. This approach also spared potential witnesses the discomfort of cross-examination. Other scholars, however, have been more critical. Hubert Picarda, who earlier in his career had suggested the Brethren were one group whose charitable status might be a candidate for rebuttal,[132] in particular, has been quite scathing. Quite apart from his wider (and very valid) criticism of the charity reform process more generally, Picarda was particularly critical of whether any court or regulatory authority should intervene in the disciplinary practices of religious groups when these did not pertain to matters of public policy or illegality.[133]

Perhaps, however, a more important aspect to be considered is the social control aspects which the PDT decision has utilized, what Pauline Ridge has referred to in her perceptive study of charity reform models as the 'state control of religious groups through charity law'.[134] In these terms, the Commission's decision could be seen to have fulfilled a number of the intentions of the reform envisioned in the Charities Act 2006, in particular the use of legislation as an 'incentive for a religious group to fashion its purposes so as to meet the legal definition of charity'.[135] Serious questions about the legal definition utilized by the Commission in its earlier guidance notwithstanding, the approach taken in the PDT case certainly appears to have partially achieved this end.

The Deed of Variation and the post-decision monitoring have had quite profound consequences for the Brethren as a group, so much so that one well-informed commentator from Partnership (a support network for Open Brethren churches) did suggest upon hearing about the decision that 'the Plymouth Brethren have given a lot of ground'.[136] The question this raises, as alluded to above, is whether this was too much and in some ways impinged upon the group's free exercise of their religious beliefs and practices. Were the Brethren to take the Commission at its word in the 2017 monitoring report, then the Deed of Variation as applied to every Brethren meeting appears to have taken on a de facto creedal status. Indeed, in these circumstances it is fair to ask whether the Commission would make a similar demand for another less controversial religious group. Would, for instance, the Commission require the average layperson in the Roman Catholic Church to demonstrate a comparable familiarity with the Code of Canon Law, or failing that, even a passing familiarity with the section dealing with disciplinary matters like excommunication?

As is often the case surrounding controversial religious groups, the question of undesirable state interference needs to be considered. Here, no doubt, matters will remain contested as to what point a regulator should take an active interest in these matters. This issue was acute in the PDT case because of the admittedly historical nature of many of the accusations of detriment and harm submitted to the Commission. In dealing with controversial religious minorities who are demonstrably subject to 'public criticism', this also brings up the question of admissible evidence and what should drive a regulatory body like the Commission in its determination to pursue legal sanctions against a group subject to its authority. While it cannot be confirmed that the issue of 'public criticism' was a decisive factor in the PDT case – and the Commission strongly maintained that it was not – this raises questions about state neutrality towards religious diversity and whether regulatory demands might impinge on religious freedom. As noted by Decker and Harding, 'the case shows that there is a risk that a heavy-handed ex ante regulatory style might cause religious communities to shift their attention from their underpinning purposes to satisfying the dictates of the Charity Commission'.[137]

The second aspect to consider pertaining to the social control is that 'conferral of charitable status also means that a religious group comes under ongoing state control'.[138] This is no small matter for a group like the Brethren who, by accepting the privileges of charity, also placed themselves under the monitoring of the Commission. Certainly the post-decision monitoring of the Brethren has shown that the Commission has been by no means negligent here, though for a group like the Brethren, whose relationship with wider society has often been tense, one must wonder whether this may eventually come to be seen by the group as an unacceptable compromise of its core doctrine of separation from evil.

This said, for those who support a *quid pro quo* argument regarding the fiscal benefits which come with charity status – or in the case of the Brethren outside of the United Kingdom, with reference to state funding for their schools – such regulatory oversight is arguably a good thing. While the more serious alleged abuses by groups like the Brethren can already be satisfactorily dealt with by reference to criminal law, an additional layer of compliance arguably functions as a further safeguard to ensure that historical abuses will not reoccur without possible legal consequences. From this perspective, critics of the PDT decision can rest in the knowledge that the Brethren cannot act with impunity with reference to how they treat former members, though they also should realize that this goes both ways.

This monitoring does *not* mean that individual Brethren members can be coerced by a regulator to associate with former members; the freedom enjoined on individual Brethren to associate with former members within the Deed of Variation without fear of censure goes both ways and also permits them to choose *not* to associate with former members. The most negative outcome of the acrimony surrounding the whole PDT case is perhaps that the decision of a number of vocal former members of the Brethren during the PDT case to publicly impugn their former co-religionists – often including immediate family still involved in the Brethren – and to lobby so publicly against the PDT may have forestalled any realistic chance that their relationships with family members still in the Brethren will return to some prelapsarian state.

Finally, the decision to negotiate confidentially, while undertaken for sensibly fiscal and pragmatic reasons, left a bitter taste in some mouths. In the face of political commentary by members of the Tory Government, this could not help but lead to accusations of political influence and religious favouritism[139] – the kind of accusations which have dogged the Brethren in a number of other jurisdictions and which cannot be easily dismissed. Certainly the Brethren lobbied to protect their interests, and arguably their viability, but given the circumstances the valid question might be asked: was this not justified? As a number of legal commentators have rightly observed, it is undesirable to allow a Commission to make or develop law relating to what constitutes public benefit, and to develop public policy theories related to charity, and the original determination arguably did just that.[140] As such, circumventing the Tribunal with reference to the PDT case can be viewed as an appropriate decision.

In this instance, a dialogue-based approach to resolving disputes, where a religious group is amenable to such an approach, may actually be a better way forward than expensive and acrimonious litigation – and perhaps should have been pursued more fully in the first instance. That said, an unwillingness to resort to the Tribunal to resolve these issues arguably failed to address one of the original drivers of charity law reform in the first place: that is, that there had been too few cases available to guide jurisprudence.[141] Moreover, if the 'detriment and harm' was there, then a more robust examination of the evidence in a more established and less beleaguered judicial forum like the High Court was arguably a more desirable approach for the sake of legal clarity; indeed, the Brethren would have preferred to have the claims tested in a higher court.[142] Regardless, whether such an approach – had it arrived at a similar conclusion – would have satisfied critics is unlikely, and perhaps an alternative approach which permitted former members more capacity to voice their concerns might have been appropriate. In the PDT case, a reconciliatory and cathartic forum for examining past mistakes by the Brethren might have been a better avenue – though certainly not in the form suggested by Baroness Berridge.[143]

Some of the most vocal critics of the group during the PDT proceedings had left the Brethren up to half a century before the case, though the wounds left by their experience are clearly still raw. The further question this raises, but which cannot be satisfactorily answered here, is whether former members should be permitted to intervene in such proceedings,[144] especially when their experiences are not such as to have demonstrably breached any criminal laws or which refer to historical (and often merely alleged) abuses. Permitting such an approach when questions of detriment and harm might be raised with reference to religious (or any other) charities may open the field for all manner of potentially vexatious and financially ruinous claims directed at organizations on historical grounds – even when organizations have made considered efforts to acknowledge and address past mistakes (as the PBCC appears to have done here). The recent experience in Australia with the Royal Commission into Institutional Responses to Child Sexual Abuse, and similar inquiries in other common law jurisdictions, has shown that many charities have been particularly culpable for past abuses. Were regulators to dredge up every historical allegation in assessing charitable status, the results could be disastrous – not least in countries like Australia where many of the religious charities who have been historically demonstrably most beneficial are the same charities which have also been historically most prolific in cases of abuse.[145] As in other instances highlighted above, legislatures and regulators would be well advised to carefully consider this question as part of the reform process.

The PDT case, whatever its merits or flaws, clearly highlights a series of problem areas in charity law reform as this has occurred in England and Wales and raises a series of issues which other common law jurisdictions would be well advised to consider as they tackle reforms. As a case study, the PDT case clearly points to a number of interesting questions regarding the assessment and regulation of religious charities and the public benefit requirement which other common law jurisdictions will need to wrestle with as they work through similar reforms. Moreover, the PDT case shines a spotlight on how regulatory frameworks might deal with questions of real or established 'detriment and harm', and, perhaps more than the other legal questions addressed by the PDT case, this aspect of the decision requires more careful and nuanced discussion, not least in how legislatures and regulators address the distinct sociological and historical contingencies and challenges posed by controversial minority religious groups like the Brethren. It is these groups, rather than the mainline churches, who will likely provide the test cases for future jurisprudence, and a more careful attention to their beliefs, practices and 'modes of insertion' in contemporary society, which takes into account wider societal factors, is paramount in underpinning any practicable legal reform in the area of charity law.

Notes

1 Charity Commission for England and Wales, *Preston Down Trust* (London: The Commission, 2014), 3 at para 5. Full report available online (pdf): <https://assets.publishing.service.gov.uk/government/uploads/system/uploads/attachment_data/file/336112/preston_down_trust_full_decision.pdf>.
2 For a brief recent overview see Bernard Doherty & Steve Knowles, 'Plymouth Brethren Christian Church' *Centre for the Critical Study of Apocalyptic and Millenarian Movements* (Bedford: Panacea Charitable Trust, 2017), online: <https://censamm.org/resources/profiles/plymouth-brethren-christian-church-1>
3 *Holmes and Others v Attorney General* [1981] The Times 12 February [*Holmes*].
4 Letter from Kenneth Dibble to Julian Smith, 7 June 2012, online (pdf): <https://www.parliament.uk/documents/commons-committees/public-administration/LetterfromKennethDibble.pdf>.
5 Kerry O'Halloran, *The Church of England – Charity Law and Human Rights* (Switzerland: Springer International, 2014), 159.
6 For an overview of these reforms see Pauline Ridge, 'Religious Charitable Status and Public Benefit in Australia' (2011) 35 MULR 1071 at 1096–98.
7 House of Commons, Public Administration Select Committee, *The Role of the Charity Commission and Public Benefit: Post-Legislative Scrutiny of the Charities Act 2006* (London: HMSO 2013), 28 at para 79.
8 J. A. Beckford, *Cult Controversies: The Societal Response to New Religious Movements* (London: Tavistock, 1985), 69–93.
9 See Stephen Mutch, 'Cults and Religious Privileges in England and Australia: Can the Wheat be Separated from the Chaff?' (2004) 3:2/3 Cultic Studies Review 135. Bernard Doherty, 'Sensational Scientology: The Church of Scientology and Australian Tabloid Television' (2014) 17:3 Nova Religio 38 at 45. Bernard Doherty, 'Quirky Neighbours or the Cult Next-Door?' An Analysis of Public Perceptions of the Exclusive Brethren in Australia' (2012) 3:2 International Journal for the Study of New Religions 163. 'The "Brethren 'Cult' Controversy": Dissecting a Contemporary Australian "Social Problem"' (2013) 4:1 Alternative Spirituality and Religion Review 25.
10 *Holmes*, *supra* note 3. On discussion surrounding the question of 'presumption of benefit' see M. Harding, *Charity Law and the Liberal State* (Cambridge: Cambridge University Press, 2014) at 25–26.
11 See e.g. Christopher Decker & Matthew Harding, 'Three challenges in charity regulation: The case of England and Wales', in *Not-for-Profit Law: Theoretical and Comparative Perspectives*, ed. Matthew Harding, Anne O'Connell & Miranda Stewart (Cambridge: Cambridge University

Press, 2014), 314 at 328–29 and 332. Hubert Picarda, 'Charities Act 2011: Dog's Breakfast or Dream Come True? A Case for Further Reform', in Mathew Harding, Anne O'Connell & Miranda Stewart, eds, *Not-for-Profit Law*, 134 at 147–48 [Picarda, 'Charities Act 2011'].
12 The two exceptions here, writing from different perspectives, are M. Introvigne, *The Plymouth Brethren* (Oxford: Oxford University Press, 2018), 90–92; and Ian McKay, 'Exclusive Brethren "The End Times"', in *Joy and Sorrow: The Story of an Exclusive Brethren Survivor*, ed. Joy Nason (Sydney: Centennial Press, 2015), 245.
13 Charity Commissioner for England and Wales, *Report of the Charity Commission in England and Wales for the Year 1974* (London: HMSO, 1975), 23 at para 80.
14 Introvigne, *supra* note 12 at 85–89. For an even-handed historical treatment of these issues see Neil Dickson, 'The Exclusive Brethren in Scotland' [unpublished manuscript]. My thanks to Dr Dickson for allowing me use of this paper pre-publication.
15 Roger Shuff, 'Open to Closed: The Growth of Exclusivism among Brethren in Britain 1848–1953' (1997) 1 Brethren Archivists and Historians Network Review 10 at 21.
16 For this period see Roger Shuff, *Searching for the True Church: Brethren and Evangelicals in Mid-Twentieth Century England* (Milton Keynes: Paternoster Press, 2005), 236–40.
17 Charity Commissioner, *supra* note 13 at 23 para 80.
18 Charity Commission for England and Wales, *Report of the Charity Commission in England and Wales for the Year 1976* (London: HMSO, 1977), 34 at para 1.
19 For various discussions of this see A. Bradney, *Religions, Rights and Laws* (Leister: Leister University Press, 1993), 122. P. Edge, *Legal Responses to Religious Difference* (London: Kluwer Law, 2002), 148. G. Dal Pont, 'Charity law and religion', in *Law and Religion: God, the State and the Common Law*, ed. Peter Radan, Denise Myerson & Rosalind F. Croucher (London: Routledge, 2005), 220 at 223. G. Dal Pont, *Law of Charity* (Chatswood, NSW: LexisNexis Butterworths, 2010), 240. Brian Lucas & Anne Robinson, 'Religion as a head of charity', in *Modernising Charity Law*, ed. Myles McGregor-Lowndes & Kerry O'Halloran (Cheltenham: Edward Elgar, 2010), 187 at 200.
20 *Thornton v Howe* (1862) 31 Beav 14; *Re Watson (deceased); Hobbs v Smith and others* [1973] 3 All ER 678 [*Re Watson*].
21 *Re Watson*, *supra* note 20.
22 Harding, *supra* note 10 at 25–26.
23 Though scholars have pointed to similarities with the Foster Inquiry into the Church of Scientology, see James A. Beckford, 'States, Governments, and the Management of Controversial New Religious Movements', in Eileen Barker, James A. Beckford & Karel Dobbelaere, *Secularization, Rationalism and Sectarianism: Essays in Honour of Bryan R. Wilson* (Oxford: Clarendon Press, 1993), 125 at 136.
24 Charity Commissioner for England and Wales, *Report of the Charity Commission in England and Wales for the Year 1979* (London: HMSO, 1980), 15 at para 32.
25 Charity Commission, *supra* note 18 at 35 para 5.
26 *Ibid*, 35 at para 6.
27 N Scotland, *Sectarian Religion in Modern Britain* (Carlisle: Paternoster Press, 2000), 101.
28 For a discussion of this action see Peter W Edge & Joan M Loughrey, 'Religious charities and the juridification of the Charity Commission' (2001) 21:1 Legal Studies 36 at 48–49.
29 Charity Commission, *supra* note 18 at 37 para 132.
30 *Ibid*, at 36 para 7.
31 House of Commons, *Hansard*, Series 5 vol. 955 (1 August 1978) at 707 (Hon. Malcolm Rifkind).
32 Charity Commissioner, *supra* note 24 at 15 para 31. Emphasis added.
33 Charity Commissioner for England and Wales, *Report of the Charity Commission for England and Wales for the Year 1981* (London: HMSO, 1982), 10 at para 23.
34 *Gilmour v Coats* [1949] 1 All ER 848 [*Gilmour v Coats*]. *Cocks v Manners* (1871) 23 LR Eq 574 [*Cocks v Manners*].

35 Steve T. Woodfield, 'Doing God's Work: Is Religion Always Charitable?' (1996–99) 8 Auckland University Law Review 25 at 30. Emphasis added.
36 A different (and to my mind incorrect) view is given in McKay, *supra* note 12 at 242. See also Bryan Wilson, 'A Sect at Law: The Case of the Exclusive Brethren' (1983) 60:1 Encounter 81 at 85 [Wilson, 'A Sect at Law'].
37 Charity Commissioner, *supra* note 33 at 11 para 29.
38 *Ibid*, at 11 para 27.
39 *Ibid*.
40 Edge, *supra* note 19 at 148. See also Harding, *supra* note 10 at 168.
41 *Thornton v Howe*, *supra* note 20.
42 *Ibid*. On the background of this case see the fascinating article of Pauline Ridge, 'Legal Neutrality, Public Benefit and Religious Charitable Purposes: Making Sense of *Thornton v Howe*' (2010) 31:2 Journal of Legal History 177.
43 *Re Watson*, *supra* note 20.
44 Charity Commissioner, *supra* note 33 at 11 para 29.
45 Wilson, 'A Sect at Law', *supra* note 36 at 85.
46 For details see Shuff, *supra* note 16 at 236–40, and Bryan R. Wilson, 'The Exclusive Brethren: A Case Study in the Evolution of a Sectarian Ideology', in *Patterns of Sectarianism: Organisation and Ideology in Social and Religious Movements*, ed. Bryan R. Wilson (London: Heinemann, 1987), 287 at 331–34 [Wilson, 'Exclusive Brethren'].
47 The account in this section relies heavily on Charity Commission for England and Wales, *supra* note 1, and the accounts in Hannah Whyatt, 'Preston Down Trust and the Plymouth Brethren: The Charity Commission's decision on public benefit and religion' Farrer & Co Briefing (2014), online (pdf):
<https://www.farrer.co.uk/Global/Briefings/01.%20Charity%20and%20Community/Preston%20Down%20Trust%20and%20the%20Plymouth%20Brethren.pdf>.
48 House of Commons, Public Administration Select Committee, *The Role of the Charity Commission and Public Benefit: Post-Legislative Scrutiny of the Charities Act 2006*, 27 at para 76.
49 Bryan Wilson, *Religious Sects: A Sociological Study* (Toronto: McGraw-Hill, 1970) at 135.
50 David Ainsworth, 'Charity Commission asked Attorney General to refer "closed religious organisations" to charity tribunal', *Third Sector* (28 January 2013), online: <https://www.thirdsector.co.uk/charity-commission-asked-attorney-general-refer-closed-religious-organisations-charity-tribunal/governance/article/1168404>.
51 Whyatt, *supra* note 47.
52 Charity Commission, *supra* note 1 at 3 para 6.
53 Public Administration Select Committee, *supra* note 7 and *Independent Schools Council v Charity Commission for England and Wales* [2011] UKUT 421, (2011) ELR 529 [*Independent Schools Council*]
54 'Analysis: The Brethren – Regulator and church settle their differences', *Third Sector* (21 January 2014), 8 (Factiva) ['Analysis: The Brethren'].
55 Rowena Mason, 'Churches not necessarily for public good, says charity watchdog' *Telegraph* (8 November 2012), online: < https://www.telegraph.co.uk/journalists/rowena-mason/9654502/Churches-not-necessarily-for-public-good-says-charity-watchdog.html>
56 Charity Commission, *supra* note 1 at 3 para 9.
57 Decker & Harding, *supra* note 11 at 333.
58 House of Commons, Public Administration Select Committee, *supra* note 7 at 22 para 59.
59 These findings were later printed in newspapers in Australia: Michael Bachelard, 'Brethren Secrets', *Sydney Morning Herald* (18 June 2018); Good Weekend Magazine, 12 at 14. It is important to note that this article is currently subject to defamation proceedings against the newspaper and author; see *Plymouth Brethren (Exclusive Brethren) Christian Church v The Age Company Ltd; Plymouth Brethren (Exclusive Brethren) Christian Church v Fairfax Media Publications Pty Ltd* [2018] NSWCA 95 (7 May 2018). For the Brethren's response to the claims see Introvigne, *supra* note 12 at 109–10.

60 House of Lords, *Debates* (22 November 2012) at 2038–39.
61 House of Commons, *Debates* (19 December 2012) at 893–94.
62 McKay, *supra* note 12 at 244.
63 See e.g. Picarda, 'Charities Act 2011', *supra* note 11 at 147–48.
64 See e.g. McKay, *supra* note 12 at 245.
65 *Ibid*, at 245.
66 An acceptable judicial practice in such cases, as indicated in *Re Watson*. Further on this topic see James T. Richardson, 'Sociology and the new religions: "Brainwashing", the courts and religious freedom', in *Witnessing for Sociology: Sociologists in Court*, ed. Pamela J. Jenkins & Steve Kroll-Smith (Westport: Praeger, 1996), 115.
67 In the interest of transparency, the author wishes to make it clear that he wrote an expert report and was reasonably offered payment for expenses and his time. He declined such payment. He is uncertain whether his report was ultimately used during the negotiations. He was provided with *all* written material requested from the Brethren to assist with his research; however, subsequently he became aware of the existence of some material – in particular searchable electronic indexes to Brethren ministry – which he was not aware of at the time. Subsequent research by the author of these indexes has satisfied him that material he requested during this case pertaining to his report was complete according to these indexes.
68 E.g. Partnership UK.
69 See Introvigne, *supra* note 12 at 107 note 38.
70 See Wilson, 'Exclusive Brethren' *supra* note 46 at 316–17.
71 Charity Commission, *supra* note 1 at 9 para 34.
72 The Trustees of Preston Down Trust, *Deed of Variation* (2014), 3 and 6, online (pdf): https://assets.publishing.service.gov.uk/government/uploads/system/uploads/attachment_data/file/336112/preston_down_trust_full_decision.pdf.
73 Charity Commission, *supra* note 1 at 9 para 35.
74 E.g. Stephen Cook, 'Will a leopard change its spots?' *Third Sector* (14 January 2014), 14.
75 Charity Commission, *supra* note 1 at 9 para 35.
76 Introvigne, *supra* note 12 at 92. McKay, *supra* note 12 at 245.
77 Charity Commission, *supra* note 1 at 17 para 78.
78 Charity Commission for England and Wales, *The Advancement of Religion for the Public Benefit* (Liverpool: Charity Commission, 2011), 20–21.
79 Charity Commission, *supra* note 1 at 16 para 67–69. See the discussion in Bernard Doherty & Laura Dyason, 'Revision or Re-Branding? The Plymouth Brethren Christian Church in Australia under Bruce D. Hales 2002–2016', in *Radical Changes in Minority Religions*, ed. Eileen Barker & Beth Singler (New York: Routledge, forthcoming).
80 On the Rapid Relief Teams generally see online: <https://uk.rapidreliefteam.org/>.
81 Charity Commission, *supra* note 1 at 17–18 para 79–81.
82 See Wilson, 'Exclusive Brethren', *supra* note 46.
83 Charity Commission, *supra* note 1 at 17 para 79.
84 *Ibid*, at 17 paras 45–53 esp. 50–53. *Neville Estates Ltd v Madden* [1962] ch 832 [*Neville Estates v Madden*]. *Joyce and Others v Ashfield Municipal Council* [1975] NSWLR 744 [*Joyce v Ashfield Municipal Council*]. On equivalence of these two cases see e.g. Harding, *supra* note 10 at 21 and Hubert Picarda, 'Thornton v Howe: A Sound Principle or a Seminal Case Past its Best Buy Date?' 2013–2014 16 CLPR 85 at 103 [Picarda, 'Thornton v Howe'].
85 Charity Commission, *supra* note 78 at 27–28.
86 O'Halloran, *supra* note 5 at 151.
87 Charity Commission, *supra* note 78 at 28.
88 *National Anti-Vivisection Society v Inland Revenue Commissioners* [1948] AC 31 at 99 [*National Anti Vivisection v IRC*].
89 Charity Commission, *supra* note 1 *at* 10–11 paras 39–43.
90 *National Anti Vivisection Society v IRC*, *supra* note 7 at 99.

91 *Ibid*, at para 59.
92 Charity Commission, *supra* note 1 at 19 para 88.
93 Charity Commission, *supra* note 1 at 19–21 paras 89–92.
94 *Ibid*, at 19–20 para 89.
95 E.g. Doherty & Knowles, *supra* note 2.
96 Charity Commission, *supra* note 1 at 20 para 90.
97 *Ibid*, at 21 para 92.
98 For this summary see Trustees of Preston Down Trust, *supra* note 71 at Schedule 2, 6 (3–7).
99 Charity Commission, *supra* note 1 at 21 para 93.
100 *Holmes*, *supra* note 2.
101 Charity Commission for England and Wales, *supra* note 1 at 13 para 96.
102 *Ibid*, at 13 para 97.
103 For various reactions see 'Analysis: The Brethren', *supra* note 54 at 8.
104 *Ibid*, at 8.
105 See online: http://wikipeebia.com/
106 Beckford, *supra* note 8 at 69–93.
107 See Laura Dyason & Bernard Doherty, 'The Modern Hydra: The Exclusive Brethren's Online Critics' (2015) 233:2 St Mark's Review 116.
108 Introvigne, *supra* note 12 at 92.
109 See e.g. Tim Smedley, 'Charity Commission and the Voluntary Sector: What has gone wrong?' *The Guardian* (14 January 2015), online: <https://www.theguardian.com/voluntary-sector-network/2015/jan/14/charity-commission-and-the-voluntary-sector-what-has-gone-wrong>.
110 See Alexi Mostrous, 'Charity at heart of massive tax avoidance scam', *The Times* (31 January 2013), online: <https://www.thetimes.co.uk/article/charity-at-heart-of-massive-tax-avoidance-scam-r3gvn0p7mrz>. For further details see National Audit Office, *Report by the Comptroller and Auditor General Charity Commission – The Cup Trust* (2013), online (pdf): <https://www.nao.org.uk/wp-content/uploads/2013/11/10299-001-Cup-Trust-Book1.pdf>.
111 Dyason & Doherty, *supra* note 107 at 125–26.
112 An example here was Frank Cranmer's detailed coverage on his *Law and Religion* UK blog, online: <http://www.lawandreligionuk.com/>.
113 Picarda, 'Charities Act 2011', *supra* note 11 at 148.
114 Bill Kember & Alexi Mostrous, 'Extreme Sect Secures £13m tax breaks', *The Times* (17 March 2015), 1. 'Inquiry at Christian sect schools that banned books', *The Times* (18 March 2015), 1.
115 See Doherty & Knowles, *supra* note 2.
116 Billy Kember, 'Religious Sect Campaigns and Prays for the Tories', *The Times* (6 May 2015), 1.
117 'Letters: Brethren decision', *The Times* (19 March 2015), 36.
118 'Letters: Brethren furore', *The Times* (21 March 2015), 28.
119 'Third Sector at Large – A clarification from the regulator and rivers of blood at WaterAid', *Third Sector* (1 May 2016), 12.
120 Charity Commission for England and Wales, *Case Report Preston Down Trust (1155382)* (15 February 2016) online (pdf): <https://assets.publishing.service.gov.uk/government/uploads/system/uploads/attachment_data/file/500364/preston_down_trust.pdf>.
121 Charity Commission for England and Wales, *Plymouth Brethren Gospel Hall Trusts: Group Case Report* (29 August 2017), online: https://www.gov.uk/government/publications/plymouth-brethren-gospel-hall-trusts-group-case-report/plymouth-brethren-gospel-hall-trusts.
122 Email correspondence of Steve Knowles to Bernard Doherty on Thursday, 5 July 2018.
123 Charity Commission, *supra* note 120 at 3.
124 *Ibid*, at 4.
125 *Ibid*, at 5.
126 Charity Commission, *supra* note 121.

127 *Ibid.*
128 *Ibid.*
129 The author has personally witnessed the activities of the Rapid Relief Team, a PBCC charity founded internationally in the wake of the PDT case, in Australia where they are fast becoming a regular fixture at community events and in times of crisis in areas where the Brethren have a sizeable numeric presence. They also make a very nice burger.
130 In the wake of the PDT decision the Brethren have threatened or initiated legal proceedings against a handful of vociferous public critics. These matters remain *sub judice* and whether they relate directly to the PDT settlement is a matter of conjecture.
131 Harding, *supra* note 10 at 169 note 61.
132 Hubert Picarda, 'New Religions as Charities' (1981) 131 New Law Journal 436 at 37.
133 Hubert Picarda, 'Religion Public Benefit and the Preston Down Trust' (2016) 1 Charity Law Bulletin, online: <http://www.bloomsburylawonline.com/2016/01/28/charity-law-bulletin/> [Picarda, 'Religion Public Benefit'].
134 Ridge, *supra* note 6 at 1071.
135 *Ibid*, at 1078.
136 Citing Neil Summerton in 'Analysis: The Brethren', *supra* note 54 at 8.
137 Decker & Harding, *supra* note 11 at 329.
138 Ridge, *supra* note 6 at 1071.
139 See e.g. Smedley, *supra* note 109.
140 Decker and Harding, *supra* note 11 at 329; Picarda, 'Religion Public Benefit', *supra* note 133.
141 O'Halloran, *supra* note 5 at 141–42.
142 As noted by Picarda, 'Thornton v Howe', *supra* note 84 at 102.
143 It suffices to say here that a process akin to a church-based heresy trial which Baroness Berridge proposed conducted by the Church of England would have been entirely inappropriate, not least in dealing with a group whose founders seceded from the Established Church.
144 The late sociologist Bryan Wilson suggested they should not. See B. R. Wilson, *The Social Dimensions of Sectarianism: Sects and New Religious Movements in Contemporary Society* (Oxford: Clarendon Paperbacks, 1992) at 19.
145 Lucas & Robinson, *supra* note 19 at 187.

Part III

PUBLIC BENEFIT AND THE ADVANCEMENT OF RELIGION IN CANADA

Chapter Six

ADVANCING RELIGION IN A 'NEUTRAL' STATE: UNDERSTANDING RELIGION AS A CONSTITUTIONAL GOOD

Derek B.M. Ross* and Ian N. Sinke**

> *It is apparent, then, that both the advancement of education and the advancement of religion are firmly and favourably rooted in the public policy of our law. Moreover, it is not stretching matters to say that even in the modern, secular age the advancement of religion is rooted in our law and in our Constitution. That policy is readily discernible in the declaratory preambles to the Canadian Bill of Rights [...] and the Canadian Charter of Rights and Freedoms which both affirm that Canada 'is founded upon principles that' acknowledge and recognize 'the supremacy of God', and 'the rule of law'. That is not to say that our country is even remotely similar to a theocracy such as have been established in past ages and in the present day in some countries. Far from it. We do not have any established church or State religion. Those Canadians who profess atheism, agnosticism or the philosophy of secularism are just as secure in their civil rights and freedoms as are those who profess religion. So it is that while Canada may aptly be characterized as a secular State, yet, being declared by both Parliament and the Constitution to be founded upon principles which recognize 'the supremacy of God', it cannot be said that our public policy is entirely neutral in terms of 'the advancement of religion' [...] The legal and constitutional recognition of God necessarily imports and involves a polity which leans in favour of belief, or faith—that is, the profession of religion among our people.*
>
> <div align="right">Justice Muldoon, Federal Court of Canada, <i>McBurney v Canada</i>[1]</div>

Part I: Introduction

Canadian law recognizes the 'advancement of religion' as a charitable purpose, such that organizations which 'advance religion' enjoy numerous advantages.[2] As reflected in the Federal Court's comments above, this has thus far been deemed constitutionally sound. However, it has been observed that recent legal trends appear to be rendering the 'advancement of religion category increasingly vulnerable to arguments for its demise'.[3] Indeed, as *Charter* jurisprudence continues to emphasize the importance of 'state neutrality', in which the state must 'neither favour nor hinder any religion'[4], the law's recognition of 'advancement of religion' as a charitable purpose may increasingly face

---

* LL.B. (Western), LL.M. (Toronto), Executive Director and General Counsel, Christian Legal Fellowship.

** B.Eng. (McMaster), J.D. (Toronto), Student-at-Law, Lawyers' Professional Indemnity Company. With great thanks and appreciation to Sarah Mix-Ross for her helpful review, feedback and input on earlier drafts, to Tatiana Emanuel and Paulina Lee for their research assistance on a number of issues discussed in this article, and to Barry Bussey, Amy Ross, Jonathan Turner and Ruth Ross for their kind review and comments.

challenges. In light of the Supreme Court of Canada's (SCC) declaration that 'the state must neither encourage nor discourage any form of religious conviction whatsoever',[5] is it still appropriate to say, as the Federal Court did in *McBurney v R*, that Canada 'leans in favour of belief, or faith'[6]?

More specifically, can organizations[7] that exist solely for the purpose of advancing religion continue to receive beneficial treatment? Can the government 'support religion over non-religion' without running afoul of the Constitution?

Academic discourse is emerging on these questions. Kathryn Chan, for example, has developed helpful scholarship on how to 'articulate the "conceptual public benefit" of religion in constitutionally "neutral" terms'.[8] This chapter seeks to contribute to the discussion by examining, from a constitutional law perspective, whether policy decisions (such as favourable tax and legal treatment for religious organizations) can be rooted in the notion that religion is a social and public good, without violating the duty of state neutrality. This analysis will explore the role that religion serves, both for individuals and society at large, through the lens of the Constitution as a *whole* rather than a single provision or precept. Specifically, it will consider whether the advancement of religion is consistent with the interests underlying the rights and freedoms guaranteed by the Constitution of Canada, as well as the societal commitments that the *Charter* expresses. The purpose of this chapter is not to conduct a detailed *Charter* analysis of any particular piece of legislation or state action but to examine how the *Charter* informs our understanding of the advancement of religion in Canada.

This chapter is divided into four sections. The first section, 'Interpreting the *Charter* Holistically', will present a brief overview of the Supreme Court's approach to 'state neutrality' in its jurisprudence and propose a holistic analytical framework for constitutional interpretation. The second section, 'Religion and Individual Freedoms', will discuss the relationship between freedom of religion and the *Charter*'s other fundamental freedoms, and how religion helps individuals pursue personal autonomy and self-realization. The third section, 'Religion and the Cultivation of a Multicultural Society', will explore religion's benefit for society as a whole, and specifically, how the advancement of religion supports 'the preservation and enhancement of the multicultural heritage of Canadians'. The final section, 'Religion and the Preservation of a "Secular Humility"', will discuss the *Charter*'s preambular references to 'the supremacy of God and the rule of law'.

This chapter concludes that, read as a whole, the Constitution recognizes religion as a public and social good. Far from undermining *Charter* rights, state support for the advancement of religion (in a non-sectarian manner) is not only consistent with the *Charter* but also a means of furthering Canada's constitutional commitments.

Part II: Interpreting the *Charter* Holistically

Although the purpose of this chapter is not to analyse the constitutionality of any specific legislative provision or state action, it is important to consider in more detail the objections that could be brought on *Charter* grounds against the advancement of religion as a discrete head of charity.

The Charter's Relevance to Charity Law

As Mayo Moran has observed, 'The relationship between the *Charter* and the definition of charity is not straightforward'.[9] The *Charter* applies to state action, chiefly legislation and administrative action.[10]

For purposes of this discussion, the *Charter* is most relevant to legislation such as the *Income Tax Act*.[11] The *Income Tax Act* confers favourable tax status on charitable organizations and those who make donations to them; the definition of 'charity', for the purposes of the *Act*, is derived from the common law.[12] The Canada Revenue Agency (CRA) indicates that, in determining whether an organization is 'charitable', it relies on the common law definition of charity[13] – specifically, the House of Lords' decision in *Commissioners for the Special Purposes of the Income Tax v Pemsel*.[14] That case determined that, in order to be considered a 'charity', an organization must further at least one of four 'charitable purposes': the relief of poverty, the advancement of education, the advancement of religion and 'other purposes beneficial to the community, not falling under any of the preceding heads'.[15] This chapter is concerned with the third head of charity: 'advancement of religion'.

Courts have interpreted 'advancing religion' to require that an organization take 'positive' and 'targeted'[16] steps towards 'the promotion of spiritual teaching in a wide sense, and the maintenance of the doctrines in which it rests, and the observances that serve to promote and manifest it'.[17] As Kathryn Chan has observed, '[w]hile the common law has never proffered a comprehensive definition of charitable "religion", the tradition has historically confined the term to belief systems that recognize a supreme deity'.[18] Thus, 'belief systems that are agnostic or hostile towards religion' do not qualify under the 'advancing religion' head of charity, nor does the 'promotion of secularism and the discouragement of supernatural belief'.[19] CRA's guidelines on the subject summarize the requirements as follows:

> Advancing religion in the charitable sense means manifesting, promoting, sustaining, or increasing belief in a religion's three key attributes, which are: faith in a higher unseen power such as a God, Supreme Being, or Entity; worship or reverence; and a particular and comprehensive system of doctrines and observances.[20]

Thus, the common law approach to advancing religion, as incorporated in Canada's laws and tax administration, appears to favour religion over anti-religion (or irreligion) by granting tax benefits and legal privileges to institutions that advance religious belief.[21] A question emerging as a result of evolving interpretations of 'state neutrality' is whether such a regime would continue to pass constitutional muster.[22] We turn now to a discussion of that question.

The Duty of State Neutrality

If the 'advancement of religion' head of charity were to be challenged under the *Charter*, it would likely be challenged on freedom of religion grounds. On initial consideration, this may seem somewhat odd; unlike the American Constitution, Canada's *Charter* lacks an 'establishment clause' or any other provision explicitly requiring a 'separation of church and state'. The SCC's early freedom of religion jurisprudence held that section 2(a) of the *Charter* served to protect freedom of religion and 'freedom from religion': in other words, section 2(a) protects the freedom to exercise whatever religion one chooses, as well as freedom from state compulsion to practice a particular religion.[23]

However, in recent decisions,[24] the Court's approach to religious freedom has been described as undergoing a 'shift' from a conception based on liberty to one based on equality.[25] Richard Moon explains that '[a]ccording to the courts, the freedom does not simply prohibit state coercion in matters of religion or conscience; it requires also that the state treat religious belief systems or communities in an equal or even-handed manner'.[26] As the Court stated in *SL v Commission scolaire des Chênes*:

> [S]tate neutrality is assured when the state neither favours nor hinders any particular religious belief, that is, when it shows respect for all postures towards religion, including that of having no religious beliefs whatsoever, while taking into account the competing constitutional rights of the individuals affected.[27]

The issue of state neutrality was further elucidated by the Supreme Court in 2015, in *Mouvement laïque québécois v Saguenay (City)*.[28] The case involved a municipal council which customarily read a Christian prayer before beginning their meetings. An atheist who attended the meetings brought a challenge under the Quebec *Charter of Human Rights and Freedoms*, and the Court found that the practice of reading the prayer violated the Quebec *Charter* due to the state's duty of religious neutrality.

However, it is important to read *Saguenay*'s discussion of religious neutrality in its specific context. The Court was concerned about the '*state's observance* of a religious practice' and its '*adhering* to a particular belief'.[29] The primary issue was that state officials were directly taking part in, and expecting others to join, a sectarian religious exercise – one which 'consciously profess[ed] a theistic faith' – during a government activity.[30] This is substantively different from the state facilitating opportunities, in an 'even-handed manner'[31] for a plurality of private, faith communities – independent of the government – to each pursue their own religious exercises. Properly read, *Saguenay* is a case that limits the state's direct and active participation in a particular religious practice but not necessarily its ability to support the enhancement of religious life for its citizens in a general and neutral sense (e.g. through tax benefits). Indeed, nothing in *Saguenay* explicitly prohibits the state from granting benefits (such as tax-exempt status) to religious organizations. As Richard Moon has observed:

> The state may also achieve a degree of neutrality by providing even-handed support to the different religious practices or institutions in the community, as well as to non-religious alternatives. Indeed, the Canadian courts have held that the Charter does not preclude the state from providing financial support to religious schools or acknowledging the practices or celebrations of different religious groups as long as it does so in an even-handed way.[32]

Regardless, in the aftermath of *Saguenay*, it is not difficult to conceive of the argument that legislation like the *Income Tax Act*, which provides financial advantages to organizations that advance religion, constitutes a *prima facie* violation of the unwritten duty of religious neutrality[33] to the extent that it favours religion over non-religion, or belief over non-belief.

This raises two questions. First, does the duty of religious neutrality require the government to be not only neutral as between and among religions but also *about* religion generally?[34] Can the government enact policies that recognize that religion is a public and social good?[35]

Second, even if the 'advancing religion' head of charity were to be found to violate section 2(a) (i.e. freedom *from* religion), can the violation be justified under section 1 of the *Charter*? That is, is there a 'pressing and substantial objective' which is served by giving favourable status to organizations which advance religion?

The answers to these questions require a careful examination of the Canadian Constitution and what it says as a whole about religion and its contribution to the public good.[36]

A Holistic Approach to Constitutional Interpretation

The duty of state neutrality is not an isolated, free-standing concept – it exists, as do all *Charter* protections, in connection with other provisions and in the context of a larger constitutional order.[37]

It is trite law that 'statutory provisions are to be read in their immediate context and in the context of the Act as a whole'.[38] The *Constitution Acts*, constitutional though they be, are Acts all the same, and Driedger's well-known and oft-recited maxim applies equally to them as to another statute. This was confirmed by the Supreme Court in *Montreal (City) v Quebec*:

> In reviewing the relevant provisions of the *Charter*, it is important to bear in mind the common rule of interpretation that statutory provisions are to be read in their immediate context *and in the context of the Act as a whole* [...] As I will explain, a holistic and purposive reading of the *Charter* leads me to the conclusion that ss. 18.2 and 20 of the *Charter* can and should be read in harmony.[39]

Supreme Court jurisprudence has consistently affirmed that constitutional provisions do not exist in a vacuum and must be interpreted in light of all provisions with which they coexist. In *Trinity Western University v British Columbia College of Teachers*, for example, the Court observed that the scope of section 15 must be interpreted in a manner consistent 'with freedom of conscience and religion, which co-exist with the right to equality'.[40] In *Amselem*, Justice Iacobucci affirmed, 'The ultimate protection of any particular *Charter* right must be measured in relation to other rights and with a view to the underlying context in which the apparent conflict arises'.[41] Justice Lamer, in *Dubois v The Queen*, also stated, 'Our constitutional *Charter* must be construed as a system where "Every component contributes to the meaning as a whole, and the whole gives meaning to its parts" [...] The courts must interpret each section of the *Charter* in relation to the others'.[42] Similarly, the Supreme Court affirmed in *Health Services and Support – Facilities Subsector Bargaining Assn v British Columbia* that the *Charter* 'should be interpreted in a way that maintains its underlying values and its internal coherence'.[43]

However, the contextual approach is not limited to the *Charter*. Rather, the entire Constitution – including both the *Constitution Act, 1867*[44] and the *Constitution Act, 1982*[45] – ought to be read as one coherent whole. Justice Louise Arbour's comments in dissent (though not on this point)[46] in *Gosselin v Quebec* also confirm this approach:

> Quite apart from its specific relation to the right to life guaranteed in s. 7, the structure and purpose of the *Charter* also provide relevant context for the interpretation of *Charter* rights more generally. This idea was implicit in this Court's dicta regarding constitutional interpretation in *Reference re Secession of Quebec* [...]:
>
>> Our Constitution has an internal architecture, or what the majority of this Court in *OPSEU v. Ontari o (Attorney General)* [...] called a 'basic constitutional structure'. *The individual elements of the Constitution are linked to the others, and must be interpreted by reference to the structure of the Constitution as a whole.*
>
> What holds for 'the Constitution as a whole' also holds for its constituent parts, including the *Charter*. *Individual elements in the Charter are linked to one another, and must be understood by reference to the structure of the Charter as a whole.* Support for this interpretive approach can be located in *Big M Drug Mart* [...]: 'the purpose of [any] right or freedom [...] is to be sought by reference to the character and the larger objects of the *Charter* itself'.[47]

From this passage, two important principles can be drawn to guide an analysis of the state's duty of religious neutrality and its relationship to the advancement of religion as a head of charity. First, the protections of the *Charter* – including the duty of state neutrality – are to be interpreted in their full context and in relation to other constitutional provisions: this includes not just the rest of the *Charter* but also the *Constitution Act, 1867* and the *Constitution Act, 1982*. Second, the provisions of the *Charter* are to be examined in relation to the 'character and larger objects of the *Charter* itself'. The former principle will be more relevant to Part IV, and the latter to Part III.

Part III: Religion and Individual Freedoms

As we have seen, the provisions of the *Charter* are to be interpreted in relation to the 'character and larger objects of the *Charter*'. What is that character, and what are those larger objects? While the *Charter* itself is largely silent as to its underlying principles (with the exception of provisions such as section 27, discussed in Part IV), there is considerable jurisprudence on the values and principles that are said to provide the basis for the *Charter*'s protections.

Discussing these values which make up the 'free and democratic society' described in section 1 of the *Charter*, Dickson CJC writes in *Oakes*:

> The Court must be guided by the values and principles essential to a free and democratic society which I believe embody, to name but a few, respect for the inherent dignity of the human person, commitment to social justice and equality, *accommodation of a wide variety of beliefs, respect for cultural and group identity, and faith in social and political institutions which enhance the participation of individuals and groups in society*. The underlying values and principles of a free and democratic society are the genesis of the rights and freedoms guaranteed by the *Charter* and

the ultimate standard against which a limit on a right or freedom must be shown, despite its effect, to be reasonable and demonstrably justified.[48]

Chief Justice Dickson does not provide a list of 'social and political institutions' which he believes 'enhance the participation of individuals and groups in society', but further jurisprudence has since expanded on the concept. More attention has been given to political, rather than social, institutions. For example, the Supreme Court has applied Dickson CJC's statement to the electoral process[49] and political parties[50] as fundamental institutions. In *R v Advance Cutting and Coring*, Bastarache J (in dissent) would have recognized labour unions as a fundamental social and political institution,[51] and in *Egan v Canada*, some Supreme Court justices would have recognized marriage and social security as fundamental institutions.[52]

Given the integral part that religion plays in Canada's multicultural heritage,[53] it is reasonable to suggest that 'religious communities' also qualify as fundamental social institutions in Canada. Indeed, religious organizations and institutions uniquely 'enhance the participation of individuals and groups in society' in at least two important ways: (1) they allow for the realization of individual freedom and personal autonomy, and (2) they facilitate the development and transmission of independent thinking and beliefs between generations.[54]

(1) Realization of Individual Freedom and Personal Autonomy

Self-definition and individual fulfilment are at the core of the *Charter*'s individual freedoms. The freedom of association, for instance, which protects religious communities,[55] has been described by the Supreme Court as existing 'to preserve and promote the existence of associations which assist in the attainment of individual goals and individual self-fulfilment'.[56] Self-fulfilment is also one of the three core human goods that underlie freedom of expression.[57]

Likewise, the Supreme Court has long recognized that religion is a path to self-definition and individual fulfilment. In *Syndicat Northcrest v Amselem*, Iacobucci J described religion as being 'about freely and deeply held personal convictions or beliefs connected to an individual's spiritual faith and integrally linked to one's self-definition and spiritual fulfilment'.[58] He quotes Dickson CJC's statement in *Big M Drug Mart* that '[w]ith the *Charter*, it has become the right of every Canadian to work out for himself or herself what his or her religious obligations, if any, should be'.[59] Justice Iacobucci states that '[t]his understanding is consistent with a personal or subjective conception of freedom of religion, one that is integrally linked with an individual's self-definition and fulfilment and is a function of personal autonomy and choice, elements which undergird the right'.[60]

Religious organizations provide the means by which this self-definition and fulfilment are pursued. As Jane Calderwood Norton states:

> Without the infrastructure provided by religious organizations, a person cannot pursue a religious way of life. If a person does not have the option of a religious way of life then they do not have an adequate range of options from which to live an autonomous life. Harm to religious organizations therefore results in harm to personal autonomy.[61]

The Supreme Court's recent comments in *Trinity Western* reflected this approach, where the majority stated, 'The ability of religious adherents to come together and create cohesive communities of belief and practice is an important aspect of religious freedom under s. 2(a)'.[62]

This is also reflected in the jurisprudence of the European Court of Human Rights, which has affirmed that religious communities facilitate 'the effective enjoyment of the right to freedom of religion by all its active members'[63] and that without protection for religious communities, 'all other aspects of the individual's freedom of religion would become vulnerable'.[64]

Religious organizations play an instrumental role in individuals' self-fulfilment: 'Without a religious group's ability to self-define, the option of a religious life is meaningless'.[65] As the Supreme Court recognized in *Big M Drug Mart*, individuals must have the ability to work out for themselves what their religious obligations should be and to freely pursue those commitments. But this cannot be done in a vacuum. It is often only with the support and direction of religious organizations that the seeking soul finds satisfaction.

(2) Formation and Transmission of Beliefs between Generations

Religious organizations not only provide a necessary support for individual self-definition and fulfilment: they also facilitate the collective formation and transmission of religious and moral beliefs between generations. This, in turn, contributes to broader societal goals such as the pursuit of truth, enhanced civic engagement and social cohesion.

As Abella J noted in *Loyola High School v Quebec (Attorney General)*, the Supreme Court has repeatedly affirmed that freedom of religion has 'both an individual and a collective dimension'.[66] She quotes *Amselem*, where Bastarache J (in dissent, but not on this point) quoted Professor Timothy Macklem:

> [R]eligions are necessarily collective endeavours. [...] It follows that any genuine freedom of religion must protect, not only individual belief, but *the institutions and practices that permit the collective development* and expression of that belief.[67]

Justice Abella concludes: 'The freedom of religion of individuals cannot flourish without freedom of religion for the organizations through which those individuals express their religious practices *and through which they transmit their faith*'.[68] As Kathleen Brady has observed, religious organizations 'play an essential role in shaping the beliefs that individuals hold as they teach and transmit ideas from one generation to the next, and they are also the vehicles for the formation and development of religious doctrine'.[69]

(a) Formation of ideas and beliefs

Doctrine is essential to every religion; it is the focal point around which adherents gather. Religious organizations are essential to the development of doctrine. Religious doctrine is seldom developed by individuals working independently; rather, it is formed through the discussion and debate that is necessary, even inherent, to life in a religious community.

As Kathleen Brady states, religion is developed by 'persons in community as group members work together to interpret, refine and reform inherited beliefs and formulate new ones'.⁷⁰ While sometimes this development of belief occurs through painful disagreement, contention and schism, 'the formulation and evolution of religious doctrine would be impossible without this conversation, debate, disagreement and sometimes deep conflict'.⁷¹

However, while the formation of doctrine is necessary for the existence of a religious group, the process of forming doctrine is also valuable to society generally. As Brady states:

> For example, who would disagree that social peace and stability, the preservation of life, the advancement of learning, the protection of health, and fairness and equality are all social and political goods. However, what do these goods require? Giving content to these values is much less obvious [...] We cannot resolve these disagreements and related questions of social benefit and harm without considering the purposes and goals of social and political life and our duties to one another. These are the truths that religion seeks to understand better [...]
>
> Indeed, religious groups do more than speak to us about social and political truth. Religious communities seek to live out their social visions in their internal community life, and it is in this form of witness that the power of new ideas may be most evident.⁷²

(b) Transmission of ideas and beliefs

Canada's international human rights obligations protect the right to transmit religious beliefs and teachings from one generation to the next.⁷³ Both the *International Covenant on Civil and Political Rights* and the *International Covenant on Economic, Social and Cultural Rights*, for example, protect parents' rights to 'ensure the religious and moral education of their children in conformity with their own convictions'.⁷⁴ This principle was also confirmed by the Supreme Court in *Loyola*.⁷⁵

The Quebec *Charter* contains similar protections, stating that '[p]arents or the persons acting in their stead have a right to give their children a religious and moral education in keeping with their convictions'.⁷⁶ The Supreme Court also confirmed in *SL* that '[t]he right of parents to bring up their children in their faith is part of the freedom of religion guaranteed by the *Canadian Charter*'.⁷⁷

Religious organizations facilitate the realization of these rights by providing the primary means by which individuals can pass on their beliefs to the next generation. Justice LeBel was cognizant of this in *Hutterian Brethren* when (in dissent, but not on this point) he stated:

> Religion is about religious beliefs, but also about religious relationships. The present appeal signals the importance of this aspect. It raises issues about belief, but also about the *maintenance of communities* of faith. We are discussing the fate not only of a group of farmers, but of a community that shares a common faith and a way of life that is viewed by its members as *a way of living that faith and of passing it on to future generations*.⁷⁸

Timothy Macklem expresses a similar view on the importance of religious institutions to the 'survival and development' of religious beliefs:

> The presence of such institutions and practices is essential to the survival and development of faith in religious beliefs, the existence and nourishment of which depends first, upon contact

with the sources of revelation, second, upon the guidance of clerics (for want of a better word), and third, upon the commitment of other believers.[79]

Religious communities are also vital to protecting and preserving the rights and identities of religious persons, especially those who are members of minority faith communities. This has been acknowledged by the European Court of Human Rights:

> [F]reedom of association is particularly important for persons belonging to minorities [...] '[A] pluralist and genuinely democratic society should not only respect the ethnic, cultural, linguistic and religious identity of each person belonging to a national minority, but also create appropriate conditions enabling them to express, preserve and develop this identity'. Indeed, forming an association in order to express and promote its identity may be instrumental in helping a minority to preserve and uphold its rights.[80]

Similarly, in the *Alberta Reference*, Dickson CJC highlighted the importance of 'various collectivities' in preserving an individual's rights and identity: 'Just as the individual is incapable of resisting political domination without the support of persons with similar values, so too is he or she, in isolation, incapable of resisting domination, over the long term, in many other aspects of life'.[81]

In short, as Jane Calderwood Norton has observed, 'religious organizations are often central to the realization of religious freedom', and '[o]ne cannot live a religious life – in other words have religious freedom – without the freedom to associate with other like-minded individuals'.[82] Such associations provide the necessary 'infrastructure' which facilitates the exercise of freedom of religion, freedom of association, and freedom of [religious] expression.[83] This, in turn, advances autonomy and individual fulfilment by supporting the 'individual's freedom to choose the path to self-actualization'.[84] A strong case can be made, therefore, that support for organizations devoted to the advancement of religion is not in opposition to the principles underlying the *Charter* but an important means of promoting them, as well as the *Charter*'s specific protections for freedom of religion, expression, and association.

Part IV: Religion and the Cultivation of a Multicultural Society

The holistic analysis of the *Charter* employed in Part III above dealt mostly with the principles which undergird the *Charter*'s substantive provisions. This section considers the application of other specific provisions of the *Charter*, and the rest of the Constitution, to an interpretation of 'state neutrality'.

An example of the Supreme Court engaging in exactly such a holistic constitutional analysis can be drawn from Dickson CJC's reasons in the *Alberta Reference*.[85] Chief Justice Dickson, holding that the *Charter* freedom of association comprehended a right to strike, called for a more expansive understanding of section 2:

> I am unable to regard s. 2 as embodying purely political freedoms. Paragraph (*a*), which protects freedom of conscience and religion is quite clearly not exclusively political in nature. It would, moreover, be unsatisfactory to overlook our Constitution's history of giving special

recognition to collectivities or communities of interest other than the government and political parties. *Sections 93 and 133 of the* Constitution Act, 1867 *and ss. 16–24, 25, 27 and 29 of the* Charter, *dealing variously with denominational schools, language rights, aboriginal rights, and our multicultural heritage implicitly embody an awareness of the importance of various collectivities in the pursuit of educational, linguistic, cultural and social as well as political ends.*[86]

Chief Justice Dickson's remarks are noteworthy for several reasons. First, as in *Oakes*, he continues to recognize 'the importance of various collectivities' in the pursuit of diverse goals, both social and political. In the following paragraph, he again stresses the foundational role that association, including religious association, plays in society: 'Through association, individuals have been able to participate in determining and controlling the immediate circumstances of their lives, and the rules, mores and principles which govern the communities in which they live'.[87]

Second, Dickson CJC's reliance on various provisions of the *Constitution Act, 1867* and the *Charter* in his interpretation of section 2(d) exemplifies a holistic constitutional analysis. He adopts a similar approach to interpreting freedom of religion in *Big M Drug Mart*, where he emphasizes that 'various provisions of the *Charter* must also be considered when analyzing the nature of the guarantee contained in s. 2'.[88] He lists three provisions in particular: section 27's affirmation of the multicultural heritage of Canada, section 29's preservation of the rights of denominational schools guaranteed under section 93 of the *Constitution Act, 1867*, and the preamble's reference to the Supremacy of God and the rule of law.[89] Each of these provisions – and their relevance to the relationship between state neutrality and public support of religious communities – is examined below.

Section 27 of the Charter

Section 27 of the *Charter* provides:

> This Charter shall be interpreted in a manner consistent with the preservation and enhancement of the multicultural heritage of Canadians.[90]

Section 27 has a somewhat unique place in the *Charter*. It is not a guarantee of any fundamental right or freedom; rather, as an interpretive provision, it serves as an indication of the importance of multiculturalism to the Canadian identity and a guide to the proper interpretation of the rights and freedoms in the rest of the *Charter*. The section was described by Cory J and Iacobucci J in *R v Zundel* (in dissent, but not on this point) as a 'magnificent recognition of the history of Canada and of an essential precept for the achievement of those elusive goals of justice and true equality':

> The section provides constitutional reinforcement of Canada's long standing policy of recognizing multiculturalism. It recognizes that all ethnic groups are entitled to recognition and to equal protection. It supports the protection of the collective rights, the cultural integrity and the dignity of Canada's ethnic groups. In doing so it enhances the dignity and sense of self worth of every individual member of those groups and thereby enhances society as a whole.[91]

A similar approach was adopted in *R v Keegstra*, where Dickson CJC (writing for the majority) described section 27 as a 'recognition that Canada possesses a multicultural society in which the diversity and richness of various cultural groups is a value to be protected and enhanced'.[92] Chief Justice Dickson further observed that section 27 had 'been used in a number of judgments of this Court, both as an aid in interpreting the definition of Charter rights and freedoms [...] and as an element in the s. 1 analysis'.[93]

Section 27 has been applied in cases involving language rights,[94] freedom of expression[95] and freedom of religion.[96] It was in the context of freedom of expression that Dickson CJC expressly connected section 27 with section 1. In *Canada (Human Rights Commission) v Taylor*, the Court was called to consider the constitutionality of hate speech laws. Chief Justice Dickson applied section 27 at the justification stage, stating that the value of multiculturalism 'further [magnified] the weightiness of Parliament's objective'[97] in enacting anti-hate-speech laws. He stated, 'These *Charter* provisions indicate that the guiding principles in undertaking the s. 1 inquiry include respect and concern for the dignity and equality of the individual *and a recognition that one's concept of self may in large part be a function of membership in a particular cultural group*'.[98]

Thus, section 27 further supports a legal understanding of religion as a public good – a religious community is a 'cultural group' advancing the democratic goods of dignity, equality, and self-identity for its individual members.

Multiculturalism and State Neutrality

In the context of freedom of religion claims, section 27 has typically been connected to the notion of state neutrality. One of the earliest applications of section 27 was in *R v Big M Drug Mart*, where the Court invoked the section to conclude that compelling Sunday Sabbath observance 'is not consistent with the preservation and enhancement of the multicultural heritage of Canadians'.[99] This connection was confirmed more recently in *SL*, where the Court stated that 'The concept of state religious neutrality in Canadian case law has developed alongside a growing sensitivity to the multicultural makeup of Canada and the protection of minorities'.[100]

Despite this connection between multiculturalism and state neutrality, however, there is an argument to be made that even-handed government support of the advancement of religion is also consistent with the *Charter*'s espousal of multiculturalism. By indirectly supporting religious communities (e.g. through tax relief), the state is contributing to the 'enhancement' of Canadian multiculturalism.

Section 27 is difficult to interpret because it 'is itself an interpretational principle'; it does not set out 'a coherent multiculturalism principle which courts can apply'.[101] However, constitutional scholar Joseph Magnet suggests that 'the key to unlocking the mysteries of section 27' is found in the development of 'mediating principles', that is, 'precepts which render useful and intelligible the words of the text'.[102]

Magnet offers several potential mediating principles. One is the principle of 'symbolic ethnicity', in which an individual 'completes a significant aspect of personality – forms a self – by voluntary identification with an ethnic group'.[103] This is reflected in Dickson CJC's observation that 'one's concept of self may in large part be a function of membership in a particular cultural group'.[104] Magnet explains that cultural activities, including 'religious occasions, provision of educational opportunities including language instruction and the like', thus implicate fundamental freedoms, and:

> [T]ouch on equality values through the allocation of governmental facilities such as school gymnasia, parks, or the expenditure of funds. In considering governmental obstruction of, or disinclination to facilitate, these and related activities, courts would have to assume an aroused sense of respect for the importance of symbolic ethnicity as a critical inspiration behind Canada's commitment to the multiculturalism principle.[105]

Another potential mediating principle is 'structural ethnicity', which refers to 'the capacity of a collectivity to perpetuate itself, control leakage in its membership, resist assimilation, and propagate its beliefs and practices'.[106] Support for structural ethnicity requires 'the creation, by the group or government, of an institutional infrastructure which can nurture the well-being of the group'.[107] Among the necessary elements of such an infrastructure, Magnet lists 'economic structures to dampen the assimilating pressures exerted by the mainstream economy' and 'mechanisms for propagation and transmission of the group's beliefs'.[108]

These understandings of multiculturalism echo the discussion in Part III. They substantiate the proposition that religion contributes to both individual fulfilment and the public good and that certain forms of state support for religious communities, whether economic or otherwise, are consistent with Canada's commitment to pursue a vibrant and pluralistic society.

Religious Communities Nurture Democracy and Enrich the Common Good

The discussion thus far has examined religious organizations primarily as social institutions. However, religious organizations also serve an important role in the 'proper functioning of democracy'[109] and therefore benefit the public as a whole.

Religious groups are instrumental in 'developing and modeling new and progressive visions for social life'.[110] As Brady states, religious groups 'develop and communicate new ideas that push the larger community forward':[111]

> Religious groups speak to us not only about the divine but also about the social and civic concerns of the larger community, and our collective progress depends upon the range of insights that different traditions provide, including insights that may initially seem unorthodox and incorrect [...] Indeed, religious groups do more than speak to us about social and political truth. Religious communities seek to live out their social visions in their internal community life, and it is in this form of witness that the power of new ideas may be most evident.[112]

The 'new ideas' that religion has helped to nurture and 'push forward' are now among some of Canada's most cherished, including some foundational principles on which our liberal democracy rests. The modern legal notion of equality, for example, is one largely developed from 'religious thought';[113] the same is true of the idea of 'human dignity', which forms the basis of our modern understanding of human rights. Consider, for example, the influential work of Jacques Maritain, a prominent Catholic scholar who played a significant role in the creation of the *Universal Declaration of Human Rights*. Maritain 'regarded human rights as correlative with moral obligations. Both rights and duties are rooted in the dignity of the person who is a spiritual whole made for God'.[114] In terms of religion's contribution to a liberal understanding of equality, Jeremy Waldron has observed, 'It may seem to us now that we can make do with a purely secular notion of human equality; but as a matter of ethical history, that notion has been shaped and fashioned on the basis of religion. That is where all the hard work was done'.[115] Indeed, Waldron concluded, 'I actually don't think it is clear that we – now – *can* shape and defend an adequate conception of basic human equality apart from some religious foundation'.[116]

The importance of religious and other communities to democracy has also been recognized by the European Court of Human Rights: '[W]here a civil society functions in a healthy manner, the participation of citizens in the democratic process is to a large extent achieved through belonging to associations in which they may integrate with each other and pursue common objectives collectively'.[117] For this reason, the European Court has repeatedly stressed that 'the autonomous existence of religious communities is indispensable for pluralism in a democratic society',[118] and this comment has been adopted by the SCC.[119]

Canadian jurisprudence has likewise affirmed the inherent value of religious association and recognized its importance to the common good. In the *Alberta Reference*, Dickson CJC emphasized that '[a]ssociation has always been the means through which [...] religious groups [...] have sought to attain their purposes and fulfil their aspirations'.[120] This passage was recently reaffirmed by the Supreme Court in *Mounted Police Association of Ontario v Canada (Attorney General)*, which described freedom of association as '[having] its roots in the protection of religious minority groups'.[121] Freedom of association for groups such as religious communities is 'essential to the development and maintenance of the vibrant civil society upon which our democracy rests' and 'permits the growth of a sphere of civil society largely free from state interference'.[122]

The Supreme Court has also recognized the valuable contributions that members of differing cultural groups can contribute to our democracy. In *R v S(RD)*, the Court considered a claim of reasonable apprehension of bias which was made against a judge who made comments about a witness based on her previous personal experiences. Justices L'Heureux-Dubé and McLachlin, in their concurring reasons, wrote:

> As discussed above, judges in a bilingual, multiracial and multicultural society will undoubtedly approach the task of judging from their varied perspectives. They will certainly have been shaped by, and have gained insight from, their different experiences, and cannot be expected to divorce themselves from these experiences on the occasion of their appointment to the bench. In fact, such a transformation would deny society the benefit of the valuable knowledge gained by the judiciary while they were members of the Bar.[123]

In the context of multiculturalism, the Supreme Court has specifically recognized the importance of religious voices to public discourse. In *R v NS*, the 2012 case where the

Court held that witnesses could wear religious head and face coverings in courtrooms in certain circumstances, LeBel J (in concurring reasons) said this:

> The religious neutrality of the state and of its institutions, including the courts and the justice system, protects the life and the growth of a public space open to all regardless of their beliefs, disbeliefs and unbeliefs. *Religions are voices among others in the public space*, which includes the courts.[124]

Finally, the free development of religious beliefs and opinions benefits democracy by nurturing independent thought, outside of the state's machinery, without which the freedom of thought, belief and opinion guaranteed by section 2(b) of the *Charter* would be impoverished. These freedoms are 'essential for the development of new and valuable ideas, including for social and political life'.[125]

As Brady observes, 'History gives us many illustrations of religious groups that have promoted ideas that were initially unpopular and divisive and, yet, are now recognised as important advances. Abolitionism and the civil rights movement come to mind'.[126] Religious groups 'are foremost among the institutions in society that address these broader ethical issues' such as 'our fundamental ethical responsibilities to one another as fellow humans and as members of a common social and political community'.[127]

The Supreme Court has thus long recognized the importance of religious freedom to both individual and community life, well before the advent of the *Charter*. As Justice Rand stated in 1953, in *Saumur v City of Quebec*, 'freedom of speech, religion and the inviolability of the person, are original freedoms which are at once the necessary attributes and modes of self-expression of human beings and the primary conditions of their community life within a legal order'.[128]

Section 93 of the Constitution Act, 1867

Another section of the Constitution relevant to a holistic analysis of state neutrality is section 93 of the *Constitution Act, 1867*, which deals with denominational schools. Section 93 is a product of the Confederation compromise between Protestants and Catholics in Upper and Lower Canada, which comprises a 'comprehensive code' of denominational school rights. It serves to protect the existing rights which were in place at the time of Confederation, namely, the right to Catholic education in Ontario and the right to Protestant education in Quebec.[129]

Section 93 has been the subject of two prominent Supreme Court decisions. The first, the 1987 *Reference Re Bill 30*,[130] arose in response to legislation proposed by the Ontario government, which extended funding to Catholic high schools in the province. Both the Ontario Court of Appeal and, on appeal, the Supreme Court, found that the Ontario government not only was permitted to fund Catholic schools but, in fact, was constitutionally required to do so, at least to the same extent as they funded the public school system.

More recently, in 1996, the Supreme Court decided *Adler v Ontario*, which involved a *Charter* challenge to the Ontario government's failure to fund private religious schools other than the Catholic school systems. The Court ruled that, because section 93 is a comprehensive code of denominational school rights, a finding that the province's failure to fund religious schools violated section 2(a) 'would be to hold one section of the Constitution violative of another'.[131]

While the majority did not find an *obligation* for the province to fund private religious education, they also did not find any impediment to the province's doing so, if it so chose. Justice Iacobucci, for the majority, said this:

> One thing should, however, be made clear. The province remains free to exercise its plenary power with regard to education in whatever way it sees fit, subject to the restrictions relating to separate schools imposed by s. 93(1). Section 93 grants to the province of Ontario the power to legislate with regard to public schools and separate schools. However, nothing in these reasons should be taken to mean that the province's legislative power is limited to these two school systems. In other words, the province could, if it so chose, pass legislation extending funding to denominational schools other than Roman Catholic schools without infringing the rights guaranteed to Roman Catholic separate schools under s. 93(1).[132]

The Supreme Court justices all agreed that the Ontario government would be constitutionally permitted to fund private schools. Going even further, L'Heureux-Dubé J, in dissent, found that the province was *obliged* to extend some public funding to private religious schools, stating that such funding would 'promote the value of religious tolerance in this context where some religious communities cannot be accommodated in the secular system'. She also observed, invoking section 27 of the *Charter*, that 'the preservation and continuation of the [religious educational] communities in question, form interests fundamental to the purposes of the *Charter*'.[133]

This is a sharp contrast to the approach taken under the American Constitution, where state funding of private religious institutions is prohibited as an infringement of the establishment clause.[134] But as Bruce Ryder states, 'ours is a different tradition, one that supports and encourages even-handed state support of religious and conscientious freedoms'.[135]

In short, section 93 jurisprudence affirms that the government has the constitutional freedom to extend financial support to religious organizations. The state's duty of neutrality must be understood in this broader constitutional context.

Part V: Religion and the Preservation of a 'Secular Humility'

This chapter's examination of 'what the Constitution says about religion' has left to the last the *Charter*'s most explicit (and perhaps most controversial) reference to the divine. The preamble to the *Charter* states:

> Whereas Canada is founded upon principles that recognize the supremacy of God and the rule of law [...][136]

In reference to the *Constitution Act, 1867*, the Supreme Court has called the preamble 'the grand entrance hall to the castle of the Constitution'[137] and the source of 'the political theory which the Act embodies'.¹³⁸ Given this seemingly large role in constitutional and *Charter* interpretation, and given the Court's repeated statements as to the secularity of Canada, the reference to the 'supremacy of God' as a founding principle of our nation may appear as somewhat of an oddity. Indeed, while the 'rule of law' half of the preamble has been an important part of *Charter* jurisprudence, the 'supremacy of God' half has been largely neglected by the judiciary.¹³⁹ Perhaps most notably, the British Columbia Court of Appeal in 1999 referred to it as a 'dead letter',¹⁴⁰ and as others have observed, Wilson J seemed to find it at odds with a 'free and democratic society' in *Morgentaler*.¹⁴¹

The preamble to the *Charter* echoes the preamble to the *Canadian Bill of Rights*, the pre-*Charter* statutory bill of rights enacted in 1960 which affirms that 'the Canadian Nation is founded upon principles that acknowledge the supremacy of God, the dignity and worth of the human person and the position of the family in a society of free men and free institutions'.¹⁴² This preamble went through many revisions before reaching its final form, with significant input from religious organizations, and George Egerton suggests that the inclusion of the phrase 'the supremacy of God' reflected and legislated a 'religiously-positive pluralism' in Canada.¹⁴³

What is to be made of this reference to the supremacy of God? The jurisprudence is clear that it does not mean that Canada is a theocracy, nor even a 'Christian nation'.¹⁴⁴ Beyond this, its treatment by the SCC has been cursory and minimal, described most recently in *Saguenay* as 'articulat[ing] the "political theory" on which the *Charter*'s protections are based'.¹⁴⁵ The Court offered no explanation as to what this means, nor what the 'political theory' referred to entails, but did observe that 'the supremacy of God does not limit the scope of freedom of conscience and religion and does not have the effect of granting a privileged status to theistic religious practices'.¹⁴⁶

Despite such scant judicial treatment to date, the 'supremacy of God' clause provides a rich 'interpretative opportunity' for future jurisprudence.¹⁴⁷ Jonathan Penny and Robert Danay suggest that the clause represents a particular vision of human rights, namely, that they do not arise from positive law but from natural law, and, thus, the *Charter* serves to affirm the rights that Canadians already have.¹⁴⁸ In the past, God was thought to be the source of such inalienable rights; in the modern era, human dignity is often cited as the source.¹⁴⁹ Penny and Danay argue that the clause is not a reference to any one religion, or to religion at all, but rather, 'to this historical premise that developed in the natural law tradition – that rights are derived from sources beyond the state – and to the fact that the *Charter* is an attempt to codify and protect those rights in a constitutional document'.¹⁵⁰

Bruce Ryder describes another approach to understanding the 'supremacy of God' clause, one which focuses more on its religious aspects. He argues it is best understood as 'a reminder of the state's role in not just respecting the autonomy of faith communities, but also in nurturing and supporting them, as long as it does so in an even-handed manner'.¹⁵¹ He states:

> The preamble represents a kind of secular humility, a recognition that there are other truths, other sources of competing world-views, of normative and authoritative communities that are profound sources of meaning in people's lives that ought to be nurtured as counterbalances to state authority. [...] *In this way, there is a complementarity, not a conflict, in the preamble's*

reference to the 'supremacy of God,' the Charter's guarantees of religious freedom and equality, and the promotion of multiculturalism. The text of the Charter as a whole suggests that the Canadian state should aim to secure a religiously positive pluralism in an even-handed manner. This is best accomplished by a secular state that is neutral between religions but not neutral about religion.[152]

Drawing on historical sources, Ryder shows that Canada, lacking the United States' establishment clause, has adopted a different view of the relationship between church and state. While a majority of the United States Supreme Court has expressed the view that the First Amendment mandates neutrality 'between religion and religion, and between religion and non-religion', Canadian law 'supports and encourages even-handed state support of religious and conscientious freedoms'.[153]

Ryder's understanding of the preamble is consistent with the holistic analysis undertaken throughout this chapter.[154] Examined as a whole, the *Charter* is unabashedly religion-positive.

At this stage an objection may be raised: many of these provisions in the Constitution might be characterized as historical artefacts, the result of political compromise. Section 93 is a well-known part of the 'Confederation compromise'.[155] The 'supremacy of God' clause is treated as an 'embarrassment' by some in academia and the judiciary,[156] and even section 27 has been described as no more than 'a rhetorical flourish'.[157] But, as Penny and Danay state,

> Many [...] would prefer a Canadian constitution without any reference to 'God' or any other notion of established religion. But this is not the Constitution we have. The Constitution must be dealt with *as* written, not as people wish it were written.[158]

We agree with Penny and Danay that Canada's legal and policy decision makers must have the 'constitutional courage'[159] to address the 'supremacy of God' clause, as well as the Constitution's other 'religiously positive' content, and consider their meaning and implications for Canadian law.

Part VI: Conclusion

According to the Supreme Court, the state's duty of religious neutrality 'results from an evolving interpretation of freedom of conscience and religion';[160] like all *Charter* principles, then, 'state neutrality' must be applied in a manner consistent with the Constitution as a whole and its interpretation informed by the broader legislative context, including all other constitutional provisions with which it coexists. In this chapter, we have attempted to provide such a contextual, holistic analysis. Our conclusion is that, far from being a paean to secularity, the Constitution and the *Charter* evince a strong preference for 'religiously positive pluralism'.[161] From the *Charter*'s explicit protections of religious freedom, association, expression and equality, to the Constitution's affirmation of minority religious education rights, to the *Charter*'s pursuit of a multicultural society, to the preamble's reference to the supremacy of God – when Canada's most fundamental legal documents are read as a unified whole, their recognition of the importance of faith to Canadian society is undeniable. Religion is not just a social good but a *constitutional* good. Any attempt to challenge 'advancing religion' as a head of charity on constitutional grounds must recognize this reality.

This is relevant to the analysis for at least two reasons. First, it confirms that the Constitution does not require the government to promote 'irreligious' policies in order to be 'neutral'; the government need not, for example, refrain from policy choices that support the ability of its citizens to pursue religious exercises. Indeed, the *Charter* itself can be fairly read as a 'pro-religion' document.[162]

Second, even if such policy choices – granting favourable legal treatment to organizations that advance religion – could be construed as limiting section 2(a), there is much the government could potentially rely on to justify the limitation under section 1. The Supreme Court has described the proportionality stage of the section 1 *Oakes* analysis – the stage at which 'most of the heavy conceptual lifting and balancing ought to be done'[163] – as being about '[weighing] the impact of the law on protected rights against the beneficial effect of the law in terms of the greater public good'.[164]

While a discussion of the tangible public benefits that religious communities provide is beyond the scope of this chapter, that topic is dealt with more extensively in other chapters of this book, as well as by other researchers and scholars.[165] Kathryn Chan provides a 'wellspring' theory of the public benefit of religion.[166] Researchers have measured the positive economic impact that religious congregations have on the cities in which they are located.[167] Recent studies reveal that Canadians largely see religion as a positive force in their local communities.[168] As just one example, religious groups play an important role in settling newcomers in Canada, with a large percentage of immigrants stating that they received material support from religious groups or relied on them for community integration.[169] Religious communities provide much-needed social and community services, including hospitals, shelters and hospices, international aid, social assistance, education, low-income housing and health services, elder care, refugee resettlement and much more. While some may argue that these services could still be considered charitable under another head of charity, they would undoubtedly be curtailed if government were to withdraw support for the communities which provide their source and motivation.[170] Indeed, charitable services provided by religious communities are not only motivated by, but also *manifestations of*, their spiritual beliefs. Advancement of religion is thus inextricably linked to the advancement of these deeply valued social goods. In short, there is plenty of weight on the 'public benefit' side of the scales of proportionality.

Finally, if the government were to decide to withdraw economic support from religious charities, it would face difficult questions – not only practical questions about how to replace the much-needed community services that religious communities provide but also philosophical questions about the scope of state neutrality in relation to irreligion. If the state has a duty to 'neither favour nor hinder any religious belief', 'including that of having no religious beliefs whatsoever' – as the Court states in *Saguenay* and *SL*[171] – it risks breaching that duty by discontinuing support for religion categorically and thus favouring *irreligion* over any and all religions. As Ravi Amarnath and Brian Bird state, 'It is difficult to identify the distinction between the duty of neutrality as defined in *Saguenay* and a duty of irreligion on the part of the state. Regardless of its purpose, the unavoidable effect of the duty of neutrality is to favour atheism or agnosticism over theistic religion in the public square'.[172] Governments should be mindful of this potential effect and ensure that religious neutrality does not morph into an irreligious or anti-religious policy default.

A similar idea was expressed by Justices Brown and Côté in their recent dissenting reasons in *Trinity Western*.[173] In that case, it was not a financial benefit being provided to a religious institution but rather approval of its proposed law school. The majority rejected Trinity Western's appeal from the Law Society's decision to deny approval. Justices Brown and Côté, however, stated that the Law Society's rejection of Trinity Western 'contravened the state's duty of religious neutrality' because it 'represented an expression by the state of religious preference which promotes the participation of non-believers, or believers of a certain kind, to the exclusion of the community of believers found at TWU'.[174]

This is consistent with the Supreme Court's recognition, in both *Saguenay* and *SL*, that neutrality must not be interpreted as state-advanced 'unbelief', noting Richard Moon's observation that 'the complete removal of religion from the public sphere may be experienced by religious adherents as the exclusion of their worldview and the affirmation of a non-religious or secular perspective'.[175] The Supreme Court acknowledged in *Saguenay* that 'absolute state neutrality is impossible to obtain' and that a 'neutrality that is non-absolute is nevertheless a true neutrality'.[176] 'In short', the Court concluded, 'there is a distinction between unbelief and true neutrality'.[177]

This distinction is an important one, especially in the present context. To interpret 'state neutrality' as denying government the ability to even-handedly support religious organizations would conflate 'state neutrality' with state-preferred 'unbelief'. It would also fail to take 'into account the competing constitutional rights of the individuals affected' such as the freedoms of expression, association and religion, discussed above.[178] This is not true neutrality.[179]

'True neutrality' has been interpreted as preventing the '*state's* profession of a clearly identified religious belief',[180] but not the state's support of initiatives designed to allow the flourishing of its *citizens*' free religious exercise and belief. Nothing in the Constitution prevents the government from making policy decisions based on the general premise that it is a social good for someone 'to have and to practice a religion'.[181] At the same time, non-religious charities can still qualify for equal benefits under any of the other three heads of charity.[182]

State neutrality does not prevent the government from creating social and legal conditions conducive to the flourishing of religious communities. As Bruce Ryder has observed, 'Canadian jurisprudence does not impose on the state a duty of neutrality *about* religion'.[183] A notion of state neutrality which asserts that *all* religious organizations automatically be denied state support is not actually 'neutral' at all: it is inherently *anti*-religious. This would undermine a Constitution which, as a whole, clearly supports a 'religiously positive pluralism'.[184] Such pluralism, along with the 'religious accommodation necessary to secure it', is 'inherently valuable'[185] and 'advances the public interest by promoting diversity' in Canada's liberal and democratic society.[186] Indeed, as the Supreme Court has recognized, 'The diversity of Canadian society is partly reflected in the multiple religious organizations that mark the societal landscape'.[187]

ADVANCING RELIGION IN A 'NEUTRAL' STATE   149

'True neutrality' is honoured by an even-handed benevolence towards religious charities which advance the public good; as argued in this chapter, this promotes,rather than undermines, Canada's constitutional commitments. The Federal Court's observation in *McBurney* remains sound today: 'It is not stretching matters to say that even in the modern, secular age the advancement of religion is rooted in our law and in our Constitution'.[188]

Notes

1. *McBurney v R*, [1984] DTC 6494 at 6496–6497 [*McBurney*]. The Federal Court of Appeal allowed an appeal of the decision on other grounds, see *Canada (Minister of National Revenue – M.N.R.) v McBurney*, [1985] F.C.J. No. 821 (F.C.A.).
2. For an overview of Canada's legislative provisions granting advantages to charities, see Terrance S. Carter, Maria Elena Hoffstein & Adam Parachin, *Charities Legislation & Commentary*, 2014 edn (Markham: LexisNexis, 2013) 'Commentary'. For the purposes of the *Income Tax Act*, two 'main advantages' were summarized by the SCC as follows: 'The first is the ability to provide receipts to donors, who, if they are individuals, are entitled to claim a tax credit for their 'total charitable gifts' […] and if corporations, may claim a deduction from their taxable income for all 'charitable gifts' […] Second, registered charities pay no tax on income (ITA, s. 149(1) (f)). The attraction of status as a registered charity is thus obvious'. See *Vancouver Society of Immigrant and Visible Minority Women v M.N.R.*, [1999] 1 SCR 10 at para 29 [*Vancouver Society*].
3. See Kathryn Chan, 'The Advancement of Religion as a Charitable Purpose in an Age of Religious Neutrality' (2017) 6 Oxford Journal of Law and Religion 112 at 113 [Chan].
4. *Mouvement laïque québécois v Saguenay (City)*, 2015 SCC 16, [2015] 2 SCR 3 at para 137 [*Saguenay*].
5. *Ibid*, at para 78.
6. *McBurney*, *supra* note 1.
7. This chapter refers to religious 'organizations' to capture both incorporated entities (such as those incorporated under not-for-profit corporate legislation) as well as unincorporated entities organized as charitable trusts.
8. Chan, *supra* note 3 at 114.
9. Mayo Moran, 'Rethinking Public Benefit: The Definition of Charity in the Era of the Charter', in *Between State and Market: Essays on Charity Law and Policy in Canada*, ed. Jim Phillips, Bruce Chapman & David Stevens (Montreal: McGill-Queen's University Press, 2001), 251 at 252 [Moran].
10. *Canadian Charter of Rights and Freedoms*, Part I of the *Constitution Act, 1982*, being Schedule B to the *Canada Act 1982* (UK), 1982, c 11, s 32 [*Charter*].
11. *Income Tax Act*, RSC 1985, c 1 (5th Supp).
12. Moran, supra note 9; see, for instance, CRA, Guidance GC-019, 'How to draft purposes for charitable registration' (25 July 2013), online: <https://www.canada.ca/en/revenue-agency/services/charities-giving/charities/policies-guidance/guidance-019-draft-purposes-charitable-registration.html> [CRA Guidance], which states that 'The CRA must therefore rely on the common law (case law, or court decisions) definition, which sets out the four broad categories (also called 'heads') of charity. The four broad charitable purposes categories were outlined by Lord Macnaghten in *Commissioners for Special Purposes of the Income Tax v Pemsel*. For a helpful summary of the common law as it relates to the third head of charity, and its interpretation by Canadian authorities, see Chan, *supra* note 3 at 115–119.
13. *Ibid*. This has long been the approach adopted in Canadian tax law. As the SCC observed in *Vancouver Society*, *supra* note 2 at para 26: 'The constantly evolving common law definition of charity has been incorporated into federal income tax legislation since charities were accorded special status under *The Income War Tax Act, 1917*, S.C. 1917, c. 28, s. 5(d)'.

14 *Commissioners for the Special Purposes of the Income Tax v Pemsel*, [1891] AC 531 (HL) [*Pemsel*].
15 *Ibid*, at 583.
16 *Fuaran Foundation v Canada (Customs & Revenue Agency)*, 2004 FCA 181 at para 15, [2004] 3 CTC 202.
17 *Keren Kayemeth Le Jisroel Ltd v Commissioners of Inland Revenue*, [1931] 2 KB 465 (CA) at 477.
18 Chan, *supra* note 3 at 117; see also CRA Guidance, *supra* note 12.
19 Chan, *supra* note 3 at 117, referencing *Bowman v Secular Society Ltd* [1917] AC 406 (HL) at 448–451; *Thornton v Howe* (1862) 31 Beav 14 at 1043.
20 CRA Guidance, *supra* note 12.
21 This framing may seem to contrast some American jurisprudence on the Establishment Clause indicating that "the government cannot favor religion over irreligion" (see, e.g., *McCreary County v. American Civil Liberties Union of Kentucky*, 545 U.S. 844 (2005), but see also notes 135 and 188 *infra* and surrounding discussion). However, it should be noted that non-religious organizations are still eligible for charitable status under any of the other three heads of charity. As Professor Chan observes, even trusts for 'the advancement of non-religious beliefs' may be recognized as

> charitable under the fourth head of charity on the basis that they tend to promote the moral or spiritual welfare of the community […] however, the charitable nature of such trusts is not assumed; the court must be persuaded on the evidence of the trust's moral worth, that it benefits the public and is within the spirit and intendment of the Preamble to the Statute of Charitable Uses of 1601. (Chan, *supra* note 3 at 117)

22 See e.g. discussion in Chan, *supra* note 3 at 114.
23 See *R v Big M Drug Mart Ltd*, [1985] 1 SCR 295 at paras 94–95, 123 18 DLR (4th) 321 [*Big M Drug Mart*].
24 See *Saguenay*, *supra* note 4; *SL v Commission scolaire des Chênes*, 2012 SCC 7, [2012] 1 SCR 235 [*SL*].
25 Richard Moon, 'The Requirement of Religious Neutrality: Civic Action and Institutional Autonomy', in *Religion, Liberty, and the Jurisdictional Limits of Law*, ed. Iain T. Benson and Barry W. Bussey (Toronto: LexisNexis Canada, 2017), 155 at 155.
26 *Ibid*.
27 *SL*, *supra* note 24 at para 32.
28 *Saguenay*, *supra* note 4.
29 *Ibid*, at paras 72 and 146 [emphasis added].
30 *Ibid*, at para 147.
31 Bruce Ryder, 'State Neutrality and Freedom of Conscience and Religion' (2005) 29 Supreme Court Law Review 169 at 176 [Ryder]. See further discussion below.
32 Richard Moon, 'The Requirement of Religious Neutrality: Civic Action and Institutional Autonomy', in *Religion, Liberty and the Jurisdictional Limits of Law*, 155 at 157. See also Terrance Carter, who, pursuant to a review of the case law, concludes:

> the courts have affirmed an indirect subsidy achieved through the granting of charitable status does not constitute an affirmation by the state that one religious view is superior to another, especially if charitable status is being granted indiscriminately to any religious organization meeting the criteria of 'advancing religion'. It follows that the government is not infringing the s. 2(a) or 2(b) Charter rights of those opposed to the views espoused by religious groups granted charitable status. Furthermore, by granting charitable status to a particular religious group, the government is not imposing a cost or burden on anyone or interfering with any other party's religious beliefs or practice.

Terrance S. Carter, 'Advancing Religion as a Head of Charity: What Are the Boundaries?' (2007) 20:4 The Philanthropist 257 at 277 [Terrance Carter].

33 The Supreme Court in *Saguenay* (*supra* note 4 at para 71) held that, although the Charter does not 'expressly' impose a duty of religious neutrality on the state, 'this duty results from an evolving interpretation of freedom of conscience and religion'.
34 See discussion in Ryder, *supra* note 31 at 174. Professor Ryder frames the question as follows: 'Must the state remain neutral about religion generally, that is, neutral as between adherents of religious and conscientious belief systems and non-adherents? Or can the state pursue policies that aid religion generally, so long as it does so in an even-handed manner that respects the duty of neutrality between religions?'
35 This approach is consistent with the common law of charities; under *Pemsel* (*supra* note 14), charitable purposes must be for a 'public benefit'. Purposes that fall under one of the first three heads are presumed to meet that requirement.
36 See following discussion, and *R v Mills*, [1999] 3 SCR 668 at para 61, which emphasized 'the importance of interpreting rights in a contextual manner – not because they are of intermittent importance but because they often inform, and are informed by, other similarly deserving rights or values at play in particular circumstances'.
37 *Ibid*. See also Guy Régimbald and Dwight Newman, *The Law of the Canadian Constitution*, 2nd ed (Toronto: LexisNexis Canada, 2017) at 550: 'The Charter is one piece of the Canadian Constitution, and it does not supplant other areas of constitutional law or other areas of law protecting rights […] The Charter does not take away from rights or freedoms arising from constitutional or other sources outside the Charter'.
38 Ruth Sullivan, *Sullivan and Driedger on the Construction of Statutes* (Toronto: LexisNexis Canada, 2002) at 281.
39 *Montréal (City) v Quebec (Commission des droits de la personne et des droits de la jeunesse)*, 2008 SCC 48 at para 57, [2008] 2 SCR 698 [emphasis added].
40 *Trinity Western University v British Columbia College of Teachers*, [2001] 1 SCR 772 at para 25 (per Iacobucci and Bastarache JJ for the majority) [*Trinity Western BCCT*].
41 See e.g. *Syndicat Northcrest v Amselem*, 2004 SCC 47 at para 62 [*Amselem*].
42 *Dubois v The Queen*, [1985] 2 SCR 350 at para 43, 23 DLR (4th) 503, citing Pierre-André Côté, *The Interpretation of Legislation in Canada* (Cowansville, QC: Yvon Blais, 1984) at 236.
43 *Health Services and Support – Facilities Subsector Bargaining Assn v British Columbia*, 2007 SCC 27 at para 80, [2007] 2 SCR 391 [*Health Services*].
44 *The Constitution Act, 1867* (UK), 30 & 31 Victoria, c 3.
45 *The Constitution Act, 1982*, being Schedule B to the *Canada Act 1982* (UK), 1982, c 11.
46 In *Gosselin v Quebec*, 2002 SCC 84, [2002] 4 SCR 429 [*Gosselin*], the Supreme Court considered a constitutional challenge to Quebec's social assistance scheme. Justice Arbour held in dissent that section 7 of the *Charter* ('Everyone has the right to life, liberty and security of the person, and the right not to be deprived thereof except in accordance with the principles of fundamental justice') established *positive* rights as against the government, including a certain minimum level of social assistance. Justice Arbour's dissent is 'widely perceived as a benchmark in progressive constitutional analysis' (Michael Plaxton, 'Foucault, Agamben, and Arbour J's dissent in *Gosselin*' (2008) 21 Can J L & Jurisprudence 411 at 411).
47 *Gosselin*, *ibid*, Arbour J (dissenting) at para 349 [references omitted] [emphasis added].
48 *R v Oakes*, [1986] 1 SCR 103 at para 64, 26 DLR (4th) 200 [emphasis added].
49 *Thomson Newspapers Co v Canada (Attorney General)*, [1998] 1 SCR 877 at para 24, 159 DLR (4th) 385.
50 *Figueroa v Canada (Attorney General)*, 2003 SCC 37 at para 27, [2003] 1 SCR 912.
51 *R v Advance Cutting and Coring Ltd*, 2001 SCC 70 at para 17, [2001] 3 SCR 209.
52 *Egan v Canada*, [1995] 2 SCR 513 at 536, 567, 124 DLR (4th) 609. See also *Reeve and Barisheff, Re*, 25 ACWS (2d) 385, 1984 CarswellOnt 2877 at para 125, in which the former Ontario Supreme Court described the family as 'the most important social institution', and *Lalonde v Ontario (Commission de restructuration des services de santé)*, [2001] OJ No 4767 at para 181, 208

DLR (4th) 577, in which the Ontario Court of Appeal described a francophone hospital as 'an important linguistic, cultural, and educational institution'.
53 See *Adler v Ontario*, [1996] 3 SCR 609 at para 85, 140 DLR (4th) 385 [*Adler*].
54 An earlier discussion of the themes and authorities examined in the following sections – and in the section 'Religious communities nurture democracy' below – can be found in Christian Legal Fellowship's intervention factum in *Highwood Congregation of Jehovah's Witnesses et al v Wall*, online: <https://www.scc-csc.ca/WebDocuments-DocumentsWeb/37273/FM090_Intervener_Christian-Legal-Fellowship.pdf> [CLF's intervention factum in *Wall*].
55 *Reference Re Public Service Employee Relations Act (Alta)*, [1987] 1 SCR 313 at paras 142, 143, 38 DLR (4th) 161 [*Alberta Reference*].
56 *Delisle v Canada (Deputy Attorney General)*, [1999] 2 SCR 989 at para 66, 176 DLR (4th) 513.
57 See *Irwin Toy Ltd v Quebec (Attorney General)*, [1989] 1 SCR 927, 58 DLR (4th) 577.
58 *Amselem*, *supra* note 41 at para 39.
59 *Ibid*, at para 40 [emphasis in original], quoting Dickson CJC in *Big M Drug Mart*, *supra* note 23 at para 35.
60 *Amselem*, *ibid*, at para 42.
61 Jane Calderwood Norton, *The Freedom of Religious Organizations* (Oxford: Oxford University Press, 2016) at 32 [Norton].
62 *Law Society of British Columbia v Trinity Western University*, 2018 SCC 32 at para 64, 292 ACWS (3d) 418 [*Trinity Western*]. See also para 130, where McLachlin CJC (concurring) discusses Canada's 'lengthy and passionately held tradition', dating back 'at least four centuries', of allowing religious communities to establish schools and institutions that 'reflect their faith and their practices'.
63 *Hasan & Chaush v Bulgaria*, No 30985/96 [2000] XI ECHR 117 [GC] at para 62 [*Hasan*]; *Sindicatul 'Păstorul cel Bun' v Romania*, No 2330/09 [2013] V ECHR 41 [GC] at para 136.
64 *Ibid*.
65 Norton, *supra* note 61 at 39.
66 *Loyola High School v Quebec (Attorney General)*, 2015 SCC 12 at para 92, [2015] 1 SCR 613 [emphasis added] [*Loyola*].
67 *Ibid*, at para 94 [emphasis added], quoting Bastarache J in *Amselem*, *supra* note 41 at para 137, quoting Timothy Macklem, 'Faith as a Secular Value' (2000) 45 McGill L.J. 1 at 25 [Macklem].
68 *Ibid*, at para 92 [emphasis added].
69 Kathleen Brady, 'Religious Group Autonomy: Further Reflections about What Is at Stake' (2006) 22 J L & Religion 153 at 156 [Brady].
70 *Ibid*.
71 *Ibid*.
72 *Ibid*, at 166–67.
73 See discussion in CLF's intervention factum in *Wall*, *supra* note 54.
74 *International Covenant on Economic, Social and Cultural Rights*, GA Res 2200A (XXI), UNGAOR, 1966, Supp No 16, UN Doc A/6316 49, Article 13(3); *International Covenant on Civil and Political Rights*, 999 U.N.T.S. 171, Article 18(4). The SCC has listed both of these documents among 'the sources most important to the understanding of s. 2(d) of the *Charter*': *Health Services*, *supra* note 43 at para 71.
75 *Loyola*, *supra* note 66 at para 66.
76 *Charter of human rights and freedoms*, CQLR c C-12, s 41.
77 *SL*, *supra* note 24 at para 50.
78 *Alberta v Hutterian Brethren of Wilson Colony*, 2009 SCC 37 at para 182, [2009] 2 SCR 567 [emphasis added] [*Hutterian Brethren*].
79 Macklem, *supra* note 67 at 52.
80 *Gorzelik and Others v Poland*, No 44158/98 [2004] I ECHR 219 [GC] at para 93, citing the preamble to the Council of Europe's Framework Convention. See also discussion in CLF's intervention factum in *Wall*, *supra* note 54.

81 *Alberta Reference, supra* note 55 at para 85. See note 85 *infra*.
82 Norton, *supra* note 61 at 13.
83 *Ibid*, at 32. Norton also cites Rex Ahdar & Ian Leigh, *Religious Freedom in the Liberal State*, 2nd edn (Oxford: Oxford University Press, 2013) at 376: 'There is an ineradicable collective or communal dimension to religion. Organizations or associations are formed to give effect to this communal aspiration. An individual's religious life is very much tied to and dependent upon the health of the religious community to which that believer belongs'.
84 *Lavigne v Ontario Public Service Employees Union*, [1991] 2 SCR 211 at para 234, 3 OR (3d) 511.
85 *Alberta Reference, supra* note 55. The *Alberta Reference* was a seminal 1987 case which established that freedom of association does not protect the right to strike; it was partially overturned by the Supreme Court in *Health Services* (*supra* note 43) which extensively referred to Dickson CJC's dissenting reasons. In *Saskatchewan Federation of Labour v Saskatchewan*, 2015 SCC 4 at para 33, [2015] 1 SCR 245, affirming the right to strike, the Court stated that 'Dickson C.J.'s dissenting reasons in the *Alberta Reference* were influential in the development of the more "generous approach" in the recent jurisprudence'. Thus, the former Chief Justice's reasons, though written in dissent, have high precedential value.
86 *Ibid*, at para 85 [emphasis added].
87 *Ibid*, at para 86.
88 *Big M Drug Mart, supra* note 23 at para 10.
89 *Ibid*, at paras 10–12.
90 *Charter, supra* note 10 at s 27.
91 *R v Zundel*, [1992] 2 SCR 731 at 817–18, 95 DLR (4th) 202. In the same passage, Justices Cory and Iacobucci affirm that section 27's conception of multiculturalism includes religious groups: 'People must be able to take pride in their roots, *their religion* and their culture. It is only then that people of every race, colour, *religion* and nationality can feel secure' [emphasis added].
92 *R v Keegstra*, [1990] 3 SCR 697 at 757, 61 CCC (3d) 1 [*Keegstra*].
93 *Ibid*.
94 *Mahe v Alberta* [1990] 1 SCR 342, 68 DLR (4th) 69.
95 *Canada (Human Rights Commission) v Taylor*, [1990] 3 SCR 892, 75 DLR (4th) 577 [*Taylor*]; *R v Sharpe*, 2001 SCC 2, [2001] 1 SCR 45; *Keegstra, supra* note 92; *R v Andrews*, [1990] 3 SCR 870, 75 OR (2d) 481.
96 *Big M Drug Mart, supra* note 23.
97 *Taylor, supra* note 95 at 920.
98 *Ibid* [emphasis added].
99 *Big M Drug Mart, supra* note 23 at para 99.
100 *SL, supra* note 24 at para 24.
101 Joseph E Magnet, 'Multiculturalism in the Canadian Charter of Rights and Freedoms', in *The Canadian Charter of Rights and Freedoms*, ed. Gérald-A Beaudoin & Errol Mendes (Toronto: Carswell, 1996), 18-1 at 18–23 [Magnet].
102 *Ibid*, at 18–24.
103 *Ibid*, at 18–27.
104 *Taylor, supra* note 95 at 920.
105 Magnet, *supra* note 101 at 18–27.
106 *Ibid*, at 18–28.
107 *Ibid*.
108 *Ibid*.
109 See *Moscow Branch of the Salvation Army v Russia*, No 72881/01, [2006] XI ECHR 1 at para 61 where the European Court of Human Rights affirmed that associations formed for the purposes of 'proclaiming or teaching religion, are also important to the proper functioning of democracy'. The Court explained: 'For pluralism is also built on the genuine recognition of, and respect for, diversity and the dynamics of cultural traditions, ethnic and cultural identities, religious beliefs, artistic, literary and socio-economic ideas and concepts. The

110 Brady, *supra* note 69 at 163.
111 *Ibid*, at 164.
112 *Ibid*, at 167.
113 *Ibid*, at 195: 'The values of political autonomy, equal political and civil liberty, equality of opportunity, economic reciprocity, and freedom of thought and conscience which Rawls finds implicit in our democratic culture all have roots in Western religious thought' [references omitted].
114 Deborah Wallace, 'Jacques Maritain and Alasdair MacIntyre: The Person, the Common Good and Human Rights', in Brendan Sweetman, ed, *The Failure of Modernism: The Cartesian Legacy and Contemporary Pluralism* (Washington: Catholic University of America Press, 1999) at 131. 'In making his case for universal human rights, Maritain explained that each soul has an eternal value and an absolute dignity. Only God, then, has an absolute claim on the human person' (at 132).
115 Jeremy Waldron, *God, Locke, and Equality: Christian foundations of John Locke's Political Thought* (New York: Cambridge University Press, 2002) at 242.
116 *Ibid*, at 13 [emphasis Waldron]. See also discussion in Derek Ross and Deina Warren, 'Religious Equality: Restoring Section 15's Hollowed Ground', (2019) 91 Supreme Court Law Review (2d) 123 at 143.
117 *Gorzelik and Others v Poland*, No 44158/98 [2004] I ECHR 219 [GC] at para 92.
118 *Hasan*, supra note 63 at para 62; *Leyla Sahin v Turkey*, No 44774/98, [2005] XI ECHR 173 [GC] at para 107; *Metropolitan Church of Bessarabia and Others v Moldova*, No 45701/99, [2001] XII ECHR 81 at para 118.
119 *Hutterian Brethren*, *supra* note 78 at para 131.
120 *Alberta Reference*, *supra* note 55 at para 87.
121 *Mounted Police Association of Ontario v Canada (Attorney General)*, 2015 SCC 1 at para 56, [2015] 1 SCR 3.
122 *Ibid*, at paras 49, 56. For an insightful discussion of freedom of association and its importance for religious minorities, see the intervention factum of the Justice Centre for Constitutional Freedoms in *The Nova Scotia Barristers' Society v Trinity Western University*, 2016 NSCA 59, online: <https://www.jccf.ca/wp-content/uploads/2013/02/Filed-JCCF-Factum-TWU-v.-NSBS-NSCA-1.pdf>.
123 *R v S(RD)*, [1997] 3 SCR 484 at para 38, 118 CCC (3d) 353.
124 *R v NS*, 2012 SCC 72, at para 73, [2012] 3 SCR 726, Lebel J, concurring [emphasis added].
125 Brady, *supra* note 69 at 155. See also Magnet, *supra* note 101, and surrounding discussion, and CLF's intervention factum in *Wall*, *supra* note 54. For further discussion on freedom of thought, see Dwight Newman, 'Interpreting Freedom of Thought in the *Canadian Charter of Rights and Freedoms*', (2019) 91 Supreme Court Law Review (2d) 107.
126 Brady, *ibid*, at 169.
127 *Ibid*, at 166.
128 *Saumur v City of Quebec*, [1953] 2 SCR 299 at 329, [1953] 4 DLR 641.
129 *Adler*, *supra* note 53 at para 33; *Reference re Bill 30, An Act to Amend the Education Act (Ont)*, [1987] 1 SCR 1148 at para 63, 40 DLR (4th) 18 [*Bill 30 Reference*].
130 *Bill 30 Reference*, *ibid*.
131 *Adler*, *supra* note 53 at para 35.
132 *Ibid*, at para 48.
133 *Ibid*, at paras 85, 106.
134 Ryder, *supra* note 31 at 178.
135 *Ibid*.
136 *Charter*, *supra* note 10.

137 *Reference re Remuneration of Judges of the Provincial Court (P.E.I.)*, [1997] 3 SCR 3, at para 109. See discussion in Jonathan W Penny & Robert J Danay, 'The Embarrassing Preamble: Understanding the 'Supremacy of God' and the *Charter*' (2006) 36 UBC L Rev 287 at 287 and 290 [Penny & Danay], who draw a connection between the preamble to the *Charter* and the preamble to the *Constitution Act, 1987*.
138 *Switzman v Elbing and A.G. of Quebec*, [1957] SCR 285 at 306; see also discussion in Penny & Danay, *ibid*.
139 Penny & Danay, *supra* note 137, at 287.
140 *R v Sharpe*, 1999 BCCA 416 at para 79, 175 DLR (4th) 1.
141 Penny & Danay, *supra* note 137, state at note 15: 'In Morgentaler, Justice Wilson stated that while she was "not unmindful" that the *Charter* "opens with an affirmation that 'Canada is founded upon principles that recognize the supremacy of God'", she was "also mindful that the values entrenched in the *Charter* are those which characterize a free and democratic society." As David M. Brown has noted, this statement suggests that "God and democracy [...] stand opposed to each other"' (citing David M Brown, 'Freedom From or Freedom For?: Religion as a Case Study in Defining the Content of Charter Rights' (2000) 33 UBC L Rev 551).
142 *Canadian Bill of Rights*, SC 1960, c 44, Preamble.
143 George Egerton, 'Writing the Canadian Bill of Rights: Religion, Politics, and the Challenge of Pluralism' (2004) 19 Can J L & Soc 1 at 2. For a fulsome account of the history of the clause, see George Egerton, 'Trudeau, God, and the Canadian Constitution: Religion, Human Rights, and Government Authority in the Making of the 1982 Constitution', in *Rethinking Church, State, and Modernity: Canada Between Europe and America*, ed. Marguerite Van Die & David Lyon (Toronto: University of Toronto Press, 2000) at 90.
144 *McBurney supra* note 1. See also *O'Sullivan v R*, [1991] 2 CTC 117, [1991] FCJ No 803 at paras 17–19: 'Did the inclusion in Canada's constitution of recognition of the supremacy of God mean to make a theocracy of Canada? Hardly [...] The preamble to the *Charter* provides an important element in defining Canada, but recognition of the supremacy of God, emplaced in the supreme law of Canada, goes no further than this: it prevents the Canadian state from becoming officially atheistic. It does not make Canada a theocracy because of the enormous variety of beliefs of how God (apparently the very same deity for Jews, Christians and Muslims) wants people to behave generally and to worship in particular. The preamble's recognition of the supremacy of God, then, does not prevent Canada from being a secular state'.
145 *Saguenay*, *supra* note 4 at para 147.
146 *Ibid*, at para 149.
147 Ryder, *supra* note 31 at 176.
148 Penny & Danay, *supra* note 137.
149 *Ibid*, at 290; see e.g. *Kindler v Canada (Minister of Justice)*, [1991] 2 SCR 779, 84 DLR (4th) 438.
150 Penny & Danay, *supra* note 137 at 290.
151 Ryder, *supra* note 31 at 176.
152 *Ibid*, at 177 [footnotes omitted] [emphasis added].
153 *Ibid*, at 178.
154 Ryder's characterization of the preamble as recognizing 'counter-balances to state authority' is consistent with the expressions, e.g., of MP David Crombie during legislative debates surrounding the *Charter*; he explained that reference to the 'Supremacy of God' had 'practical democratic value' because it reflected a legal order which 'allows for diversity and dissent': 'The roots of democratic dissent have always begun with religious dissent [...] The way in which generations of western people have been able to overcome tyranny was by being able to appeal over the head of the government which oppressed them'. *House of Commons Debates*, 32nd Parl, 1st Sess, No 7 (18 February 1981) at 7441.

155 *Bill 30 Reference*, *supra* note 129 at para 62.
156 See discussion in Penny & Danay, *supra* note 137.
157 Peter W Hogg, *Canada Act 1982: Annotated* (Toronto: Carswell, 1982) at 72.
158 Penny & Danay, *supra* note 137 at 289 [footnotes omitted].
159 *Ibid*, referencing Harry Arthurs, 'Constitutional Courage' (2004) 49 McGill LJ 1.
160 *Saguenay*, *supra* note 4 at para 71.
161 Ryder, *supra* note 31 at 177.
162 *McBurney*, *supra* note 1.
163 *Hutterian Brethren*, *supra* note 78 at para 149 per Abella J. This comment was affirmed by Karakatsanis J for the majority of the Court in *R. v K.R.J.*, 2016 SCC 31, [2016] 1 SCR 906 at para 78.
164 *Carter v Canada (Attorney General)*, 2015 SCC 5 at para 122, [2015] 1 SCR 331.
165 See e.g. discussion in Terrance Carter, *supra* note 32, especially at 261–63.
166 Chan, *supra* note 3 at 126.
167 Milton Friesen & Mike Wood Daly, 'Phase 1 – The Halo Project' (2016), online: Cardus <https://www.haloproject.ca/phase-1-toronto>.
168 Angus Reid Institute, 'Canada at 150: Religion seen to have played a positive role in local communities, less so on the national stage' (2017), online: <http://angusreid.org/religion-in-canada-150-part-three/>.
169 Angus Reid Institute, 'Faith and Immigration: New Canadians rely on religious communities for material, spiritual support' (2018), online: <http://angusreid.org/faith-canada-immigration/>.
170 As Kathryn Chan has observed, 'the strong normative universes of religion tend to encourage the transfer of charitable resources to (religious and non-religious) charitable objects in ways that the weaker normative universe of the civic community does not' (Chan, *supra* note 3 at 124).
171 *Saguenay*, *supra* note 4 at para 72; *SL*, *supra* note 24 at para 32.
172 Ravi Amarnath & Brian Bird, 'Prayer for Relief: Saguenay and State Neutrality toward Religion in Canada' (2016) 1 Cambridge L Rev 176 at 183.
173 *Trinity Western*, *supra* note 62.
174 *Ibid*, at para 324.
175 *Saguenay*, *supra* note 4 at para 131, and *SL*, *supra* note 24 at para 30, citing Richard Moon, 'Government Support for Religious Practice', in Richard Moon, ed, *Law and Religious Pluralism in Canada* (Vancouver: UBC Press, 2008), 217 at 231.
176 *Saguenay*, *supra* note 4 at para 132.
177 *Ibid*, at para 134 [emphasis added].
178 *SL*, *supra* note 24 at para 32.
179 *Ibid*.
180 *Saguenay*, *supra* note 4 at para 134 [emphasis added].
181 *Gilmour v Coats*, [1949] AC 426 (H.L.), at 458–9 per Lord Reid who observed that, in showing 'favour to gifts for religious purposes', the law of England still remained neutral as it did not 'prefer one religion to another'.
182 *Supra* note 21.
183 Ryder, *supra* note 31 at 174 [emphasis added].
184 *Ibid*, at 177.
185 *Trinity Western*, *supra* note 62 at para 337, Brown and Côté JJ, dissenting.
186 *Ibid*, at para 327, Brown and Côté JJ, dissenting.
187 *Trinity Western BCCT*, *supra* note 40 at para 33.

188 *McBurney, supra* note 1 at 6496. See also *Walz v. Tax Commission of City of New York*, 397 U.S. 664 (1970), where the US Supreme Court, in finding that property tax exemptions for religious organizations did not violate the Constitution, observed the following:

> The general principle deducible from the First Amendment and all that has been said by the Court is this: that we will not tolerate either governmentally established religion or governmental interference with religion. Short of those expressly proscribed governmental acts there is room for play in the joints productive of a benevolent neutrality which will permit religious exercise to exist without sponsorship and without interference. […] The legislative purpose of the property tax exemption is neither the advancement nor the inhibition of religion; it is neither sponsorship nor hostility […] it is simply sparing the exercise of religion from the burden of property taxation levied on private profit institutions.

Chapter Seven

MAKING REGISTERED CHARITABLE STATUS OF RELIGIOUS ORGANIZATIONS SUBJECT TO '*CHARTER* VALUES'

Barry W. Bussey*

Abstract

The Supreme Court of Canada has held that government actors must ensure that their decision-making process considers '*Charter* values'. This has led to a growing opinion, within the legal community, that Canada Revenue Agency's decisions on the registered charitable status of religious organizations ought to ensure such charities are compliant (in belief and action) with '*Charter* values' such as equality and 'reproductive rights'. In some circles, '*Charter* values' are seen as a necessary part of the evolving definition of 'public benefit'. This chapter explores that perspective in the context of current law and liberal democratic philosophy. It argues that fundamental human life issues (FHLI) such as equality of all, definition of marriage and the value of human life, have been the subject of religious thought and teaching for millennia, and such beliefs have inspired the legal, political and philosophical traditions of liberal democracies. FHLI are part and parcel of the religious enterprise that seeks to understand what it means to be human. Denying public benefit recognition to charities that advance religion merely because they have unpopular beliefs or practices will not only have a negative effect on civic engagement, it will also have a negative philosophical impact on our traditional and scientific understanding of human nature. Liberal democracy demands that the state recognize it has no role in denying the complexity of religious identity's framing of fundamental human life issues upon which reasonable people may disagree.

Introduction

It was an 'A-ha!' moment heard around the country. On 1 December 2017, the Supreme Court of Canada (SCC) hearing was in its second day of the Trinity Western University (TWU) law school case.[1] Justice Malcolm Rowe questioned Canadian Bar Association (CBA) lawyer Susan Ursel about the CBA's position that accreditation of TWU's law school would amount to government actors condoning discrimination.

---

* B.A., LL.B., M.A., LL.M., MPACS, PhD; Director, Legal Affairs at Canadian Council of Christian Charities and Adjunct Associate Professor, University of Notre Dame Australia (Sydney).

'How about my theoretical Jesuit institute?' Justice Rowe inquired. 'You can't get in unless you're a Jesuit. You can't become a Jesuit unless you're a Catholic priest. And you can't become a Catholic priest unless you're a man. Should their tax-exempt status be struck down because of that?'

'It's not the case before us', Ursel replied, deflecting.

'But is it not the logic of what you're putting to us?' Justice Rowe pressed.

'It is the logic of what I am putting to you', Ursel agreed. 'There are limits to what the state should be called upon to support [...] you are right, we are at that threshold, and we can't back away from it'.[2]

That exchange is telling not only for what it reveals about the legal profession's view of the tax-exempt status of religious organizations but also, more broadly, for what it reveals about the profession's view on the granting of any 'public support' of religious organizations that do not accept the profession's moral views on fundamental human life issues (FHLI).[3]

There is a growing opinion among the societal and legal elite that, in order to obtain any public authorization to operate and/or receive government benefits, a religious entity must be compliant with certain ideological positions on human nature. This is an imposition of 'correct' worldviews. It is justified in large part by the controversial '*Charter* values' doctrine that has captivated a majority on the Supreme Court and a sizeable following among legal academics. The doctrine presupposes that the judiciary and the legal academy intuitively know what '*Charter* values' are and how they should be applied in light of the 'public interest'. What constitutes 'public interest' is another brewing controversy. Such 'values' are not enumerated in the *Charter* but rather seem to flow from it like mist on a lake at sunrise. And like those floating tendrils of fog, '*Charter* values' are notoriously difficult to capture: it would seem that only judges and legal academics are able to discern which '*Charter* values' are relevant or applicable in any given case. In cases where religious communities hold unpopular views, the net result is almost invariably to deny the enumerated rights of the religious community in favour of the mystical '*Charter* values' that only the judges can see. It is indeed a mystery wrapped up in enigma.[4]

The elites perceive their ideological positions as de facto 'in the public interest'. Therefore, any recipient of government largess (whether in the form of funding or mandatory regulatory approval to carry out the recipient's operation) who espouses an opposing view to the elites is holding that 'benefit' or approval against the public interest. The 'public interest' has also become a turn of phrase that is monopolized by the elites.

Such a perception is not only improper but also potentially dangerous as it violates the basic principle of equality of every citizen and denies the strength gained from diversity of viewpoints in public policy making. A free and democratic society is predicated on the ability of every individual and civic group to speak their minds on any subject of interest and to lawfully carry out life based on their views without any fear or hindrance, subject only to reasonable limits that are demonstrably justified.[5]

These bedrock principles are eroded by the troubling concept of '*Charter* values' currently being advocated among leading academics and members of the judiciary. This concept diminishes the legal protection of enumerated constitutional rights and is a justification for the removal of public benefit to lawful citizens and groups whose only offense is having the wrong opinion.

When we hop on a train of thought we need to look carefully at our ticket to make sure we know where we are going.[6] For that reason, this chapter is necessary to explain more fully where the current trajectory of the anti-religious opinion is leading us. We must ask, 'Where do we want to end up?' For those outspoken critics of religion, the goal is obvious: we want to arrive at a societal destination where religious organizations with unpopular views are denied tax exemptions or charitable status.[7] While this prospect might be alluring to some, we must exercise caution as we consider the full ramifications. What might this contested future look like? What would we have to sacrifice to reach this objective? And what might it mean for the tens of thousands of charities who currently strive to advance religion while serving their communities in many tangible, beneficial ways?

This chapter will analyse some of the most prominent and problematic arguments which are being made against the advancement of religion as a charitable head. First, we will address the troubling argument that traditional religious beliefs on FHLI can be equated to racial discrimination and that charitable status for religious organizations can be removed according to a framework provided by the Bob Jones University case in the United States.[8] This approach, though latent, was evident in the *TWU* 2018 cases. This chapter contends that the *TWU* 2018 decisions laid the groundwork for further challenges to the religious communities' registered charitable status because of their refusal to adopt the ever-changing, 'progressive' sexual moral views. Second, we will discuss the growing controversy over the use of *'Charter* values' and how they can be applied as a tool to remove registered charitable status. To counter these arguments, I assert that the issuance of public regulatory approval was never meant to condone, approve or disapprove of the beliefs of authorized charities that contribute to the public good. Finally, this chapter concludes with a practical and positive way forward.

The Bob Jones University Case's Influence on Trinity Western University Law School Case

The *TWU* 2018 cases illustrate two of the most troubling arguments used against religious institutions, both of which are addressed in this chapter. First, through false analogies to racism, the opposition characterizes certain politically incorrect (FHLI) beliefs as reprehensible. This then provides the social, political and legal will to infringe on religious freedom when the offense taken to these beliefs is depicted as a 'harm' that must be recompensed, as opposed to recognizing the value and benefit of religious charities to society at large. The second misleading argument involves the application of *'Charter* values' reasoning to deny the enumerated *Charter* rights of religious freedom; the legal accommodation of religious practice as contained in legislation, such as human rights codes; and common law precedent.

On 15 June 2018, a majority of the SCC rejected TWU's bid to open a law school. The SCC held that the British Columbia (BC) and Ontario law societies had the authority to deny TWU's accreditation based on the societies' subjective view that TWU's mandatory Community Covenant Agreement (CCA) dishonoured *'Charter v*alues'.[9] This was because of the CCA's requirement that students respect TWU's religious teaching of traditional marriage as being one man and one woman.

In the SCC's majority view, the CCA, which was deemed 'degrading and disrespectful', was sufficiently repugnant to justify the infringement of TWU's religious freedom as protected under human rights legislation and the *Charter*.[10] Conspicuously, the SCC's emotive characterization failed to appreciate the whole context. TWU is a private university; no one is required to attend. Yet the majority objected to the prospect of students being 'required by someone else's religious beliefs to behave contrary to [their] sexual identity' – a clear *non sequitur* given the facts.[11] In other words, the Court gave considerable weight to speculative 'harm' to a hypothetical future student rather than the obvious, concrete effect of preventing TWU from operating its law school. Moreover, the SCC's assertion wrongly presumed that TWU has state authority to compel action.[12] The relationship TWU has with its students is best characterized as a voluntary contract. As the SCC stated in its *Trinity Western University v British Columbia College of Teachers* 2001 decision, 'TWU is not for everybody; it is designed to address the needs of people who share a number of religious convictions'.[13] Additionally, it is 'a private institution that is exempted, in part, from the British Columbia human rights legislation and to which the *Charter* does not apply'.[14] Amazingly, the SCC majority in its *TWU* 2018 decisions did not address its *TWU* 2001 decision. It simply ignored it. This is a most puzzling response to one of its own decisions that was so similar on the facts, it causes one to question the political nature of the *TWU* 2018 decisions.[15]

Throughout the litigation in three different provinces,[16] two of which led to the *TWU* 2018 SCC decisions, argument was made concerning the United States Supreme Court decision in the Bob Jones University (BJU) case.[17] Though the SCC decision did not reference BJU, it was discussed in the BC Court of Appeal[18] and the Ontario Court of Appeal[19] decisions. It was also referenced in several legal academic articles[20] and was alluded to in oral argument by the CBA[21] and by Justice Gascon[22] at the SCC. It is perplexing that the SCC did not refer directly to the BJU case in its decisions, because the *TWU* 2018 decisions only make sense when seen in light of the BJU framework. It is my view that one can reasonably conclude that the SCC majority fully adopted the BJU reasoning but failed to acknowledge the influence that BJU had on its decision. BJU hovers over *TWU* 2018 like an unwelcome ghost. Indeed, then Chief Justice McLachlin in her concurring opinion specifically stated that 'the most compelling law society objective is the imperative of refusing to condone[23] discrimination against LGBTQ people, pursuant to the Law Society of British Columbia's (LSBC's) statutory obligation to protect the public interest'.[24] As we will see, that is the very spirit and sentiment of the BJU decision.

The Bob Jones University Case[25]

Background

The decades after the Second World War saw the internal politics of the United States preoccupied with resolving the issues of racial segregation and civil rights. The response of many white Southerners to desegregation in public schools that resulted from the

1954 *Brown v Board of Education*[26] decision was to move their children into whites-only private schools.[27] Southern state governments supported them by 'enacting legislation mandating or allowing the closing of public schools to resist desegregation or providing state tax credits and tuition grants to students attending private schools'.[28]

By the 1980s, two cases arrived at the Supreme Court of the United States (SCOTUS) that brought the segregation issue to the doors of private schools. The cases involved Bob Jones University in Greenville, South Carolina, and the Goldsboro Christian School in Goldsboro, North Carolina. Both had racially discriminatory admissions policies. BJU maintained that its policy that prohibited interracial dating among its students was based on its religious beliefs. So, too, did Goldsboro make similar claims. To better understand these cases, and the distorted parallels made to TWU, it is important to first recognize the historical context.

In 1968, the *Columbia Law Review* observed that in the 'process of articulating the boundaries of national policy, requirements of equal protection [became] more stringent, and [the] conceptions of state action and responsibility [were] broadened, so that hitherto private domains [became] subject to scrutiny'. It continued to observe that '[t]he pressure to eradicate racial discrimination is now being felt in the area of federal tax benefits to private, charitable institutions which discriminate – in particular, those to segregated private schools'.[29]

With the coming into effect of Title VI of the 1964 *Civil Rights Act*,[30] which prohibits discrimination on the basis of race, colour and national origin in programmes and activities receiving federal financial assistance, and the rise in segregated private schools, there was a concerted effort to limit all support of segregated private schools. Therefore, the Internal Revenue Service (IRS) announced in an August 1967 press release that 'exemptions will be denied and contributions will not be deductible' to contributors 'if the operation of the school is on a segregated basis and its involvement with the state or political subdivision is such as to make the operation unconstitutional or a violation of the laws of the United States'.[31]

However, the IRS did not solve the problem of private school segregation. First, the IRS's position only worked for situations where the state had unconstitutionally supported the segregated private schools as noted by the courts.[32] Second, the Tax Code generally permitted private religious schools to receive tax exemptions and allow tax deductions for their financial donors.[33] Private schools, like BJU, met the Code's definition of being 'organized and operated exclusively for religious, charitable, [...] or educational purposes' despite their segregated policies, and there was nothing the IRS could do. There had to be a legislative change or a court ruling on its constitutionality to say otherwise.

Congressional legislators proved to be ineffectual and it was the courts that brought the change. On 12 January 1970, a three-judge District Court for the District of Columbia issued a preliminary injunction prohibiting the IRS from granting tax-exempt letters to private schools in Mississippi that 'operated on a racially segregated basis as an alternative to white students seeking to avoid desegregated public schools'.[34] The IRS did not wait for a permanent injunction but changed its policy in the aftermath of that court's decision. By 30 June 1970, the District Court granted the permanent injunction wherein Judge Harold Leventhal stated, '[w]hile in the past the traditional law of charities embraced educational trusts for the benefit of a racially defined class, there is grave doubt whether this rule has continuing vitality in view of current values which govern the application of charitable trust law'.[35]

The legislators had not changed the law, but the District Court did, based on the Court's understanding of 'current values'. This proved to be an important framework that would be similarly applied at the SCOTUS. It is likewise a common method applied by the SCC as part of the 'living tree' doctrine discussed later in this chapter. Law is deemed to be malleable on the basis of 'values'.[36]

Further litigation[37] and congressional debate carried on throughout the 1970s as it related to the increasingly robust desegregation stance of IRS tax-exempt policies. In the meantime, the BJU and Goldsboro cases made their way through the courts, and on 13 October 1981, the SCOTUS granted review of them both. Ten years of multiple cases and congressional debates laid the background for the highest court in the United States to determine whether the IRS tax-exempt policy was going to be subject to positive tax law or subject to the Court's interpretation of public policy and the 'current values' against desegregation.

The inauguration of President Reagan in 1981 brought further complications. Incumbent Jimmy Carter supported the IRS policy, but Ronald Reagan campaigned against IRS's removal of BJU's tax exemption and promised to change it. The government's position was that 'IRS lacked power to revoke the school's tax-exempt status'.[38] For the Republicans, it was an issue of legislative intent and building a check against the expanding judicial and administrative power of government. The Reagan administration's policy was that '[t]he IRS would no longer revoke the charitable status of "religious, charitable, or scientific organizations on the grounds that they don't conform with certain fundamental public policies"'.[39]

This resulted in significant public outcry and forced Reagan's administration to reaffirm its opposition to discrimination based on race. But it still framed the issue as government actors usurping the constitutional role of Congress. To shore up the position, the President proposed legislation to Congress that supported IRS's prohibition of tax exemption for discriminatory organizations.[40] This would put into law the IRS policy. However, it was opposed by critics who argued that it was not necessary since IRS had broad legislative authority to make the decision in the first place. Meanwhile, Reagan's supporters did not like the proposed legislation because they saw it as a betrayal of his campaign promise. On 18 February 1982, the DC Court of Appeals enjoined IRS from granting or restoring tax-exempt status to segregated schools as defined by *Green*.[41] The uncertainty of opposing decisions would be settled once and for all by the BJU case.

The Decision

On 24 May 1983, the SCOTUS ruled 8–1 that IRS had the authority to deny tax exemptions to segregated schools and its policy was not a violation of the First Amendment.

Chief Justice Burger noted, '[t]he sponsors of the University genuinely believe that the Bible forbids interracial dating and marriage. To effectuate these views, Negroes were completely excluded until 1971. From 1971 to May 1975, the University accepted no applications from unmarried Negroes, but did accept applications from Negroes married within their race'.[42] Burger was of the view that '[i]t is a well-established canon of statutory construction that a court should go beyond the literal language of a statute if reliance on that language would defeat the plain purpose of the statute'.[43]

Burger's analysis highlighted the role of trusts to provide public benefit, noting 'that the purpose of a charitable trust may not be illegal or violate established public policy'.[44] He continued:

> When the Government grants exemptions or allows deductions all taxpayers are affected; the very fact of the exemption or deduction for the donor means that other taxpayers can be said to be indirect and vicarious 'donors.' Charitable exemptions are justified on the basis that the exempt entity confers a public benefit – a benefit which the society or the community may not itself choose or be able to provide, or which supplements and advances the work of public institutions already supported by tax revenues.[45]

'The institution's purpose', said Burger, 'must not be so at odds with the common community conscience as to undermine any public benefit that might otherwise be conferred'.[46] The Court's jurisprudence since *Brown v Board of Education* established 'beyond doubt this Court's view that racial discrimination in education violates a most fundamental national public policy, as well as rights of individuals'.[47] Burger opined that:

> [g]iven the stress and anguish of the history of efforts to escape from the shackles of the 'separate but equal' doctrine of *Plessy v. Ferguson* [...] it cannot be said that educational institutions that [...] practice racial discrimination, are institutions exercising 'beneficial and stabilizing influences in community life,' [...] or should be encouraged by having all taxpayers share in their support by way of special tax status.[48]

On the issue of the IRS overstepping its 'lawful bounds', Burger held that the IRS did not overstep. Congress vested 'those administering the tax laws very broad authority to interpret those laws', and in a complex tax system, 'the agency Congress vests with administrative responsibility must be able to exercise its authority to meet changing conditions and new problems'.[49] As Congress cannot be expected to anticipate every conceivable problem, it relies on its administrators to implement its will.[50] When the IRS made its 1970 ruling, 'the position of all three branches of the Federal government was unmistakably clear. The correctness of the Commissioner's conclusion that a racially discriminatory private school 'is not "charitable" within the common law concepts' outlined in the Code is 'wholly consistent with what Congress, the Executive, and the courts had repeatedly declared before 1970'.[51]

As far as the failure of Congress to amend the Code to conform with the IRS policy, Burger held that such 'failure to act on the bills proposed on this subject provides added support for concluding that Congress acquiesced in the IRS rulings of 1970 and 1971'.[52] This, combined with the Congressional passage of legislation denying tax-exempt status to social clubs that discriminated on the basis of race, and Congressional reports from both houses, established that 'discrimination on account of race is inconsistent with an educational institution's tax-exempt status'.[53]

Finally, the governmental interest in the case was compelling – it 'has a fundamental, overriding interest in eradicating racial discrimination in education [...] That governmental interest substantially outweighs whatever burden denial of tax benefits places on petitioners' exercise of their religious beliefs'.[54]

Analysis of the SCOTUS Decision

The Court reached its decision based on policy rather than law. There was no direct legislative tool given to the IRS to change its policy from permitting religious organizations charitable status even though they held socially unacceptable views. The concept of the courts being the source of law or changing the law to satisfy what it considers important public policy concerns, or its understanding of the changing societal 'values', is a matter of some controversy and debate. On the one hand, proponents of court intervention suggest that it is the only way forward when political pressure prevents legislators from doing 'the right thing'. On the other hand, those who oppose court intervention point out that courts usurp the constitutional role of the legislature when they amend or create law out of whole cloth. They thus create a precedent for future courts to become embroiled in political lawmaking, all the while having neither the political competence nor the constitutional jurisdiction to create or change the law. To legitimize this practice of court intervention would, say the opponents, create role confusion among governmental branches. This then leads to societal instability as the different branches get in each other's way exercising political power.

This is a serious conundrum. At times, it would appear, courts must intervene when the legislature refuses to address a vital social concern. Indeed, most reasonable people would agree that the judiciary was right to 'advance' or 'nudge'[55] the law in assisting the desegregation of American society. According to this view, racial segregation was so egregious that when the legislature would not intervene, the courts were left with no choice but to act. However, who is to say that society would not have arrived at such a consensus without the courts' intervention? After all, as we saw with the IRS policy, Congress did not challenge IRS's policy to refuse registered charitable status to racist religious charities. Congress's refusal to act against the IRS was itself an acquiescence of the legislature to the government actor's policy change, and the courts were merely in agreement (as we discuss below).

However, it is arguably a much better scenario for the legislature and executive branches to make acts of commission than omission in making law rather than allowing the courts to legislate by fiat. That is because the legislature and executive are the political branches of power, whereas the judiciary is, or ought to be, the least political branch in its arbiter role. A court embroiled in politics rather than law loses legitimacy to be the independent arbiter of legal disputes.

The sociopolitical climate was very clear that segregation policies were totally unacceptable – and for good reason. It could be argued that the IRS showed courage to step up and remove the charitable status of BJU because of its racist policies.

In its decision, the Court stepped back and considered the presuppositions of granting religious institutions special tax status. It was assumed that religion provides a public benefit; however, religion that practices racism cannot be said to provide a public benefit as it causes civil strife, and no amount of racism can bring about any public good.

Therefore, the logic of the SCOTUS decision is readily discernible. First, the purpose of the Tax Code exemption for religious organizations, such as universities, is tax relief for agencies that provide public benefit; second, there is no public benefit from racism; and, third, there is an adamant sociopolitical demand that no public funding, directly or indirectly, go to a racist school as it taints whatever good might come from the provision of university education. This is the case even if it is cheaper for the public purse, which does not have to provide funding for students attending a private university. Therefore, even though the institution was private and religious, and there was no direct authorization in the law for the IRS policy, taken as a whole, the Court concluded that the IRS was within its authority to make a decision within the spirit of the law and society's 'current values' for the greater public benefit.

Anti-TWU Activists See BJU as a Template

The argument of using BJU as a comparator case for attacking TWU's religious position on marriage has a long history. In her dissent in *TWU* 2001, Justice L'Heureux-Dubé referenced the BJU case as being relevant. She asserted the BJU case of miscegenation 'is difficult to distinguish in a principled way from the ban on homosexual behaviour at issue here [with TWU] […] there can no longer be any doubt that sexual orientation discrimination in education violates deeply and widely accepted views of elementary justice'.[56] For L'Heureux-Dubé J, it was the religious practice that offended the law, not the religious belief.[57]

Legal academics and anti-TWU activists in the *TWU* 2018 litigation used the BJU case as a template to condemn TWU's law school accreditation based on TWU's CCA concerning marriage. Professor Elaine Craig, one of the most outspoken and influential opponents of TWU, stated that '[a] religiously based anti-miscegenation policy is analogous to TWU's anti-gay policy'.[58] Likewise, Ontario Bencher Gavin MacKenzie, in a 10 April 2014 Law Society meeting, referenced BJU when he said that 'we can draw a useful analogy between public attitudes towards interracial dating and interracial marriage in 1985 and discrimination based on sexual orientation in 2014'.[59]

Similarly, Jena McGill, Angela Cameron and Angela Chaisson of the University of Ottawa noted in submissions to the Law Society of Upper Canada (LSUC) that TWU wanted a 'public benefit from a public body statutorily obligated to act in the public interest' in the same way BJU wanted tax exempt status. Like BJU, TWU relies on 'on the constitutional guarantee of freedom of religion to insulate its discriminatory Covenant from critique and constitutional scrutiny'.[60]

The Ontario Court of Appeal agreed with Craig and other academics that BJU was a comparable situation. Claimed Justice MacPherson:

> TWU, like Bob Jones University, is seeking access to a public benefit – the accreditation of its law school. The Law Society of Upper Canada (LSUC), in determining whether to confer that public benefit, must consider whether doing so would meet its statutory mandate to act in the public interest. And like in Bob Jones University, the LSUC's decision not to accredit TWU does not prevent the practice of a religious belief itself; rather it denies a public benefit because of the impact of that religious belief on others – members of the LGBTQ community.[61]

By contrast, the British Columbia Court of Appeal (BCCA) firmly rejected the BJU comparison. 'TWU is not seeking a financial public benefit [like the tax break sought in BJU] from this state actor', said the BC court.[62] Instead, 'Accreditation is not a "benefit" granted in the exercise of the largesse of the state; it is a regulatory requirement to conduct a lawful "business" which TWU would otherwise be free to conduct in the absence of regulation'.[63] There is a practical benefit to TWU from regulatory approval, but that is not a funding benefit. The BC court observed that 'the reliance on the comments of a single concurring justice in the Bob Jones case is misplaced'. Finally, the court did not see the BJU case 'as supporting a general principle that discretionary decision-makers should deny public benefits to private applicants'.[64]

However, this position did not prevent the LSBC and multiple interveners at the Supreme Court from relying yet again on the BJU case. The LSBC factum to the SCC argued that the only difference between BJU and TWU was 'the particular religious belief at issue, which is entirely contingent on the purely subjective commitments of the community in question'.[65] Of course, TWU rejected that position.[66]

The CBA argued the applicability of the BJU case throughout the *TWU* 2018 litigation,[67] and at the SCC it said that the SCOTUS decision in BJU tracks the SCC's 'emphasis on reasonable and proportionate impairment of constitutionally protected rights, including in situations where' the exercise of religious beliefs and the state interest of eradicating discrimination compete.[68] EGALE Human Rights Trust referenced BJU when it argued that the treatment of LGBTQ students at TWU was 'similar to [the costs] historically borne by students who enrolled in schools that prohibited interracial dating and marriage, and who faced expulsion if they entered into relationships that violated school policy'.[69] Lesbians, Gays, Bisexuals and Trans People of the University of Toronto (LGBTOUT) observed that 'if TWU sought to exclude a different historically marginalized group from accessing legal education – for example, inter-racial couples – there can be little doubt that LSUC and other government actors would categorically refuse to approve or accredit the institution'.[70]

I argue below that the SCC applied the BJU case as a template in reaching its decision that denying accreditation for TWU was reasonable. I make that assertion even though the Court did not reference BJU directly. However, I suggest that the presuppositions of the SCC in *TWU* 2018 are so similar to the BJU case that it is reasonable to suggest BJU provided a model or template for the TWU reasoning. I suggest that the BJU case is an analytical framework, in light of the *TWU* 2018 decisions, for a legal challenge against the registered charitable status of religious organizations that, in the minds of various elites, discriminate and are in violation of '*Charter* values' and of 'public interest' as the elites define those two concepts.

BJU's Influence on *TWU* 2018 Decisions

TWU's Marriage Position Wrongly Equated to Racism

Despite the fact that the SCC did not explicitly mention the BJU case, it did frame TWU's policy as being on par with racism, suggesting that '[t]he Covenant singles out LGBTQ people as less worthy of respect and dignity than heterosexual people, and reinforces negative stereotypes against them'.[71] Noticeably, there was no evidence on the record that supported those assertions of the Court. However, there was evidence in the CCA itself that TWU students were called upon to 'treat all persons with respect and dignity, and uphold their God-given worth from conception to death'.[72] That hardly qualifies as singling out LGBTQ people for anything but the utmost respect.

'Drawing distinctions on the basis of certain traits in certain contexts', observes Professor Deborah Hellman, 'has meaning that distinguishing on the basis of other traits would not'.[73] This was lost on the SCC in *TWU* 2018. A private religious university that maintains religious teachings on traditional marriage is a context where one would expect a student admissions policy that would be in harmony with the school's religious position. Hellman posits that discrimination is wrong when it demeans another person; '[w]hether classification demeans depends on the social or conventional meaning of drawing a particular distinction in a particular context'. She goes on, 'Context and culture play a significant role in determining the meaning of actions'.[74] 'To demean', according to Hellman, 'is to treat someone in a way that denies her equal moral worth [...]. To demean is to not merely to insult but also to put down, to diminish and denigrate. It is to treat another as lesser'.[75]

It should also be noted that prior to its April 2014 Benchers meeting, the LSBC had commissioned its own investigation into whether TWU graduates were involved in discriminatory conduct at BC's three public law schools. They came up empty. What they did find, inter alia, from the University of Victoria was that the 2011 gold medallist was a TWU alumnus.[76] The fact that the Law Society felt that this investigation was even necessary shows a stereotypical anti-religious bias against TWU. It is reasonable to imagine the public outcry if a similar investigation were conducted on undergraduates of public universities.

Therefore, for the SCC to suggest that the Covenant 'singles out LGBTQ' students as inferior is factually incorrect on the face of the document and in practice. The SCC's position is perplexing. From both a legal and a logical perspective, to suggest that the TWU law school case is analogous to the BJU case is suspect. Professor Mary Ann Waldron argues that the history of black students' access to education in the United States is a very different issue than the history of the LGBTQ community's access to education in Canada.[77] While not diminishing the struggles the LGBTQ community has had in Canada, Waldron notes 'no school and no public policy have ever barred LGBTQ students from attending a school or university'.[78] Individuals 'with differing sexual orientations or genders are not under-represented in the well-educated or the professional classes'.[79] Therefore, there is no 'remedial need for punitive public policy to require all institutions to accept same-sex marriage'.[80]

Yet, given the Court's portrayal of the CCA as reinforcing 'negative stereotypes', it is reasonable to conclude that the Court understood TWU's belief and practice of traditional marriage as analogous to racism. And it would appear that the SCC saw itself in an analogous position to that of the SCOTUS in the 1950s–1980s. Just as SCOTUS broke new ground in eradicating racist policies at both public and private universities, the SCC evidently saw itself in the vanguard of eliminating discrimination on the basis of sexuality. Therefore, the SCC took upon itself the mantle to push back against TWU and its allegedly 'degrading and disrespectful' admissions policies against sexual minorities.

Times They Are a Changin'

The emphasis on 'changing values' concerning racial discrimination in the BJU case conjures up the 'living tree' doctrine of Canadian constitutional law, as alluded to earlier. That doctrine originated with Lord Sankey's comments in a 1930 decision of the British House of Lords in which the Privy Council ruled that 'person' in the *Constitution Act, 1867*, also included 'women'. Sankey described our Constitution as 'a living tree capable of growth and expansion within its natural limits'.[81] In other words, the metaphor is not endless – growth or evolution must be 'within its natural limits'. Unfortunately, as Bradley W. Miller pointed out, 'The concept of natural limits has not received much sustained attention from either the Court or its commentators and it is reasonable to conclude that it lacks any real explanatory power'.[82] Does the 'living tree' doctrine apply to the BJU and TWU cases?

Certainly, there are similarities. Just as the Berger Court in BJU took judicial notice of the changing societal views on racism, the McLachlin Court in TWU took note of changing sexual moral ethics. It goes without saying that the social and legal changes in the United States regarding racism and segregation were necessary and positive developments, just as it was a positive movement to ensure that LGBTQ persons were treated with respect in Canada.

However, to make race and sexual identity analogous is to assert that sexuality is an unassailable or involuntary biological reality, like skin colour – a characterization that is disputed by proponents of non-binary or gender fluidity[83] and by the proliferation of identities represented by variations of the LGBTQ acronym itself.[84] While the SCOTUS has accepted, in the *Obergefell* decision,[85] the arguments of the American Psychological Association[86] that sexual orientation is immutable, there nevertheless is a recognition that sexual orientation is different than race. For example, as we have seen, the SCOTUS does not countenance any view that there is a valid religious position in support of race discrimination that the state could accept. But, on the matter of religious conscience and sexual orientation, Justice Kennedy, speaking for the five-member majority held:

> The right to marry is fundamental as a matter of history and tradition, but rights come not from ancient sources alone. They rise, too, from a better informed understanding of how constitutional imperatives define a liberty that remains urgent in our own era. *Many who deem same-sex marriage to be wrong reach that conclusion based on decent and honorable religious or philosophical premises, and neither they nor their beliefs are disparaged here.* But when that sincere, personal opposition becomes enacted law and public policy, the necessary consequence is to put the imprimatur of the State itself on an exclusion that soon demeans or stigmatizes those whose own liberty is then denied. Under the Constitution, same-sex couples seek in marriage the same legal treatment as opposite-sex couples, and it would disparage their choices and diminish their personhood to deny them this right.[87]
>
> *Finally, it must be emphasized that religions, and those who adhere to religious doctrines, may continue to advocate with utmost, sincere conviction that, by divine precepts, same-sex marriage should not be condoned. The First Amendment ensures that religious organizations and persons are given proper protection as they seek to teach the principles that are so fulfilling and so central to their lives and faiths, and to their own deep aspirations to continue the family structure they have long revered.* The same is true of those who oppose same-sex marriage for other reasons. In turn, those who believe allowing same-sex marriage is proper or indeed essential, whether as a matter of religious conviction or secular belief, may engage those who disagree with their view in an open and searching debate. The Constitution, however, does not permit the State to bar same-sex couples from marriage on the same terms as accorded to couples of the opposite sex.[88]

The unmistakable reality is that the SCOTUS recognized that religious communities were not only permitted to hold their views in support of traditional marriage but were also constitutionally protected to do so.

Opponents might nonetheless maintain that while religious groups may be entitled to hold discriminatory views, that does not mean the state must give its imprimatur by granting a public benefit or other recognition such as registered charitable status.

Such a criticism fails on several counts. First, in the US context, the SCOTUS was clear that (1) the beliefs of religious communities holding the traditional definition of marriage were characterized as 'decent and honorable' and not 'disparaged' by the Court; and (2) religious organizations and individual persons are protected in advocating for 'the family structure they have long revered'. Thus, under *Obergefell*, the SCOTUS is not taking the position that the status of religious organizations, including registered charities, is subject to state rejection in the same way that the racial policies of BJU were. As Professor Frank S. Ravitch states, the tone between *Obergefell* and BJU was markedly different. He suggests that 'the Court sees value in specifically acknowledging the right of religions to exercise their freedom of religion and freedom of speech in the same-sex marriage context but did not see any benefit to doing so in the anti-miscegenation context'.[89] And then there is the difference between racism based in religion that has a peculiar American association with slavery, whereas '[t]heological notions that marriage is between a man and a woman go back thousands of years and have existed even in traditions that did not exhibit broader antigay ideals'.[90]

Second, there is a parallel with the SCC in its *Marriage Reference*[91] decision. Academic opinion held that legal recognition of same-sex marriage was a major contextual difference between *TWU* 2001 and *TWU* 2018. However, what this view failed to appreciate were the explicit exemptions or protections given to religious individuals, clergy and institutions. The LGBTQ Coalition before the BCCA was wrong in law to argue that traditional marriage is 'an unconstitutional definition of marriage'.[92] As TWU argued, this distinguishes BJU; the racist practices espoused by BJU in the 1980s were not defensible in the way that traditional marriage remains a completely valid practice.[93]

In recognizing the constitutional authority of the Parliament of Canada to define marriage, the SCC was emphatic that all government entities must accommodate clergy who will not perform marriages that violate their beliefs,[94] as well as religious communities who decline the use of their 'sacred places' for 'compulsory celebration of same-sex marriages'.[95] Further, it must also be noted that the *Income Tax Act* was amended in 2005 to protect religious charities from losing their charitable status because of their beliefs and practices on marriage.[96]

The *TWU* 2018 decisions of the SCC have marked, in my view, a turning away by the Court from the reality of the differences between race and sexual orientation. It now appears that sexual politics has come to be a major force in the constitutional litigation of religious freedom.

Indeed, the SCC showed itself to be hypersensitive to any criticism from the LGBTQ movement. This was exhibited by the Court's unprecedented reversal of its decision on the intervener applications. An initial decision by Justice Wagner excluded LGBTQ intervener applicants, among others. Out of 26 applications, only nine were granted leave to intervene. The outcry was immediate and intense: Jacques Gallant of *The Toronto Star* explained, 'Wagner's order Friday faced backlash throughout the weekend on social media, with lawyers and LGBTQ activists expressing outrage over the exclusion of LGBTQ groups'.[97] Within days, Chief Justice McLachlin responded with a decision allowing all intervener applicants and opening an additional day of hearing to accommodate the about-turn. It was a remarkable event because it was without precedent.[98]

Light can be shown on this development when we consider the first press conference of newly appointed Chief Justice Richard Wagner, held only a few days after the SCC's release of its *TWU* 2018 decisions. 'When you talk about interpretation', he observed in his extrajudicial comments, 'context is paramount. And when you are looking issues that come up long after the original text has been drafted, as in the Constitution for example, there are principles of interpretation that you apply'. In Wagner CJC's view, the Court may reach a different conclusion not because of legal reasons but because 'society has evolved'; such rulings 'take context into account as a backdrop to the legal rulings that we arrive at'.[99]

Evidently, the courts are increasingly concerned about 'public' opinion. In the majority decision of the *LSBC v TWU* 2018 case, the Court so feared that TWU accreditation would erode 'public confidence' that they referenced it no less than five times.[100] This raises a number of issues that we must question. First, in its phrase 'public confidence', what does the Court mean by 'public'? After all, the SCC is not an elected body and it does not take periodic polls as to how well the Canadian public takes to their decisions. How can the Court claim with certainty that it knows the views of the 'public'? The only 'public' that gives feedback to the SCC is the legal profession and the media.

But are those two institutions rightly the all-inclusive 'Canadian public?' It does not seem probable. What appears to be happening is that the Court is caught in its own feedback loop where it mistakenly takes what the media and the legal profession say as being indicative of 'public'[101] sentiment.

Consider also the statements of Justice Karakatsanis who, during oral hearing, was piqued with the BCCA's approach to addressing the claim that LGBTQ students would suffer loss of equality if the TWU law school were approved. The BCCA suggested that the LGBTQ community might have access to more, not fewer, law school seats because evangelical students would go to TWU law school, relaxing the demand on public law schools. Karakatsanis was not convinced since this argument was not 'from the perspective of substantive equality; they don't consider whether they have less opportunity than others for those seats. Is that the way we approach equality?' She insisted, 'it's not a numbers game'.[102]

While Justice Karakatsanis was emphatic that equality is 'not a numbers game', the SCC majority's decision was particularly interested in highlighting the numbers of the LSBC membership that were against TWU's bid for a law school. It noted that at the 10 June 2014 Special General Meeting, '[b]y a vote of 3,210 members for and 968 members against, the members voted to adopt the proposed resolution not approving the law school'.[103] It also underscored the LSBC's subsequent referendum wherein '5,951 members voted to implement the resolution through a declaration that TWU's proposed law school was not an approved faculty of law, while 2,088 members voted against the resolution'.[104]

The overwhelming numbers within the BC legal profession were against TWU and were of such significance to the SCC majority that the particulars of that voting warranted mention. But, as the SCC dissent so aptly noted, 'the Benchers abdicated their duty as administrative decision-makers by deferring to a popular vote'.[105] The LSBC counsel admitted as much in oral hearing before the SCC when he said the LSBC's 'failure' to 'determine the proportionate balancing in this situation' meant that the SCC had to decide whether the decision of the referendum was an appropriate balance between the LSBC's statutory mandate and TWU's *Charter* rights. In other words, the SCC had to fill in the blanks left by the LSBC. In normal situations courts would send the matter back to the government actor to carry out the work they failed to complete. That was not done here. The SCC did the proportionate analysis for the LSBC. Such a proposal, as the dissent noted, was totally against previous SCC precedent, but that did not stop this SCC from replacing 'the (non-) reasons of the LSBC with its own, and [making] the outcome [of the referendum] the sole consideration'.[106]

It was indeed a numbers game – a game to take away TWU's enumerated *Charter* right to religious freedom in favour of the nebulous '*Charter* value' that TWU not discriminate against the LGBTQ community. The erosion of 'public confidence' the Court feared most was, in reality, the confidence of the legal community. It had no problem with those numbers infringing on the religious freedom right of the religious minority. Where then is the 'substantive equality' for the evangelical community wanting its own law school in accordance with its own enumerated *Charter* right to practice its religious beliefs? There is none.

To conclude, in this section I have argued that racial discrimination, being the subject of the BJU case, is very different from discrimination based on pro-traditional marriage beliefs and practices, as in the *TWU* 2018 cases. Therefore, it is without merit to suggest, as some do, that religious organizations who advocate for traditional marriage are discriminating in the same manner as the racial discrimination in the BJU case. It is a false and misleading comparison, especially given the exemptions in legislative acts and jurisprudence for religious communities who affirm traditional marriage.

Further, when courts seek to harmonize the law with their perception of societal expectations, they are involved in a feedback loop that is reinforcing the views of the elites – the academic, the media and the legal profession. The courts' obsession with the changing times has resulted in a failure to accommodate religion.[107]

Government Actors Interfering in the Private Sphere

During oral argument in the TWU case, questions and comments from the bench suggested that the BJU analysis was top of mind in allowing a government actor, in this case the law societies, to interfere with the private operations of a religious university. The following exchange is illustrative of this point.

Justice Wagner used the logic of BJU when he asked TWU Counsel, Kevin Boonstra, in oral hearing:

> Assuming that you are right [...] that as a private enterprise you are not submitted to some discrimination provisions of the *Charter*, but is the situation different when a private enterprise like your client goes on to [...] need some kind of recognition or approval or help [...] from the state – and I mean the state being the Law Society or a public entity which is submitted to the *Charter of Rights*? You know, is the situation not different then?[108]

Boonstra replied that the issue was the religious accommodation necessary for TWU and its students to practice their faith and not be burdened with *Charter* obligations. Religious institutions are not subject to the *Charter* – it is the law societies which have *Charter* obligations. Justice Abella immediately questioned him within the BJU framework as to whether the law society 'in its accreditation role' has the right 'to determine whether [...] the entrance requirements posed by the proposed new law school meet certain standards?'[109]

Abella's question was fixated not on the role of the law society to ensure that law graduates are competent to practice law, but whether religious law schools are entitled to limit entrance based on religious beliefs and practice. Boonstra replied that the authority of the society only commences at the point at which a law graduate 'shows up with their credentials and asks to be admitted into the legal profession'.[110]

'So if the particular religious community had policies, entrance requirements that said certain religions or genders, not sexual orientation, were not eligible to come in to the law school', Justice Abella continued her inquiry, 'your argument would be that religious autonomy[111] of the community means that the Law Society has no role in regulating what those entrance requirements are, as long as that religious community law school can demonstrate that their graduates will be able to be good lawyers notwithstanding the entrance requirements'.¹¹² To which Boonstra replied, 'Yes. Provided that the context of that hypothetical [situation] is the same, and that is the reasons for articulating those entrance requirements as you have posed are based on sincerely held religious beliefs [...] [and] that there is [...] no evidence of specific concrete harm in relation to the graduates that emerge from the program'.¹¹³

As noted above, the SCC ruled against TWU. It evidently had no qualms allowing the state to interfere with the private, internal religious beliefs and practices of a religious university. This was made possible, I suggest, in no small part because of the influence of the BJU decision of the SCOTUS – an influence, I suggest, that was unwarranted, due to the marked difference between race discrimination and lawful discrimination based upon pro-traditional marriage.

The logic of the SCC's decisions on TWU follows a similar pattern as the BJU case. First, part of the law society's mandate is to act in the 'public interest' (as it chooses to define 'public interest') by accrediting universities that provide public benefit by means of university education; second, there is no public benefit from discrimination based on sexual orientation; third, there is an adamant sociopolitical demand that no public approval go to a discriminatory school as it taints whatever good might otherwise come from educating future lawyers; fourth, even though the institution is private and religious, and there is no direct authorization in the law to outright deny TWU a law school, the denial of accreditation by the law societies was reasonable because it advanced their statutory mandate to act in the 'public interest' and to support '*Charter* values'.

TWU Decisions Form a Backdrop to Deregister 'Discriminatory' Religious Charities

Canadian law presumes that the 'Advancement of Religion'¹¹⁴ provides a public benefit. However, in recent years, there has been a growing call to re-evaluate that presumption.¹¹⁵ In the United Kingdom, for example, new legislation abolished the presumption,¹¹⁶ and the Charity Commissioner now requires religious charities to provide 'an identifiable, positive, beneficial moral or ethical framework that is promoted by religion which demonstrates that the religion is capable of impacting on society in a beneficial way'.¹¹⁷

The SCC's *TWU* 2018 decisions have laid the groundwork for activists' demand that religious charities holding to traditional marriage should be deregistered. This is not meant to be alarmist but, I would argue, follows logically from the '*Charter* value' of equality – which ought not to be confused with the *Charter* right to equality. Refashioning CRA policy to meet such a radical departure from the historical presumption of benefit would take little effort. Current CRA policy maintains that any restriction of 'benefits must always ensure that the restrictions proposed are not illegal or contrary to public policy'. Organizations

> with purposes that are discriminatory or based on notions of racism, may, depending on the nature of the discriminatory purpose, offend the norms in the Canadian Charter of Rights and Freedoms. They may also be in contravention of the various human rights regimes either

federally or provincially, or contrary to public policy as expressed in those constitutional and legislative regimes.[118]

Critics argue that it is not the 'belief' of the organization but the 'exercise' or the 'practice' of the belief that causes a discriminatory effect on, in the case of traditional marriage, sexual minorities. This was common parlance among those who argued against TWU in the 2018 litigation. All religious charities that require a lifestyle agreement of their employees – or, in the case of schools, from their students as well – are potential targets for activists to pressure government to remove their charitable status.[119]

Indeed, it is not so much a matter of speculating *whether* a political challenge against the charitable status of religious organizations will be made. It is a matter of *when*, and preparing for the inevitable. Consider the stridency with which religious communities' beliefs and practices are being challenged by anti-religious activists, as in the cases of TWU, the CSJ scandal[120] and the BC Humanist property tax campaign[121] and its call for the removal of advancement of religion as a head of charity.[122]

The underlying purpose of these challenges to religious charities that have 'discriminatory' policies is to pressure them to change their non-compliant religious practices to conform to the mainstream or, at the very least, adjust them in a way that is not dissonant with the mainstream. This strategy not without justification.

There is ample evidence to suggest that strong-arm tactics do produce results. For example, in the *Reynolds*[123] case, the Church of Jesus Christ of Latter-Day Saints lost its appeal at the SCOTUS to maintain the practice of polygamy. It subsequently changed its position.[124] The BJU decision also led that university to change its position 17 years after the SCOTUS 1985 decision; and three decades later, BJU regained its charitable status.[125]

Commentators on the *TWU* 2018 litigation argued that TWU might well change its view in time. BC lawyer Mark Meredith noted in a 2014 email to the LSBC, '[c]hilling as the position then espoused by BJU is, it seems to me that the position taken by TWU is little different with respect to sex and sexual orientation. Even BJU dropped its interracial dating policy in 2000; perhaps, in the fact of public light, TWU might do the same with its condemnation of same-sex relationships'.[126]

Peter Rogers, counsel for the Nova Scotia Barristers' Society (NSBS), argued that part of the rationale for the NSBS not to accept TWU law graduates was that the refusal would hopefully compel TWU to change its admissions policies. During oral argument he suggested:

> It may induce TWU to make what the Society submits is a very small adjustment to its process that would remove the situation where we now have a new law school coming in that is reserving places, in effect, for heterosexual students and increasing the disadvantages experienced by LGB students.[127]

So, the point of refusing TWU's accreditation was to force the university to abandon its anachronistic beliefs and wake up to modern reality. As BC law society bencher David Mossop argued, while TWU has a legal right to maintain its Community Covenant, 'it doesn't mean you should do it'.[128] 'The present trend in Christian churches is to accept gay marriage', Mossop continued; 'it's happened in the Anglican Church'. By implication, his message is that TWU will follow suit, given enough time and pressure.

As it turned out, on 9 August 2018, less than two months after the SCC decisions, TWU's Board of Governors voted to make the CCA voluntary for students.[129] It was a dramatic development given the extent to which TWU fought not once, but twice, all the way to the SCC. There was speculation that this was not only a response to the SCC ruling but also a defensive move to protect the school from harassment by other professional regulators for their nursing and education degree programmes.[130]

However, even with the change in policy, commentators made it clear that the concession did not go far enough. There were demands for TWU to remove the requirement entirely, not only for the students but also for the faculty and staff.[131] Further, Professor Richard Moon expressed concern that even preserving the Christian character of the school would 'favour Evangelical students and, in effect, disfavour non-Evangelicals'. Moon was concerned that 'discriminating based on religious commitment raises similar problems as discriminating based on sexual orientation'.[132]

Professor Moon's sentiment is indicative of the problem when the strong arm of the state is applied against religious communities because their religious practices are seen as being out of the mainstream. Despite attempts to paint them as 'unlawful', religious beliefs and practices on traditional marriage are entirely lawful.

Can we truly be a free society if non-conforming religious communities are pressured to conform to elite opinion under threat of tax policy or regulatory changes? How does that compare with former Chief Justice Brian Dickson's opinion[133] that a 'truly free society is one which can accommodate a wide variety of beliefs, diversity of tastes and pursuits, customs and codes of conduct'? Citizens must be free to practice their beliefs as they choose 'without fear of hindrance or reprisal'; in short, '[f]reedom can primarily be characterized by the absence of coercion or constraint. If a person is compelled by the state or the will of another to a course of action or inaction which he would not otherwise have chosen, he is not acting of his own volition and he cannot be said to be truly free'.

A major purpose of the *Charter*, said Dickson CJC:

> is to protect, within reason, from compulsion or restraint. Coercion includes not only such blatant forms of compulsion as direct commands to act or refrain from acting on pain of sanction, coercion includes indirect forms of control which determine or limit alternative courses of conduct available to others. Freedom in a broad sense embraces both the absence of coercion and constraint, and the right to manifest beliefs and practices [...] no one is to be forced to act in a way contrary to his beliefs or his conscience.

Despite our history of respecting differences of opinion and religious practices, we appear to be headed toward state-coerced conformity. Tax policy is only one tool in the government arsenal to enforce compliance. There are other mechanisms, from regulatory approval of religious institutions, as in the TWU case, to the extreme of criminal sanctions. The state is virtually limitless. That is why liberal democracy has built in safeguards against the capricious use of political power. The *Charter* is one safeguard, as are the independent judiciary and the rule of law. Even then, liberal democracies are not without their own internal weaknesses, and constant vigilance is required to maintain freedom.

The *TWU* 2018 decisions laid the groundwork for legal challenges to the registered charitable status of religious communities that do not fall into line with the current thinking of the activists, government and legal elites on such issues as changing sexual moral views concerning marriage; or abortion; or medical assistance in dying (MAiD).[134] Political pressure will build until government acts to satisfy its base of support.

Under such a scenario, the government will have to address several legal hurdles. First, 'advancement of religion' as a charitable category[135] is a common law construct. To remove or change definitions of such a category would require a legislative enactment – or, under the post-*TWU* 2018 framework, a constitutional argument to a court could be made that registration of religious charities would be in violation of '*Charter* values'.[136] Second, as noted above, the *Income Tax Act* was amended in 2005 to protect religious charities from losing their charitable status because of their beliefs and practices on marriage.[137] Again, a legislative enactment will be necessary to remove that protection, or, alternatively, a court may hold that legislative provision unconstitutional for violating '*Charter* values'. Third, it goes without saying that any action by government to remove the charitable status of these religious organizations will be met with a robust legal response from the religious community. One can anticipate long and extensive litigation grounded in religious freedom rights and the state's duty of neutrality.

It is beyond the scope of this chapter to provide an analysis on every legal nuance of the possible legal challenges to a government action against a religious charity in this regard. However, one can be certain that whatever challenge arises, it will involve, to one degree or another, a claim that the subject religious charity violates '*Charter* values'.

The Growing Controversy of '*Charter* Values'

The majority in *TWU* 2018 stated that the use of '*Charter* values' in constitutional interpretation is '[f]ar from controversial'.[138] However, the concurring and dissenting opinions belie that assertion.[139] If anything, the use of '*Charter* values' is more controversial than ever as a result of *TWU* 2018. Justices Côté and Brown's robust dissent criticized the doctrine which elevates 'the idiosyncrasies of the judicial mind' to such an extent that these judicially imposed 'values' limit a constitutionally protected right.[140] A cursory look at the legal literature makes it indisputable that '*Charter* values' are controversial.[141] Even the Ontario Court of Appeal has recognized that '*Charter* values lend themselves to subjective application because there is no doctrinal structure to guide their identification or application'.[142] This 'is particularly acute when *Charter* values are understood as competing with *Charter* rights'.[143]

In highly unusual fashion at the SCC, Justices Côté and Brown were vigorous and forceful in their dissent. '[R]esorting to *Charter* values as a counterweight to constitutionalized and judicially defined *Charter* rights', they said, 'is a highly questionable practice'.[144] Côté and Brown observed that, unlike *Charter* rights, '*Charter* values' are unsourced. Rather, they are entirely the product of the idiosyncrasies of the judicial mind that pronounces them to be so. And, perhaps one judge's understanding of 'equality' might indeed represent a 'shared value' with all Canadians, but perhaps another judge's might not. This in and of itself should call into question the legitimacy of judges or other state actors pronouncing certain 'values' to be 'shared'.[145]

These comments express the extent to which '*Charter* values' as a doctrine in constitutional analysis is not only controversial but ought to be abandoned. The nub of the problem, Côté and Brown argue, 'is the imposition of judicially preferred "values" to limit constitutionally protected rights, including the right to hold other values'.[146]

The second issue that Côté and Brown observe is that '*Charter* values' are amorphous and undefined. They lack the structure of substantive meaning and application that the Courts have given to *Charter* rights over 35 years of jurisprudence. '*Charter* values like "equality", "justice", and "dignity"', Côté and Brown aptly note, 'become mere rhetorical devices by which courts can give priority to particular moral judgments, under the guise of undefined "values", over other values and over *Charter* rights themselves'.[147] This damning rebuke is worthy of note given the serene and respectful ambiance that is usually associated with the SCC. The audacious majority decision not to ground '*Charter* values' in an articulate philosophical foundation while taking away TWU's enumerated religious freedom merited the blistering criticism of Côté and Brown JJ who were appalled at the lack of judicial discipline. It was, regrettably, a court that preferred a political decision rather than a well-reasoned legal analytical decision that is bound to mark this case as a low point in Canadian religious freedom jurisprudence.

Côté and Brown JJ also criticized the majority's application of the 'value of equality' in the case. Legally, under s.15 of the *Charter*, the claim of equality 'relates to differential application of *a specific rule* to a certain group of people in a certain legal context'; however, the majority cannot 'point to a specific legal rule or right to ground the application of a value of equality here'.[148] Instead, the majority's assertion of 'equality' is abstract and 'it could mean almost anything'. It could mean that 'all are equal before and under the law' or it could mean equality in 'an absolute sense' which 'is also perfectly compatible with a totalitarian state'; it could even mean a 'tolerance of difference'. By relying on this abstraction, 'the majority avoids actually making explicit its moral judgment, its premises and the legal authority on which it rests'.[149]

Concurring with the outcome, Chief Justice McLachlin observed, 'to adequately protect the right, the initial focus must be on whether the claimant's constitutional right has been infringed. *Charter* values may play a role in defining the scope of rights; it is the right itself, however, that receives protection under the *Charter*'.[150] The former Chief Justice made a point of reminding the Court that it is the *Charter* rights, not '*Charter* values', that are protected. The focus on '*Charter* values' is misplaced.

Justice Rowe observed that the 'reliance on values rather than rights has muddled the adjudication of *Charter* claims in the administrative context'.[151] They 'have no independent function in the administrative context'.[152] While they may assist in adjudication of claims based on *Charter* rights, they bring about confusion when they are used as a standalone basis for the adjudication of *Charter* claims. This is because the scope of *Charter* values is often undefined in the jurisprudence. In some cases, a *Charter* value aligns with a particular *Charter* right. In other cases, the value does not line up with earlier *Charter* jurisprudence. This lack of clarity heightens the potential for unpredictable reasoning.[153]

Rowe disagreed with the majority's use of '*Charter* values' because it denies the proper structural analysis that the *Charter* requires. He explains:

> The point is this. In cases where *Charter* rights are plainly at stake, courts and other decision-makers have a constitutional obligation to address the rights claims as such and to do so explicitly. An analysis based on *Charter* values should not eclipse or supplant the analysis of whether *Charter* rights have been infringed. Where *Charter* rights have been infringed by administrative actors, reviewing courts must determine whether the state meets the burden of justifying the infringement according to s. 1. This is not a matter of doctrinal preference. It is a constitutional obligation imposed by the *Charter*.[154]

Justice Rowe's 10 paragraphs explaining 'The Problem With *Charter* Values',[155] along with the caution of former Chief Justice McLachlin, and the incisive wit of Justices Côté and Brown, makes the majority's assertion even more puzzling.

The legal literature on the '*Charter* values' controversy already occupies significant shelf space.[156] Justices Lauwers and Miller, of the Ontario Court of Appeal, have also recognized the problems with '*Charter* values' as they do not have 'doctrinal structure to guide their identification or application' and are therefore subjective.[157] Their comments were assimilated by Justice Rowe in the TWU decisions.

Despite the considerable and, I would suggest, growing opposition toward the '*Charter* values' doctrine, the SCC, for the time being, is intent on using it as a tool of constitutional interpretation. With that in mind, we must consider how this doctrine will impact the field of charity law as it relates to religious organizations. There is a strong probability that the ill-advised doctrine has the potential to take away the necessary accreditations, tax exemptions and registered charitable status of religious charities across Canada. That is because it weighs religious teachings and practices (on topics such as marriage, abortion and MAiD) in the balance of political correctness and finds them wanting: in short, they are politically incorrect; they are offensive; they are unbecoming of our modern world.

The fundamental problem with the use of '*Charter* values' is that they are not objective and only can be implemented by those who hold power to enforce their interpretation on others. As Justice Lauwers discerns, '[i]nvariably, the concept is used to identify a particular moral commitment that the sponsor asserts is not only desirable but should be given additional or decisive weight in legal reasoning [...]. Labelling a moral commitment as a "*Charter* value" is, in practice, a rhetorical move – a result-selective conclusion – and not the outcome of a transparent analytical process'.[158] In other words, '*Charter* values' are subjective opinion, which is why we must be concerned.

Law professor Iain Benson observes that the term 'values' is often used as a proxy for objective moral norms.[159] But, as he notes, that is a mistaken application, because 'values' are subjective. A better approach would be to address issues of morality within the 'richer frame' of 'virtues'.[160] For Benson, '[t]he choice to use the language of values to mean something that was believed to be inherently good, at a time when the term was rising to mean "personal choices" free from moral evaluation or its use within educational frameworks that sought to avoid ethics or morals, has led to wide-scale confusion about the meaning of "values".[161] Canadian philosopher George Grant, often referred to by Benson, explains:

> Everybody uses the word 'values' to describe our making of the world: capitalists and socialists, atheists and avowed believers, scientists and politicians. The word comes to us so platitudinously that we take it to belong to the way things are. It is forgotten that before Nietzsche and his immediate predecessors, men did not think about their actions in that language. They did not think that they made the world valuable, but that they participated in its goodness.[162]

In quoting Grant, Benson points out that '"values" is a false sort of moral language – a trickster, one that offers what it does not and cannot deliver'.[163] And its use is ubiquitous. Virtues, on the other hand, argues Benson, 'entail and always have, a shared moral tradition'.[164] Benson makes a compelling argument that the 'values' language has played a similar role in our culture as the cuckoo's egg.[165] Some cuckoo bird species practice a brood parasitism where they lay their eggs in another bird's nest. The cuckoo fledglings then push any non-cuckoo fledgling out of the nest to its death. The cuckoo thereby survives at the expense of the other. This, says Benson, is what has happened with the introduction of 'values' in our language and it is now pushing out the long moral tradition of virtues. The use of 'values' implies that 'nothing is intrinsically good and no one is intrinsically worthy'.[166]

Benson argues that '[a]uthoritarianism, subjectivism and relativism are checked not by vagueness but by moral clarity'.[167] Moral clarity comes from a recognition that there is such a thing as moral truth. It is fascinating to observe that the SCC made a value judgement on TWU's bid for a law school by noting that TWU's CCA was 'degrading and disrespectful'. That judgement was meant to align with its understanding of *Charter* values', as if such an expression was based on a moral truth. However, it was not based on a truth but on a mere expression of the Court's 'values'. The Court was expressing its own subjective offense taken against TWU's lawful expression and practice of religious belief. In essence, the Court, like the ONCA, was persuaded that the existence of TWU's Community Covenant Agreement caused 'hurt', as discussed below.[168]

As the Sexular Age[169] gains traction among secular elites, the differences between those religious communities that maintain traditional sexual norms and those who advocate a further loosening of those norms will become more, not less, prominent. The opposing opinions of what ought to be considered 'proper' in how sexual expression is manifested in any given context will remain a challenge for liberal democratic societies to navigate in allowing maximum individual freedom while also maintaining civil peace.

Those whose sexual orientation did not fit within the binary heterosexual model were, until recent decades, at a distinct disadvantage in gaining societal acceptance of their lifestyle and sense of self. Over the last few decades, academic studies have documented the extent of oppression such groups and individuals have faced historically.[170] Recently,

Western culture has shown empathy with their plight and has sought to make amends by removing criminal sanctions and implementing human rights protections. Public institutions such as the media, government bureaucracies, academia and the law advocate general acceptance of diverse sexual lifestyles. For example, the legal profession and the law schools consistently go to great lengths to encourage LGBTQ individuals to enter the profession.[171]

Nonetheless, within many religious communities, traditional moral teachings on marriage remain. Liberal democracies must now contend with the problem of sexual minorities who are offended by knowing and interacting with the traditional moral beliefs and practices of religious institutions. The offense is said to be exacerbated by the fact that government agencies grant regulatory approval that allows these 'discriminatory' institutions to operate.

Yet, it must be recognized that religious institutions and religious communities still provide high social capital[172] and social benefit[173] to their respective constituencies and to the public at large. Demanding systematically forced closure of these institutions by the state for not respecting a diversity of sexual expressions is bound to be met with pushback from the religious community and their supporters.

In the TWU law school case, the unaddressed 'elephant in the room' was the fact that the law societies sided with the argument that they could not be seen to 'endorse' a traditional moral view of marriage by granting accreditation to TWU, even in the face of robust SCC jurisprudence that presumed significant public benefit of religious institutions and that understood religious freedom was among 'the original freedoms'.[174] The SCC's majority approach to the 'elephant' was to ignore it completely, just as it ignored the *TWU* 2001 precedent. The net effect of this refusal has only made the situation more precarious. Religious communities are now faced with an existential threat because they hold views on marriage that differ from government actors, societal elites, and the SCC.

The poignant question to be answered is, 'Do religious organizations with traditional moral views and practices on marriage no longer have the support of public regulators?' The religious organizations that operate elementary and high schools, radio stations, refugee programmes, literature distribution charities, international development programmes, churches and more all require government regulation in one form or another. Are they considered so 'degrading and disrespectful' that the law is willing to eliminate their enumerated rights in favour of the 'idiosyncrasies of the judicial mind' under the rubric of '*Charter* values'? Is having such views now considered the great blasphemy of our secular ideology?

When religious communities maintain traditional moral beliefs and practices, those who hold more ideologically 'progressive' views often take offense that their views are not universally accepted. That is self-evident, but it goes much deeper. Describing individuals whose confirmation bias is strengthened when they are 'embedded in groups that are locked in combat with other groups', Jonathan Haidt explains that '[i]ntense tribalism is fundamentally incompatible with open mindedness and the search for truth because changing your mind – or merely acknowledging nuance – becomes treason'.[175]

Indeed, there is great irony in the uncompromising absolutism of the 'sexular' elites. While such 'progressives' purport to be inclusive and tolerant, they are in fact as dogmatic as any religious extremist when it comes to establishing and enforcing the 'right' opinions and practices. Heresy, in this view, must be called out and shamed.[176] Not only was TWU's CCA postulating wrong views, it was the source of harm. It actually 'hurt' those who had a different view.[177] 'The refusal to approve TWU's proposed law school', said the SCC majority, 'prevents concrete, not abstract, harms to LGBTQ people and to the public in general'.[178] Yet, there was not an iota of evidence that TWU's proposal created any concrete harm. It was a proposed law school. No law school yet existed. How then could there be concrete harm? It was judicial fiction to elevate offense to 'hurt' as per Justice MacPherson of the Ontario Court of Appeal, who wrote, 'My conclusion is a simple one: the part of TWU's Community Covenant in issue in this appeal is deeply discriminatory to the LGBTQ community, and it hurts'.[179]

The courts in Nova Scotia or British Columbia were not so convinced about the notion of 'harm'. The BCCA addressed the issue head on:

> While there is no doubt that the Covenant's refusal to accept LGBTQ expressions of sexuality is deeply offensive and hurtful to the LGBTQ community, and we do not in any way wish to minimize that effect, there is no *Charter* or other legal right to be free from views that offend and contradict an individual's strongly held beliefs, absent the kind of 'hate speech' described by the SCC in *Whatcott* that could incite harm against others. [...] Disagreement and discomfort with the views of others is unavoidable in a free and democratic society.[180]

As the BCCA noted further, 'the language of "offense and hurt" is not helpful in balancing competing rights. The beliefs expressed by some Benchers and members of the Law Society that the evangelical Christian community's view of marriage is "abhorrent", "archaic" and "hypocritical" would no doubt be deeply offensive and hurtful to members of that community'.[181]

The BCCA's view, however, was rejected outright by the SCC, who claimed that more is at stake than simple 'disagreement and discomfort' with views that some will find offensive. Religious freedom can be justifiably limited where its beliefs or practices injure the rights of others to hold their own opinions and where it 'offends the public perception that freedom of religion includes freedom from religion'.[182] That, of course, presumes the Court has a very good understanding and knowledge of 'public perception' beyond the echo chamber that is the legal profession – and that this is even a legitimate legal principle by which to measure the level of protection afforded by law to religious freedom. University professors and administrators – and now appeal court judges – appear to be 'circling the wagons' around those who claim to be offended. There is little tolerance for any questioning of 'the reasonableness (let alone the sincerity) of someone's emotional state, particularly if those emotions are linked to one's group identity'.[183]

Scholars Lukianoff and Haidt note, '"I'm offended" becomes an unbeatable trump card'.[184] They suggest that '[s]chools may be training students in thinking styles that will damage their careers and friendships, along with their mental health',[185] not to mention irreparable damage done to freedom and democracy when this thinking infiltrates legal analysis.

There is virtually no limit to where this perceived right of not being offended may lead. Consider our cultural moment when the University of Virginia president was openly chastised for having the temerity to quote from Thomas Jefferson, the university's founder.

The opposition came from the university's professors and students who were offended that the founder was a slave owner.[186] Gone is the critical ability to appreciate the dissonance of the past with today's morality to understand Jefferson's own ideal. His aspiration for the university was that 'this institution will be based on the illimitable freedom of the human mind. For here we are not afraid to follow truth wherever it may lead, nor to tolerate any error so long as reason is left free to combat it'.[187] The current logic that rejects these words of Jefferson based on a retroactive sense of morality would presumably also reject the legitimacy of the American Declaration of Independence since it, too, was written by Jefferson.

Yet, as author Bruce Bawer observed, even though America has not lived up to its creed as stated in the Declaration – 'that all men are created equal, that they are endowed by their Creator with certain unalienable Rights, that among these are Life, Liberty and the pursuit of Happiness' – that creed 'was in fact the very thing that made moral progress in America not only possible but inevitable'.[188]

Likewise, Professor Amanda Harman Cooley[189] vividly illustrates the same cultural tendency with the juxtaposition of two student protests at the University of North Carolina (UNC), one in 1966 and the other in 2009. In 1966, UNC students protested a law that would not allow any Communist to speak at a state-funded sponsored university, even though many did not agree with the speakers' views. They also filed, and won, a lawsuit against the UNC Board of Trustees for banning public speakers. In 2009, UNC students protested so vehemently to silence a speaker with whom they disagreed that the disturbance cut short US Representative Tom Tancredo's speech on campus. They opposed his position on illegal immigration.[190]

Observes Justice Lauwers, of the Ontario Court of Appeal:

> *Charter* values such as dignity, equality, and liberty engage our deepest instincts about right and wrong. They engage our sympathies, our emotions, our passions, and, most importantly, our sense of justice. The common understanding and expectation is that decision-makers are independent, impartial, and objective, especially judges. But human beings are fallible, and judges and tribunal members must be attentive to their own cognitive infirmities when they carry out their public responsibilities, if they are to do justice consistent with the demands of the rule of law. The task of a decision-maker exercising public responsibilities is to do the right thing for the right reason, regardless of personal feelings.[191]

The problem with personal feelings, whether cloaked in the phrase '*Charter* value' or in the notion of dignitary harm, as the basis of judicial decision making is that it inevitably creates inconsistency in the law and leads to 'concept creep' or 'interest creep'. By that I make reference to the work of Dov Fox who explains:

> When a court of last resort invokes an underspecified interest without clarifying which among the more particular meanings it plausibly conveys, litigants, lawmakers, lower courts, and others who rely on it are […] left only to guess what that instruction means. In law as in life, these seemingly trivial equivocations can take us afield of our destination.[192]

'*Charter* values' is a creeping, evolving concept that has limited value in assisting the law to be just. It is indeed a product of the 'idiosyncrasies of the judicial mind' that is used as a reasoning tool to justify a judge's decision.[193]

Professor Jonathan Haidt reminds us that when we make decisions, there are two distinct acts that occur: judgement and justification. We tend to intuitively make decisions and then justify why we made the decision.[194] Recognizing this basic impulse in decision making, says Lauwers, should humble judges as they seek rational explanations for their decisions, being mindful of how influenced they are by feelings.[195]

Abortion and the Canada Summer Jobs Controversy

Consider, for example, the Abortion Rights Coalition of Canada's (ARCC) call to the Liberal government to remove the charitable status of 'anti-abortion agencies'. ARCC claimed that these religious charities were misrepresenting their expense reports[196] to the government but also, more importantly, that their mission and activities 'are inherently political and biased, which should disqualify them from charitable status. They work to stigmatize abortion, constrain individuals' access to it, and ultimately to recriminalize it. They seek to subvert the *Charter* rights of Canadians through deception and misinformation'.[197]

It is important to note that since ARCC's call for action against pro-life charities, the federal government has removed limitations on a charity's ability to engage in public policy (i.e. political) activities.[198] Therefore, ARCC's position on that political front is moot. However, the other part of their objection is very much in play – the argument that anti-abortion charities 'subvert the *Charter* rights of Canadians through deception and misinformation'. That position has resonance with the current government, and it resonates with those who argue that such charities are in violation of '*Charter* values'.

In 2017, ARCC was dismayed that 'anti-abortion' groups and churches received funding from the Canada Summer Jobs (CSJ) programme, the fact of which was inimical to ARCC and the current government's public commitment to the so-called feminist agenda. Acting upon ARCC's complaint, the government required all applicants to 'attest' to government ideology on '*Charter* values', support a 'pro-choice' position and have anti-discrimination policies acceptable to the government's view in order to be eligible to apply for the 2018 CSJ programme. The ensuing controversy meant that some 1,500 religious charities could not apply and/or were denied CSJ funding because they did not attest to the government's ideology.[199] While the government did reverse course, to a degree, in 2019, the matter nevertheless provides a case study as to how politics could drive government itself to challenge the charitable status of religious organizations.

During the CSJ debate, opposition MPs raised concerns that the government's aggressive approach towards non-conforming religious groups was bound to lead to a similar attack on registered charitable status. Lisa Raitt declared, '[t]he Prime Minister has opened the door, and it is going to be part of other programs. I am sounding the alarm right now. We could be in for a major problem with charitable status in this country and ripping the carpet out from so many vulnerable people who depend on charities and their good work'.[200]

Indeed, ARCC's response confirmed the predictions of opposition MPs. In a March 2018 statement, ARCC observed that the '"charitable" purpose of anti-choice groups to oppose abortion no longer has any public benefit and their status should be revoked'.[201]

After all, '[t]he work of anti-abortion groups [...] no longer has any public benefit (if it ever did) and is now detrimental to society'.²⁰² In particular, 'no "crisis pregnancy centre" should be registered as a charity', says ARCC, because, '[t]heir mission is literally that – a "mission" to stop abortion based on religious doctrine'.²⁰³

Importantly, the beliefs and practices complained of in the CSJ controversy were not illegal but simply out of step with the government's partisan ideology. That was sufficient for government supporters to call for the removal of charitable status. The CSJ controversy provides an example of how a politically charged public policy issue can quickly and readily transform into a call for removing charitable status of non-conforming religious organizations.

Conclusion: Moving Forward

The law's synchronization with changing sexual moral views has had a major impact on the legal accommodation of religious entities. The SCC expressed its opinion, in the *TWU* 2018 decisions, that state actors are now empowered to deny religious organizations accreditation for religious practices that are deemed 'degrading and disrespectful'²⁰⁴ and that violate '*Charter* values'.²⁰⁵ By virtue of the two TWU decisions, the SCC has put in jeopardy the law's traditional accommodation of religious practice and has dramatically increased the likelihood of further assaults on the ability of religious organizations, primarily conservative Christian charities, to carry out their work as registered charities. The Court's subjective understanding of '*Charter* values' is now eclipsing the enumerated right of religious freedom.

I have argued that the BJU case explains the intellectual framework for understanding how the SCC arrived at its *TWU* 2018 decisions. That framework considers only current 'societal values', even in the absence of specific statutory or positive legal authority. In the Canadian context, the justification comes down to the Court using the questionable concept of '*Charter* values' to arrive at its conclusion.

The dramatic change in the moral landscape has put pressure on religious communities to conform to elite opinion. In the *Obergefell* hearing, Associate Justice Alito asked US Solicitor General Donald Verrilli, 'in the Bob Jones case, the Court held that a college was not entitled to tax-exempt status if it opposed interracial marriage or interracial dating. So would the same apply to a university or a college if it opposed same-sex marriage?' Solicitor General Verrilli replied, 'You know, I – I don't think I can answer that question without knowing more specifics, but it's certainly going to be an issue. I – I don't deny that. I don't deny that, Justice Alito. It is – it is going to be an issue'.²⁰⁶

As we have seen in this chapter, there is a growing chorus of voices calling on government to remove the registered charitable status of religious organizations that are dissonant with the evolving, normative moral views among society's elite. Views on traditional marriage are only one contentious issue – there are at least two others: abortion and MAiD. Such moral flashpoints are expected to increase in intensity.

Liberal democracies, like Canada, are at a reflection point on how best to realise the promises of individual freedom while maintaining the public good. Religious charities have done and continue to do much public good.[207] Putting in jeopardy their registered charitable status – indeed, their very existence – because they no longer reflect the worldviews and practices of Canadian elites on the fundamental human life issues is a denial of liberal democratic aspirations of respecting diversity and ways of being.

The 'public good' is best served when religious communities are given the opportunity to carry out their religious beliefs and practices on FHLI as historically understood. In other words, teachings within the religious community and their organizations must be respected, not penalized. This has been broadly understood in the law. To say that we, as a society, respect diversity means we accept a wide and sometimes conflicting spectrum of views and practices on FHLI – religious and non-religious, conservative and liberal, right and left. To favour one at the expense of the other is hardly tolerant of diversity.

In the past, the SCC affirmed the accommodation of religious practices and viewpoints. Consider two examples. First, in the *Multani*[208] case, the SCC granted accommodation to a Sikh boy to wear his kirpan (a ceremonial dagger) to school because of its religious significance. Other students were concerned with this arrangement, to which the Court said, '[r]eligious tolerance is a very important value of Canadian society'. Therefore, 'it is incumbent on the schools to discharge their obligation to instil in their students [that] this value [...] is [...] at the very foundation of our democracy'.[209] Religious tolerance being the very foundation of our democracy is a statement with which I agree wholeheartedly. If only the SCC were consistent in that sentiment.

The second example involves the role of religious views in the public square. In its 2002 *Chamberlain*[210] decision, the SCC held that the term 'secular' includes the religious. It held that the *British Columbia School Act*'s requirement that schools be conducted on 'strictly secular [...] principles' did not mean decisions by the school trustees could not be motivated by religious views.[211] Justice Gonthier pointed out in his dissenting judgement:

> In my view, Saunders J. below erred in her assumption that 'secular' effectively meant 'non-religious'. This is incorrect since nothing in the *Charter*, political or democratic theory, or a proper understanding of pluralism demands that atheistically based moral positions trump religiously based moral positions on matters of public policy.[212]

Gonthier J obtained his inspiration from Professor Iain T. Benson who argued:

> The term 'secular' has come to mean a realm that is neutral or, more precisely, 'religion-free.' Implicit in this religion free neutrality is the notion that the secular is a realm of facts distinct from the realm of faith. This understanding, however, is in error. Parse historically the word 'secular' and one finds that secular means something like non-sectarian or focused on this world, not 'non-faith.' States cannot be neutral towards metaphysical claims. Their very inaction towards certain claims operates as an affirmation of others. This realization of the faith-based nature of all decisions will be important as the courts seek to give meaning to terms such as secular in statutes written some time ago.[213]

Political philosopher William Galston notes, 'A liberal democracy is, among other things, an invitation to struggle over the control of civil associations'.[214] He argues:

> It is necessary to reconsider the understanding of politics that pervades much contemporary discussion, especially among political theorists – an understanding that tacitly views public institutions as plenipotentiary and civil society as a political construction possessing only those liberties that the polity chooses to grant and modify or revoke at will. This understanding of politics makes it all but impossible to give serious weight to the 'liberal' dimension of liberal democracy.[215]

Galston illuminates the struggle of our time. Those in power seek to control and (re)make civil associations in their image. However, if we do not allow civil organizations the ability to be different from the powerful, they are not free. Society becomes homogenous and bland. The vibrancy of liberal democracies is due in no small part to healthy civil groups such as religious communities.

Religious educational institutions that require teachers and students to share the same ethics on marriage, pro-life principles and rules on sexual intimacy 'are not gratuitous or controlling'; instead, '[t]hey empower incoming students and scholars by giving them the freedom – the live option – to join a community that offers support for living by a demanding moral vision of their own choice'.[216] Context is important, as was noted above by Professor Hellman.

Indeed, this is reflected in s.27 of the *Charter* itself: 'This *Charter* shall be interpreted in a manner consistent with the preservation and enhancement of the multicultural heritage of Canadians'.[217] The appeal to a 'multicultural heritage' is a recognition that the state cannot simply dismiss religious beliefs and practices as inconsequential.[218] Enumerated rights must be understood within the context of Canada's multicultural reality – that includes religion and the public expression of religious views – even as they affect public policy.[219] In *R v Videoflicks*, Tarnopolsky JA was referring to s.27 of the *Charter* when he stated:

> Religion is one of the dominant aspects of a culture which it is intended to preserve and enhance [...] Section 27 determines that ours will be an open and pluralistic society which must accommodate the small inconveniences that might occur where religious practices are recognized as permissible exceptions to otherwise justifiable homogenous requirements.[220]

If we are to maintain a truly free and liberal society, the modern nation-state must resist that homogenizing tendency in order to provide room for diverse, religious communities to operate their respective charities. Religion is the manifestation of humanity's quest to understand the meaning of life: who we are and what our core purpose is. It is, by nature, intensely personal and yet inherently public. Since other people have come to their own conclusions about life, they may feel threatened if our expressed thought contradicts their personal views. That is the risk we take in a free society. Not to take that risk means we are not free.

Moving Forward

So, then, how do we move forward?

First, we must state the obvious: given that registered charitable tax status is granted by Parliament, there must be a political will that supports true diversity – a diversity that allows religious communities to remain true to their faith commitments on the fundamental human life issues. We cannot avoid this political reality and must prepare to address the political challenges as they arise. Registered charitable status for religious charities is not a constitutional right. It is a privilege, granted to charities advancing religion, in accordance with the CRA's stringent guidelines, maintained at the sole discretion of the government in power. Given the CRA's recently relaxed political activities policy,[221] religious charities now have greater latitude when it comes to advocating for registered charitable status among government bureaucrats and politicians.

Second, there is a need for greater exposure to the work of religious charities among three secular elite groups – academics, media, and legal professionals. Sociologist Peter L. Berger observed:

> There exists an international subculture composed of people with western-type higher education, especially in the humanities and social sciences that is indeed secularized. This subculture is the principle 'carrier' of progressive, enlightened beliefs and values. While its members are relatively thin on the ground, they are very influential, as they control the institutions that provide the 'official' definitions of reality, notably the educational system, the media of mass communication and the higher reaches of the legal system.[222]

'What this means', suggests Iain T. Benson, 'is that when we are dealing with the law and the media we must recognize that these sectors are heavily over-represented by those, such as many Western journalists, judges and lawyers, who have little time for religion at best and actively wish to attack it at worst'.[223]

Given that these three groups (academics, media personnel, and members of the legal profession) are 'thin on the ground' but 'are very influential', it behooves the religious charities to ensure these groups are aware of the work that religious charities do. Just as importantly, these elite groups need to appreciate why religious charities do what they do. After all, it is the religious motivation that undergirds the charitable work to begin with. If religious charities are forced to fit the secular mould – that is to say, if they are called upon to deny their religious beliefs and practices – then they lose the 'why' of the enterprise. The religious 'why' is the oxygen of religious charities. Religious charities, as others in this volume make abundantly clear, are a very significant player in the charitable sector. Losing them would be an unfathomable loss to society.

Third, the law of religious accommodation needs to be revisited. The SCC's recent incursion against religious accommodation as shown in the *Hutterian Brethren*[224] and the *TWU* 2018 cases must be countered. The lack of respect the Court has shown towards religious groups is unprecedented. It appears to be bolstered by a wave of identity politics that threatens to impoverish our society, as it will inevitably lead to religious charities being forced to stop programming or even 'close shop'.[225] It is time we remember that religious tolerance is the very foundation of our society.

Fourth, the legal accommodation of religious charities functions well to promote beneficial programmes while also allowing a measure of regulatory oversight, both of which could be lost with the removal of registered charitable status for the advancement of religion. Given the tangible and intangible benefits that religious charities provide, the onus is on critics like the CBA to show why deregistration is in the public interest. This is worth emphasizing.

Finally, religious charities have to continue maintaining a presence before the courts by intervening in key cases that affect their registered status. If we have learned anything in recent years, it is that incremental legal developments can have long-term, dramatic implications. Therefore, religious charities need to be vigilant and consistent in advocacy. That will require charities, along with the broader religious community, to seek and develop competent expertise to be persuasive in court, in the political arena, in the media and in academic circles.

Given the current obsession with '*Charter* values' that have been used in diminishing enumerated *Charter* rights, there is little doubt that they can be used to take away the unenumerated privileges of tax exemption that religious communities currently enjoy at the sole discretion of our political leaders.

Concluding Remarks

The growing controversy over the SCC's use (and abuse) of '*Charter* values' shows no sign of abating anytime soon.[226] As Professor Waldron, QC, observes:

> Ultimately, the moral principles of the judiciary shape the 'values' they have found in the *Charter* and, rather than using them to protect a morally diverse population, they succumb to the temptation to create from their values the same 'moral legalism' they condemned in *Butler*,[227] leaving Canadian society at the mercy of an elite group whose markers of cultural superiority are enforced as universal.[228]

The SCOTUS used 'values' as a justification for the support of the IRS's denial of registered charitable status to BJU for racial discrimination. Similarly, the SCC, though it did not overtly admit to using the BJU case as a template, nevertheless used similar reasoning to rule against TWU's law school proposal. This paper argues the SCC's approach is inherently wrong in law and in policy. The SCC failed to observe its own *TWU* 2001 precedent or the enumerated *Charter* protection of TWU's religious freedom s.2(a) right. Further, it applied an amorphous, undisciplined and inherently subjective doctrine of '*Charter* values' to arrive at a decision that was supported by Canada's legal profession, media and academics.

As discussed, the SCC's dedication to the '*Charter* values' doctrine logically threatens the registered charitable status of any registered charity that does not comply with the Court's understanding of '*Charter* values'. This chapter is primarily concerned with the registered status of religious charities that maintain traditional moral views on pro-life, traditional marriage and end-of-life issues. Such charities have every reason to fear a negative treatment if they face a challenge to their registered charitable status before Canadian courts dedicated to the '*Charter* values' doctrine. As Justice Lauwers observes, the use of '*Charter* values' 'tends to dispense with disciplined decision-making and to facilitate result-selective reasoning by tribunals and judges'.[229] That was clearly seen in the *TWU* 2018 decisions.

CHARITABLE STATUS SUBJECT TO *CHARTER* VALUES   191

Given that the SCC shows no sign of reducing its reliance on this controversial doctrine, it has now become abundantly clear that the only sure way that registered religious charities will be successful in maintaining their status is if they can convince their fellow citizens that such status is worth preserving. In other words, this issue has become political. The chapters in this volume – including this one – are meant to make that public policy case.

Notes

1 The SCC made two decisions in the TWU case: *Law Society of British Columbia v Trinity Western University*, 2018 SCC 32 [*LSBC v TWU* 2018] and *Trinity Western University v Law Society of Upper Canada*, 2018 SCC 33 [*TWU v LSUC* 2018]. Together, the cases are referred to hereinafter as *TWU* 2018.
2 *TWU* 2018, *supra* note 1 (transcript of oral hearing, SCC vol. 2, 1 December 2017, at 282).
3 Fundamental human life issues (FHLI), for the purposes of this chapter, are those issues that have been, up until recently, culturally understood concepts, principles, and axioms. They include abortion, marriage and end-of-life principles. Western culture, influenced as it was by Judaeo-Christian beliefs, understood that human life was to be respected such that intentional killing of the pre-born and the elderly was morally wrong, and that marriage was a commitment of one man and one woman for life. There are other FHLI but they are not the subject of this chapter.
4 As Winston Churchill would say.
5 See, *R v Big M Drug Mart Ltd.*, [1985] 1 SCR 295, 1985 CanLII 69 (SCC), para 94, <http://canlii.ca/t/1fv2b#par94>, and s.1 of *Canadian Charter of Rights and Freedoms*, Part 1 of the *Constitution Act*, 1982, being Schedule B to the Canada Act 1982 (UK), 1982, c 11 (hereinafter '*Charter*').
6 I first heard this illustration from a talk by Christian apologist Ravi Zacharias.
7 E.g. see the campaign of the BC Humanist Association, 'Fair Property Tax Exemptions', online: <https://www.bchumanist.ca/property_taxes>.
8 *Bob Jones University v United States*, 461 U.S. 574 (1983).
9 In August 2018, TWU announced that the CCA would no longer be mandatory for students, although it remains mandatory for employees. See Bob Kuhn, 'TWU Reviews Community Covenant' (14 August 2018), online: <https://www.twu.ca/twu-reviews-community-covenant>.
10 *LSBC v TWU* 2018, *supra* note 1 at para 101.
11 As McLachlin CJC observed, 'students who do not agree with the religious practices do not need to attend these schools. But if they want to attend, for whatever reason […] it is difficult to speak of compulsion' (*LSBC v TWU* 2018, *supra* note 1 at para 133).
12 The SCC did not rebut the mischaracterization of the Ontario Court of Appeal that TWU's CCA violated s.15 of the Charter. TWU is not subject to the Charter, therefore cannot violate the Charter.
13 *Trinity Western University v British Columbia College of Teachers*, [2001] 1 SCR 772, 2001 SCC 31 (CanLII), para 25, <http://canlii.ca/t/dmd#par25>, hereinafter '*TWU* 2001'. In the 2001 case, the British Columbia College of Teachers (BCCT) argued that TWU's admissions requirement was discriminatory against LGBTQ student applicants to TWU and asserted that TWU's education graduates would likely discriminate against LGBTQ students under their care in the public-school system. The SCC rejected those arguments and ordered the BCCT to accredit TWU's education degree.
14 *Ibid*, at para 25.
15 Barry W Bussey, 'Law Matters but Politics Matter More: The Supreme Court of Canada and Trinity Western University' (2019) 7 Oxford Journal of Law and Religion, 559–68, <https://doi.org/10.1093/ojlr/rwy046>.
16 British Columbia: *Trinity Western University v The Law Society of British Columbia*, 2015 BCSC 2326 (CanLII), http://canlii.ca/t/gmh9k; *Trinity Western University v The Law Society of British Columbia*, 2016 BCCA 423 (CanLII), http://canlii.ca/t/gvd6q [*TWU* BCCA 2016]. Ontario: *Trinity*

Western University v The Law Society of Upper Canada, 2015 ONSC 4250 (CanLII), http://canlii.ca/t/gjxpw; *Trinity Western University v The Law Society of Upper Canada*, 2016 ONCA 518 (CanLII), http://canlii.ca/t/gs9d5 [*TWU* ONCA 2016]. Nova Scotia: *Trinity Western University v Nova Scotia Barristers' Society*, 2015 NSSC 25 (CanLII), http://canlii.ca/t/gg386; *The Nova Scotia Barristers' Society v Trinity Western University*, 2016 NSCA 59 (CanLII), http://canlii.ca/t/gsng6.

The SCC heard appeals only from BC and Ontario as the Nova Scotia Court of Appeal decision was not appealed.

17 *Bob Jones University v United States*, 461 U.S. 574 [hereinafter 'BJU']. See below the extent of the references to BJU throughout the *TWU* 2018 litigation.

18 *TWU* BCCA 2016, *supra* note 16, at para 182.

19 *TWU* ONCA 2016, *supra* note 16, at paras 136–38.

20 Elaine Craig, 'The Case for the Federation of Law Societies Rejecting Trinity Western University's Proposed Law Degree Program' (2013) 25 Can. J. Women & L., 148; Elaine Craig, 'TWU Law: A Reply to Proponents of Approval' (2014) 37 Dalhousie LJ, 621; Pippa Feinstein & Sarah E. Hamill, 'The Silencing Of Queer Voices In The Litigation Over Trinity Western University's Proposed Law School' (2017) 34:2 Windsor Yearbook on Access to Justice 156, 2017 CanLIIDocs 161, <http://www.canlii.org/t/792>; Blair Major, 'Translating the Conflict over Trinity Western University's Proposed Law School' (2017) 43:1 Queen's LJ.

21 Susan Ursel, of the Canadian Bar Association, in *TWU* 2018, *supra* note 1 (transcript of oral hearing, SCC vol. 2, 1 December 2017, at 282).

22 Justice Gascon, in *TWU* 2018, *supra* note 1 (transcript of oral hearing, SCC vol. 1, 30 November 2017, at 47).

23 To suggest that the state gives its imprimatur to the teachings of a religious entity solely because it issues a regulatory approval for the granting of a license to operate a nursing home, a hospital or a school, is a very troubling concept. It makes no practical sense. For example, of the 86,234 registered charities in Canada, 33,020 (38.3%) are religious charities registered under the charitable head of the advancement of religion (as of March 2018). Are we to assume that the Canada Revenue Agency (CRA) has vetted all 33,020 Christian charities for their beliefs and practices before it issued registered charitable status for each of them?

24 *LSBC v TWU*, *supra* note 1 at para 137.

25 *Supra* note 8.

26 347 U.S. 483 (1954).

27 Olati Johnson, 'The Story of Bob Jones University v United States: Race, Religion, and Congress' Extraordinary Acquiescence' (2010) Columbia Public Law & Legal Theory Working Papers, Paper 9184, at 4, online: <http://lsr.nellco.org/columbia_pllt/9184>. See also, David Nevin & Robert E. Bills, *The Schools That Fear Built: Segregationist Academies in the South* (Washington, DC: Acropolis Books, 1976).

28 Johnson, *supra* note 27 at 4.

29 'Federal Tax Benefits to Segregated Private Schools' (1968) 68:5 Columbia Law Review, 922–58, at 922, doi:10.2307/1121037 ['Tax Benefits'].

30 *Civil Rights Act* of 1964, Pub.L. 88–352, 78 Stat. 241 (1964).

31 'Tax Benefits', *supra* note 29 at 924, quoting from the IRS News Release, August 2, 1967, 7 CCH 1967 STAND. FED. TAX REP. fn 673.

32 'Tax Benefits', *ibid*:

> in *Poindexter II*, Judge Wisdom wrote that '[a]ny aid to segregated schools that is the product of the State's affirmative, purposeful policy of fostering segregated schools and has the effect of encouraging discrimination is significant state involvement in private discrimination'. [Poindexter II, 275 F. Supp. 833, 854 (E.D. La. 1967), aff'd per curiam, 389 U.S. 571 (1968)] He rejected any reliance on the amount of aid. The public school remains just as segregated, by means of state-encouraged separation of the races into

public and private schools, as it was under the dual system of public schools invalidated by Brown; the state's action is, therefore, just as impermissible constitutionally.

33 Section 501(c)(3) of the US Tax Code exempted from tax '[c]orporations, and any community chest fund or foundation, organized and operated exclusively for religious, charitable, scientific, testing for public safety, literary or educational purposes, or to foster national or international amateur sports competition [...] or for the prevention of cruelty to children or animals'.[33] Section 170(a) of the tax code provided deductions for 'charitable contributions', defined in 170(c) as contributions to corporations 'organized and operated exclusively for religious, charitable, scientific, literary or educational purposes'.
34 *Green v Kennedy*, 309 F. Supp. 1127, 1140 (D.D.C 1970).
35 *Green v Connally*, 330 F. Supp. 1150, 1160 (D.D.C 1970).
36 In a 25 March 2006 interview with *Western Standard*, then Chief Justice Beverley McLachlin said, 'in interpreting the constitutional provisions, from time to time the court can have and must have recourse to unwritten values'. See Terry O'Neill, 'The right to make new rights: Chief Justice Beverley McLachlin defends the Supreme Court's power to transcend the Constitution', *Western Standard* (24 April 2006), 23 at 24.
37 Plaintiffs in *Green* reopened the litigation, and a nationwide class action lawsuit was started by parents of black children in *Wright v Regan*, 65 F.2d 820, 822–26 (D.C. Cir. 1981).
38 Johnson, *supra* note 27 at 15.
39 *Ibid*, at 16, quoting: Department of the Treasury News Release, 8 January 1982, Treasury Establishes New Tax-Exempt Policy.
40 Johnson, *supra* note 27 at 17, noting the Proposed Legislation to Amend Internal Revenue Code, Communication from the President of the United States, No. 97–132, 97th Congress 2d Session (18 January 1982).
41 *Wright v Regan, Sec. of the Treasury*, Order (No. 76–1426), (D.C. Cir., 18 February 1982).
42 BJU, *supra* note 8 at 580.
43 *Ibid*, at 586.
44 *Ibid*, at 591.
45 *Ibid*.
46 *Ibid*, at 592.
47 *Ibid*, at 593.
48 *Ibid*, at 595.
49 *Ibid*, at 596.
50 *Ibid*, at 597.
51 *Ibid*, at 598.
52 *Ibid*, at 601.
53 *Ibid*.
54 *Ibid*, at 604.
55 See the work of Cass Sunstein, *Why Nudge?: The Politics of Libertarian Paternalism*, Storrs Lectures on Jurisprudence (New Haven, CT: Yale University Press, 2015); Cass R. Sunstein and Lucia A. Reisch, *Trusting Nudges: Toward a Bill of Rights for Nudging* (Abingdon, Oxon: Routledge, 2019).
56 *TWU* 2001, *supra* note 13 at para 70.
57 *Ibid*, at para 71.
58 Craig, 'The Case for the Federation of Law Societies Rejecting Trinity Western University's Proposed Law Degree Program' (2013) 25 Can. J. Women & L. 159. In her letter to Rene Gallant of the Nova Scotia Barristers' Society (NSBS), 5 February 2014, at 6, she asks:

[W]ould the NSBS give the stamp of approval to a law school that prohibited interracial couples? The analogy is direct and apt. There are examples of American schools, such as Bob Jones University, that have done precisely this and have done so on the basis of religious belief. The Internal Revenue Service had the courage to revoke Bob Jones

University's tax-exempt status on the basis that such a policy was contrary to public interest – a decision that was upheld by the Supreme Court of the United States. (See online at <https://nsbs.org/sites/default/files/ftp/TWU_Submissions/2014-02-05_Craig_TWU.pdf>.)

59 Gavin MacKenzie, Transcript, Convocation of the Law Society of Upper Canada, Public Session (10 April 2014), at 27–28, online (pdf): <https://lawsocietyontario.azureedge.net/media/lso/media/legacy/pdf/c/convocationtranscriptapr102014twu.pdf>.
60 Jena McGill, Dr Angela Cameron & Angela Chaisson, of the University of Ottawa, letter to the LSUC Convocation, 28 March 2014, at 23–24.
61 *TWU* ONCA 2016, *supra* note 16 at para 138.
62 *TWU* BCCA 2016, *supra* note 16 at para 182.
63 *Ibid*.
64 *Ibid*.
65 Factum of Appellant, The Law Society of British Columbia, SCC File No. 37318, at para 200 (p. 5), online: https://www.scc-csc.ca/case-dossier/info/af-ma-eng.aspx?cas=37318.
66 Factum of the Respondents, Trinity Western University and Brayden Volkenant, SCC File No. 37318, at paras 163–65 (p. 37), online https://www.scc-csc.ca/case-dossier/info/af-ma-eng.aspx?cas=37318:

> This case is not like the American case of *Bob Jones University v United States*. *Bob Jones* involved state financial support (i.e., a tax exemption) for a school. TWU is not seeking financial assistance or other support. It seeks only recognition for its graduates. In *Bob Jones*, a penalty was imposed on the school for conduct of the university. No one refused to recognize its graduates' qualifications. That case does not support a principle 'that discretionary decision-makers should deny public benefits to private applicants.' In any event, the anti-miscegenation, segregationist ethos reflected in *Bob Jones* is not comparable to evangelical beliefs on marriage. TWU and its community hold beliefs that are long-standing and protected in Canadian law, unlike those in *Bob Jones*. Unlike antimiscegenation rules, the purpose of evangelical beliefs and rules were not to '[force] segregation on an oppressed minority.' TWU's beliefs about marriage are widely held and have been inherent in the Christian and Western legal tradition for thousands of years and are recognized in the *Civil Marriage Act*. *The Income Tax Act* also protects the status of religious charities for exercising their religious position on marriage, which alone distinguishes *Bob Jones*.

67 E.g. the Canadian Bar Association / SOGIC wrote a letter to Gerald Tremblay, 18 March 2013, and cited BJU in Section E, p. 6.
68 Factum of the Intervener, Canadian Bar Association, SCC File No. 37209 & SCC File No. 37318, at paras 23–27.
69 Factum of the Intervener, EGALE Human Rights Trust, SCC File No. 37209, fn 18, p. 6.
70 Factum of the Intervener Lesbians, Gays, Bisexuals and Trans People of the University of Toronto (LGBTOUT), SCC File No. 37209.
71 *LSBC v TWU* 2018, *supra* note 1 at para 138.
72 Trinity Western University, Community Covenant Agreement (CCA), section 3.
73 Deborah Hellman, *When Is Discrimination Wrong?* (Cambridge, MA: Harvard University Press, 2008) at 7.
74 *Ibid*, at 29.
75 *Ibid*.
76 See Memorandum from the Law Society of British Columbia, Policy and Legal Services Department, to The Benchers (31 March 2014), Subject: 'Follow up to Enquiries from February 28, 2014 Benchers Meeting', Appendix 9, online (pdf): <https://www.lawsociety.bc.ca/Website/media/Shared/docs/newsroom/TWU-memo1.pdf>.

77 Mary Anne Waldron, 'Analogy and Neutrality: Thinking about Freedom of Religion', in *Religious Freedom and Communities*, ed. Dwight Newman (Toronto: LexisNexis, 2016) at 252.
78 *Ibid*.
79 *Ibid*.
80 *Ibid*.
81 *Edwards v Attorney General of Canada* [1930] A.C. 124 at 136.
82 Bradley W. Miller, 'Beguiled By Metaphors: The 'Living Tree' and Originalist Constitutional Interpretation in Canada' (2009) 22 Can. J. L. & Jurisprudence 331 at 353.
83 See, for instance, Dylan Vade, 'Expanding Gender and Expanding the Law: Toward a Social and Legal Conceptualization of Gender That Is More Inclusive of Transgender People' (2005) 11 Mich. J. Gender & L. 253 at 267: 'Like so many things in life, and in fact, like every moment of life, gender can change, and it can change more than once'. Brenda Picard, in 'Gender Identity: Developments in the Law and Human Rights Protections' (2018) 69 U.N.B.L.J. 126 at 127, asserts that 'we now understand that gender is not binary. It is on a spectrum', further explaining that '[s]exual orientation and gender identity are distinct concepts which are protected separately in human rights legislation. We must challenge stereotypes' (at 128).
84 Elizabeth K. Ehret, 'Legal Loophole: How LGBTQ Nondiscrimination Laws Leave out the Partners of Transgender People' (2015) 67 Rutgers U. L. Rev. 469 at 478 acknowledges that '[w]ays to describe different conceptions of sexuality are continuously being created and added to the 'alphabet soup' of sexual categories, resulting in a list far too cumbersome to be used understandably as a consistent term or phrase in a written work'. As a result, some activists and scholars prefer alterative labels such as 'queer' or 'gender and sexual minorities' (see also Adam R. Chang; Stephanie M. Wildman, 'Gender In/sight: Examining Culture and Constructions of Gender' (2017) 18 Geo. J. Gender & L., 43).

For consistency, this chapter adopts the SCC's use of LGBTQ to denote Lesbian, Gay, Bisexual, Transgender and Queer/Questioning persons.
85 In *Obergefell v Hodges*, 135 S. Ct. 2584 (2015) ['*Obergefell*'].
86 Brief for the American Psychological Ass'n et al. as Amici Curiae Supporting Petitioners at 7, *Obergefell, supra* note 85, online (pdf): https://www.apa.org/about/offices/ogc/amicus/obergefell-supreme-court.pdf.
87 *Obergefell, supra* note 85 at 18–19, emphasis added.
88 *Ibid*, at 27, emphasis added.
89 Frank S. Ravitch, *Freedom's Edge: Religious Freedom, Sexual Freedom, and the Future of America* (New York: Cambridge University Press, 2016) at 171.
90 *Ibid*.
91 *Reference re Same-Sex Marriage*, [2004] 3 S.C.R. 698, 2004 S.C.C. 79 (S.C.C.), at paras 55–60 ['*Reference*'].
92 *TWU* BCCA 2016, *supra* note 16. My personal notes at the time of the hearing.
93 See, for instance, *Civil Marriage Act*, SC 2005, c 33, assented to 20 July 2005. The Preamble states unequivocally:

> WHEREAS nothing in this Act affects the guarantee of freedom of conscience and religion and, in particular, the freedom of members of religious groups to hold and declare their religious beliefs and the freedom of officials of religious groups to refuse to perform marriages that are not in accordance with their religious beliefs; WHEREAS it is not against the public interest to hold and publicly express diverse views on marriage [...]

94 *Reference, supra* note 91 at para 58.
95 *Ibid*, at para 59. Note the *Human Rights Code*, R.S.O. 1990, c. H.19, at s.18.1 (1), which exempts clergy from the Act when they refuse to solemnize a marriage or allow a marriage to use a sacred place if such a marriage would violate their religious beliefs; the doctrines,

rites, usages, or customs of the religious body to which the person belongs. Further, *Marriage Act*, R.S.O. 1990, c. M.3, at s.20 (6) provides the same protection and s. 20 (7) defines 'sacred place' as a place of worship and any ancillary or accessory facilities.

96 *Income Tax Act* RSC, 1985, c 1 (5th Supp) (6.21):

> For greater certainty, subject to subsections (6.1) and (6.2), a registered charity with stated purposes that include the advancement of religion shall not have its registration revoked or be subject to any other penalty under Part V solely because it or any of its members, officials, supporters or adherents exercises, in relation to marriage between persons of the same sex, the freedom of conscience and religion guaranteed under the Canadian Charter of Rights and Freedoms.

97 Jacques Gallant, 'Supreme Court reversal allows LGBTQ groups to take part in case involving B.C. Christian university', *The Star* (2017), online: <https://www.thestar.com/news/gta/2017/08/01/supreme-Court-reversal-allows-lgbtq-groups-to-take-part-in-case-involving-bc-christian-university.html>.

98 Barry W. Bussey, 'The Law of Intervention after TWU Law School Case: Is Justice Seen to Be Done?' (2019) 90 Supreme Court Law Review, 2d Series, 265–96.

99 Richard Wagner Holds First News Conference as Canada's Chief Justice', *Headline Politics* (22 June 2018), online: *cpac.ca*, <http://www.cpac.ca/en/programs/headline-politics/episodes/62857192>.

100 *LSBC v TWU*, *supra* note 1, at paras 47, 95, 98, 103.

101 Court are 'ill-equipped to "assess public consensus, which is a fragile and volatile concept"'. See *Everywoman's Health Centre* at 68–69, cited in CRA 'Guidelines for registering a charity: Meeting the public benefit test', Policy Statement CPS-024, effective 10 March 2006, last modified 23 January 2019, online: <https://www.canada.ca/en/revenue-agency/services/charities-giving/charities/policies-guidance/policy-statement-024-guidelines-registering-a-charity-meeting-public-benefit-test.html#fn30:>.

102 *TWU* 2018, *supra* note 1 (transcript of oral hearing, SCC vol. 1, 30 November 2017, at 58).

103 *TWU* 2018, *supra* note 1 at para 18.

104 *Ibid*, at para 21.

105 *Ibid*, at para 298.

106 *Ibid*, at para 300.

107 See also CRA: 3.1.3 Variation of public benefit over time:

> What was once considered a public benefit for a charitable purpose may not necessarily always be so. What is beneficial is considered in light of prevailing standards current at the time and accordingly, the court's notion of what constitutes public benefit may vary with the passing of time. Previous recognition or rejection of a type of public benefit does not end the issue for all time,
>
> online: <https://www.canada.ca/en/revenue-agency/services/charities-giving/charities/policies-guidance/policy-statement-024-guidelines-registering-a-charity-meeting-public-benefit-test.html#fn45-44-rf>.

108 *TWU* 2018, *supra* note 1 (transcript of oral hearing, SCC vol. 1, 30 November 2017, at 7–8).

109 *Ibid*, at 10.

110 *Ibid*.

111 It is worth noting that Justice Abella used the term 'religious autonomy'. It is not a coincidence, I suggest, that her term is similar to the term 'church autonomy' commonly referred to in the American legal academic context analysing the American religious freedom jurisprudence. Professor Douglas Laycock is credited with raising the notion of 'church autonomy' in his seminal law review article, 'Towards a General Theory of the Religion Clauses: The Case of Church Labor Relations and the Right to Church Autonomy' (1981) 81 Colum.

L. Rev. 1373, 1388–92. He subsequently updated his position in Douglas Laycock, 'Church Autonomy Revisited' (2009) 7 Geo JL & Pub Pol'y, 253.
112 *TWU* 2018, *supra* note 1 (transcript of oral hearing, SCC vol. 1, 30 November 2017, at 11).
113 *Ibid*, at 11–12.
114 *Income Tax Act*, RSC 1985, c 1 (5th Supp), does not define what is charitable. The CRA must therefore rely on the common law definition, which sets out the four heads of charity including the advancement of religion, most recently confirmed in the Supreme Court of Canada decision in *Vancouver Soc'y of Immigrant & Visible Minority Women v Minister of Nat'l Revenue*, [1999] 1 S.C.R. 10, at paras 42, 144.
115 Donovan Waters, QC, 'The advancement of religion in a pluralist society (Part I): Distinguishing religion from giving to "charity"' (2011) 17:7 Trusts & Trustees, 652–67.
116 *Charities Act* 2011 (c 25) UK Act of Parliament, at 4(2): 'it is not to be presumed that a purpose of a particular description is for the public benefit', online: http://www.legislation.gov.uk/ukpga/2011/25
117 Charity Commission 2011: The Advancement of Religion for the Public benefit, D2L, p. 11, online (pdf): https://assets.publishing.service.gov.uk/government/uploads/system/uploads/attachment_data/file/358531/advancement-of-religion-for-the-public-benefit.pdf
118 CRA, 'Guidelines for registering a charity: Meeting the public benefit test', CPS-024 (10 March 2006), online: <https://www.canada.ca/en/revenue-agency/services/charities-giving/charities/policies-guidance/policy-statement-024-guidelines-registering-a-charity-meeting-public-benefit-test.html#toc10/>.
119 See: 'For example, a restriction imposed on eligibility based on a person's religion when the purpose of the undertaking is not religious in nature (for example, the establishment of a science museum) will likely fail the public benefit test and disentitle the applicant from being registered as charitable', CRA CPS-024, *supra* note 118.
120 For a more detailed discussion of the CSJ controversy, see Section III of this chapter.
121 BC Humanist Association, *supra* note 7.
122 For example, see Ian Bushfield, Executive Director of the British Columbia Humanist Association, 'Toward a Modernized Charity Framework for Canada', Submission to Special Senate Committee on the Charitable Sector (17 September 2018), online (pdf): https://d3n8a8pro7vhmx.cloudfront.net/bchumanist/pages/2297/attachments/original/1537216366/2018_BCHA_CSSB_Submission.pdf?1537216366. According to Bushfield, the simplest path forward is to omit 'advancement of religion' in a new statutory definition. Religious organizations that contribute to the public good in other ways may be recognized under other purposes, such as relief of poverty'. (As an alternative, he was also in favour of redefining religion to include non-theist beliefs.) There are also other examples of politically motivated campaigns to get rid of religious funding. Consider the manner in which the Newfoundland Governments of Premier Clyde Wells and then later Brian Tobin used public referenda to remove the right of churches to receive government funding for their schools. Clearly, even a constitutionally protected right to a status can be removed given the right context and determination of the political actors.
123 *George Reynolds v United States*, 98 U.S. 145 (1878).
124 See Elizabeth Harmer-Dionne, 'Once a Peculiar People: Cognitive Dissonance and the Suppression of Mormon Polygamy As a Case Study Negating the Belief-Action Distinction' (1998) 50:4 Stanford Law Review, 1295–1347.
125 Nathaniel Cary, 'Bob Jones University regains nonprofit status 17 years after it dropped discriminatory policy', *Greenville News* (16 February 2017), online: <https://www.greenvilleonline.com/story/news/education/2017/02/16/bju-regains-nonprofit-status-17-years-after-dropped-discriminatory-policy/98009170/>.
126 Mark Meredith, email to Justine Clark, LSBC Senior Executive Assistant to the CEO, 18 February 2014, Re: CBA resolution, at 2.

127 Peter Rogers, counsel for NSBS, in *Trinity Western University v Nova Scotia Barristers' Society*, 2015 NSSC 25 (Transcript of 18 December 2014 hearing, by Angèle Poirier, legal transcriptionist).
128 See Law Society of British Columbia Bencher Meeting, Transcript (11 April 2014) at 21, online (pdf): <https://www.lawsociety.bc.ca/docs/newsroom/TWU-transcript.pdf>.
129 Kuhn, *supra* note 9.
130 During an interview with an Ottawa area journalist in August 2018, the reporter suggested this as a possibility. I concurred that indeed that would be a plausible explanation for the turnabout.
131 Aline Bouwman, 'Trinity Western University drops contentious covenant, but LGBTQ staff still face discrimination', *CBC News* (16 August 2018), online: <https://www.cbc.ca/news/canada/british-columbia/trinity-western-university-drops-contentious-covenant-but-lgbtq-staff-still-face-discrimination-1.4786673>. Bouwman made a fascinating admission in the piece, noting that she attended the school with the mandatory covenant, stating,

> I chose TWU at a time when my values aligned with those described in the Community Covenant. I might have even found it a bit too 'liberal'. But I changed. As an institution of higher learning, I would expect TWU to encourage its students to experience such change and development and start to question and criticize its leaders when they see or experience discrimination within their community.

She continued, 'But as long as TWU cannot itself call into question the Community Covenant it has held onto for decades, I don't foresee any real change'. This author is emblematic of the Sexular Age – change in sexual identity can be made at any time and religious institutions must 'get with the program' and likewise change with the times.
132 Joseph Brean & Chris Selley, 'Still seeking law school, Trinity Western drops sexual "covenant" for students', *National Post* (14 August 2018), online: <https://nationalpost.com/news/canada/still-seeking-law-school-trinity-western-drops-sexual-covenant-for-students>.
133 The following quotes of Dickson CJC are from *R. v Big M Drug Mart Ltd.*, [1985] 1 SCR 295, 1985 CanLII 69 (SCC), paras 94–96, <http://canlii.ca/t/1fv2b#par94>.
134 Consider the pressure on Catholic hospitals in the MAiD debate. See, Barry W. Bussey, 'The Right of Religious Hospitals to Refuse Physician-Assisted Suicide, Supreme Court Law Review' (2018) 85 Supreme Court Law Review (2d) 1. Available at SSRN: https://papers.ssrn.com/abstract=3183767.
135 In legal terms we refer to charitable categories as 'heads'.
136 The use of the term 'values', as noted below, is a means of avoiding the enumerated rights in the *Charter* that have fallen out of fashion. Among those anachronistic enumerated rights are s.2(a), s.15 religious equality right, the s.27 multiculturalism emphasis that would favour religious communities. Section 27 was canvassed in this work by Derek Ross, who observed, 'certain forms of state support for religion, whether economic or otherwise, are consistent with Canada's commitment to pursue a rich, vibrant, pluralistic and multicultural society'. Justice Rowe in *LSBC v TWU* 2018 warned at para 175, 'In cases where *Charter* rights are plainly at stake, courts and other decision-makers have a constitutional obligation to address the rights claims as such and to do so explicitly. An analysis based on *Charter* values should not eclipse or supplant the analysis of whether *Charter* rights have been infringed'.
137 See *Income Tax Act*, *supra* note 96.
138 *LSBC v TWU* 2018, *supra* note 1, para 41.
139 *Ibid*, Chief Justice McLachlin, para 115; Justice Rowe, paras 166–75; dissent of Justices Côté and Brown, paras 307–11.
140 *Ibid*, para 308.
141 For example, see: Audrey Macklin, 'Charter Right or Charter-Lite? Administrative Discretion and the Charter', in J. Cameron, B. Berger & S. Lawrence, eds, (2014) 67 Supreme Court Law Review (2d) 561; Mark S. Harding & Rainer Knopff, 'Constitutionalizing Everything: The Role of "Charter Values"' (2013) 18 Rev. Const. Stud. 141; Iain T. Benson, 'Do "values"

mean anything at all? Implications for law, education and society' (2008) 33:1 Journal for Juridical Science 1–22; Matthew Horner, 'Charter Values: The Uncanny Valley of Canadian Constitutionalism' (2014) Supreme Court Law Review: Osgoode's Annual Constitutional Cases Conference, 67 at 361.
142 *Gehl v Canada (Attorney General)*, [2017] O.J. No. 1943, 2017 ONCA 319 (Ont. C.A.), para 79 ['*Gehl*'].
143 *Ibid*. See also *E.T. v Hamilton-Wentworth District School Board*, 2017 ONCA 893 ['E.T.'] at paras 103–104.
144 *LSBC v TWU*, *supra* note 1 at para 307.
145 *Ibid*.
146 *Ibid*, at para 308.
147 *Ibid*, at para 309.
148 *Ibid*, at para 310.
149 *Ibid*, at paras 310–311.
150 *Ibid*, at para 115.
151 *Ibid*, at para 166.
152 *Ibid*, at para 169.
153 *Ibid*, at para 171.
154 *Ibid*, at para 175.
155 *Ibid*, at paras 166–175.
156 *Supra* note 141.
157 *Gehl*, *supra* note 142 at para 79. See also *E.T.*, *supra* note 143, at paras 103–104. See also the Honourable Justice Peter Lauwers, 'What Could Go Wrong with Charter Values?' (2019) 91 Supreme Court Law Review (2d) 1–84.
158 *E.T.*, *supra* note 143, at paras 103–4.
159 Iain T. Benson, ' "Values Language": A Cuckoo's Egg or Useful Moral Framework?' in *Creative Subversion: The Liberal Arts and Human Educational Fulfilment*, ed. David Daintree (Redland Bay, QLD: Connor Court Publishing, 2018), 2 ['Values Language'].
160 *Ibid*, at 2.
161 *Ibid*, at 5.
162 George Grant, *Time as History* (Toronto: Canadian Broadcasting Corporation, 1969) at 44–45.
163 Benson, 'Values Language', *supra* note 159 at 6.
164 *Ibid*, at 6.
165 *Ibid*, at 8.
166 Edward Andrews, *The Genealogy of Values: The Aesthetic Economy of Nietzsche and Proust* (Lanham, MD: Rowman & Littlefield, 1995) at 170.
167 Benson, 'Values Language', *supra* note 159 at 13.
168 See *TWU* ONCA 2016, *supra* note 16 at para 119.
169 I use this term to describe a socially complex convergence of sexual identity politics and radical individualism that demands societal approval and accommodation of sexual identity even at the expense of other identities such as religious identity. See Bussey, *The Legal Revolution against the Accommodation of Religion: The Secular Age v the Sexular Age* (PhD Dissertation, University of Leiden, 2019).
170 Tommy Dickinson, 'Oppression and Suppression of the Sexual Deviant, 1939–1967', in *Curing Queers': Mental Nurses and Their Patients, 1935–74* (Manchester: Manchester University Press, 2015), 39–90.
171 See e.g. Yamri Taddese, 'LSUC revamps guidance on LGBT inclusion at law firms', *Law Times* (4 November 2013), online: <https://www.lawtimesnews.com/author/yamri-taddese/lsuc-revamps-guidance-on-lgbt-inclusion-at-law-firms-10865/>.
172 Robert Putnam defines 'social capital' as 'norms of generalized reciprocity and networks of civic engagement [that] encourage social trust and cooperation because they reduce incentives to defect, reduce uncertainty, and provide models for future cooperation'. See Robert

Putnam, *Making Democracy Work* (Princeton, NJ: Princeton University Press, 1993) at 177. It calls our 'attention to the ways in which our lives are made more productive by social ties'. See Putnam, *Bowling Alone: The Collapse and Revival of American Community* (New York: Simon & Schuster, 2000) at 19.

173 Social benefit has been aptly addressed in Dr John Pellowe's chapter in this volume.

174 Per Justice Ivan Rand, *Saumur v City of Quebec*, [1953] 2 S.C.R. 299 at 330.

175 Jonathan Haidt, 'Why Concepts Creep to the Left' (2016) 27:1 Psychological Inquiry, at 43. Similarly, Jordan Peterson notes that '[i]t's in the best interest of the radical left types – best psychological and strategic interest – to refuse to admit to the possibility that reasonable people can object to their ideological staff (sic). Because if reasonable people objected, that would imply that their ideological stance is not reasonable'. See Saagar Enjeti, 'Jordan Peterson on the Media Obsession to Cast Him as Alt-Right', *The Daily Caller* (6 May 2018), online: <https://dailycaller.com/2018/05/06/jordan-peterson-on-the-media-obsession-to-cast-him-as-alt-right/>.

176 Contrast this mindset with that of Justice Ivan Rand who stated in 1951:

> Freedom in thought and speech and disagreement in ideas and beliefs, on every conceivable subject, are of the essence of our life. The clash of critical discussion on political, social and religious subjects has too deeply become the stuff of daily experience to suggest that mere ill-will as a product of controversy can strike down the latter with illegality. [...] Controversial fury is aroused constantly by differences in abstract conceptions; heresy in some fields is again a mortal sin; there can be fanatical puritanism in ideas as well as in mortals; but our compact of free society accepts and absorbs these differences and they are exercised at large within the frame-work of freedom and order on broader and deeper uniformities as bases of social stability. Similarly in discontent, affection and hostility: as subjective incidents of controversy, they and the ideas which arouse them are part of our living which ultimately serve us in stimulation, in the clarification of thought and, as we believe, in the search for the constitution and truth of things generally. (*Boucher v the King*, [1951] S.C.R. 264 at 288)

177 For an analysis of expanding notions of harm, see Nick Haslam, 'Concept Creep: Psychology's Expanding Concepts of Harm and Pathology' (2016) 27:1 Psychological Inquiry 1–17. Haslam observes at 14, 'In essence, the concept creep phenomenon broadens moral concern in a way that aligns with a liberal social agenda by defining new kinds of experience as harming and new classes of people as harmed, and it identifies these people as needful of care and protection'.

178 *LSBC v TWU*, *supra* note 1 at para 103.

179 In *TWU* ONCA 2016, *supra* note 16 at para 119.

180 *TWU* BCCA 2016, *supra* note 16 at para 188. See also *Saskatchewan (Human Rights Commission) v Whatcott*, [2013] 1 SCR 467, 2013 SCC 11, paras 82, 89–90 and 111 [*Whatcott*].

181 *TWU* BCCA 2016, *supra* note 16 at para 189.

182 *LSBC v TWU* 2018, *supra* note 1 at para 101.

183 Greg Lukianoff & Jonathan Haidt, 'The Coddling of the American Mind', *The Atlantic* (September 2015), 42 at 47.

184 *Ibid*. This links to the notion of *Charter* values, as noted by Justices Miller & Lauwers in *E.T.*, *supra* note 143.

185 *Ibid*, at 48.

186 Kate Bellows, 'Professors ask Sullivan to stop quoting Jefferson: Faculty, students believe Jefferson shouldn't be included in emails', *Cavalier Daily* (13 November 2016), online: <http://www.cavalierdaily.com/article/2016/11/professors-ask-sullivan-to-stop-quoting-jefferson>.

187 Letter from Thomas Jefferson to William Roscoe (27 December 1820), University of Virginia Press, online: *Founders Early Access*, <http://rotunda.upress.virginia.edu/founders/default.xqy?keys=FOEA-print-04-02-02-1712>.
188 Bruce Bawer, *The Victims' Revolution: The Rise of Identity Studies and the Closing of the Liberal Mind* (New York: HarperCollins, 2012), xiii.
189 Amanda Harmon Cooley, 'Inculcating Suppression' (2019) 107:365 Georgetown Law Journal 366–68.
190 For more on the incidence and reasons for 'deplatforming', see also the Disinvitation Database maintained by the Foundation for Individual Rights in Education (FIRE), online: <https://www.thefire.org/research/disinvitation-database/#home/?view_2_sort=field_6|desc>.
191 Lauwers, *supra* note 157 at 28.
192 Dov Fox, 'Interest Creep' (2014) 82 Geo. Wash. L. Rev. 273, 285.
193 Also consider a slightly different point of view of Nick Haslam, 'Concept Creep: Psychology's Expanding Concepts of Harm and Pathology' (2016) 27:1 Psychological Inquiry at 10:

> to count perceived discrimination and ambiguous microaggressions as unqualified instances of prejudice is to subjectivize the concept. In addition to this subjectivity, the concept of microaggression extends the concept of prejudice by encompassing acts of omission and phenomena that reflect anxiety rather than hostility. […] Prejudice is no longer exclusively blatant, but can be subtle and nonconscious. It is not necessarily hostile, but can be anxiously avoidant or patronisingly positive. It may not even be inherent in the acts or attitudes of a prejudiced person, existing instead in another person's perception. This expansion of the meaning of prejudice reflects a process of vertical concept creep in which the concept's elastic boundaries stretch to include increasingly mild and subtle phenomena.

> Haslam further notes at 10 that 'most of the concepts have stretched to include milder, subtler, or less extreme phenomena than those to which they referred at an earlier time'.

194 Jonathan Haidt, 'Moral Psychology and the Law: How Intuitions Drive Reasoning, Judgment, and the Search for Evidence' (2013) 64 Ala. L. Rev. 867, at 868.
195 Lauwers, *supra* note 157 at 31.
196 An unfounded allegation.
197 ARCC, 'Revoke Charitable Status of Anti-choice Groups, says Pro-choice Group' (11 January 2018), online (pdf): http://www.arcc-cdac.ca/press/ARCC-CDAC-release-Jan-11-18-english.pdf. See also ARCC, 'Position Paper #80 Why Anti-Choice Groups Should Not Have Charitable Tax Status', online (pdf): <http://www.arcc-cdac.ca/postionpapers/80-Charitable-Tax-Status.pdf>.
198 Canada Revenue Agency, 'Public policy dialogue and development activities by charities, CG-027', 21 January 2019, online: https://www.canada.ca/en/revenue-agency/services/charities-giving/charities/policies-guidance/public-policy-dialogue-development-activities.html.
199 For a full account of the CSJ controversy see, Barry W. Bussey, 'The Canada Summer Jobs Debate and The Democratic Decline' (2019) 91 Supreme Court Law Review (2d) 245–96.
200 House of Commons Debates, 42nd Parliament, 1st Session, 11 March 2018, online: <https://www.ourcommons.ca/DocumentViewer/en/42-1/house/sitting-269/hansard>.
201 ARCC, 'Conservative Party's Bad Faith on Canada Summer Jobs Attestation' (14 March 2018), online (pdf): http://www.arcc-cdac.ca/csj/docs/con-party-bad-faith.pdf.
202 ARCC, 'Position Paper #80 Why Anti-Choice Groups Should Not Have Charitable Tax Status', online (pdf) at 4: http://www.arcc-cdac.ca/postionpapers/80-Charitable-Tax-Status.pdf.
203 ARCC, 'Position Paper #82 Anti-Choice "Crisis Pregnancy Centres" Should Not Have Charitable Tax Status', online: http://www.arcc-cdac.ca/CPC-study/8-CPCs-should-not-have-charitable-status.pd, p 2. See also Amanda Connolly, 'Should anti-abortion groups be

allowed to register as charities?' Global News, 16 January 2018, online: https://globalnews.ca/news/3961321/anti-abortion-groups-registered-charity/y.
204 *LSBC v TWU* 2018, *supra* note 1 at para 101.
205 *Ibid*, at para 41.
206 *Obergefell*, *supra* note 85, Supreme Court of the United States Official Transcript, 28 April 2015, at 38, online (pdf): https://www.supremecourt.gov/oral_arguments/argument_transcripts/2014/14-556q1_l5gm.pdf.
207 This is strongly evidenced by Rev. Dr John Pellowe's piece in this collection. Note, however, the arguments of Professor Luc Grenon, 'An Analysis of ohe Tangible Public Benefits Provided By Religious Charities' (2014) 44 R.D.U.S. 531–67 who argues (at para 5): 'the majority of religious organizations do not provide any, or provide very little, public tangible benefits to society' and that 'there is a large disparity between religious organizations that offer tangible public benefits and those that don't, meaning that the majority of the benefits are provided by a very small number of organizations' (para 6). His conclusion is that 'a substantial portion of charities profit unduly from the good reputation forged by the most active of charities' (para 6). Grenon points out that on average religious charities invest only 15% of their resources to non-religious purposes (para 27). Hence, 'the social engagement of religious charities with society does not support or justify the tax privileges are accorded to them' (para 27). Pellowe's work suggests otherwise. Further, even if Professor Grenon's statistics are correct, he assumes that religious charities spending the bulk of their resources on religious activities is not a net public benefit. That does not follow. There is ample evidence that even the religious activity that the religious community does is beneficial. For example, Professor Jonathan Haidt in *The Righteous Mind: Why Good People Are Divided by Politics and Religion* (New York: Pantheon Books, 2012) at 248, 227, observes that religion makes community possible as it brings people together.
208 *Multani v Commission scolaire Marguerite-Bourgeoys*, [2006] 1 S.C.R. 256, 2006 SCC 6 [*Multani*].
209 *Ibid*, at para 76.
210 *Chamberlain v Surrey School District No. 36*, [2002] S.C.J. No. 87, [2002] 4 S.C.R. 710 [*Chamberlain*].
211 See also David M. Brown, 'Neutrality or Privilege? A Comment on Religious Freedom' (2005) 29 Supreme Court Law Review (2d) 220 at 230.
212 *Chamberlain*, *supra* note 210 at para 137.
213 Iain T. Benson, 'Notes Towards a (Re)Definition of the Secular' (2000) 33 UBC L. Rev. at 519.
214 William Galston, 'Religion and the Limits of Liberal Democracy', in *Recognizing Religion in a Secular Society: Essays in Pluralism, Religion, and Public Policy*, ed. Douglas Farrow (Montreal: McGill-Queen's University Press, 2004), 41 at 42.
215 *Ibid*.
216 John Corvino, Ryan T. Anderson & Sherif Girgis, *Debating Religious Liberty and Discrimination* (Oxford: Oxford University Press, 2017) at 117.
217 *Charter*, *supra* note 5, s.27.
218 It is interesting to note that the role of religious communities promoting pluralism was one of the justifications that the US Congress has used in providing religious charities tax exempt status. See Grant M. Newman, 'The Taxation of Religious Organizations in America' (2019) 42:2 Harvard Journal of Law & Public Policy 681 at 685, quoting Joint Comm. On Tax'n, Historical Development and Present Law of the Federal Tax Exemption for Charities and Other Tax-Exempt Organizations 8 (2005). The complete list includes: (1) Charitable and religious organizations serve the public and therefore should be supported through provision of tax benefits; (2) Charitable and religious organizations provide goods and services that otherwise would have to be provided by the Government and therefore should be supported by the Government; (3) It is difficult to measure the net income of charitable and religious

organizations, and therefore they should be exempt from tax; (4) Charitable and religious organizations promote pluralism; (5) Charitable and religious organizations are efficient providers of services but have inherent limits on their ability to raise capital compared to for-profit entities and therefore need government support in the form of tax exemption (and charitable contributions); and, (6) Exemption is afforded to those organizations that can prove their worth through sustained donations'.

219 See also Ross & Sinke in this collection.
220 *R. v. Videoflicks Ltd.* (1984), 48 O.R. (2d) 395 at 427–8.
221 CRA, 'Public policy dialogue', *supra* note 198.
222 Peter L. Berger, *The De-Secularization of the World* (Grand Rapids, MI: Eerdmans, 1999), 34.
223 Iain Benson, 'The Attack on Western Religions by Western Law: Re-Framing Pluralism, Liberalism and Diversity' (2013) 6:1–2 Int'l J Religious Freedom at 11, http://ssrn.com/abstract=2328825.
224 *Alberta v Hutterian Brethren of Wilson Colony*, [2009] 2 SCR 567, 2009 SCC 37.
225 E.g., in the case of Catholic adoption agencies when the government required them to adopt secular norms. In other cases, Catholic hospitals transferred ownership and ceased to be Catholic or simply refused to follow the law. See United States Conference of Catholic Bishops, 'Discrimination Against Catholic Adoption Services', online: <http://www.usccb.org/issues-and-action/religious-liberty/discrimination-against-catholic-adoption-services.cfm>; Matthew W. Clark, 'The Gospel According to the State: An Analysis of Massachusetts Adoption Laws and the Closing of Catholic Charities Adoption Services' (2007–2008) 41 Suffolk U. L. Rev. 871 [hereinafter 'Clark']; Staff writers, 'We will not kill patients: Catholic hospitals to defy euthanasia laws', *Catholic Weekly* (25 October 2017), online: <https://www.catholicweekly.com.au/we-will-not-killpatients-catholic-hospitals-to-defy-euthanasia-laws/>.
226 Lauwers, *supra* note 157; and Professor Mary Anne Waldron, QC, 'The Intolerant State: The Use and Misuse of Charter Values in the Supreme Court of Canada', (2019) 91 Supreme Court Law Review (2d) 85–106.
227 *R. v Butler*, [1992] 1 SCR 452 (S.C.C.).
228 Waldron, *supra* note 226 at 88.
229 Lauwers, *supra* note 157 at 83.

Chapter Eight

JUST CHECK THE BOX: WHY RELIGIOUS INSTITUTIONS STILL MAKE CANADA A BETTER PLACE TO LIVE AND FLOURISH

Janet Epp Buckingham*

Abstract

Pierre E. Trudeau observed a 'golden thread of faith' was 'woven throughout the history of Canada'. Indeed, religion has long been part of the public life of Canada; many schools, universities, hospitals and humanitarian aid organizations were founded by religious institutions. In addition, religion is a head of charity because religious institutions by their nature and practice contribute to the common good. Religious institutions fulfil three functions: (1) connect seekers and adherents to the transcendent; (2) provide rites of passage – birth, marriage, death and community; (3) provide care and service to their own and the broader community.

Yet, secular policymakers and academics argue that religious freedom does not apply when religious organizations engage in 'public' activities such as education. The logical extension of this position is that religion must remain in the private sphere and that religious freedom only guarantees freedom of worship. This view violates religious protection of the Canadian *Charter* and international human rights standards; it restricts the positive societal impact of religious institutions; and it brings into question whether religious organisations should have charitable status. This is illustrated in the recent Supreme Court of Canada decisions which permitted a regulatory body to deny accreditation of a Christian law school (Trinity Western University) because of its religious beliefs and practices on marriage. Similar tensions were highlighted when the federal government required religious organisations to agree with its ideology on abortion, marriage and '*Charter* values' in order to receive student summer job grants. In short, this approach denies religious freedom to adherents in the 'commons'. That is the very point of religious freedom to begin with. There is collective amnesia on the part of academics and government concerning the 'golden thread' running through Canadian society.

---

* BA, LLB, LLD, *Professor, Trinity Western University.*

Introduction

Religion has long been part of the fabric of Canadian life. Prime Minister Pierre Elliott Trudeau, in a speech to thousands of believers participating in David Mainse's 'Salute to Canada' on Parliament Hill in 1981, acknowledged that the 'golden thread of faith is woven throughout the history of Canada from its earliest beginnings up to the present time'.[1]

This history has been all but forgotten in today's secular Canada. Several recent examples show that secular policymakers and academics recommend restricting religious activity in order to achieve other secular goals. These include restrictions on Christian universities and restrictions on a wide variety of religious organizations that hire summer students to minister to the vulnerable in society.

University administrator Peter MacKinnon argues in his 2018 book, *University Commons Divided*,[2] that faith-based universities that are open to the general public must comply with secular social norms. This is the prevailing, but illogical, argument against approval for a law school at Trinity Western University that has now been embraced by a majority of Supreme Court of Canada (SCC) justices.[3] This argument, taken to its logical extension, is that religious charities must 'comply with secular norms' or lose their charitable status. Legal counsel for the Canadian Bar Association admitted as much in the SCC hearing on Trinity Western's proposed law school.[4]

What does it mean for a religious charity to be forced to 'comply with secular norms'? We do not have to speculate in this area as there is already a case study in the secularization of Canadian universities in order to receive public funds. Few students at Acadia University or McMaster University would detect any vestiges of the Baptist foundations of these institutions. There are similarly no vestiges of the Roman Catholic foundations of Laval University or the University of Ottawa. Thus, compliance with secular norms leads to loss of religious identity. Is this what was intended by Canadians? Is this good for Canada? Is the public role of religion in Canada dead? I argue no, no and no. Religious institutions, including universities, have important roles to play in the public life of Canada, including in the commons. These institutions have shaped Canada, and to obliterate religious identity from public life in Canada will make Canada poorer.

Religious identity is the heart and soul of a religious charity. It is not a dispensable feature. The religious motivation behind these charities affects participation, funding and style of service delivery.

Canada is a diverse, multifaith country. P. E. Trudeau concluded his speech to 'Salute to Canada' thus:

> Faith played a large part in the lives of so many men and women who have created in this land a society which places a high value on commitment, integrity, generosity and, above all, freedom. To pass on that heritage, strong and intact, is a challenge worthy of all of us who are privileged to call ourselves Canadians.[5]

The religious element, far from being diminished, should be cultivated and encouraged as part of our vibrant, pluralistic nation. Those who argue for the privatization of religion would keep the salt of religion in the proverbial saltshaker. But it can do no good in society in the saltshaker. It needs to be poured out of the saltshaker to have a positive impact in the commons.

Contributions of Religious Institutions to Canadian Society

Religious institutions fulfil three functions in Canadian society. The first is to connect seekers and adherents to the transcendent, usually a supreme being. The second is to provide rites of passage, including birth, marriage and death, and to create a community for human flourishing. The third is to provide care and service to its own and to the broader community, particularly to the vulnerable in society.

Seeking the Meaning of Life

A preamble to the *American Declaration of the Rights and Duties of Man* affirms: 'Inasmuch as spiritual development is the supreme end of human existence and the highest expression thereof, it is the duty of man to serve that end with all his strength and resources'.[6] The primary contribution of religious institutions to Canadian society, therefore, is to provide avenues to the transcendent. As theologian Miroslav Volf affirms, 'With their feet firmly planted in ordinary realities, human beings always extend their hand beyond the stars into the transcendent realm'.[7] Further, 'Reference to transcendence isn't an add-on to humanity; rather, it defines human beings'.[8] As humans, we need religious institutions to aid us in the quest to fulfil our deepest human longings.[9]

Rites of Passage and Creating Community

Religions each have a vision for human flourishing.[10] In addition, they show a way, or a path, to follow to attain the good. Religions therefore generally promote strong character and moral behaviour. Religions teach good citizenship, including adherence to the law. While religious adherents may criticize the law and seek changes, they will generally use peaceful means to seek social justice. Religious institutions also provide a collective identity and a place of community for adherents.

Cities and towns across Canada have an abundance of churches with growing numbers of mosques, temples and synagogues. These religious institutions provide a wealth of support for their communities. They not only provide for spiritual needs but also give new immigrants communities of support.[11] They host community events. Their buildings are used for life transitions such as marriages, celebrating new babies and mourning death.

Care and Service to the Broader Community

Religious organizations have founded hospitals, schools and universities. At Confederation, most hospitals, schools and universities were run by religious orders or Christian denominations. It was religious organizations that supplied most of the education and healthcare in Canada until the mid-twentieth century. Religious charities continue to run homeless shelters, food banks and after-school programmes. Today, churches, mosques, temples and synagogues often provide free counselling services and emergency financial assistance. Some churches have language classes for refugees. Some have community gardens. Far from being enclaves to support their members, houses of worship usually offer a great deal to the surrounding community.[12]

An essential attribute of many religious institutions is a desire to make the world a better place. Christians, for example, seek to love God and love their neighbours. The love of neighbour can be manifested on an individual basis or an institutional basis. Churches care for the poor and homeless. They provide shelter for those on the streets on winter nights. They provide hot meals for those in need.

Religious organizations have also played significant roles in social justice in Canada. Churches have raised awareness and campaigned against slavery, for equal rights for women, for refugees and immigrants, for improved working conditions and for better conditions in prisons and penitentiaries. It is part of the religious impulse to care for the vulnerable in society.

A Short History of Faith-Based Universities in Canada

At Confederation in 1867, 13 of the 17 degree-granting universities were denominationally based. Roman Catholics founded St. Francis Xavier University and St. Mary's University in Nova Scotia, University of Ottawa and St. Michael's College in Ontario, and Laval University and Université de Montréal in Quebec. Presbyterians founded Dalhousie University in Nova Scotia, McGill University in Quebec and Queen's University in Ontario. Baptists founded Acadia University in Nova Scotia and McMaster University in Ontario. Anglicans founded Bishop's University in Quebec and Trinity College in Ontario. Methodists founded Mount Allison University in Nova Scotia and Victoria College in Ontario.

With respect to universities, the process of secularization happened over a long period of time.[13] The province of Ontario started this process early by withdrawing funding for denominational universities in 1868. This gave rise to three religious colleges affiliated with University of Toronto: St. Michael's (Catholic), Victoria (United Church) and Trinity (Anglican).

By the 1960s, every one of the above-noted religious universities was secularized, although some of the universities created or affiliated religious colleges. Today, all of them receive considerable government funding.

With the secularization of religious universities, a new generation of religiously affiliated colleges and universities was founded. Trinity Western University, located in Langley, British Columbia, was founded by the Evangelical Free Church in 1962 as a junior college and gained full accreditation in 1985. Christian Reformed denominations founded The King's University in Alberta (1979) and Redeemer University College in Ontario (1982). Ambrose University was founded in Alberta in 2007 when an Alliance college and a Nazarene college joined to form one university. St. Stephen's University in New Brunswick (1975) and Tyndale University College in Ontario (2003)[14] are both non-denominational Christian universities. Mennonites founded Canadian Mennonite University in Manitoba in 2000 when several Mennonite institutions amalgamated.[15]

This history shows that when religiously affiliated institutions secularize, new ones rise up to take their place. An apt conclusion to draw, therefore, is there has always been – and continues to be – in Canada consistent motivation on the part of academics and students to have higher education in a religious context.

All the Christian universities noted above are private institutions. All are accredited by provincial governments. All have mechanisms for receiving charitable donations, either directly or through a foundation. However, universities in Canada, even public universities, are private organizations. They are not considered to be government agents, even though many receive substantial government funding. The SCC has held repeatedly that universities in Canada are not subject to the *Canadian Charter of Rights and Freedoms*.[16]

Religious Organizations in International Law

Religious freedom is one of the pillars of international human rights law. It is protected in the *Universal Declaration of Human Rights*, Article 18:

> Everyone has the right to freedom of thought, conscience and religion; this right includes freedom to change his religion or belief, and freedom, either alone or in community with others and in public or private, to manifest his religion or belief in teaching, practice, worship and observance.

This emphasizes that religious freedom includes the right to practice one's faith in community with others and in public. It is echoed in the more expansive *International Covenant on Civil and Political Rights*, Article 18, which further allows limitation of the rights only if 'necessary to protect public safety, order, health, or morals or the fundamental rights and freedoms of others'.

The most detailed formulation of international human rights norms for religious adherents is found in the *UN Declaration on the Elimination of all Forms of Intolerance and Discrimination Based on Religion or Belief*. Article 6(b) specifies the right to establish and maintain appropriate charitable or humanitarian institutions. Articles 2 and 3 state that religious freedom is to be enjoyed by all without discrimination. Article 3 states:

> Discrimination between human beings on grounds of religion or belief constitutes an affront to human dignity and a disavowal of the principles of the Charter of the United Nations, and shall be condemned as a violation of the human rights and fundamental freedoms proclaimed in the Universal Declaration of Human Rights and enunciated in detail in the International Covenants on Human Rights, and as an obstacle to friendly and peaceful relations between nations.

Canada has ratified or acceded to all these international documents and has long been considered a beacon of human rights protection.

The right to religious freedom protected in international human rights law includes the right to found religious institutions. This does not mean that they must be given any preferential tax status, as is currently the case in Canada. However, once the government has established preferential tax treatment for charitable organizations, it would violate international human rights standards to discriminate against religious institutions on the basis of their religious beliefs and practices.[17]

Religious Organizations and Charity Law in Canada

The *Constitution Act, 1867*, s. 92(7) lists charities as a provincial responsibility. However, the Canada Revenue Agency (CRA), an agency of the federal government, is the de facto regulator of charities in Canada under its taxation powers. The first federal income tax act, in 1917, included an exemption for 'religious, charitable, agricultural and educational institutions'.[18] In 1948, the *Income Tax Act* was made permanent and included a deduction for charitable organizations.[19] There was no definition of what constituted a charity but it was clearly understood. Granting a tax deduction for donations to charities was a way to encourage philanthropy.

Registered charities enjoy certain tax privileges, most important of which is that donations can be claimed on a donor's tax return as tax credits. This is a significant advantage in fundraising. In order to register as a charity, an organization must fall within one of four heads of charity as defined in common law: advancement of religion, relief of poverty, advancement of education or other activities for public benefit.[20] Registered charities must complete annual filings and are subject to being audited by the CRA.

The CRA has set out policies on what it considers to be objects and activities that are charitable under each head of charity. For advancement of religion, the CRA says,

> Advancing religion in the charitable sense means manifesting, promoting, sustaining, or increasing belief in a religion's three key attributes, which are: faith in a higher unseen power such as a God, Supreme Being, or Entity; worship or reverence; and a particular and comprehensive system of doctrines and observances.[21]

The CRA has revoked the charitable status of organizations registered under advancement of religion if it determined that they were advocating for a cause rather than advancing religion per se.[22]

Faith-based universities fall under two heads of charity: advancement of education and advancement of religion. Mere registration of a faith-based university as a charity under the head of education, as is Trinity Western University, does not diminish its religious identity.

Other chapters in this book outline the incredible contributions religious charities have made to the social fabric of Canada and, indeed, other nations around the world. These contributions are ongoing but would be restricted by religious organizations being forced to relinquish part of their religious beliefs and practices in order to retain charitable status. This applies equally to religious organizations that have their charitable registration under education, relief of poverty or public benefit, rather than under 'advancement of religion'.

Religious adherents have contributed beyond their share to their communities. While this chapter has focused on universities, religious institutions include the provision of services as varied as palliative care homes or community gardens. But religious institutions can only contribute to society as they are empowered to do so. When the state places significant restrictions on religious participation in the commons, these institutions cannot flourish but rather must retreat to the four walls of houses of worship. Unfortunately, this seems to be the view of the majority of justices of the SCC as expressed in its recent jurisprudence.[23]

Limits on Charitable Religious Institutions

If we acknowledge that religious institutions work for the common good in Canada and must be given a place in the commons to flourish, it raises the question whether there are any legitimate limits on religious participation. The answer is clearly yes, there must be reasonable limits, particularly if the government grants charitable status as a means of encouraging these institutions.

Yet unreasonable restrictions have been placed on religious belief and expression in Canada. The most egregious restriction on a religious institution on the basis of its religious practices was the banning of the Jehovah's Witnesses. After the Second World War began, Jehovah's Witnesses refused to participate in military service. Further, they distributed literature denouncing churches that encouraged young men to join the military. After pressure from the Roman Catholic clergy, the Attorney General of Canada banned the Jehovah's Witnesses and the Watch Tower Society.[24] Possession of Jehovah's Witness literature was made a criminal offence. Jehovah's Witness children who refused to participate in patriotic exercises were expelled from school.[25]

During times of war, patriotism runs high and tolerance and common sense can fall victim to such patriotism. It is politically expedient to restrict organizations that do not share patriotic fervour. It is not uncommon for government to be pressured to restrict organizations on hot button issues. It is precisely because there is such pressure that religious institutions are protected. Religious practice does not change with the current political winds. Banning of the Jehovah's Witnesses clearly goes far beyond revocation of charitable status. But it is a reminder that the state can be heavy-handed under certain circumstances.

The charitable registration system has within it several restrictions on registered charities. There are restrictions on the level of political activity to ensure that charities do not become lobbyist associations. Charities cannot become businesses, although they can have some forms of businesses to support the mission of the organization. The final catch-all limit on charities is they can be deregistered if they carry on activities that are contrary to public policy. It is clear that charitable registration will be revoked if an organization is carrying on illegal activities.

Must religious institutions be consistent with Canadian public policy? It is a very broad requirement. As Justice Robins says, 'public policy is an unruly horse'.[26] It is often difficult to determine Canadian public policy. Both the majority and dissent wrestled with this issue in a 2002 Federal Court of Appeal case on whether a charitable registration should be revoked for an organization providing humanitarian assistance in Israel.[27] The public policy issue arose because some of the funds were distributed in the Occupied Territories. Justice Sharlow, for the majority, found that there was not a 'definite and somehow officially declared and implemented policy' and refused to revoke charitable status on that basis.

When the definition of civil marriage was expanded to 'two persons' rather than a man and a woman, religious organizations made strong arguments before both the SCC and the parliamentary committee considering the issue that they would face discrimination for maintaining a traditional, religious definition of marriage. The SCC in the *Reference re Same-sex Marriage* considered that these concerns were hypothetical.[28] The unanimous court said, 'The protection of freedom of religion afforded by s. 2 (a) of the Charter is broad and jealously guarded in our Charter jurisprudence'.[29] The Supreme Court was certain that conflicts between the right to same-sex marriage and the right to freedom of religion would be resolved under the *Charter* 'by way of internal balancing and delineation'.[30]

The Special Committee on Bill C-38, the *Civil Marriage Act*, heard from a wide variety of religious leaders who were concerned about the potential for future discrimination against religious institutions. As a response to these concerns, Bloc Quebecois MP Richard Marceau proposed amendments to the bill to make it clear that there would be no discrimination. Preambles were added to affirm religious freedom and to make it clear that it is 'not against the public interest to hold and publicly express diverse views on marriage'.[31] The following substantive clause was also added:

> 3.1 For greater certainty, no person or organization shall be deprived of any benefit, or be subject to any obligation or sanction, under any law of the Parliament of Canada solely by reason of their exercise, in respect of marriage between persons of the same sex, of the freedom of conscience and religion guaranteed under the *Canadian Charter of Rights and Freedoms* or the expression of their beliefs in respect of marriage as the union of a man and woman to the exclusion of all others based on that guaranteed freedom.

This section was added to ensure that religious charities would not lose their charitable status based on their religious definition of marriage.

While at the time Bill C-38 was being considered, revocation of charitable status seemed far-fetched; the concern was based on a 1990 Ontario Court of Appeal decision, *Canada Trust Co. v Ontario Human Rights Commission*.[32] The case was not about charitable status but about whether a scholarship trust was contrary to public policy. The terms of the trust excluded Roman Catholic, non-British and non-Christian people and placed restrictions on how many female students could benefit. The court found that the trust violated public policy, since '[t]o say that a trust premised on these notions of racism and religious superiority contravenes contemporary public policy is to expatiate the obvious'.[33] The trust was amended *cy-pres* by removing the exclusions.[34]

This is part of a broader issue at play: whether government officials can deny an institution charitable status, or any other government benefit, because it holds unpopular beliefs. From 2012 to 2014, some charities critical of government policy on the environment faced CRA audits and were threatened with loss of charitable status.[35] The Liberal government suspended the political audit programme in 2017.[36] But for five years, charities felt a chill in speaking publicly on certain controversial issues. Today, the current unpopular beliefs relate to the definition of marriage and abortion, but religious institutions have been restricted on the basis of other beliefs, past and present.

Similar arguments to those raised in the above-noted case have been used in relation to Trinity Western University and similar educational institutions be they universities or schools. This is despite the provisions of the *Civil Marriage Act* that were intended to protect religious institutions from this threat.

Trinity Western University

As noted above, Trinity Western University was founded by provincial charter in 1962. Under this charter, the university is required to offer a university education 'with an underlying philosophy and viewpoint that is Christian'.[37] It is affiliated with the Evangelical Free Church and is considered an 'arm of the church'.[38] Although it was originally a junior college, offering a two-year programme, it was granted full degree-granting status in 1979. It was one of four British Columbia universities to be granted 'exempt status' by the British Columbia Minister of Advanced Education. This provides an expedited review process to trusted institutions that meet certain academic criteria. Trinity Western has been a member of Universities Canada since 1984.

Like most universities in Canada, Trinity Western is a registered charity. It is registered under the 'education' head of charity.

The religious impulse impacts on how Trinity Western University functions. In addition to offering a liberal arts university programme, Trinity Western both connects students to the transcendent and ministers to the broader community. The university has daily chapel services, which are available to students but not required, and weekly bible study groups. The university supports student outreach programmes to minister to the vulnerable. This includes ministries in the Lower East Side of Vancouver, home to many who are homeless, who are in the sex trade, or who are drug addicts; and ministries to inmates in a local prison. During break weeks, there are student humanitarian trips to developing countries. Recent student-led initiatives have included awareness campaigns on human trafficking[39] and launching a new charity to sponsor a refugee family.[40]

Trinity Western is a liberal arts university but also has professional programmes in education, nursing, counselling psychology and business. In 2001, the SCC ruled 8–1 in favour of accreditation of a School of Education at the university. Accreditation had been denied on the basis of the university's policies on homosexuality. In 2012, Trinity Western sought accreditation of a School of Law. It was granted by the Federation of Law Societies and the British Columbia Minister of Advanced Education in 2013. However, three provincial law societies refused to approve graduates to article and be licenced in their provinces.

The Council of Canadian Law Deans (CCLD) was the first to raise serious concerns about the law school proposal, particularly with reference to the university's Community Covenant.[41] This document must be signed by all administration, faculty, staff and students on an annual basis. The covenant includes the following controversial statement: members of the community agree to voluntarily abstain from a variety of activities including 'sexual intimacy that violates the sacredness of marriage between a man and a woman'. The CCLD raised questions about the discriminatory impact on gay, lesbian and bisexual students.

When the law societies of Ontario, Nova Scotia and British Columbia denied approval for graduates of Trinity Western's law school to have their degrees recognized in those provinces, Trinity Western sought judicial review of those decisions. The cases from Ontario and British Columbia were appealed to the SCC, which heard them on 30 November and 1 December 2017.

The proposed law school at Trinity Western University had been one of the most hotly debated issues in academia, in the media and on social media for several years. One of the more extreme arguments was that Trinity Western should lose its charitable status. Saul Templeton raised this in a special issue of the Alberta branch of the Canadian Bar Association magazine, *Law Matters*, in 2015.[42] Justice Malcolm Rowe asked the question of Susan Ursel, legal counsel for the Canadian Bar Association, on 1 December of the SCC hearing on the Trinity Western University cases. Ursel conceded that the extension of her argument before the court was that any religious institution that discriminates, including Roman Catholic exclusion of women from clergy, should lose its charitable status.[43]

The SCC released its ruling in the Trinity Western University cases on 15 June 2018.[44] The court issued separate decisions in the two cases, each with four sets of reasons. Five justices concurred in the majority judgement with Chief Justice McLachlin, as she then was, and Justice Rowe, each writing separate judgements concurring in the result. Two justices wrote a strong dissent. None of the justices addressed the issue of charitable status.

In essence, the majority judgement ruled that the law societies could refuse to approve the proposed law school on the basis of Trinity Western's mandatory Community Covenant. 'By interpreting the public interest in a way that precludes the approval of TWU's law school governed by the mandatory Covenant, the LSBC has interfered with TWU's ability to maintain an approved law school as a religious community defined by its own religious practices'.[45] It went on to rule 'that members of the TWU religious community are not free to impose those religious beliefs on fellow students, since they have an inequitable impact and can cause significant harm'.[46]

This ruling seems to place new restrictions on the ambit of religious freedom in Canada. While the majority recognized Trinity Western as 'a private religious institution created to support the collective religious practices of its members', it did not rule on the issue of institutional religious freedom.[47] This is a step back from the court's position in the *Loyola* case.[48] Just weeks before this decision, the Supreme Court ruled in a unanimous judgement that a Jehovah's Witness congregation is a voluntary, religious organization that can apply its own standards of conduct and morality.[49] This approach does not apply to a faith-based university, however. With respect to charities law, a religious institution is left with a conundrum: its ability to define and apply religious standards can only apply to its own members while to gain or maintain charitable status it must minister beyond its own community.

The majority judgement did not reference the *Civil Marriage Act* provisions that were intended to protect religious charities from sanctions on the basis of maintaining their traditional, religious definition of marriage. This may be because the issues in the case were not within federal jurisdiction. The dissenting judgement did find the provisions of that Act persuasive.⁵⁰ It is disturbing to see the majority simply ignore legislation that was intended to delineate the balance between religious freedom and equality rights for LGBTQ persons.

Canada Summer Jobs Grant Attestation

The government of Canada has been providing funds to non-profit organizations and small businesses for many years for the Canada Summer Jobs programme. It subsidizes summer students and is intended to help university students gain skills to enter the job market on graduation. It also helps organizations and businesses that might not otherwise be able to afford to hire summer students. Over the years, some charities, including religious charities, have become dependent on this funding to run summer camps and sports programmes for underprivileged children.

In December 2017, the federal government announced a new requirement for an organization to be eligible for funding for the summer of 2018. This was that the organization must make an attestation affirming that

> the core mandate of the organization must respect individual human rights in Canada, including the values underlying the Canadian Charter of Rights and Freedoms (Charter) as well as other rights. These include reproductive rights and the right to be free from discrimination on the basis of sex, religion, race, national or ethnic origin, colour, mental or physical disability, sexual orientation or gender identity or expression.⁵¹

Many religious organizations, particularly Christian organizations, could not make this attestation, as it was antithetical to the individual and collective beliefs of their community members in that it appeared to support abortion and same-sex marriage.

The background to this new requirement was an issue that arose in relation to funding for this programme in the summer of 2017. Minister Patricia Hajdu, Minister of Employment, Workforce Development and Labour, said that her office received complaints that pro-life groups had previously received funding and that students hired distributed anti-abortion literature. The government refused funding to The Canadian Centre for Bioethical Reform, Guelph Right to Life and Toronto Right to Life. These three organizations commenced lawsuits against the government. In November 2017, the government settled these lawsuits and paid the organizations the amounts they would have received for summer students.

The new attestation requirements were intended to prevent pro-life organizations from applying for funding for summer 2018. The attestation requirement inadvertently applied to a much broader range of religious organizations. Some 1,500 organizations were denied funding because they did not check the attestation box.⁵² Several lawsuits have been launched to challenge the attestation requirement as a violation of religious freedom under the *Charter*.⁵³

Again, charities are concerned that if the government can require this kind of attestation in order to be eligible for a funding programme, it can attach this kind of requirement to charitable status. Given the number of organizations denied funding for refusing to check the box of the attestation, a similar requirement for charitable status would impact on many religious charities.

Secular Arguments against Religious Institutions

Trinity Western University has attracted considerable controversy throughout its almost fifty-five-year history. It is astonishing that the university has been required to take legal challenges to the SCC twice to get approval to start new programmes. Trinity Western also has faced challenges to its membership in Universities Canada, the association that coordinates standards for university education and advocates for universities with various levels of government.[54] It has also been reprimanded by the Canadian Association of University Teachers for an allegation of violating academic freedom. If there is to be a challenge to charitable status of religious institutions, it seems likely that Trinity Western University would be a target test case.

Peter MacKinnon, who from 2003 to 2005 was chair of what is now Universities Canada, has written a book, *University Commons Divided*,[55] discussing a variety of contentious issues relating to universities in Canada. This includes academic freedom, freedom of expression and the freedom of religion of Christian universities. MacKinnon's views are widely held among those who share a progressive, secular perspective that dominates Canadian public universities.

MacKinnon includes a chapter considering the debate over accreditation of a law school at Trinity Western University. It should be noted at the outset that MacKinnon's legal specialization is the law of evidence. He is neither a constitutional lawyer nor a charities expert. While many academics have written on the issues involved with approval of the Trinity Western University law school, MacKinnon is paradigmatic in his approach to the issues. In his concluding chapter, he proposes the following to resolve this dispute:

> A preferable one might be to recognize that freedom of religion is not engaged here. In moving from its faith-based community to offer education in the public commons, TWU changes arenas from one in which it can practise its discriminatory beliefs to one in which it cannot. Quite simply, its discriminatory religious beliefs should not be at play in the commons.[56]

Justice Rowe of the SCC appears to have been convinced by this type of approach in the recent Trinity Western University cases.[57]

Such a proposal would limit religious participation to within the four walls of churches, synagogues, mosques and other houses of worship. Once a faith-based initiative moves out of the saltshaker of the building, it must abide by MacKinnon's 'rules of the commons'. And if the rules of the commons are set by non-religious people, any inclusion of religion, quickly and without reflection or exception, will be strictly forbidden.

This is evidenced by the attestation requirement for Canada Summer Jobs grants. Religious organizations launched a lobbying campaign to encourage the government to remove the attestation requirement. National Christian associations, including the Evangelical Fellowship of Canada, the Canadian Council of Christian Charities and the Canadian Conference of Catholic Bishops met with Minister Hajdu. The minister repeatedly affirmed that religious groups were encouraged to apply; they simply had to check the box.[58] She did not understand that religious organizations cannot check a box affirming things that violate their religious beliefs.

Problems with a 'Rules of the Commons' Approach

As noted above, there are several problems with limiting religious activities to within the four walls of the church. First, it violates both the *Charter* protection for religious freedom guaranteed in s. 2(a) and the international human rights standards detailed above. Second, it restricts the positive impact of religious institutions on the broader community. Third, it would bring into question whether religious institutions should have charitable status. If religious adherents cannot participate in the commons, they cannot make a positive contribution there. Charitable status is for organizations contributing to the public benefit. Fourth, MacKinnon's argument is deeply flawed and incoherent.

In his chapter devoted to Trinity Western, MacKinnon details the path for approvals of the law school proposal. He mentions the 2001 SCC decision approving Trinity Western's School of Education. MacKinnon acknowledges that there is 'a lot of room' for Trinity Western in teacher education in British Columbia.[59] The university commons is large enough and diverse enough to include a faith-based university programme. However, he adds the proviso that for Trinity Western to participate, it must not discriminate. Thus, if there are no competing rights and values, the *Charter* protects the religious beliefs of Trinity Western and its students. But if there are competing rights and values, Trinity Western must be excluded because it does not comply with the 'rules of the commons'.

But in the Trinity Western case in 2001 and again in 2018, there are competing rights at issue, as there are in many *Charter* cases. The main reason religious freedom is protected in the *Charter* is that religious beliefs are often unpopular, even contentious. Religious freedom did not suddenly become an issue when the *Charter* came into force in 1982. Religion had long been controversial in Canada, from religious education issues to distribution of religious literature.[60]

MacKinnon goes on to posit that religious individuals and communities clearly enjoy religious freedom; '[w]e become hesitant only when they move beyond their worshipful activities and into a public domain shared with others who do not believe and worship as they do'.[61] MacKinnon claims that there is an absolute prohibition on discrimination in any activities in the public domain. Interestingly, Minister Hajdu made the same assertion, that it is 'against labour law' in Canada to discriminate in hiring.[62] In fact, religious organizations are exempted from anti-discrimination laws with respect to hiring.[63] This allows religious organizations to maintain their religious identities by hiring staff that are committed to maintaining the religious mission.

MacKinnon raises the issue of academic freedom at Trinity Western University as another reason to refuse approval for a law school. He references several chapters in a book edited by James Turk, then executive director of the Canadian Association of

University Teachers (CAUT), on academic freedom. These chapters go further than MacKinnon to question the legitimacy of a faith-based university as a university.[64]

CAUT developed a policy in 2006 that any institution that has an ideological or faith test as a requirement of employment violates academic freedom. CAUT then proceeded to 'investigate' Christian universities that have faith tests, even though none of their faculty are members of CAUT. The first of these investigations was of Trinity Western University, which CAUT found, not surprisingly, violates academic freedom.

Again, the issue of academic freedom comes back to the ability of a religious organization to maintain its religious character. There are several aspects to academic freedom, one of which is freedom for professors to teach, research and publish. Universities also have institutional academic freedom, as against state control.[65] Students also have a measure of academic freedom with respect to their research and writing. They should not be penalized for writing on unpopular topics or coming to conclusions that may differ from that of the professor. There is obviously tension among these three aspects of academic freedom. While this may appear evident for a Christian university such as Trinity Western with its Statement of Faith and Community Covenant, these tensions exist at all universities. For example, Robert Buckingham, Dean of the School of Public Health, was dismissed from the University of Saskatchewan for publicly criticizing the university regarding budget cuts. He was reinstated on the basis of academic freedom but removed from his position as dean.

All the criticisms of Trinity Western University relate to its religious identity, yet its statement of faith is that of its founding denomination. The Community Covenant reflects the deeply held religious beliefs and practices of the religious community. It would not be the university it is if not for its Christian character. If it is required to adhere to society's secular values in order to be a university, to obtain accreditation of its programmes, to be a member of Universities Canada or to have charitable status, it would be required by the state to abandon its purpose, its mission and its legislative charter and become a different institution altogether.

Conclusions

There appears to be collective amnesia on the part of academics and government officials concerning the important 'golden thread of faith' that runs through the fabric of Canadian history. Yet as then Prime Minister Pierre Trudeau acknowledged, faith plays a large role in the lives of many Canadians. It is also an essential element of many institutions that contribute to the common good of Canada. Canada is a pluralist, tolerant and multifaith country that is enriched by its diversity. The many religious institutions that are hard at work day in and day out to make our communities better are an important part of this diversity.

The inclusion of 'advancement of religion' as a head of charity has always recognized the importance of religious institutions in the common life of Canada. This also recognizes that religious institutions are of public benefit to society. It is unhistorical, not to mention unconstitutional and illogical, then to subject them to rules and regulations that restrict their activities to houses of worship, thereby limiting religious freedom to 'freedom of worship'. Religious institutions cannot and should not be required to conform to secular norms that strip them of their religious identities.

The two examples used in this paper, Trinity Western University and the Canada Summer Jobs attestation requirement, both show ways that religious institutions can be restricted in their ability to contribute to Canadian society. For religious institutions to maintain their religious definitions of marriage and to oppose unrestricted abortion runs contrary to current secular standards. The fact that both these issues ended up in court shows that religious institutions are not about to relinquish their religious beliefs and practices. It seems that modern, progressive Canada in its quest for new 'Canadian values' is jettisoning some of the old 'Canadian values' upon which its educational, healthcare and poverty-reduction institutions were founded.

Notes

1 Don Page, 'From Private to Public Religion: The History of the Public Service Christian Fellowship', unpublished at 9, online (pdf): <http://www.pscf-acfp.ca/From_Private_to_Public_Religion-Don_Page.pdf>.
2 Peter MacKinnon, *University Commons Divided: Exploring Debate & Dissent on Campus* (Toronto: University of Toronto Press, 2018).
3 *Trinity Western University v Law Society of Upper Canada*, 2018 SCC 33 [*TWU v LSUC*]; *Law Society of British Columbia v Trinity Western University*, 2018 SCC 32 [*LSBC v TWU*].
4 See the introduction to Barry W. Bussey's chapter, 'Making Registered Charitable Status of Religious Organizations Subject to "Charter values"'.
5 Page, *supra* note 1 at 9–10.
6 Inter-American Commission on Human Rights (IACHR), *American Declaration of the Rights and Duties of Man*, 2 May 1948.
7 Miroslav Volf, *Flourishing: Why We Need Religion in a Globalized World* (New Haven, CT: Yale University Press, 2015) at 81.
8 *Ibid.*
9 Augustine addresses God in *Confessions*, 'our hearts are restless till they find rest in you' *(Lib 1,1-2,2.5,5: CSEL 33, 1–5)*.
10 Volf, *Flourishing*, *supra* note 7, ch. 2.
11 See Angus Reid Institute, 'Faith and Immigration: New Canadians Rely on religious communities for material, spiritual support', 9 July 2018, online (pdf): <http://angusreid.org/wp-content/uploads/2018/07/2018.06.22_CardusWave1_2018.pdf>.
12 See Michael Van Pelt & Richard Greydanus, *Living on the Streets: The Role of the Church in Urban Renewal* (Hamilton: Work Research Foundation, 2005) at 20–24.
13 Much of this history is found in Catherine Anne Gidney, *A Long Eclipse: The Liberal Protestant Establishment and the Canadian University, 1920–1970* (Montreal: McGill-Queen's University Press, 2004).
14 Tyndale University College was founded in 1894 as Toronto Bible Training School. It went through several evolutions before gaining university status in 2003. See 'Tyndale's History Timeline' (2019) online, *Tyndale University College and Seminary*: <https://www.tyndale.ca/about/timeline>.
15 The three colleges were Concord College, Canadian Mennonite Bible College and Menno Simons College. The university is supported by both the Mennonite Church Canada and the Mennonite Brethren Church of Manitoba. See 'About CMU' (2019) online, *Canadian Mennonite University*: <http://www.cmu.ca/about.php?s=cmu&p=facts>.

16 *BC Civil Liberties Association v University of Victoria*, 2016 BCCA 216 (BCCA), leave to appeal to SCC denied 1 December 2016; *McKinney v University of Guelph*, [1990] 3 SCR 229.
17 See *Waldman v Canada*, Communication No. 694/1996; UN Doc, /CCPR/C/67/D/694/1996 (1999) (UN Hum. Rts. Ctte.).
18 *Income War Tax Act*, (1917), 7–8 Geo. 5, c. 29, 5(d).
19 *Income Tax Act*, SC 1948, c. 52.
20 See *Pemsel v Special Commissioners of Income Tax*, [1891] AC 531.
21 Canada Revenue Agency, 'How to draft purposes for charitable registration' (25 July 2013), online: <https://www.canada.ca/en/revenue-agency/services/charities-giving/charities/policies-guidance/guidance-019-draft-purposes-charitable-registration.html>.
22 Human Life International and Alliance for Life are pro-life organizations that had their charitable status revoked.
23 See *TWU v LSUC* and *LSBC v TWU*, *supra* note 3 and further discussion of these judgements infra.
24 M. James Penton, *Jehovah's Witnesses in Canada: Champions of Freedom of Speech and Worship* (Toronto: Macmillan of Canada, 1976) at 134–45.
25 William Kaplan, *State and Salvation: The Jehovah's Witnesses and their Fight for Civil Rights* (Toronto: University of Toronto Press, 1989) at 131–40.
26 *Canada Trust Co. v Ontario Human Rights Commission*, [1990] O.J. No. 615, 74 OR (2d) 481 (C.A.).
27 *Canadian Magen David Adom for Israel v Minister of National Revenue*, 2002 FCA 323, 218 DLR (4th) 718.
28 [2004] 3 SCR 698, para 52.
29 *Ibid*, para 53.
30 *Ibid*, para 52.
31 *Civil Marriage Act*, SC 2005, c. 33.
32 *Supra* note 26.
33 *Ibid*, at 491 (OR).
34 The *cy-pres* doctrine allows a court to amend the terms of a trust to keep it from failing.
35 See Dean Beeby, 'Conservative government steps up scrutiny of charities' political activities', *Globe and Mail* (10 July 2014), online: https://www.theglobeandmail.com/news/politics/study-cites-chill-from-tax-agency-audits-of-charities-political-activities/article19551584/.
36 Dean Beeby, 'Political activity audits of charities suspended by Liberals', *Globe and Mail* (4 May 2017), online: <http://www.cbc.ca/news/politics/canada-revenue-agency-political-activity-diane-lebouthillier-audits-panel-report-suspension-1.4099184>.
37 *Trinity Junior College Act*, SBC 1969, c. 44, s. 3(2).
38 See Trinity Western University's Mission Statement online: <https://www.twu.ca/mission-statement-statement-faith-community-covenant>.
39 Tara Teng, who was Miss World Canada in 2012, was a strong advocate against human trafficking when she was a student at Trinity Western. David Punnamanil founded Lighthouse Voyage, a charity to fund victims of human trafficking in India, while a student at Trinity Western.
40 Jordan Koslowsky founded Trinity Refugee Awareness Campaign to sponsor a refugee family.
41 See online (pdf): <http://www.docs.flsc.ca/_documents/TWUCouncilofCdnLawDeansNov202012.pdf>.
42 Saul Templeton, 'Re-Framing the Trinity Western University Debate', *Law Matters* (Summer 2015), online: <https://www.cba-alberta.org/Publications-Resources/Resources/Law-Matters/Law-Matters-Summer-2015-Issue/Re-Framing-the-Trinity-Western-University-Debate>.
43 *LSBC v TWU* and *TWU v LSUC*, *supra* note 3 (transcript of oral hearing, SCC vol. 2, 1 December 2017, at 282).
44 *Supra* note 3.
45 *LSBC v TWU*, *supra* note 3, para 75.
46 *Ibid*, para 103.

47 *Ibid*, para 61.
48 *Loyola High School v Quebec (Attorney General)*, 2015 SCC 12.
49 *Highwood Congregation of Jehovah's Witnesses (Judicial Committee) v Wall*, 2018 SCC 26.
50 *LSBC v TWU*, *supra* note 3, para 336.
51 Barry W. Bussey, 'Summer Jobs Program: Further Evidence of The Government of Canada's Ideological Approach toward Religious Charities' (19 December 2017), online: <https://www.cccc.org/news_blogs/barry/2017/12/19/summer-jobs-program-further-evidence-of-thegovernment-of-canadas-ideological-approach-toward-religious-charities/>.
52 See Monique Scotti, '1,559 applications for summer jobs money rejected after groups refuse to check box on abortion, LGBT rights', *Global News* (15 May 2018), online: <https://globalnews.ca/news/4209375/summer-jobs-abortion-applications-lgbt-rights/>.
53 The Toronto Right to Life Association filed an application for judicial review of the programme in Federal Court in January 2018. A second challenge was brought by small business owners Rhea Lynn and William Anderson in southern Alberta. Their application for funding was denied because they did not check the attestation box.
54 See Universities Canada, 'About Us', online: <https://www.univcan.ca/about-us/>.
55 MacKinnon, *supra* note 2.
56 *Ibid*, 117.
57 *LSBC v TWU*, *supra* note 3, paras 241–42.
58 See e.g. John Geddes, 'Trudeau government stands firm in clash with faith-based groups over summer jobs', *Maclean's* (19 January 2018), online: <https://www.macleans.ca/politics/ottawa/trudeau-government-stands-firm-in-clash-with-faith-based-groups-over-summer-jobs/>.
59 MacKinnon, *supra* note 2 at 80.
60 See Janet Epp Buckingham, *Fighting Over God: A Legal and Political History of Religious Freedom in Canada* (Montreal: McGill-Queen's University Press, 2014).
61 MacKinnon, *supra* note 2 at 81.
62 Amanda Connolly, 'Canada Summer Jobs attestation specifically targets activities, not beliefs: Hajdu', *Global News* (23 January 2018), online: <https://globalnews.ca/news/3981525/canada-summer-jobs-attestation-came-after-complaints-about-anti-abortion-anti-gay-groups-hajdu/>.
63 See e.g. *Human Rights Code*, RSBC 1996, c. 210, s. 41.
64 John Baker, 'Academic Freedom as a Constraint on Freedom of Religion', in James L. Turk, ed, *Academic Freedom in Conflict: The Struggle over Free Speech Rights in the University* (Toronto: James Lorimer, 2014) at 127–44.
65 Fascist and Communist dictatorships exerted control over European universities. See Ralph F. Fuchs, 'Academic Freedom – Its Basic Philosophy, Function, and History' (Summer 1963) 28 Law and Contemporary Problems 431–46, 434, fn. 17.

Part IV
CONCLUSION

Chapter Nine

THE GOAL OF EXCLUDING RELIGION FROM THE IDEA OF PUBLIC BENEFIT: SOME ASPECTS OF NEO-SECULARIST STRATEGIES

Iain T. Benson*

Abstract

It is no longer obvious that religion *ought* to be in the public sphere. Law has become ideology and religion has lost respect, despite being close to the centre of how we understand justice and the common good. Instead, forced conformity under 'equality' or 'non-discrimination' is used to monitor the public and private places of religious activities. Liberty is now presumed to be a grant from the state and any public license for religious activities must follow the state, as seen in the Trinity Western University law school case.

Religious freedom rights are not solely private and individual but communal. Much depends on the context. Religion is an equality right and to suggest it is at odds with equality rights is simply inaccurate. Further, to suggest that 'secular' means 'non-religious' is to imply that that 'secular' people have no 'faith'. That is also untrue. Everyone has faith; the question is what is believed. When 'secular' is read as non-religious, then the beliefs of atheists and agnostics are accorded representation but 'religious' beliefs are not. That is neither representative nor fair. Only through an inclusive approach can accommodation and diversity have their proper application and meaning. The term 'secular' must not be used when speaking of the public sphere and religion's role in it.

---

* BA, MA, JD, PhD (Wits), Professor of Law, School of Law, University of Notre Dame Australia, Sydney; Extraordinary Professor of Law, Department of Public Law, University of the Free State, Bloemfontein, South Africa. A version of this chapter was originally presented as a paper, 'A Cookbook of Ways to Dissolve Religious Associations Through Law', at a conference entitled, 'Religion and Civil Society, the Changing Faces of "Religion" and "Secularity"' hosted by The Institute for Culture and Society of the University of Navarra and The School of Law Harvard University, Cambridge, Massachusetts, USA, 7–8 June 2012. The author would like to thank Mary Ann Glendon and the late Jean Bethke Elshtain for helpful encouragement and advice after this paper was presented. This version, much shortened and reframed, is published here in memory of Jean Bethke Elshtain whose works illuminated critical concepts in relation to many areas of philosophy and culture including religion and the state. The author also acknowledges his friends Robert Royal and Russell Hittinger, who were also present at the Harvard Conference; Barry Bussey, who is responsible for its appearance in this volume; and Tara Veness, who assisted with editing.

Once we grasp the importance of religion to culture and to the continued understanding of moral rights and duties, our approach to the law of charities – and our understanding of the public benefit of religious charities – ought to bolster the role religions play in relation to ideas of conscience and justice in open societies. Charitability towards religion will lead to benefits from the charitable dimensions of religion.

Introduction

A version of the paper upon which this conclusion is based was given elsewhere, and when originally presented, styled itself as 'a cookbook of ways to dissolve the freedom of religion'. It was written in the style of C. S. Lewis's *The Screwtape Letters* in the sense that it purported to give advice from a senior devil to a junior devil about how one opposed to religion might wish to minimize the place of religion in the public sphere. It was intended to be somewhat humorous. In the years since then, however, I have thought better about trying to be satirical about this topic because, frankly, it is now more of a problem than ever and it is not the case that it is obvious anymore why such recipes should be amusing.

As Dame Helen Gardner said in a lecture at Cambridge University almost forty years ago,[1] comedy only 'works' in a setting where the moral horizons are in place – Swift's 'A Modest Proposal' only makes sense because we recognize that eating the young is preposterous as a solution to the hunger problems in Ireland. Similarly, pointing out how to limit religion in the public sphere only makes sense if one understands that religion *ought* to have a place in the public sphere and that religious purposes are close to the centre of how we should understand justice and the common good: neither of these things are obvious any longer, judging by how some courts and legislators are dealing with religion and related rights (such as conscience) in many places.[2]

Unfortunately, as the various chapters in this book show, settled understandings about the public and common good dimensions of religion are quite likely to have been forgotten in our time even if they were once held. In referring to 'religion' I include all faiths, though Christianity in particular played a formative role in the West – a fact that was once undisputed, as Justice Sachs notes, but which no Canadian jurist has yet dared to assert.[3] Works of history referring to religion being the 'vital element' in a culture are no longer *de rigueur*. Prior periods understood matters differently.

Consider the much-celebrated historian of an earlier era – Christopher Dawson. In his Gifford Lectures from 1938, *Progress and Religion*, generally considered his most important work, he noted the tension between immanent and transcendent law, referred to as 'material' and 'spiritual'. Dawson's insights are remarkably prescient and useful in relation to our situation today. He wrote:

> We have come to take it for granted that the unifying force in society is material interest, and that spiritual conviction is a source of strife and division. Modern civilization has pushed religion and the spiritual elements in culture out of the main stream of its development, so that they have lost touch with social life and have become sectarianized and impoverished. But at the same time this has led to the impoverishment of our whole culture [...] It has borne fruit in that 'plebeianism of the European spirit' which Nietzsche regarded as the necessary consequence of the disappearance of the spiritual power.[4]

These are grave and important matters and so, on reflection, what is covered below will be put forward, not in the manner of the *Screwtape Letters*, not in the nature of comedy or irony or satire, though each, in its way, could describe some of the truly horrendous decisions and developments on view. It is sadly the case that in relation to religion and contemporary societies, cultures that once understood and respected the important place of religions do so less and less confidently, if at all.

The Slide to Law as Ideology and the Loss of Respect for Religion

It is likely no longer the case that readers of this volume will come to the problem of charitable status in general and religious charitable status in particular, and the notion of public benefit, with commitments about two key things: (1) that religions are important to central moral ideas essential to society and, related to that, (2) that the nature and role of religion matters a great deal to individual and community wellbeing.

Just how far we have come from what was widely understood as essential even a generation ago may be seen by charting, as some of the authors in this volume have, the inroads that law has made in relation to restrictions governing religious associations. Public licences, such as accreditation at issue in the 2018 Trinity Western University decisions (*TWU* 2018)[5] or public funding as in the Canada Summer Jobs programme discussed by both Barry W. Bussey and Janet Epp Buckingham, may be used as proxies to enforce ideological viewpoints.[6] Instead of recognizing the valid places for different moral viewpoints, forced conformity under the general language of 'equality' or 'non-discrimination', even in relation to issues such as the nature of marriage or the legitimacy of abortion, are used to monitor the public and private places of religious activities. Instead of liberty being the base condition (as is essential in the common-law tradition), it is presumed that the state grants us our freedoms and law gives us freedoms rather than recognizes them, thus getting the priority of freedom backwards. Any public licence must be built, implicitly or expressly, upon the extent to which the society understands coexistence and disagreement. Where it is understood that people will disagree about fundamental matters, and that an open society will maximize the legitimate legal space for such disagreements, then freedoms can coexist.

Consider the following with regard to TWU. The five-justice division of the British Columbia Court of Appeal (BCCA) in *Trinity Western University v The Law Society of British Columbia*[7] held in favour of the university and they did so unanimously. Canada's highest court, in all its euphemistic judicializing about hurt and exclusion, simply avoided dealing with the extremely strong language from the BCCA about the illiberal use of law by the LGBTTIQQPA activists. Nowhere in the three Supreme Court of Canada (SCC) majority judgements[8] do the seven judges (including the now-retired former Chief Justice McLachlin) deal with this passage from the BCCA:

> A society that does not admit of and accommodate differences cannot be a free and democratic society – one in which its citizens are free to think, to disagree, to debate and to challenge the accepted view without fear of reprisal. This case demonstrates that a well-intentioned majority acting in the name of tolerance and liberalism, can, if unchecked, impose its views on the minority in a manner that is in itself intolerant and illiberal.[9]

In every respect, the judges of the BCCA argued a deeper conception of a plural and diverse society than the majority judges of the SCC whose sanctimonious elevation of 'hurt feelings' and 'exclusion' and '*Charter* values' failed utterly to deal with what should have been addressed. Given the superficiality of their reasoning, it is not surprising that the above passage from the BCCA went completely uncommented upon by the majority judges of the SCC – to their shame: it is more likely that they could not deal with the argument and simply avoided it.

In such a setting, law has been overtaken by ideology.[10] In the SCC decision in *TWU* 2018 and the Ontario Court of Appeal's lamentable *Christian Medical and Dental Society of Canada v College of Physicians and Surgeons of Ontario* decision[11] denigrating 'conscience', we can see how the 'new moralities' of abortion, euthanasia, gender identity and similar developments will all too easily become tests for other sorts of inclusions and exclusions and the granting or withholding of public benefits. It is already evident that under this new kind of law (for the shift between TWU at the BCCA and at the SCC is a difference of kind) there is no tolerance for dissenting viewpoints. Now there are required beliefs for 'attestations', 'accreditations', 'licencing requirements', 'public interest standards', 'exemption restrictions', 'conscience exercise limits' and 'reference requirements', and, in a charitable context, we can expect 'public benefit' to be adjudged in line with these new sexual and identity orthodoxies.

Ours is now – and we should not be under any illusion here – a situation in which law is, frankly, in political freefall and these sorts of exclusions of religious believers and their communities will follow from these decisions in future just as surely as the communists used 'atheist pledges' to exclude the religious from graduate schools or academic teaching positions in the past. In the end, it's all about how the idea of God or gods influences how one understands culture. It has always been like that, but contemporary 'schooling' (it is not properly termed 'education') has robbed many elites in the media, education, law and politics of any meaningful horizon against which to measure decontextualized concepts such as 'inclusion', 'exclusion' and 'hurt feelings'.[12]

However, once fundamental matters about which people may legitimately disagree are reduced to singular conceptions, then society becomes explicitly or implicitly coercive.

We think, generally, that we can do without religion and that law is competent to tell religion what to do. This is a serious mistake. Again, Christopher Dawson notes the error by observing that the exclusion of religion and 'the spiritual element' from culture is not a lasting or permanent or, in fact, healthy condition. He argues:

> This, however, is but a temporary phenomenon; it can never be the normal condition of humanity. For, as we have seen, the vital and creative power behind every culture is a spiritual one. In proportion, as the spiritual element recovers its natural position at the centre of our culture, it will necessarily become the mainspring of our whole social activity. This does not, however, mean that the material and spiritual aspects of life must become fused in a single political order which would have all the power and rigidity of a theocratic state. Since a culture is essentially a spiritual community, it transcends the economic and political orders. It finds its appropriate organ not in a state, but in a Church, that is to say a society which is the

embodiment of a purely spiritual tradition and which rests, not on material power, but on the free adhesion of the individual mind.[13]

The authors in this volume have noted this development away from religion in various ways. I would like to place these concluding observations in the context of a justly celebrated quotation from a South African jurist, now retired: Justice Albie Sachs, formerly of the Constitutional Court of South Africa. His statement sets out rather well the general nature of the importance of religion itself as follows:

> [I]n the open and democratic society contemplated by the Constitution, although the rights of non-believers and minority faiths must be fully respected, the religious beliefs held by the great majority of South Africans must be taken seriously. As this Court pointed out in *Christian Education*, freedom of religion goes beyond protecting the inviolability of the individual conscience. For many believers, their relationship with God or creation is central to all their activities. It concerns their capacity to relate in an intensely meaningful fashion to their sense of themselves, their community and their universe. For millions in all walks of life, religion provides support and nurture and a framework for individual and social stability and growth. Religious belief has the capacity to awaken concepts of self-worth and human dignity which form the cornerstone of human rights. Such belief affects the believer's view of society and founds a distinction between right and wrong. It expresses itself in the affirmation and continuity of powerful traditions that frequently have an ancient character transcending historical epochs and national boundaries. For believers, then, what is at stake is not merely a question of convenience or comfort, but an intensely held sense about what constitutes the good and proper life and their place in creation. Religious bodies play a large and important part in public life, through schools, hospitals and poverty relief programmes. They command ethical behaviour from their members and bear witness to the exercise of power by state and private agencies; they promote music, art and theatre; they provide halls for community activities, and conduct a great variety of social activities for their members and the general public. They are part of the fabric of public life, and constitute active elements of the diverse and pluralistic nation contemplated by the Constitution. Religion is not just a question of belief or doctrine. It is part of a people's temper and culture, and for many believers a significant part of their way of life. Religious organisations constitute important sectors of national life and accordingly have a right to express themselves to government and the courts on the great issues of the day. They are active participants in public affairs fully entitled to have their say with regard to the way law is made and applied.[14]

For Justice Sachs, religion is cultural, and its importance is, in a sense, upstream of law and politics, both of which are framed by the essential background that religion (and other culture-forming dimensions such as race) provide. No Canadian judgement of any court has set out a passage showing this sort of understanding of religion. Why an atheist judge from South Africa has been willing to express what Canadian judges will not or cannot must remain a mystery. Canada awaits its Justice Albie Sachs.

In several of his judgements, Justice Sachs was also at pains to point out the coexistent spheres recognized under the South African Constitution, noting that these spheres must be kept in play alongside one another without subordinating one group to another. This approach is, however, not being followed in Canada and from issue to issue one hears abstract languages of 'equality' and 'non-discrimination' and new terms 'inclusivity' and 'exclusion' used to bleach other differences in beliefs and the lived lives of different human communities. When language is used in Orwellian ways, the result can only be Orwellian.

It is important to recognize that associational diversity (and public diversity as well) requires various viewpoints to coexist. This is, in fact, the law in both Canada and South Africa and is made clear with respect to 'equality' in the following passage from Justice Sachs:

> [E]quality should not be confused with uniformity; in fact, uniformity can be the enemy of equality. Equality means equal concern and respect across difference. *It does not presuppose the elimination or suppression of difference.* Respect for human rights requires the affirmation of self, not the denial of self. *Equality therefore does not imply a levelling or homogenisation of behaviour but an acknowledgment and acceptance of difference.*[15]

Canadian and South African jurisprudence tends *in theory* to favour both a religiously inclusivist and plural conception of the public sphere along the lines that we saw various authors urging in the previous chapters. Whether it does so in practice is, however, quite another matter as we are starting to see with some regularity. In terms of theory at any rate, the Constitutional Court of South Africa in the *Fourie* decision dealing with same-sex marriage in that country held that

> [T]here are a number of constitutional provisions that underline the constitutional value of acknowledging diversity and pluralism in our society, and give a particular texture to the broadly phrased right to freedom of association contained in section 18. Taken together, they affirm the right of people to self-expression without being forced to subordinate themselves to the cultural and religious norms of others, and highlight the importance of individuals and communities being able to enjoy what has been called the 'right to be different'. In each case, space has been found for members of communities to depart from a majoritarian norm.[16]

It should be noted, as Janet Epp Buckingham observes in her chapter 'Just Check the Box: Why Religious Institutions Still Make Canada a Better Place to Live and Flourish', that 'religious freedom is one of the pillars of international human rights law' (and see, also, Derek Ross and Ian Sinke in their chapter 'Advancing Religion in a "Neutral" State: Understanding Religion as a Constitutional Good'). The *International Covenant on Civil and Political Rights* (ICCPR) (in force 1976) that brought into law the *Universal Declaration of Human Rights* (1948), at Articles 18 and 19, sets out the general framework which ought to be considered in relation to the role and nature of the rights and freedoms in that Covenant. Article 18 protects the 'right to freedom of thought, conscience, and religion', which includes the freedom to manifest religious beliefs 'either individually or in community with others and in public or private'. Article 19 stipulates that '[e]veryone shall have the right to hold opinions without interference', subject only to such restrictions as are necessary 'for respect of the rights or reputations of others' and 'for the protection of national security or of public order'.

Religion Is Both a Public as well as a Private, a Group and a Personal Right: Different Views of Equality Can Only Be Resolved by Context

We should note here that religious freedom rights are not limited to the private sphere nor are they limited to individuals. They are private and public, personal and communal. This is important when we come to consider the implications of moves to limit the public dimension (restriction of public charitable work, for example) or group involvement (threatening the associational dimension of religious liberty).

Religion is an equality right and so to place religion as if it were against equality is an erroneous formulation of what is a tension that may only be resolved by *context*.[17]

Quite apart from the international provisions, we should also consider the *Canadian Charter of Rights and Freedoms* in terms of how religion appears not simply as a key enumerated right (along with 'conscience') in section 2(a) but also that religion is listed as one of the rights in relation to the equality or non-discrimination provision, section 15. Yet it is not at all uncommon to see people argue that religion is in competition with, or somehow opposed to, equality. What this sort of analysis then does is, typically, to suggest that equality or some other right 'weighs' more on the constitutional balancing scales. So prevalent is this formulation (with all its built-in assumptions about there being one sort of equality, etc.) that it seems to be scarcely noted or commented upon. This article attempts a corrective to this oversight and hopes to influence future politicians and judges not under the thrall of the contemporary malaise.

Misunderstanding the Nature of the 'Secular' and 'Faith'

Many of the key words we use to describe the nature of the state can hide preconceptions that are unfair. We have seen that Article 18 of the ICCPR recognizes that the freedom of religion applies in both the public as well as the private. For reasons I have discussed elsewhere, the term 'secular', like the term 'secularism', has to be understood in relation to historical changes. Where 'secular' once referred to a particular orientation to 'the world' in relation to eternity, it has come to mean 'non-religious' – or even anti-religious – in general language. This becomes a problem when we put it alongside the public nature of religious freedom. Much of our terminology, such as how we discuss 'faith', for example, tends to assume that only religious people have 'faith', when that is untrue. What religious people have is religious faith; what non-religious people have is non-religious faith. In short, everyone has faith; the question is not whether they believe but, rather, what they believe in. Unless we understand the terminology accurately, we can tend to leave religious belief systems at a public disadvantage (in terms of such things as public funding or charitable status) in relation to the unexamined faiths of atheism and agnosticism.

Legal cases in Canada and South Africa suggest that, for the reasons just given, we are at a time when the settled understanding of 'secular' as 'non- religious' needs to be revised. In the *Chamberlain*[18] decision, the SCC upheld the unanimous BCCA which had determined that the meaning of 'secular' in Canadian law must be inclusive of religious believers (and by inference their communities) rather than excluding them from participation. Perhaps because this shift in understanding has been so radical, it is the case that, even now, many years later, the new interpretation of 'secular' for the purposes of Canadian law is not widely known in Canada. Hence, it is frequently missed by counsel who should be using this in legal arguments and by judges who should be applying it in making their decisions. Again, it should happen in relation to a rigorous understanding of genuine pluralism and diversity.

In addition, the fact that there is, and should be, no such thing as a non-religious secular can be somewhat threatening to those who have assumed this unquestioningly. The recognition that all positions, including atheism and agnosticism, are positions of 'faith',[19] even though not of religious faith, can prompt a re-understanding of the public sphere in a more accurate manner. How this happens depends on the definition of the public sphere as this determines how we eventually accommodate or fail to accommodate differing beliefs, regardless of whether these beliefs are religious or non-religious in nature. The principles of accommodation and diversity, both well established and recognized in the law *in theory*, are of practical importance in terms of how they work out in culture and politics.

Much of the language that is used to characterize the public sphere virtually insulates it from religion and insulates religion from its proper public influence. Thus, if 'secular' is equivalent to 'non-religious', and 'secular' means all those public things like government, law, medical ethics, public education and so on, then these major aspects of culture are outside religion and religion is outside them. This important aspect of the foundational language is rarely commented upon and shows the dominance of the exclusivist (religion excluded from the 'secular' as public) position.

But what about the beliefs of the citizens who are in government, law, medicine and public education? When the 'secular' is read as 'non-religious' in its exclusivist position, then the beliefs of atheists and agnostics, who define themselves as 'non-religious', are accorded representation, but those who define themselves as 'religious' are not. This is neither representative nor fair, yet it is the dominant and largely unexamined result of assuming the 'public' as 'secular' and the 'secular' as 'non-religious'.

This chapter is a counter-reading to this common but erroneous construction of the public sphere. If 'secular' means 'the opposite of religious' or 'non-religious', and if the public realm is defined in terms of the 'secular', then the public sphere has only one kind of believer removed from it – the religious believer. I suggest that this way of using 'secular' is deeply flawed and will tend to lead us in the direction of religious exclusivism. An express meaning to 'secular' or 'public' that rules out religion without arguments based on fairness and justice leaves those realms distorted in relation to principles of accommodation. If we start off with an implicit idea that the public is secular, and thus 'non-religious', then it is difficult to balance or reconcile the various interests held by religious claimants and others in a public setting.

In contrast to this exclusivist position, this chapter suggests a different approach, that of 'religious inclusivism'. Only within an inclusive approach can accommodation and diversity have their proper application and meanings. Proper understanding of the public sphere requires a more explicit acknowledgment of the beliefs of those within it, whether these beliefs come from religion or not.[20] The SCC decision in *Chamberlain*[21] is an illustrative example of the new way in which the term 'secular' can be understood, since it shows the development from the common usage of 'secular' to one that is more accurate and fair. At the same time, however, the decision handed down by the SCC in *Chamberlain* still failed to address properly the concept of 'secularism', a term it seemed to endorse when doing so was inconsistent with how it reconfigured the understanding of the term 'secular'.[22]

The Need to Move Away from 'Religion AND the Secular'

For many people, including politicians and religious leaders, the phrase 'religion and the secular' contains the implicit assumption that whatever the 'secular' is, it is somehow completely separate from religion. Yet, if religion (religious persons and their communities) are to have a role in the public sphere (that includes, at the very least, public education, medical ethics, politics and law), then a bifurcation of this sort is destructive to the idea of an interpenetration between religion and the wider culture that we have seen in the legal decisions just referred to, that the law has begun to recognize.

Certainly, the original and older uses of secular as *saeculorum*, meaning in relation to 'the age' or 'the times' or 'the world', did not necessarily import a desacralized conception of the public sphere; but this has certainly changed in commonly understood usage today. Indeed, in Roman Catholic usage, both the clergy and certain sorts of institutes have been understood to be properly 'secular' in this earlier use. Thus, the clergy are divided between 'secular' and 'regular' clergy, and there can be 'secular institutes', none of which are non-religious. The shift from a former religiously inclusive secular to a religiously exclusive one, therefore, is of the utmost importance to understand at a time when the term 'secular' is being used so widely in relation to the public sphere. We would do better, in fact, to banish the use of the term 'secular' entirely when what we really mean is the public sphere and the relation of religion to that sphere. The term 'secular', with its deeply ambiguous usages in our contemporary age, simply confuses our analysis at the outset.[23]

Religion Is Not Just a Private Right; the Public Place of Religion; 'Separation of Church and State' and Laicism Rejected; Cooperation of Religions and the State Affirmed in Both Canada and South Africa and USA Approach Rejected

It had been commonly understood, at least since the *Big M Drug Mart* decision of the SCC (1985), that the essence of the freedom of religion was not just the right to have a religion in private but also 'the right to declare religion openly and without fear of hindrance or reprisal, and the right to manifest religious belief by worship and practice or by teaching in dissemination'.[24]

Note that the words employed are active, public words and reflect the International Covenant discussed above: 'declare', 'manifest', 'practice', 'teaching', 'dissemination'.

Further insight about the public nature of religious freedom may be found in South African jurisprudence. There it has been recognized that religion is not always merely a matter of private individual conscience or communal sectarian practice. Thus, Justice Sachs has stated:

> Certain religious sects do turn their back on the world, but major religions regard it as part of their spiritual vocation to be active in the broader society. Not only do they proselytize

through the media and in the public square, religious bodies play a large part in public life, through schools, hospitals and poverty relief. They command ethical behaviour from their members and bear witness to the exercise of power by State and private agencies; they promote music, art and theatre; they provide halls for community activities, and conduct a great variety of social activities for their members and the general public. They are part of the fabric of public life, and constitute active elements of the diverse and pluralistic nation contemplated by the Constitution.[25]

Neither country accepts the American conception of 'separation' (as that has come to be defined) nor the French conception of *läicité*. This does not mean, however, that arguments based in whole or in part on these concepts are not made in courts or heard in political or popular rhetoric; they, and comments regarding the equally misunderstood concept of 'secularism', are as ubiquitous as they are confused and confusing.

Diversity is a principle that has been recognized as important to Canadian society and is often recognized by virtue of the principle of accommodation which has been held to be one of the core 'values and principles essential to a free and democratic society'. The phrase 'free and democratic society' is one of the foundational concepts against which all *Charter of Rights and Freedoms* limitations are measured in section 1 of the *Charter*.

This linking of accommodation and diversity may be seen in the following passage from the Court's decision *R v Oakes* where then Chief Justice Dickson discussed the 'ultimate standard' of section 1 as follows:

A second contextual element of interpretation of s. 1 is provided by the words 'free and democratic society'. Inclusion of these words as the final standard of justification for limits on rights and freedoms refers the Court to the very purpose for which the *Charter* was originally entrenched in the Constitution: Canadian society is to be free and democratic. The Court must be guided by the values and principles essential to a free and democratic society which I believe embody, to name but a few, respect for the inherent dignity of the human person, commitment to social justice and equality, accommodation of a wide variety of beliefs, respect for cultural and group identity, and faith in social and political institutions which enhance the participation of individuals and groups in society. The underlying values and principles of a free and democratic society are the genesis of the rights and freedoms guaranteed by the *Charter* and the ultimate standard against which a limit on a right or freedom must be shown, despite its effect, to be reasonable and demonstrably justified.[26]

It may be seen from the above that accommodation of 'a wide variety of beliefs' and respect for 'cultural and group identity', both of which resonate with a robust recognition of the place of associations and diversity, has been seen to be at the core of the understanding of the kind of free and democratic society Canada is.

How have we done in this recognition? Until recently, not too badly. A review of the history of the cases argued and decided under the Canadian *Charter* since 1985 shows a long series of challenges to the scope and relevance of religious institutions and, on some occasions, questions about the continued ability of religious believers and organizations to play a part in the tapestry of Canadian life. Thus, *Chamberlain v Surrey School Board*[27] considered whether the term 'secular principles' ruled out of relevance decisions based or significantly influenced by religion. *Trinity Western University v British Columbia College of Teachers*[28] (*TWU* 2001) determined whether a religious institution could achieve accreditation from a provincial monitoring body in education despite the fact that attendance at the university required adherence to a Christian lifestyle clause.

In *TWU* 2001, it was stated on behalf of the majority of eight judges that '[t]he diversity of Canadian society is partly reflected in the multiple religious organizations that mark the societal landscape and this diversity of views should be respected'.[29]

This theory of diversity and accommodation, however, could not, as the second *TWU* decision showed, withstand the relentless threats from those who view public expressions of dissent or disagreement as constituting 'hatred' or attacks on dignity. Thus, it is sometimes argued that to resist, for example, claims for the acceptability of same-sex marriage amounts to a rejection of the dignity of same-sex couples. Hence, groups that advocate traditional marriage (or heterosexist conceptions as some might argue it) should not be tolerated.

At the time of the changes to the federal marriage act in Canada, it was argued successfully that the *Income Tax Act* should be amended to ensure that charities which continued to uphold a heterosexual definition of marriage should not have their charitable status removed as a result. The reason for that amendment was that at the time of the hearings in Ottawa, there were those who were advocating just that – the removal of charitable tax status for those who were opposed to same-sex marriage. Time has shown that civic totalism is the new modus of so-called equality seeking groups when it is evident that the only 'equality' they seek is their own.[30]

Accommodation is the practical principle which ensures that diversity is actualized in particular settings. When an employee lodges a conscientious or religious objection to something, the employer, if conscience is being respected rather than ignored, must try to accommodate the employee up to the point of undue hardship. Thus, if a person adheres to the belief that Saturday is a holy day of obligation on which he or she must not work and the employer has scheduled the employee for Saturday work, the employer must attempt to accommodate the employee's beliefs by adjusting the schedule. Similarly, if an employee objects to a particular practice – and these may be across a very wide spectrum – the employer must, in theory, seek to accommodate the employee.

But some requests for accommodation bring us into conflict with movements that desire recognition such that the request for accommodation can be perceived as an attack on the identity claim seekers' rights. It is this kind of concern that underlies pressure on physicians to refer for abortions or marriage commissioners to officiate marriages that they do not wish to perform. Recent decisions from the highest courts show scant regard for functional pluralism or the importance of conscience protection.[31]

Taken together, what the chapters in this volume represent are a series of concerns about the proper role of the state in relation to the differing beliefs of citizens – some of the beliefs of which will quite rightly manifest in actions to benefit the wider society. The risk in an age characterized by an increasingly unrecognized 'secularism' is that the restrictive animus behind the exclusions of secularism will be masked by a series of strategies themselves playing into the privatization and marginalization of religion that the International Covenant is structured against.

We are far along the road of increasing exclusion of religion and conscience, which were once understood as important in the public imagination. We want to have justice but without any understanding that it is, in fact, a virtue. We want (see Barry Bussey's chapter 'Making Registered Charitable Status of Religious Organizations Subject to "Charter Values"') to endorse 'values' which are nothing but subjective preferences. It is the long traditions of virtues and natural law (kept alive primarily by religions) that, as Justice Sachs understood in *Fourie*, frame for millions of people their conceptions of 'right and wrong' on which justice itself depends.

The American political theorist William Galston has understood well the relationship between politics and other dimensions of culture. He sets out a clear recognition of the importance of religion and the limits of politics and law:

> *Like all politics [and the principles would apply to law as well] democratic politics is legitimate to the extent that it recognizes and observes the principled limits to the exercise of democratic power.* The liberties that individuals and the associations they constitute should enjoy in all but the most desperate circumstances go well beyond the political rights that democratic politics requires. We cannot rightly assess the importance of politics without acknowledging the limits of politics. The claims that political institutions can make in the name of the common good co-exist with claims of at least equal importance that individuals and civil associations make, based on particular visions of the good for themselves or for human kind. *Liberal democracy rightly understood must steer a course between theocratic claims that subject politics to a single religious orthodoxy and a civic republicanism that subordinates faith to the functional requirements of the polity. This means acknowledging that there are multiple sources of authority within a shared social space and that the relation amongst them is not straightforwardly hierarchical.* As Chief Justice Hughes rightly observed in *Macintosh*, *our conception of religious liberty implies that for some purposes, religious authority is higher than political authority and should take priority in cases of conflict between them.* [...] A key aim of liberal democratic politics is the creation of social space within which individuals and groups can freely pursue their distinctive visions of what gives meaning and worth to human existence. There is a presumption in favour of the free exercise of this kind of purposive activity which I call 'expressive liberty', and a liberal democracy bears and must discharge a burden of proof whenever it seeks to restrict expressive liberty.[32]

Students of history and philosophy who have attended to developments in the twentieth century that culminated in the judgement of German laws at Nuremburg know the limits of positive law that sees itself supposedly freed from metaphysics.[33] Yet it is in natural law and the traditions of religion that rationality and reasonableness were most richly framed.[34] Once we understand the importance of religions to culture and to the continued maintenance of our understanding of moral rights and duties, our approach to the law of charities and our proper understanding of the *public benefit of religious charities* ought to make us more aware of the importance of bolstering rather than limiting the roles that religions play in relation to ideas of conscience and justice in open societies. On 'public benefit', see the chapter in Part I of this volume by John Pellowe, 'The Public Benefit of "Advancing Religion" as a Charitable Purpose'.

Law and religion and respectful politics need each other, and the nature of their multi-level interrelationships are important to keep in mind and practice (see the chapters by

Juliet Chevalier-Watts and Raymond B. Chiu on the relationship between legal systems and religions).

The ultimate irony about the proper relationship between charity and religion is that the only relationship that will last is if one is first charitable *to* religion in order to benefit *from* the charitable dimensions *of* religion. This will require a considerable course-correction from the drift of contemporary culture and its aggressive new approaches to law which show a marked tendency towards the denigration of religious communities and their charities rather than the encouragement of both. The contemporary crises of liberal societies are deep and relate in key ways to loss of traditions that nurture shared meanings and purposes: chief among these are religions. In order to understand religion as a public benefit, therefore, it is essential that those who practice implicit or explicit bigotry towards religious believers and their communities, or who have been complicit in not recognizing the problems described above, begin to recognize the bigotries and change the practices that support them. It will be a great public benefit to do so, and sooner rather than later.[35]

Notes

1 Subsequently published as Helen Gardner, 'Happy Endings: Literature, Misery, & Joy' (August 1981) *Encounter*, 39–50, online: <https://www.unz.com/print/Encounter-1981aug/>. In this essay, she notes, quoting Ian Donaldson:

> the existence of a generally accepted social order is necessary for laughter to be possible at the comic inversions by which social order is flouted, and the distinctions of degree, priority, and place are impertinently reversed by the sight of beggars on horseback and justices in the stocks. A strongly ordered society can afford to find matter for laughter in what cannot be tolerated in a society in which authority is weak and threatened. (45)

Ours is a society notably increasingly brittle about comedy as evidenced by leading comedians no longer wishing to appear at University campuses because of the hostility they encounter there. It is increasingly true that the youth of today literally, as the saying goes, 'cannot take a joke'. The culture of victimhood and identity politics combines increasing fragility of the self (such things as campus 'safe spaces', 'trigger warnings' and disagreement characterized as 'hate speech' abound) with a lack of the self-abnegating humour that is essential for healthy life in community. The psychological and therapeutic dimensions of these new 'gnostic' movements is well described in the work of Eric Voegelin. In particular, see *The New Science of Politics* (Chicago: University of Chicago Press, 1952, 1987) and *Science, Politics and Gnosticism* (Chicago: Henry Regnery, 1968). These works well describe the background to what is being seen in current cultures and point to the general malaise as one needing therapeutic and spiritual/religious treatment.

2 The recent decision of the Ontario Court of Appeal in the *Christian Medical and Dental Society of Canada v College of Physicians and Surgeons of Ontario*, 2019 ONCA 393 (15 May 2019), in which that court upheld a lower court decision requiring physicians to make 'effective referrals' in relation to abortion, euthanasia or gender reassignment surgery, shows that scant regard can be given to the important place of conscience in society. Suggesting that conscientiously opposed physicians choose other types of medical practice strikes many commentators as a complete abrogation of the court's duty to ensure accommodation and protection of conscience. Perhaps on a proper set of facts (this case was argued in the abstract as a challenge to the legal framework itself), another court might come to a more nuanced and acceptable conclusion.

3 See CBC coverage of MP Michael Cooper being vilified for asserting that Canada was founded on Judaeo-Christian principles: Evan Dyer, 'MP Michael Cooper disparaged "goat herder cultures" in 2008 law class discussion, lawyers claim', *CBC News* (18 June 2019), online: <https://www.cbc.ca/news/politics/michael-cooper-goat-herder-cultures-1.5179039>.
4 Christopher Dawson, *Progress and Religion* (New York: Sheed and Ward, 1938) at 261–62.
5 *Law Society of British Columbia v Trinity Western University*, 2018 SCC 32, [2018] 2 S.C.R. 293 and *Trinity Western University v Law Society of Upper Canada*, 2018 SCC 33, [2018] 2 S.C.R. 453. Hereinafter '*TWU* 2018'.
6 As this chapter was being written, a leading Australian rugby player, Israel Folau, who is a self-confessed fundamentalist Christian, had his employment contract terminated by the Australian Rugby Union (ARU) due to his failure to support their requirements for 'inclusivity'. His 'high-level breach' consisted of him posting scriptural quotations on his Instagram page critical of a list of sins including drunkenness, adultery, idolatry and homosexual conduct alongside the statement that such sinners 'will go to hell'. Folau was then hounded for his 'homophobia' and his multimillion dollar sports contract terminated. Following this, he quickly raised significant sums for his looming court battle with the ARU but then had his 'GoFundMe' page on the popular crowd funding site cancelled due to the 'community standards' of GoFundMe. Thus, the rugby player is not able to use this otherwise generally available website to support his legal challenge against the Rugby Association, with both the website and the association citing 'inclusivity', 'community standards' and the Christian position as 'homophobic'. On 4 December 2019 the two sides settled out of court for an undisclosed but significant amount (see Georgina Robinson, 'Rugby Australia and Israel Folau reach settlement, both apologise for "for any hurt or harm caused"', *Sydney Morning Herald* (4 December 2019), online: <https://www.google.com.au/amp/s/amp.smh.com.au/sport/rugby-union/rugby-australia-reaches-settlement-with-folau-20191204-p53gr6.html>). The joint statement published as a result reads:

> The Social Media Post reflected Mr Folau's genuinely held religious beliefs, and Mr Folau did not intend to harm or offend any person when he uploaded the Social Media Post.
>
> Mr Folau wants all Australians to know that he does not condone discrimination of any kind against any person on the grounds of their sexuality and that he shares Rugby Australia's commitment to inclusiveness and diversity.
>
> Rugby Australia and NSW Rugby do not in any way agree with the content of the Social Media Post. Inclusiveness is one of Rugby's core values and it welcomes all people to the game, including all members of the LGBTI community. While it was not Rugby Australia's intention, Rugby Australia acknowledges and apologises for any hurt or harm caused to the Folaus.

For its part, the ARU has an entire part of its website dedicated to 'Rugby Pride', indicating a strongly pro-LGBT position. This is an interesting application of Plato's insight that as it goes with the games, so it goes with the city: see Gavin Ardley, 'The Role of Play in the Philosophy of Plato' (July 1967) 42:161 Philosophy 226–44. It shows that, for the new ideologues, no area of culture is immune from their policing and punishments.
7 2016 BCCA 423.
8 *TWU* 2018, *supra* note 5.
9 *Ibid*, at para 193.
10 By 'ideology' here, following Jacques Ellul, I subscribe to Raymond Aron's statement that 'an ideology is any set of ideas accepted by individuals or peoples without attention to their origin or value'. Ellul develops this to note the distinction between myths (which are deeper in the soul, less doctrinaire and, paradoxically, less passive than ideologies) and ideologies which are more flexible and fluid. On Ellul's reading, socialism, democracy and communism are ideologies and work, progress and happiness, myths. Presumably, though Ellul does not develop this sufficiently, religions form and are formed by myths and have longer and shared traditions not matched by less stable ideologies. The long and shared nature of traditions is one of C. S.

Lewis's central insights in *The Abolition of Man* (referred to below, *infra* note 34). It is the rhetorical thinness and disconnection of the language of the new ideologies that are part of their characteristic nature. Thus, these contemporary debates focus on the identities of 'individuals' rather than 'persons', 'gender' rather than 'sex', 'values' rather than 'virtues' and 'inclusivity' and 'equality' without proper attention to lived *contexts*. See Jacques Ellul, *Propaganda: the Formation of Men's Attitudes* (New York: Vintage, 1965) at 116–17.

11   2019 ONCA 393.
12   I have, elsewhere, discussed the importance of differential contexts in relation to the diversity that logically precedes assessment of equality or discrimination: see Iain T. Benson, 'The Necessity for a Contextual Analysis for Equality and Nondiscrimination', in *Equality and Nondiscrimination: Catholic Roots, Current Challenges*, ed. Jane F. Adolphe, Robert L. Fastiggi & Michael A. Vacca (Eugene: Pickwick, 2019) at 63–75.
13   *Ibid*, at 262 [emphasis added].
14   *Minister of Home Affairs and Another v Fourie and (Doctors for Life International and Others, amici curiae); Lesbian and Gay Equality Project and Others v Minister of Home Affairs* 2006 1 SA 524 (CC) at paras 89–90.
15   *National Coalition for Gay and Lesbian Equality v Minister of Justice* (1998) 1517, 1574–1575 (Sachs J) [emphasis added].
16   *Minister of Home Affairs v Fourie* at paras 60–61 per Sachs J [emphasis added].
17   See Benson, *supra* note 12.
18   *Chamberlain v Surrey School District No. 36* [2002] 4 S.C.R. 710 (SCC) ['*Chamberlain*'].
19   John Henry Cardinal Newman recognized that everyone who acts must take matters on faith and wrote: 'Life is for action. If we insist on proofs for everything, we shall never come to action: to act you must assume, and that assumption is faith'. See Newman, 'Tamworth Reading Room Letters', in *Discussions and Arguments on Various Subjects* (London: Longmans, 1899) at 295. Closer to our own day, philosopher, R. F. A. Hoernlé, wrote that 'every bona fide judgment is characterised by belief. [...] [and] if "faith" is firm belief, conviction of truth, then faith in this context is indistinguishable from knowledge', in 'Knowledge and Faith', in Daniel S. Robinson, ed., *Studies in Philosophy* (Cambridge: Harvard University Press, 1952) at 55–61.
20   See Iain Benson, 'The Case for Religious Inclusivism and the Judicial Recognition of Associational Rights: A Response to Lenta. Case Comment' (2008) 1 Constitutional Court Review [South Africa] 297–312.
21   *Chamberlain v Surrey School District No. 36*, [2002] S.C.J. No. 87, [2002] 4 S.C.R. 710 [*Chamberlain*].
22   This is addressed elsewhere. See Iain T. Benson, 'Considering Secularism', in *Recognizing Religion in a Secular Society*, ed. Douglas Farrow (Montreal: McGill-Queens University Press, 2004) at 83–98. It should be said that failure to properly define what is meant by 'secularism' has become an ever-greater problem in the years since this chapter appeared.
23   I have written about this in 'Towards a (Re) Definition of the Secular' (2000) 33 University of British Columbia Law Review 519–49 (cited with approval by Gonthier J in *Chamberlain*).
24   *R. v Big M Drug Mart Ltd.* [1985] 1 S.C.R. 295 at 336 (SCC).
25   *Christian Education South Africa v Minister of Education* [2000] ZACC 11; 2000 (4) SA 757; 2000 (10) BCLR 1051 at para 33.
26   *R. v Oakes*, [1986] 1 S.C.R. 103 at para 64.
27   *Chamberlain, supra* note 21.
28   *Trinity Western University v British Columbia College of Teachers* [2001] 1 S.C.R. 772, 2001 SCC 31.
29   *Ibid*, at para 33. Unfortunately, respect for the diversity that marked the first Trinity Western University decision (*TWU* 2001) disappeared in *TWU* 2018. The University was forced to litigate through the courts a second time, in this case for accreditation of a law school, only to lose in a decision that was, in its reasoning, inconsistent with the earlier case, which demonstrated a genuine understanding of diversity and reconciliation of conflicting interests. For a useful commentary on the decision, its background and likely effects, see: Barry W. Bussey, 'Law

Matters but Politics Matter More: The Supreme Court of Canada and Trinity Western University' (2018) 7 Oxford Journal of Law and Religion 559–68, and Barry W. Bussey, 'The Legal Revolution against the Accommodation of Religion: The Secular Age v the Sexular Age' (unpublished PhD Dissertation, Universiteit Leiden, 2019) at 135–209. Respect for diversity has become a concept paid lip service only. Liberal elites have shown themselves unable and/or unwilling to defend genuine diversity, placing, in every case, the tribal concerns of identity politics ahead of those of religious believers and associations.

30 The nature of 'civic totalism' is well described by William Galston. See: Galston, 'Religion and the Limits of Liberal Democracy', in *Recognizing Religion in a Secular Society*, ed. Douglas Farrow (Montreal: McGill-Queens University Press, 2004), 41–50 at 43–45.

31 In *Carter v Canada (Attorney General)* 2015 SCC 5, [2015] 1 S.C.R. 331, the Supreme Court of Canada mandated euthanasia (euphemistically termed MAiD or 'medical assistance in dying') over the express intervention against the practice by, among others, the Canadian Medical Association. The judges thought they knew better what the nature of the therapeutic framework was as they applied the jurisprudential scalpel of autonomous individualism to medicine. The Ontario Court of Appeal in the *CMDS* decision (discussed above) saw that court dominate the wishes of the medical community with respect to 'effective referrals' and conscience. In South Africa, the Gauteng High Court Pretoria in the *Gaum v Dutch Reformed Church*, Case No. 40819/17, 9 March 2019, decision ruled that the Dutch Reformed Church must change its *doctrine* on same-sex marriage and the ordination of gay and lesbian clergy. Settled jurisprudence in which internal doctrine or specialized expertise would be deferred to or not interfered with by courts is now being ignored. Law has become a wall-to-wall form of dogmatism – it is a return to a kind of theocracy by law.

32 William A. Galston, *The Practice of Liberal Pluralism* (Cambridge: Cambridge University Press, 2005) at 128–29 [emphasis added]. I have written about the jurisdictional limits of law itself: Iain T. Benson, 'Foreword: The Limits of Law and Religious Associations', in *Religion, Liberty and the Jurisdictional Limits of Law*, ed. Iain T. Benson & Barry G. Bussey (Toronto: Lexis Nexus, 2018), xxi–xlvi.

33 See e.g. Gustav Radbruch 'Five Minutes of Legal Philosophy', in *The Natural Law Reader*, ed. Jacqueline A. Laing & Russell Wilcox (Oxford: Blackwell, 2014) at 232–33.

34 Two works in this area make important reading: C.S. Lewis, *The Abolition of Man* (New York, Macmillan, 1943), and George Grant, *Philosophy in the Mass Age* (Toronto: Copp Clark, 1959, 1966), particularly chapter 3, 'Natural Law'.

35 I catalogue various contemporary theorists from a wide variety of perspectives who discuss the 'crisis of liberalism' in Iain T. Benson, 'Civic Virtues and the Politics of Full Drift Ahead', Annual Acton Lecture, Centre for Independent Studies, Sydney, Australia, 26 April 2017, online (pdf): <https://www.cis.org.au/app/uploads/2017/06/op155.pdf> (last accessed 24 June 2019).

CONTRIBUTORS

General Editor

Barry W. Bussey – Making Registered Charitable Status of Religious Organizations Subject to 'Charter Values'

Barry W. Bussey, BA (Burman University, Union College), LLB (Western University), MA (Memorial University), LLM (York University), MPACS (University of Waterloo), PhD (Leiden University), is Director, Legal Affairs, at the Canadian Council of Christian Charities and Associate Adjunct Professor of law at the University of Notre Dame, Sydney. He is the co-editor of *Religion, Liberty and the Jurisdictional Limits of Law* (Toronto, Ontario: LexisNexis, 2017). Prof. Bussey has many years of experience in the charitable and non-profit sectors and has written extensively on law and religion.

Contributors

Iain T. Benson – The Goal of Excluding Religion from the Idea of Public Benefit: Some Aspects of Neo-Secularist Strategies

Iain T. Benson, BA (Hons) (Queen's University), MA (Cambridge University), JD (University of Windsor), PhD (Wits University), is a professor of law at University of Notre Dame, Sydney, and Professor Extraordinary, Faculty of Law, University of the Free State, Bloemfontein, South Africa. He teaches legal philosophy, legal history, human rights, public international law and contemporary legal issues.

Janet Epp Buckingham – Just Check the Box: Why Religious Institutions Still Make Canada a Better Place to Live and Flourish

Janet Epp Buckingham, BA (Western University), LLB (Dalhousie University), LLD (Stellenbosch University), is a professor at Trinity Western University and the director of the Laurentian Leadership Centre, an Ottawa-based, live-in extension programme focusing on leadership in public policy, business and communications. Janet researches and publishes on religious freedom in Canada and internationally. She is also interested in the relationship between faith, public policy and the legal system.

Juliet Chevalier-Watts – Have a Little Faith: The Advancement of Religion and Public Benefit

Juliet Chevalier-Watts, BA (Hons), LLB (Hons), LLM (Distinction), PGCLT, PhD candidate, is Associate Dean Research and Senior Lecturer in Law at Te Piringa – Faculty of Law, University of Waikato, and specializes in charitable trusts and charity law. She is considered one of New Zealand's leading charity law academics, lecturing and publishing extensively nationally and internationally. Juliet's latest monograph, *Charity Law: International Perspectives*, was recently published with the international publisher Routledge. Juliet has worked extensively with the Department of Internal Affairs – Charities Services, as well as carrying out consulting for charitable organizations and legal practitioners. Juliet spent many years as the editor-in-chief of the *Waikato Law Review*, a peer-reviewed journal. Juliet further sits on a number of editorial boards and frequently undertakes editing work for the *New Zealand Law Journal*.

Raymond B. Chiu – Religion and Public Benefit: Social Scientific Perspectives and Critiques

Raymond B. Chiu, BASc (University of Toronto, Civil Engineering), MBA (Schulich School of Business, York University), MTS (Tyndale University College & Seminary), PhD (DeGroote School of Business, McMaster University), is an assistant professor at the Goodman School of Business, Brock University, where he teaches business ethics. His ongoing research in organizational behaviour and human resource management focuses on religious and spiritual beliefs in the workplace, truth and trust in leadership, the influence of moral beliefs on perception of leaders and ethical objectives in personnel selection.

Frank Cranmer – Religion and Public Benefit in United Kingdom Charity Law

Frank Cranmer, BA, MA (Dunelm), LLM (University of Wales), STh (Lambeth), is Director of Central Lobby Consultants, Secretary of the Churches' Legislation Advisory Service, a Fellow of St Chad's College, Durham, and Honorary Research Fellow at the Centre for Law and Religion at Cardiff University. He specializes in UK and EU legislation as it affects churches, UK charity law and religion and human rights.

Bernard Doherty – Back at the Bar: Charity Law, Public Benefit and a Case of Legal *déjà vu* for the Exclusive Brethren

Bernard Doherty, BA (Ancient History, Macquarie University), MA (Early Christian and Jewish Studies, Macquarie University), PhD (Macquarie University), is Course Director at the School of Theology, and Research Fellow of the Centre for Public and Contextually Theology, Charles Sturt University, Canberra. He is also an adjunct lecturer in the School of Law at the University of Notre Dame, Sydney, and Honorary Fellow at the Information Network Focus on Religious Movements (INFORM) based at King's College London. Bernard's research interests are wide-ranging and include new religious movements, patristics, Australian religious history, Church and State issues, and religion and the media.

John Pellowe – The Public Benefit of 'Advancing Religion' as a Charitable Purpose: A Canadian Perspective

John Pellowe, BBA (Wilfrid Laurier University), MBA (Wilfrid Laurier University), MDiv (Tyndale University College & Seminary), DMin (Gordon-Conwell Theological

Seminary), is Chief Executive Officer at the Canadian Council of Christian Charities. John is the author of three books and a blog, all related to good governance and organizational leadership. He is passionate about using his expertise to help Christian ministries become exemplary, healthy and effective for the benefit of our entire society.

Derek B. M. Ross – Advancing Religion in a 'Neutral' State: Understanding Religion as a Constitutional Good

Derek B. M. Ross, LLB (Western University), LLM (University of Toronto), is Executive Director and General Counsel for Christian Legal Fellowship. He has acted for public interest interveners in numerous Charter cases, including several before the Supreme Court of Canada. He has also presented before legislative and parliamentary committees on constitutional and legal issues. Derek has served as an executive member of the Charity and Not-for-Profit Law sections and the Constitutional, Civil Liberties and Human Rights Law sections of both the Canadian Bar Association and the Ontario Bar Association. He is the editor-in-chief of *Christian Legal Journal*, a periodical examining the relationship between law and religion. He also served as General Editor of *Assisted Death: Legal, Social and Ethical Issues after Carter* (Toronto, Ontario: LexisNexis Canada, 2018) and *Canadian Pluralism and the Charter: Moral Diversity in a Free and Democratic Society* (Toronto, Ontario: LexisNexis Canada, 2019).

Ian Sinke – Advancing Religion in a 'Neutral' State: Understanding Religion as a Constitutional Good

Ian N. Sinke, BEng (McMaster University), JD (University of Toronto), is a student-at-law at Lawyers' Professional Indemnity Company (LawPRO). He recently graduated from the University of Toronto Faculty of Law and hopes to develop a litigation practice, with a particular interest in professional liability, construction law and the intersection of law and technology.

Seminary), is Chief Executive Officer at the Canadian Council of Christian Charities. John is the author of three books and a blog, all related to good governance and organizational leadership. He is passionate about using his expertise to help Christian ministries become exemplary, healthy and effective for the benefit of our entire society.

Derek B. M. Ross – Advancing Religion in a 'Neutral' State: Understanding Religion as a Constitutional Good

Derek B. M. Ross, LLB (Western University), LLM (University of Toronto), is Executive Director and General Counsel for Christian Legal Fellowship. He has acted for public interest interveners in numerous Charter cases, including several before the Supreme Court of Canada. He has also presented before legislative and parliamentary committees on constitutional and legal issues. Derek has served as an executive member of the Charity and Not-for-Profit Law sections and the Constitutional, Civil Liberties and Human Rights Law sections of both the Canadian Bar Association and the Ontario Bar Association. He is the editor-in-chief of *Christian Legal Journal*, a periodical examining the relationship between law and religion. He also served as General Editor of *Assisted Death: Legal, Social and Ethical Issues after Carter* (Toronto, Ontario: LexisNexis Canada, 2018) and *Canadian Pluralism and the Charter: Moral Diversity in a Free and Democratic Society* (Toronto, Ontario: LexisNexis Canada, 2019).

Ian Sinke – Advancing Religion in a 'Neutral' State: Understanding Religion as a Constitutional Good

Ian N. Sinke, BEng (McMaster University), JD (University of Toronto), is a student-at-law at Lawyers' Professional Indemnity Company (LawPRO). He recently graduated from the University of Toronto Faculty of Law and hopes to develop a litigation practice, with a particular interest in professional liability, construction law and the intersection of law and technology.

INDEX

1964 *Civil Rights Act* 163

Abella, Justice 136, 174
Abortion Rights Coalition of Canada (ARCC) 185–86
ACNC. *See* Australian Charities and Not-for-profits Commission (ACNC)
advancing religion 41–96, 130–31, 133, 147, 189
Alito, Justice 186
Amarnath, Ravi 147
American economy 5, 49
American Grace 55
American Psychological Association 23, 170
Ammerman, Nancy 54, 58
Arbour, Louise 133
ARCC. *See* Abortion Rights Coalition of Canada (ARCC)
Argyle, Michael 23
Australia 3–4, 7, 11–14, 114–15, 117, 120
Australian Charities and Not-for-profits Commission (ACNC) 102

Bahá'í International Community 60
Barna study 43
Barro, Robert 26
Bastarache, Justice 135–36
Bawer, Bruce 184
BCCA. *See* British Columbia Court of Appeal (BCCA)
Beit-Hallahmi, Benjamin 23
Benson, Iain T. xvi, xx, 180–81, 187, 189, 225–37
Berger, Peter L. 189
Bhatt, Ela 46
Bibby, Reginald 42, 49
Biblical financial principles 9
Bird, Brian 147
The Bob Jones University Case 161–69, 186
  anti-TWU activists using 167
  current values, Court interpretation of 164
  deregister 'discriminatory' charities 175–78
  equating to discrimination on basis of sexuality 170
  emphasis on 'changing values' 170
  failure of Congress 165–66
  Goldsboro case and 163–64
  government interference in private sphere 174–75
  Green definition of tax-exemption 164
  injunction prohibiting IRS 163–64
  IRS tax-exempt policy 163–64
  issues of racial segregation 162–63
  Canadian Courts reliance on 170–74
  SCOTUS decision in 163–4, 166–67
Bologun, Funmi 61
Bond, Michael 27
Boonstra, Kevin 174–75
Bowen, Kurt 42, 44, 50–51, 53
Brady, Kathleen 61–62, 136–37, 141, 143
Brethren, see Exclusive Brethren
British Columbia Court of Appeal (BCCA) 168, 172–73, 183, 227–28, 231
Brian Dickson, Justice xxv, 59, 134–35, 138–40, 142, 177, 234
British Columbia School Act 187
Brown, Justice 148, 178–80
Buckingham, Janet Epp xix, 205–19, 227, 230
Buddhism 87, 91, 93
Burger, Justice 165
Bussey, Barry W. xix, 159–203, 227, 236, 241
Butterfield, Kenneth 23

Cameron, Angela 167
Campbell, David 43
Canada 5, 21–22, 25, 31, 41–43, 47, 50–52, 54–56, 59, 63
  advancement of religion 129–31, 138, 140, 149, 161, 175–76, 178, 189, 210
  charity law in 210–16
  federal marriage act 235
  freedom of religion 131
  golden thread of faith in 206
  granting tax benefits 131

Canada (*cont.*)
  history of faith-based universities 208–9
  narrowing freedom of worship 218–19
  preferential tax status 209
  religiously-positive pluralism in 145–46, 148
  role of religious institutions to 207–8
  rule of interpretation holistically 133–34
  securalization of religious universities 208
  Special Senate Committee on the Charitable Sector xx–xxi
  state neutrality 129, 131–33
  state observance of religious practice 132
  Summer Jobs programme 215–16
  TWU law school cases 206, 213–15. *See also* Trinity Western University
Canada Revenue Agency (CRA) xiv, 131, 175, 210, 212
Canada Summer Jobs (CSJ) programme 185–86, 215–16, 219, 227
Canadian Association of University Teachers (CAUT) 217–18
Canadian Bar Association (CBA) 159, 162, 168, 190, 206, 214
Canadian Bill of Rights 145
Canadian Charter of Rights and Freedoms 22, 129–35, 137, 140, 143–45, 147, 159–91, 212, 215, 231
  approach to religious freedom 132, 135, 138, 143
  cases 217
  free and democratic society 234
  individual fulfilment 135
  interpretation in character and larger objects of 134
  lacks 'establishment clause' 131
  preamble of 144–45
  protections of 134
  provisions of 134
  purpose of 177
  self-definition 135
  state neutrality 146
  'supremacy of God' clause 145–46
  values' doctrine 159–60, 178–85
canon law 5
Carter, Jimmy 164
Carter xii–xiii, xv, xvi–xvii
causal relationship 26
CAUT. *See* Canadian Association of University Teachers (CAUT)
CBA. *See* Canadian Bar Association (CBA)
CCA. *See* Community Covenant Agreement (CCA)

CCLD. *See* Council of Canadian Law Deans (CCLD)
Chaisson, Angela 167
Chalmers, Thomas 86
Chan, Kathryn 35, 85, 94, 130–31, 147
Charitable Incorporated Organisation (CIO) 93
Charitable Purposes 6–8. *See also* Public benefit, Religion
  advancing religion 41–68
    better personal outcomes 44
    business and economy, effects on 62–63
    categories 41
    civic engagement 57–58
    community services 58–59
    declining religiosity 42–43
    economic impact of 49
    epidemiologist reports 45
    good behaviour 50–51
    good citizens 49–50
    government policy, support for 63–64
    greater opportunity 46–47
    improved health 47–48
    increased longevity 48
    investment, religion's return on 56
    liberal democracy, foundational freedom for 59
    neighbourhood viability index 56–57
    non-religious 50–52
    other-centredness 57
    personal outcomes 49
    places of worship 46
    pluralistic culture 59–60
    positive effect religion 44
    positive social capital 54–56
    prosocial attitudes 49–57
    prosocial behaviours 49–53
    public discourse 61–62
    public, benefits for 57–60
    refugees 63, 147, 182, 207–8, 213
    religion 60–67
    religiosity and philanthropy, relationship between 52–53
    religious attendance 48
    religious benefits 41–42, 44–47
    responsible choices 44–46
    sense of identity 47
    social buffer 58
    social intercourse 47
    Syrian refugees 68
    tangible community benefits 53–57
    volunteering 51

INDEX 247

women 60–67
  in Canada 41–68
  places of worship 65–66
    build strong family bonds 66
    coherent and cohesive 66
    drive behaviour 65–66
    self-reinforcing social networks 65
  religion 65–67
    'works' 64–67
    comprehensive 64
    shapes identity 64–65
    strong motivation 64
Charitable Uses Act 1601 xii, 6, 81
Charities Act (Northern Ireland) 2008 83
Charities Act 2005 7
Charities Act 2006 81, 101–2
Charities Act 2011 82, 91
Charities and Trustee Investment (Scotland) Act 2005 82
charity 1–117, 130–31, 133–48, 176, 178, 185, 190, 213
  definition of 131
  economics of 5
  Pemsel heads of xii, xvii, 6–7, 21, 35, 81–82, 131, 148, 210
  principle divisions 6–9
  religion and 206, 210, 236
  religion, advancement of xi, xvii–xxi, 3–4, 7, 8, 10, 15, 31, 34–35, 67, 81–82, 84–86, 88–89, 91, 94, 102, 111, 117, 129–31, 134, 138, 140, 147, 149, 161, 175–76, 178, 189, 210, 218
  to education 5
charity law. *See also* Charity, Public benefits
  in Canada 41–68
  in United Kingdom 81–100
  incremental changes to 22
Charter rights 25, 33
Charter values xvi, xix–xx, 22, 159–91, 205, 228, 236
Chatters, Linda 47
Chiu, Raymond B. xii, xviii, 21–40
Chevalier-Watts, Juliet xvii 3–19, 241
Christian theology of revelation 4
Church of Scientology
  recognized as a religion: xviii, 86–87, 90, 95
  Church of the New Faith v Commissioner of Pay-Roll Tax 11–13
  Decision of the Charity Commissioners re: Church of Scientology, 84–85
  Hodkin 81, 90–91
  Segerdal 90–91

Churches xiii, xiv–v, xix, xxi, 6, 10, 28, 45–46, 51–52, 54–57, 63, 65, 81, 92, 105, 177, 182, 185, 207, 211, 216–17
  African American 60
  attendance 45–46, 58
  civic engagement 57–58
  contributions to communities 27, 54, 207–8
  membership xiv, 51–52
  neighbourhood viability 56
  property tax exemptions 6
CIO. *See* Charitable Incorporated Organisation (CIO)
Civil Marriage Act 212–14
Civil Rights Movement xiii, xx, 143, 162–63
civil society xiv, 15, 142, 188
Cnaan, Ram 27
Columbia Law Review 163
Common law 5, 7, 86
  jurisdictions 21–22, 34, 94, 101–2, 115, 117, 120–21
Community Covenant Agreement (CCA) 161–62, 169–70, 177, 181, 183
Confederation compromise 143, 146
Constitution Act, 1867 133–34, 139, 170, 210
  Section 93, 143–44
Constitution Act, 1982 133–34
Cooke, Gresham 103
Cooley, Amanda Harman 184
correlative relationship 26
Côté, Justice 148, 178–80
Council of Canadian Law Deans (CCLD) 213
Cranmer, Frank xi, xviii, 81–100
CRA. *See* Canada Revenue Agency (CRA)
Craig, Elaine 167–68
CSJ. *See* Canada Summer Jobs (CSJ) programme
Cup Scandal 114

D'Cunha, Jean 61
Daly, Michael Wood 55, 57
Danay, Robert 145–46
Dawkins, Richard 6
Dawson, Christopher 226, 228
dead letter 145
Deed of Variation 92, 109, 112–13, 116–19
Dibble, Kenneth 113
Dickson CJC 134–35, 138–40, 142, 177
discrimination 22, 24–25, 61, 159, 161–70, 174–75, 185, 190, 192n32, 198n131, 201n193, 209, 212, 215, 217, 238n6
Dillon, Justice 91

Doherty, Bernard xi, xviii, 101–26
Du, Xingquiang 27, 62
Dyck, Bruno 34

earnings management 62
Eddy, Mary Baker 87
EGALE Human Rights Trust 168
Egerton, George 145
Eichler, Stefan 27
Elias CJ 10
England and Wales 7, 21–22, 25, 81–85, 101–3, 105, 107
England and Wales, Charities Act 2006 82
equality xix, xx, xxii, 31, 61–62, 91, 132–34, 137, 139–42, 146, 154n113, 159–60, 173, 175, 179, 184, 215, 227, 230–31, 234–35
European civil law 5
European Court of Human Rights 59, 95, 136, 138, 142
Exclusive Brethren 91–93, 101–17
  in conflict 113–17
  members 105
  trust 104–5, 110

Faith 3–20, 28. *See also* charity, religion
faith-based universities 206, 208–10, 214, 217
Farr, Thomas 59
female genital mutilation (FGM) 61
FGM. *See* female genital mutilation
FHLI. *See* fundamental human life issues (FHLI)
Finke, Roger 59
First-tier Tribunal (FTT) 107
Fox, Dov 105, 184
Fox, Justice 105
Francis, H. E. 103, 114
FTT. *See* First-tier Tribunal (FTT)
fundamental human life issues (FHLI) 159–61, 187
fundamentalism 24

Galston, William xvi–vii, 187–88, 236
Gardner, Dame Helen 226
Gary, Lawrence 47
Gervais, Ricky 6
Gender xvi, 170, 174
  equality / inequality 60–62
  fluidity 170, 195n83-84
  identity or expression 215, 228
Gonthier, Justice 187
Grana, Sheryl 34
Grant, George 181
Greater Toronto Area (GTA) 55

Greenpeace decision 10, 13
Grim, Brian 59
GTA. *See* Greater Toronto Area (GTA)

Haidt, Jonathan 182–83, 185
Hajdu, Patricia 215, 217
Hales, Bruce David 109
Halo Effect 53, 55
Halo Project 55–56
Handy, Femida 27
Harding, Matthew 67
Hebrew Scriptures 50
Hellman, Deborah 169, 188
Hill, Peter 24, 48
Hitchens, Christopher 6
Hodkin 81, 90–91, 94
Holmes 92, 103, 106–7, 110–14
Holyoake, George Jacob xiii
Hood, Ralph 24
Horsforth Gospel Trust 107
Horwitz, Paul xvii
Hubbard, L. Ron 11
Hughes, Justice 236

Iacobucci, Justice 133, 135, 139, 144
Iannaccone, Laurence 27
ICCPR. *See* International Covenant on Civil and Political Rights (ICCPR)
inclusive 35, 182, 225, 231–33, 238n6
Income Tax Act 131–32, 172, 178, 210, 235
Individual-level religiousness (RI) 28
Individualism 32
inference 26
intangible belief systems 4
Internal Revenue Service (IRS) 163–7
International Covenant on Civil and Political Rights (ICCPR) 137, 209, 230
international human rights law 209, 230
Ireland 5, 83–84
IRS. *See* Internal Revenue Service (IRS)

Jeavons, Thomas 24
Jedi Doctrine 93
Jediism 93
Jefferson, Thomas 183–84
Jewish religion 85
Jim Crow Laws 60
Joseph, Peniel 60
Juneau, Carl 67

Karakatsanis, Justice 173
Kennedy, Justice 170

INDEX 249

Keren Kayemeth 85
Koran 50
Kristof, Nicholas 61

L'Heureux-Dubé, Justice 142, 144, 167
Lamer, Justice 133
Lauwers, Justice Peter 180, 184–85
Law Matters 214
Law Society of British Columbia (LSBC) 162, 168–69, 172–73, 176
Law Society of Upper Canada (LSUC) 167–68
Lawmakers 15, 21, 32, 34–36
leaked documents 115
LeBel, Justice 137, 143
legal *déjà vu* 103–6
legal environment 22
Lesbians, Gays, Bisexuals and Trans People of the University of Toronto (LGBTOUT) 168
Leung, Kwok 27
Leventhal, Harold 164
Lewis, C. S. 225
LGBTOUT. *See* Lesbians, Gays, Bisexuals and Trans People of the University of Toronto (LGBTOUT)
LGBTTIQQPA activists 227
Liberty Trust 8–11
  funds 9
Lin, Xinyu 26
'living tree' doctrine 164, 170
Lord Denning MR 82
Lord Macnaghten 6
Lord Toulson 81, 91, 94
LSBC. *See* Law Society of British Columbia's (LSBC)
LSUC. *See* Law Society of Upper Canada (LSUC)
Lucke, Navina 27
Lukianoff, Greg 183
Lyon, Jo-Ann 59

MacKenzie, Gavin 167
MacKinnon, Peter 206, 216–18
Macklem, Timothy 136–37
MacPherson, Justice 168, 182
Magnet, Joseph 140–41
MAiD. *See* medical assistance in dying (MAiD)
Mainse, David 205
Mallon Justice 9–10
Marceau, Richard 212
Maritain, Jacques 142

Marriage Reference decision 171
Mayahana tradition 50
McCleary, Rachel 26
McConnell, Michael 66
McFadden, Jean 83
McGill, Jena 167
McLachlin, Beverley, CJC 142, 162, 170, 172, 179, 180, 214, 227
Measures of Religiosity catalogues 24
medical assistance in dying (MAiD) 178, 180, 186
Medieval legal system 5
Mertz, Elizabeth 36
Miller, Justice Bradley W. 170, 180
Monsma, Stephen 24
Moon, Richard 132, 148, 177
Moon, Sun Myung 84
Moonies. *See also* Unification Church 84
morality test 104
Moran, Mayo 130
mortgage-free lending scheme 8
Murphy, Justice 12

natural law 4–5, 145, 236
normative universes 35
Norton, Jane Calderwood 135, 138
Nova Scotia Barristers' Society (NSBS) 176
NSBS. *See* Nova Scotia Barristers' Society (NSBS)
Northern Ireland 83–84
New Zealand 3–5, 7–9, 114–15

O'Fallon, Michael 28
O'Halloran, Kerry 94
Oakes 134, 139
Obergefell decision 170
Office of the Scottish Charity Regulator (OSCR) 102
Ogilvie, M. H. 32
Old Testament law 30
Omer, Thomas 26
Organizational research 22
OSCR. *See* Office of the Scottish Charity Regulator (OSCR)

Parachin, Adam xxi
Pargament, Kenneth 23
PASC. *See* Public Administration Select Committee (PASC)
PBCC. *See* Plymouth Brethren Christian Church (PBCC)
PDT. *See* Preston Down Trust (PDT)
Pellowe, John xii, xviii, 41–79, 236
Pemsel 81

Penny, Jonathan 145–46
Places of Worship Registration Act 1855 91
Plowman, Justice 104, 106
Plymouth Brethren Christian Church
 (PBCC) 101–2
Preamble of *Statute of Elizabeth* 6–7, 81
Preston Down Trust (PDT) 81, 101
Preston Down Trust Decision 106–13
 charitable purpose 109–10
 detriment and harm 111–13
 extent of public benefit 110–11
 public benefit 110
 the decision 113
Progress and Religion 226
Protestant era 30
Protestant Ethic 30
Protestantism 30
Public Administration Select Committee
 (PASC) 102
Public benefit 6–8, 21–117. *See also* Charity,
 Religion
 advancing religion 41–68
 Canadian perspective 41–68
 in Canada 129–219
 public criticism 113
Putnam, Robert 43, 55

Quebec *Charter of Human Rights and Freedoms*
 132, 137

Raitt, Lisa 185
Rand, Justice 143
Ravitch, Frank S. 171
Re Shaw's Wills Trusts 12
Re South Place Ethical Society 86
Reductionism 32
Regan, Ronald 164
Religion 3–6, 21–36. *See also* Charity
 advancement of 3–6
 atheist pledges 228
 benefit relationship 26
 benefit the public 31–32
 incongruence 32–33
 misconstrual disrespects humanity 33–35
 reductionism 32
 broader implications 31–35
 charity and 236–37
 contributions of cultural groups 142
 critiques 21–29
  complexity of relationships 28–29
  realities of religious effects 30–31
 definition of 90–91

development of Western law 3
economic gains 3
effect on divorce rates 5
epistemological concerns 35
facing forced conformity under equality and
 non-discrimination 227
health benefits 3, 5
importance of 236
in Canada 41–68
in United Kingdom 81–100
inclusivism 232
individual freedoms and 134–38
is equality right 230–31
law, relationship between 6
legal history of 3
liberty, the base condition 227
limits of politics and law in 236
loss of respect for 226–30
multicultural society and 138–44
multiculturalism
no longer allow moral views on marriages or
 abortion 227
not a private right 233
ontological questions 35
personal autonomy 138
physiological or *corporeal* concerns 35
preservation of a 'secular humility' 144–46
public place of 227, 233
purposes of 131
reality 29–31
related businesses and institutions 5
religious concepts 23–29
religious levels 23–24
 culture level 24
 individual level 24, 26
 organizational level 24, 26
 quantitative research 27
 relationships between 25–28
 societal level 23, 26
religious participation, impacts in 5
religious system, integrity of 29
right to manifest xxvn66, 10, 24, 26,
 67, 95, 131, 147, 177, 209, 230,
 233, 235
scientific *theory* 29
secular and 231–33
self-definition and 135
social scientific perspectives 21–36
society, contribution to 5
society, relationship between 6
state neutrality 140–41
theory 29–31

undertake charity work 5
voices 142–43
religious adherents 210, 217
religious charity 25, 32, 104, 178, 206
religious freedom 13, 32–33, 41, 59–60, 62, 119, 132, 135, 138, 143, 146, 161–62, 173, 178–79, 182–83, 186, 190, 205, 209, 212, 214–15, 217–18, 225, 230–31, 233
religious groups. *See* religious organizations
religious identity 21, 28, 159, 206, 210, 218
religious organizations (RO) 27, 137
  anti-abortion groups 185–86, 205, 215
  attestation requirements 215–16
  care and services, providing 207–8
  charity law and 210
  Christian Reformed denominations 208
  civil marriage and 212
  connect seekers and adherents 207
  creating community for human flourishing 207
  definition of marriage 159, 171–72, 212, 214, 235
  discrimination in 212
  facilitate formation of ideas and ideas 136–37
  freedom of association for 142
  hosting community events 207
  importance to common good 142
  in international law 209
  instrument role in self-definition 135–36
  Jehovah's Witnesses 211, 214
  Mennonites institutions 208
  new and progressive ideas 141–42
  non-denominational Christian universities 208–9
  preferential tax treatment 209
  process of secularizations 208
  proper functioning of democracy 141–43
  protect and preserve rights 138
  public policy and 211
  realization of religious freedom 138
  registered charities 210
  registration system 211
  restrictions on 211
  rites of passage 207
  role in social justice 208
  'Rules of Commons' approach 217–18
  secular arguments against and 216–17
  secular social norms and 206
  status of 212
  structural ethnicity principle 141
  'survival and development' of religious beliefs 137–38

transmissions of ideas and beliefs 137–38
  without discrimination 209
Religiousness 23, 48
return on investment (ROI) 56
RI. *See Individual-level religiousness* (RI)
Rifkind, Malcolm 105
RO. *See religious organizations*
Robins, Justice v 211
Rogers, Peter 176
ROI. *See* return on investment (ROI)
Roman law 4
Romilly, John M. R. 106
Rorty, Richard xii, xvi
Ross, Derek B. M. xii, xix, 59, 106, 129–57, 230
Rowe, Malcolm 159–60, 179–80, 214
Royal Society for the Prevention of Cruelty to Animals (RSPCA) 116
RSPCA. *See* Royal Society for the Prevention of Cruelty to Animals (RSPCA)
Ryder, Bruce 144–46, 148

'symbolic ethnicity' principle 140
Sachs, Justice Albie 226, 228–29, 233, 236
Sacred 23
Sacred Hands 85
Safayeni, Justin 33
Sandberg, Russell 94
Sankey, Lord 170
SCC. *See* Supreme Court of Canada
Scholasticism 4
Schroeder, David 34
Scientology 11–13, 81, 85–87, 91, 95
Scotland 82–4, 103
SCOTUS. See Supreme Court of the United States (SCOTUS)
The Screwtape Letters 225–26
secularism xi, xiii, xiv, 24, 43, 108, 129, 131, 231, 233–35
Segerdal 90–1
self-definition 135
self-fulfilment 135
sexually transmitted infections (STIs) 45
Sexular Age 181
Sharlow, Justice 211
Sheker, Manini 61
Sider, Ronald 24–25
Sinha, Jill 27
Sinke, Ian xii, xix, 129–57, 230
Social science 24, 30, 36, 189
South Africa 229–31, 233

South Place Ethical Society 91
Southcott, Joanna 106
Statute of Elizabeth 6–7, 81
STIs. *See* sexually transmitted infections (STIs) v
Stout, Jeffrey xv
Supreme Court of Canada (SCC) xix, xx, 59, 130–33, 135–38, 142–45, 146–48, 159–62, 164, 168–73, 175, 177–83, 186–87, 189–91, 206, 209, 211–14, 216–17, 227–28, 231–33
Supreme Court of the New Zealand 10, 13
Supreme Court of the United Kingdom 81, 91, 95
Supreme Court of the United States (SCOTUS) xix, 163–64, 166, 168, 170–71, 175–76, 190

Taiwanese study 52
Tancredo, Tom 184
Tarnopolsky, J. A. 188
Taylor, James Jr 103–6
Temple of the Jedi Order 81, 93
The Druid Network 89–90
The Gnostic Centre 88
The Pagan Federation 90
The Way of the Livingness 89
Third Sector 116
Tocqueville, Alexis de 57
Toulson, Lord 81
Trinity Western University (TWU) xix, 22, 148, 159–63, 167–91, 205–6, 210, 213–14, 216–19, 225, 227, 234
Trinity Western University (TWU) 2018 law school case 159
  application of '*Charter* values' 161
  BJU influence on xix, 161–62
  FHLI issues 161
  SCC rejection of bid 161
Trudeau, Pierre Elliott 205–6, 218
true neutrality 148–49. *See also* state neutrality
Trump, Donald 4
Tun, Hla 61
Tushnet, Mark xvii
TWU. *See* Trinity Western University (TWU)

U Aye Lwin, Al Haj 61
UNC. *See* University of North Carolina (UNC)
Unification Church 84
Universal Declaration of Human Rights 142, 209, 230
University Commons Divided xix, 206, 216

University of North Carolina (UNC) 184
United Kingdom 81–100
  advancement of religion 81–100
  charitable purposes 81–82
  charity commission 85–86
  commission's decisions on religious charities 91–94
  consultation, outcome of 87–88
  decisions on registration 84–5, 88–90
  Preston Down Trust (PDT) xviii–xix, xxv, 84, 91–3, 101–21
  presumption, abolition of xi, 82, 83, 85–86, 175
  public benefit 81–100
  registration post-*Hodkin* 91–94
  regulator, role of 86
  religion, nature of 86–87
  Scottish act, influence of the 84
Unruh, Heidi 24–25
Ursel, Susan 159–60, 214
US Metropolitan Statistical Areas 26

Vaaler, Margaret 45
Vaisey, Justice 12
VanderWeele, Tyler 48
Vedas 4
Verrilli, Donald 186

Wagner, Richard 172, 174
Waldron, Jeremy 142
Waldron, Mary Ann 169–70, 190
Walton, Justice 105–6
Wales 7, 22, 81–85, 93, 95, 101–3, 105, 107, 120
Wang, Qunyong 26
Waters, Donovan xii, 32
Weber, Max 26, 30
Wellspring theory of public benefit 35, 147
Welsh, David 86
Western law 4
Wickens, Sir John 82
Wiepking, Pamela 51–52
Wilson, Justice Bertha 145
Wilson, Bryan R. 106–7
Wilson, Erin 62
Word 13–14
Wuthnow, Robert 49–50
Wycliffe Bible Translators 13–14

Yates, Joshua 27, 43, 48, 62, 64
Young, Justice Ronald 9

www.ingramcontent.com/pod-product-compliance
Lightning Source LLC
Chambersburg PA
CBHW021821300426
44114CB00009BA/272